The Comic Turn in Contemporary English Fiction

The Comic Turn in Contemporary English Fiction

Who's Laughing Now?

Huw Marsh

BLOOMSBURY ACADEMIC
LONDON • NEW YORK • OXFORD • NEW DELHI • SYDNEY

BLOOMSBURY ACADEMIC
Bloomsbury Publishing Plc
50 Bedford Square, London, WC1B 3DP, UK
1385 Broadway, New York, NY 10018, USA
29 Earlsfort Terrace, Dublin 2, Ireland

BLOOMSBURY, BLOOMSBURY ACADEMIC and the Diana logo are trademarks of
Bloomsbury Publishing Plc

First published in Great Britain 2020
This paperback edition published in 2022

Copyright © Huw Marsh, 2020

Huw Marsh has asserted his right under the Copyright, Designs and
Patents Act, 1988, to be identified as Author of this work.

For legal purposes the Acknowledgements on p. ix constitute an extension of
this copyright page.

Cover design: Eleanor Rose
Cover image © Getty Images

All rights reserved. No part of this publication may be reproduced or transmitted
in any form or by any means, electronic or mechanical, including photocopying,
recording, or any information storage or retrieval system, without prior
permission in writing from the publishers.

Bloomsbury Publishing Plc does not have any control over, or responsibility for, any third-
party websites referred to or in this book. All internet addresses given in this book were
correct at the time of going to press. The author and publisher regret any inconvenience
caused if addresses have changed or sites have ceased to exist, but can accept no
responsibility for any such changes.

A catalogue record for this book is available from the British Library.

A catalog record for this book is available from the Library of Congress.

ISBN: HB: 978-1-4742-9303-7
PB: 978-1-3502-4938-7
ePDF: 978-1-4742-9305-1
eBook: 978-1-4742-9304-4

Typeset by Deanta Global Publishing Services, Chennai, India

To find out more about our authors and books visit www.bloomsbury.com and
sign up for our newsletters.

For Hannah

Contents

Acknowledgements	ix
Introduction: A comic turn in contemporary English fiction?	1
The comic turn	3
Contemporary English fiction	8
Who's laughing now?	19
1 'Sinking giggling into the sea'?: Jonathan Coe and the politics of comedy	21
Jokes and/as innovative action	29
From satire to comedy	40
Metacomedy	45
2 'A grave disquisition': Style, class and comedy in the novels of Martin Amis	53
The ethics of style	53
High and low: Hierarchies of comic style	57
Comedy, class and style from *The Information* to *Lionel Asbo*	62
3 'Talking about things we didn't want to talk about': Zadie Smith and laughter	77
What's so hysterical about hysterical realism?	79
Mixed emotions: Laughter and tears	86
Comedy and community	94
4 'Like a monkey with a miniature cymbal': Magnus Mills and the comedy of repetition	101
Comedy, surprise and repetition	101
Magnus Mills	104
Deadpan; dead bodies: *The Restraint of Beasts*	106
Working to rule, ruling the workplace: *The Scheme for Full Employment* and *The Maintenance of Headway*	112
Funny as hell: Beckett, O'Brien, Mills	121

5	'Simple high jinks'?: Nicola Barker and the comedy of paradox	131
	Pooterism, pedantry and the logic of the absurd: Incongruity as comic practice	132
	'Is the fucking carnival in town or what?': Satire, the grotesque and the carnivalesque	140
	Laughter and redemption: From comedy to humour	153
	Rabbit-duck/Duck-rabbit	164
6	'No drawing of lines': Howard Jacobson and the boundaries of the comic	167
	Lancing the boil: *Zoo Time*, *Coming from Behind* and the necessity of offence	170
	'Jew know why'?: *The Finkler Question*, Jewish jokes and the politics of joke-telling communities	180
	'Not *only* funny': *Kalooki Nights* and Holocaust comedy	186
	Comedy Trumped? *Pussy* and the challenge for contemporary satire	196

Conclusion: The comic turn in contemporary English fiction — 201
  Selling the past as the future: Nationhood, work and performance in Julian Barnes's *England, England* — 204

Bibliography — 211
Index — 238

Acknowledgements

This book has been several years in the writing, but its origins go back a good deal further. In fact, I can pin them down to a precise moment. It was during a supervision meeting in the early stages of my PhD on the novels of Beryl Bainbridge. My supervisor, Mary Condé, was giving feedback on my most recent chapter. With customary tact and insight, she told me that she had enjoyed the chapter but didn't get any sense that the novels I was discussing were actually *funny*. This started me thinking about the comic voice in Bainbridge's fiction, which became a chapter of the thesis and the eventual book. It also made me realize that that there was a lot more to be said about comedy, and that I wanted to return to it as a subject. Mary passed away in 2018, and I didn't get the opportunity to tell her, but I owe this book to her. Thank you, Mary.

Since those early stages, I have benefitted from the generosity of many friends and colleagues at Queen Mary University of London and elsewhere, who have contributed their thoughts at conferences and seminars, on work submitted for publication, or more typically during snatched conversations in the staff room, waiting for the kettle to boil or the coffee to percolate. Thank you to Nadia Atia, Nick Bentley, Leonid Bilmes, Andrew Dean, Zara Dinnen, Robert Eaglestone, Bridget Escolme, Howard Finn, Katie Fleming, Niall Gildea, Sam Halliday, Matthew Ingleby, David James, Sam McBean, Molly Macdonald, Aoife Monks, Daniel O'Gorman, John Osborne, Jake Poller, kitt price, Peggy Reynolds, Charlotta Salmi, Berthold Schoene, Katy Shaw, Matthias Somers, Philip Tew, Jane Thomas, Tiffany Watt-Smith, Patricia Waugh and Kate Wilkinson. I am particularly indebted to Suzanne Hobson, Nadia Valman and Andrew van der Vlies for their feedback on draft chapters of the book, and to Bill Schwarz for reading the full manuscript – the generous and attentive suggestions of these readers have been invaluable and I hope I have done them justice in the final version.

This kindness and generosity is typical of the School of English and Drama at Queen Mary, and I am grateful to successive heads of school and department for fostering such a collegial and intellectually stimulating working culture. Thank you to Michèle Barrett, Warren Boutcher, David Colclough, Mark Currie, Markman Ellis, Rachael Gilmour and Paul Hamilton. I would also like to offer my heartfelt thanks to Julia Boffey, Jen Harvie and Scott McCracken, each of whom has gone above and beyond their role as directors of research to offer advice and support at different points in the lifecycle of this project. I have benefitted enormously from discussions with the superb students on my module 'Laughing Matters: Comedy and Contemporary Culture', who have helped shape my thinking about many aspects of this work, confirming my belief in teaching-led research as well as research-led teaching. And I am fortunate to have shared comradeship, laughter and puns of variable quality with my colleagues in the School Administrative Team: Faisal Abul, Jonathan Boffey, Richard Coulton, Rupert Dannreuther, Rob Ellis, Lara Fothergill, Jenny Gault, Eszter Gillay, Patricia Hamilton, Suzi Lewis, Hari Marini, Matthew Mauger, Afsana Nishat, Kate Russell and, last but by no means least, Beverley Stewart.

I am grateful to the Queen Mary Faculty of Humanities and Social Sciences for granting me a period of research leave, which enabled me to finish the book. I also thank the editorial team at Bloomsbury, David Avital, Lucy Brown and Mark Richardson, for their initial enthusiasm about the project and their ongoing support.

Finally, I owe a huge debt of gratitude to my family. To my loving and supportive parents, Robert and Rosie, to Katy and Matt, and to all my family on the Long side. Thank you.

This book is for Hannah, with whom I am lucky enough to have shared all of the best years my life. Thank you Hannah, for everything.

* * *

Elements of the Introduction and Chapters 2 and 3 appear in a different form in 'Comedy', in *The Routledge Companion to Twenty-First Century Literary Fiction*, eds Daniel O'Gorman and Robert Eaglestone (Abingdon: Routledge, 2019), pp. 67–79. I am grateful for permission to reproduce this material here.

Introduction

A comic turn in contemporary English fiction?

In the spring of 2018, there was a brief literary controversy, one of a regular series that accrete around the 'posh bingo' of UK literary prizes and inspire opinion pieces in the broadsheet and literary press.[1] For the first time in its history, the Wodehouse Prize for best comic novel would not be awarded. The prize committee had been unable to find a book they felt was worthy of the accolade, citing the failure of the nominated books to incite 'unanimous laughter'; the best they could muster was a 'wry smile', which was deemed insufficiently prizeworthy.[2] Putting to one side the inherent vagaries of prizes for the arts, this decision might be read as an indication that 2018 was a fallow year for comic writing, or perhaps it represents a judgement on the state of contemporary comedy more generally speaking. I would locate its significance elsewhere and would suggest that the desire for unanimity of laughter and the dismissal of the wry smile indicate something more fundamental about the nature of the comic and the genre of comedy. As Andrew Stott writes, laughter is 'the most obvious barometer' of comedy's success or failure, but the two are not synonymous.[3] Judith Roof echoes this sentiment when she notes that 'not all comedy results in laughter and not all laughter is a response to the comic',[4] emphasizing that we may find something funny and not express this through laughter, and that laughter can also have non-comic meanings and functions. Whether our amusement manifests in laughter depends not only on the nature of the comic text – scatological or witty, linguistic or physical, and so on – but

---

[1] The novelist Julian Barnes, whose novel *England, England* is discussed in the final chapter of this book, discussed the vicissitudes of literary prizes in a 1987 article for the *London Review of Books*. He characterized the Booker Prize as a version of 'posh bingo'. Julian Barnes, 'Diary', *London Review of Books*, 12 November 1987. Available online: https://www.lrb.co.uk/v09/n20/julian-barnes/diary (accessed 8 May 2019).

[2] Heloise Wood, 'Bollinger Everyman Wodehouse Prize Withheld for First Time', *Bookseller*, 16 May 2018. Available online: https://www.thebookseller.com/news/bollinger-everyman-wodehouse-prize-comic-fiction-withheld-first-time-786381 (accessed 8 May 2019).

[3] Andrew Stott, *Comedy*, 2nd edn (Abingdon: Routledge, 2014), p. 2.

[4] Judith Roof, *The Comic Event: Comedic Performance from the 1950s to the Present* (New York: Bloomsbury, 2018), p. 22.

also on situational factors such as our own background and preferences, and whether we are alone or in a social group.[5] Moreover, as many writers including Roof have noted, laughter is not always a response to amusement and may be borne of nervousness, embarrassment, politeness or a desire to ridicule, as well as a range of other affective states and social stimuli.[6] Nor is there a fixed sense of what constitutes comedy, and although some accounts stick to a more rigid definition, identifying a lineage from Ancient Greek forms,[7] I agree with Stott's formulation that comedy 'is better understood as a tonal quality rather than a structural one'.[8] Agnes Heller adopts Wittgenstein's terminology to speak of a 'family resemblance' between the multiple forms of the comic, aptly summarizing their overlapping but non-identical commonalities.[9] As is attested by the range of previous nominees and winners of the Wodehouse Prize,[10] this tonal quality or family resemblance covers strikingly different texts and approaches to humour, and this, combined with other complicating factors such as the multiple forms comic writing can take, the personal and situational factors affecting its reception, and the numerous ways in which amusement can express itself, means it is unsurprising that the Wodehouse Prize committee did not find itself erupting in 'unanimous laughter'. I argue throughout *The Comic Turn in Contemporary English Fiction* that comic writing is in excellent health, and the comic voice is central to much of the most interesting, and sometimes interestingly problematic, contemporary fiction. It is not a single genre in terms of form, plot, style, politics or the affective responses it elicits and seeks to elicit, and these complexities of intention, addressivity and genre inform many of the

---

[5] See Robert R. Provine, *Laughter: A Scientific Investigation* (New York: Penguin, [2000] 2001), pp. 43–8.
[6] For recent discussions of the multiple meanings of laughter see, for example, Michael Billig, *Laughter and Ridicule: Towards a Social Critique of Humour* (London: Sage, 2005); Alfie Bown, *In the Event of Laughter: Psychoanalysis, Literature and Comedy* (London: Bloomsbury, 2019); Alexander Kozintsev, *The Mirror of Laughter*, trans. Richard P. Martin (New Brunswick, NJ: Transaction, [2007] 2012); and Anca Parvulescu, *Laughter: Notes on a Passion* (Cambridge, MA: MIT Press, 2010). And for useful digests of scientific perspectives, see Peter McGraw and Joel Warner, *The Humor Code: A Global Search for What Makes Things Funny* (New York: Simon and Schuster, 2014); Provine, *Laughter*; and Scott Weems, *Ha! The Science of When We Laugh and Why* (New York: Basic Books, 2014).
[7] See, for example, Dmitri Nikulin, *Comedy, Seriously: A Philosophical Investigation* (New York: Palgrave Macmillan, 2014); and Erich Segal, *The Death of Comedy* (Cambridge, MA: Harvard University Press, 2001).
[8] Stott, *Comedy*, p. 2.
[9] Agnes Heller, *Immortal Comedy: The Comic Phenomenon in Art, Literature, and Life* (Oxford: Lexington, 2005), p. 4.
[10] Previous winners include Helen Fielding's romantic comedy *Bridget Jones's Baby: The Diaries* (2017), Gary Shteyngart's dystopian *Super Sad True Love Story* (2010), and Geoff Dyer's witty fictionalized travelogue *Jeff in Venice, Death in Varanasi* (2009), each of which offers a distinctive version of the comic. Two recipients of the Prize, Jonathan Coe and Howard Jacobson (who has been awarded it twice), are the subject of later chapters of this book.

questions addressed in the following discussion of novelists including Jonathan Coe, Martin Amis, Nicola Barker, Zadie Smith, Magnus Mills, Howard Jacobson and Julian Barnes. This book makes a claim for comedy as an often-neglected mode that plays a significant and critically generative role in much of the most interesting contemporary writing, creating sites of rich stylistic, cognitive, political and ethical contestation whose analysis offers a new perspective on the present.

The comic turn

To begin with the question of genre, for Erich Segal, the premiere of Samuel Beckett's *Waiting for Godot* 'marks the end of the life cycle of a genre—the death of comedy'; the intellectualism of Beckett, Ionesco and the Theatre of the Absurd sounds the death knell for comedy because while it engages with the models established by Greek playwrights such as Aristophanes, it also seeks systematically to dismantle those same models, substituting fecundity for sterility and denying its characters the required happy ending.[11] Segal defines comedy as dramatic comedy, and as dramatic comedy that adheres to a template in which 'new' refers to a form developed in Greece in about 300 BC. Clearly, comedy as it is conventionally understood has not died, but Segal's comments are suggestive of the fact that it is no longer helpful or indeed possible to identify a set of plot, character or stylistic traits that mark a piece of work as comedy. As I have already suggested in the opening discussion of the 2018 Wodehouse (non-) Prize, definitions of comedy are peculiarly slippery. The same can of course be argued for other contemporary genres, which in Theodore Martin's words 'lead distinctly double lives, with one foot in the past and the other in the present',[12] but in comedy this is especially pronounced. It is not only a question of historicism and the developing nature of the form, but also a question of its adaptability and relative formlessness. The classical reliance on the happy ending having long since been jettisoned as an essential element, comedy is associated with laughter but not dependent on it; it often exists in combination with other genres such as romance, horror, fantasy, science fiction or even tragedy;[13] and as Erich Segal's

---

[11] Segal, *Death of Comedy*, p. 450.
[12] Theodore Martin, *Contemporary Drift: Genre, Historicism and the Problem of the Present* (New York: Columbia University Press, 2017), p. 6.
[13] As Lauren Berlant and Sianne Ngai put it, 'Contemporary comedy suffuses so many genres that are not comedy it is hard to draw lines.' Lauren Berlant and Sianne Ngai, 'Comedy Has Issues', *Critical Inquiry*, 43:2 (2017), 233–49 (p. 239).

comments on Beckett indicate, even classics of the form are not universally accepted as comedy. I therefore avoid rigid, formal definitions of comedy and instead define it as work that is intended to amuse. This definition overlaps with, but is distinct from, the broader term 'humour', which can include unintentional amusement and other forms of social interaction that may be funny but that are not, strictly speaking, examples of comedy. Intention is something of a dirty word in many sectors of literary studies,[14] but it plays an important role here in separating that which is funny because it is intended to be funny from that which is accidentally humorous. There is a significant difference between *I, Partridge* (2011), the 'autobiography' of the fictional radio and television presenter Alan Partridge, a comic character played by Steve Coogan, and *Poptastic!* (2007), the often unintentionally hilarious autobiography of real-life radio DJ Tony Blackburn, on whom aspects of the Partridge character are based: both inspire laughter, but there is an important difference in intent.[15] Reading contemporary fiction *as* comedy, with a focus on the elements of comic narrative and the moments at which the comic voice interposes in the text, offers a new picture of contemporary English fiction and suggests a series of original frameworks for thinking about and discussing questions of genre, style, affect and politics.

This book makes a claim for the significance of comedy in contemporary English fiction, arguing that it has taken an identifiable funny turn. By funny turn I mean not only that much of the most interesting contemporary writing is funny and that there is a comic tendency in contemporary fiction, but also that this humour, this comic licence, allows writers of contemporary fiction to do peculiar and interesting things – things that are funny in the sense of odd or strange and that may in turn inspire a funny turn in readers. To have a funny turn is to feel peculiar or light-headed, to feel that something is awry, and at its

---

[14] Kaye Mitchell's *Intention and Text* offers a valuable history and analysis of intentionality in literary studies, arguing for a reconsideration of intention as a 'structural or linguistic feature of texts, a feature of the way that they themselves "intend" meaning'. Kaye Mitchell, *Intention and Text: Towards an Intentionality of Literary Form* (London: Continuum, 2008), p. xi. And for a detailed and insightful discussion of intentionality in the context of narrative humour, see Jeroen Vandaele, 'Narrative Humor (I): Enter Perspective', *Poetics Today*, 31:4 (2010), 721–85; and Jeroen Vandaele, 'Narrative Humor (II): Exit Perspective', *Poetics Today*, 33:1 (2012) 59–126.

[15] Blackburn's autobiography was one of the sources of inspiration for *I, Partridge*, and it is full of lines that could easily be spoken by Partridge, Coogan's un-self-aware and often pompous comic masterpiece. In a further turn of the intertextual screw, stand-up comedian and radio DJ John Robins has written his own autobiography, *A Robins Amongst the Pigeons* (2015), a pitch-perfect homage to both Partridge and Blackburn. See Tony Blackburn, *Poptastic!: My Life in Radio* (London: Cassell, 2007); Rob Gibbons, Neil Gibbons, Armando Iannucci and Steve Coogan, *I, Partridge: We Need to Talk about Alan* (London: HarperCollins, 2011); and John Robins, *A Robins amongst the Pigeons*, 2015. Available online: https://arobinsamongstthepigeons.tumblr.com/ (accessed 15 May 2019).

best and most powerful, comic writing can inspire just such peculiar feelings.[16] 'Turn' can also be used to refer to a performance, which as Eric Weitz argues, 'plays an undeniable role in any comic construction ... and such is the case even in a political cartoon, comic novel or email, where the competent performance is crafted for the specific relationship between the author's output on the page and the mind's eye of the reader'.[17] A comic turn, then, is performed, and it can bring about a transformation of mood or perspective. In the novels of Magnus Mills, for example, the repetitions of labour are pushed to deadpan comic extremes in ways that serve to question the norms and iniquities of contemporary working life. Or in the twisted picaresques of Nicola Barker, comic laughter can move between shock and revulsion, through uneasy recognition to eventual understanding or even identification. As I discuss in more detail later in this Introduction, any selection of texts is necessarily limiting, and my focus here is on contemporary English fiction, but the comic turn I identify is part of a wider turn, which could include US writers such as Paul Beatty, Michael Chabon, Junot Diaz, Jennifer Egan, A.M. Homes, Jarett Kobek, Gary Shteyngart and many more besides, or British and Irish writers such as Damian Gough, Niall Griffiths, A.L. Kennedy, Paul Murray, Ali Smith and Irvine Welsh, along with an even larger body of writers from other nations and a corpus of texts that include comic moments in the context of narratives whose prevailing tone is not comic.[18] This literary turn also speaks to the increasing prevalence of other forms of comedy and of the comic mode in contemporary Western society, or what Lauren Berlant and Sianne Ngai describe as the '"commedification" of modern social life', where 'it is comedy that people increasingly come to expect in the kinds of social interaction that take place in all zones of modern life – politics, education, journalism, even religion'.[19] In the context of comedians' prominence as both entertainers and spokespersons, for example, or in the rise of satirical programmes such as the *Daily Show* as sources of news and investigative journalism as well as

---

[16] The word 'funny' contains a similar ambiguity within it, and can mean peculiar as well as amusing. For a discussion of these dual meanings of the word and their significance for our understanding of the incongruity theory of humour, see John Morreall, 'Funny Ha-Ha, Funny Strange, and Other Reaction to Incongruity', in *The Philosophy of Laughter and Humor*, ed. John Morreall (Albany, NY: State University of New York University Press, 1987), pp. 188–207.

[17] Eric Weitz, *The Cambridge Introduction to Comedy* (Cambridge: Cambridge University Press, 2009), p. ix.

[18] Barbara Puschmann-Nalenz also identifies a comic turn in contemporary fiction in her introduction to a special issue of the journal *Anglistik* on 'Comic Representations in Post-Millennial British and Irish Fiction'. Barbara Puschmann-Nalenz, 'Introduction', in 'Focus on Comic Representations in Post-Millennial British and Irish Fiction', ed. Barbara Puschmann-Nalenz, special issue *Anglistik: International Journal of English Studies*, 27:1 (2016), 5–17.

[19] Berlant and Ngai, 'Comedy Has Issues', pp. 237, 240.

amusement, or in the ubiquity of comic interactions on social media platforms, communication and information are increasingly taking the form of jokes or other forms of comic 'event', to use Roof's formulation.[20] The comic turn in contemporary fiction, then, is part of a cultural turn towards comic modes of expression.

Despite the significance and prominence of comedy in contemporary culture, however, relatively little scholarly work has been conducted in this area, particularly from a literary studies perspective. Recent research on the contemporary moment has tended to focus on a mood of crisis, bleakness, cruelty, melancholia, environmental catastrophe and collapse,[21] with affect-orientated readings focusing on negative emotions such as trauma, fear, rage and shame.[22] Indeed, such is the prevalence of this mood of disaster and imminent collapse that there is a growing body of work specifically on apocalyptic and post apocalyptic fiction.[23] My focus on the comic is not to deny the importance of such work and of the texts and real-world crises with which it engages, nor is it to suggest that comedy is unable to respond to crisis and the contemporary structures of feeling associated with this reality. In fact, the chapters that follow

---

[20] See Roof, *Comic Event*. In Chapter 6 I discuss Howard Jacobson's idea in *Zoo Time* (2012) that stand-up comedians have overtaken novelists in terms of cultural reach and significance. The same chapter concludes with a discussion of 'internet humour at the end of the world' in the context of Mark Doten's *Trump Sky Alpha* (Minneapolis, MN: Graywolf Press, 2019).

[21] See, for example, Amanda Anderson, *Bleak Liberalism* (Chicago: University of Chicago Press, 2016); Lauren Berlant, *Cruel Optimism* (Durham, NC: Duke University Press, 2011); Astrid Bracke, *Climate Crisis and the 21st-Century British Novel* (London: Bloomsbury, 2019); Judith Butler, *Precarious Life: The Power of Mourning and Violence* (London: Verso, 2004); Amitav Ghosh, *The Great Derangement: Climate Change and the Unthinkable* (Chicago: University of Chicago Press, 2017); Paul Gilroy, *After Empire: Melancholia or Convivial Culture?* (Abingdon: Routledge, 2004); Ursula K. Heise, *Imagining Extinction: The Cultural Meanings of Endangered Species* (Chicago: University of Chicago Press, 2016); and Adam Trexler, *Anthropocene Fictions: The Novel in a Time of Climate Change* (Charlottesville, VA: University of Virginia Press, 2015).

[22] See, for example, Sara Ahmed, *The Cultural Politics of Emotion*, 2nd edn (Edinburgh: Edinburgh University Press, 2014); Douglas Dowland and Anna Ioanes (eds), 'Violent Feelings: Affective Intensities in Literature, Film, and Culture', special issue *Lit: Literature Interpretation, Theory*, 30:1–2 (2019), 1–169; Heather Houser, *Ecosickness in Contemporary U.S. Fiction: Environment and Affect* (New York: Columbia University Press, 2016); David James, *Discrepant Solace: Contemporary Literature and the Work of Consolation* (Oxford: Oxford University Press, 2019); and Sianne Ngai, *Ugly Feelings* (Cambridge, MA: Harvard University Press, 2005). This tendency to concentrate on negative affect is further evident in the focus of the volumes in the series Palgrave Studies in Affect Theory and Literary Criticism, whose subjects include mourning, shame, tragedy and reparation, but little or no mention of laughter, happiness or joy, for example.

[23] See, for example, Monica Germanà and Aris Mousoutzanis (eds), *Apocalyptic Discourse in Contemporary Culture: Post-Millennial Perspectives of the End of the World* (New York: Routledge, 2014); Paul Crosthwaite (ed.), *Criticism, Crisis, and Contemporary Narrative: Textual Horizons in an Age of Global Risk* (New York: Routledge, 2011); Diletta De Cristofaro, *The Contemporary Post-Apocalyptic Novel: Critical Temporalities and the End Times* (London: Bloomsbury, 2019); Heather J. Hicks, *The Post-Apocalyptic Novel in the Twenty-First Century: Modernity beyond Salvage* (Basingstoke: Palgrave Macmillan, 2016); and Andrew Tate, *Apocalyptic Fiction* (London: Bloomsbury, 2019).

are concerned with questions of political despair, class and labour inequalities, community relations, the possibility of sincerity after postmodernism and the limits of representation, all of which are 'serious' topics that are at the centre of many debates within the discipline and the wider society. My argument is that contemporary fiction is as likely to treat these subjects humorously as it is to treat them gravely, and that the recognition and proper analysis of this humour opens up new ways to think about these debates. The division between comedy and seriousness is a false one, and the focus on conventionally serious topics and modes of expression at the expense of the comic represents a diminution of critical vocabulary and understanding.[24]

However, although comedy has undoubtedly been marginalized in thinking about contemporary fiction, as well as contemporary culture more broadly, there is a growing and valuable body of work in this field. In 2018, Lauren Berlant and Sianne Ngai, two of the thinkers noted earlier for their association with the analysis of negative affect, edited a special issue of the influential journal *Critical Inquiry*, which along with a 2016 special issue of *Angelaki* on philosophy and comedy is representative of a burgeoning engagement with comedy and humour in the humanities. A forthcoming issue of *ASAP*, the house journal for ASAP: The Association for the Study of the Arts of the Present, will take this further by publishing contributions that use humour as a style and methodology. The establishment in 2010 of the journal *Comedy Studies*, in 2013 of the Centre for Comedy Studies Research at Brunel University London and in 2016 of the Palgrave Macmillan series Palgrave Studies in Comedy also speaks to the development of a discernible upturn of interest in this area, particularly in relation to television, film and comic performance. And this work joins a long-standing strand of humour studies most prominently represented by the International Society for Humor Studies and its journal *Humor*, which was established in 1988 and publishes interdisciplinary work on humour, comedy and laughter, with a particular focus on social scientific perspectives. The book series Humor Research shares a publisher with *Humor* and has a similar focus. There are also a number of individual volumes that focus wholly or in part on literary comedy, such as James English's path-breaking *Comic Transactions* (1994), Margaret Stetz's *British Women's Comic Fiction, 1890–1990* (2001), Simon

---

[24] For a fascinating discussion of the false division between comic and serious discourse, with a particular focus on the reproduction of this division in pedagogy, see Allon White, '"The Dismal Sacred Word": Academic Language and the Social Reproduction of Seriousness', in *Carnival, Hysteria and Writing: Collected Essays and Autobiography* (Oxford: Clarendon Press, 1993), pp. 122–34.

Critchley's *On Humour* (2002), Michael Ross's *Race Riots: Comedy and Ethnicity in Modern British Fiction* (2006) and Andrew Stott's *Comedy* (2014), as well as a number of recent theoretically minded works that make valuable interventions across multiple disciplines, including Alenka Zupančič's *The Odd One In* (2008), Judith Roof's *The Comic Event* (2018) and Alfie Bown's *In the Event of Laughter* (2019).[25] *The Comic Turn in Contemporary English Fiction* engages with work from all of these areas and seeks to bring together disciplinary perspectives that too often speak past one another rather than working in dialogue. It also engages with multiple versions of the three 'classic' theories of laughter – superiority, relief and incongruity – as well as more recent attempts to explain humour such as Peter McGraw and Caleb Warren's theory of benign violation.[26] I will spare the reader from the synopsis of these theories that seems all but compulsory in introductions to works on comedy, but each is discussed and contextualized where relevant in the chapters that follow, and I would direct readers to John Morreall's books *Taking Laughter Seriously* (1983) and *Comic Relief* (2009) for useful summaries of these concepts, their origins and exponents, and to Magda Romanska and Alan Ackerman's *Reader in Comedy* (2017) for wide-ranging excerpts from classic and more recent works on the topic. No single theory of humour can account for the multiple ways in which it is manifested in the comic text, let alone across multiple texts, and the approach throughout this book is to engage with work from cross-disciplinary perspectives both within and without humour and comedy studies in order to understand how comedy works and what it does in contemporary English fiction and beyond.

Contemporary English fiction

In *The Art of Fiction* (1992), David Lodge describes the comic novel as 'a very English, or at least British and Irish, kind of fiction, that does not always travel well'. He goes on to quote John Updike's review of Kingsley Amis's novel *Jake's Thing* (1978), and Updike's dismissive conclusion that Amis suffers from being 'in thrall to the "comic novel"', that 'there is no need to write "funny novels" when life's actual juxtapositions, set down attentively, are comedy enough'.[27] Lodge, a

---

[25] Jeroen Vandaele offers a valuable review of developments in comic theory and an analysis of the concept of narrative humour in his two-part essay 'Narrative Humor'.
[26] For an explanation of McGraw and Warren's theory, see Peter McGraw and Caleb Warren, 'Benign Violations: Making Immoral Behavior Funny', *Psychological Science*, 21:8 (2010), 1141–9.
[27] David Lodge, *The Art of Fiction* (London: Penguin, 1992), p. 110.

writer of comic novels himself, and understandably somewhat defensive, goes on to list the strength of the comic tradition in both acknowledged classics of comic writing (Fielding, Sterne, Smollett, Austen, Dickens and Waugh) and in fiction that contains comic episodes within a structure whose prevailing tone is not necessarily comic (Eliot, Hardy and Forster). He develops a persuasive defence against Updike's charges, but Updike is far from alone in his withering dismissal of comic writing, and James Wood has made a similar point about the distinction between the comic dimension of human experience and the comic novel:

> There is comedy, and then there is something called the Comic Novel, and these are related to each other rather as the year is related to a pocket diary – the latter a meaner, tidier, simpler version of the former. Comedy is the angle at which most of us see the world, the way that our very light is filtered.[28]

On this view, the comic novel is a simplification, an unnatural refraction of the pure light of actually occurring humour, and these brief comments by Lodge, Updike and Wood serve to emphasize some of the difficulties inherent to any discussion of comedy and fiction, or in comic fiction more narrowly defined. In Lodge's remarks we see the suggestion of particularity and regionality, even parochialism, followed by a list of precursors that both reinforces this sense of parochialism by naming only British and Irish authors, and then stretches the definition of comic novel almost to breaking point. And in Updike's and Wood's scornful reviews we can see a suspicion of, even snobbery against, writers who work in a comic tradition; comic fiction is not, it seems, sufficiently literary: rather than being a structure imposed upon fiction, comedy should inhere in the representation of everyday life. More recently, Howard Jacobson – who, as a writer of comedies, has his own agenda – again reminded readers of comedy's centrality to the history of the novel. He is similarly dismissive of the term 'comic novelist', finding it 'as redundant and off-putting as the term "literary novelist"', but he makes a strong claim both for the importance of the comic tradition and for its gradual denigration in the literary marketplace and intellectual life more broadly: 'we have created a false division between laughter and thought', he argues, 'between comedy and seriousness, between the exhilaration that the great novels offer when they are at their funniest, and whatever else it is we

---

[28] James Wood, 'Member of the Tribe: Howard Jacobson's *The Finkler Question*', *New Yorker*, 1 November 2010. Available online: https://www.newyorker.com/magazine/2010/11/08/member-of-the-tribe (accessed 4 June 2019).

now think we want from literature.'[29] Jacobson's views on the state of comedy are discussed at greater length in Chapter 6, and the division he identifies is perhaps not as pronounced as he suggests, but his comments, as well as his work in the 1997 book and television series *Seriously Funny*, do gesture towards the historical significance of comedy and its continued importance in the present. As I have already indicated in the opening discussion of genre, I too am wary of the unhelpful term 'comic fiction' or the 'comic novel' because like many such classifications, it falls apart under scrutiny, making it hard to identify a series of features that would align the writers discussed here to a particular genre or style. And after all, the English novel is comic from its inception.

From its emergence in England in the eighteenth century, the process influentially described by Ian Watt as the 'the rise of the novel' also represents the rise of the novel as the dominant form of literary comedy.[30] As Richard Keller Simon argues, in the novels of Henry Fielding in particular 'the history of laughter enters a new phase, one dominated by the novel, not the drama';[31] during this era, the novel took over as the preeminent form of English comedy and many of the most significant early novels in English were comic. Cervantes's *Don Quixote* (1605–15) was an important and influential precursor, but in Fielding, Smollett and Sterne, for example, as well as in less obvious but still significant ways in Defoe, Richardson, Burney and others, the development of a new genre of Anglophone writing happened in tandem with the development of new forms of comedy.[32] The English novel is, in a meaningful sense, a comic form, and although this is by no means the only way of framing its history, I agree with V.S. Pritchett that 'the comic tradition in the English novel is a powerful one' that offers 'an alternative to the Puritan tradition'.[33] This influence continues even through what Franco Moretti has described as the 'serious' nineteenth century,[34]

---

[29] Howard Jacobson, 'Howard Jacobson on Taking Comic Novels Seriously', *Guardian*, 9 October 2010. Available online: https://www.theguardian.com/books/2010/oct/09/howard-jacobson-comic-novels (accessed 21 March 2019).

[30] Ian Watt, *The Rise of the Novel: Studies in Defoe, Richardson and Fielding* (London: Penguin, [1957] 1972).

[31] Richard Keller Simon, *The Labyrinth of the Comic Theory and Practice from Fielding to Freud* (Tallahassee, FL: Florida State University Press, 1985), p. 17.

[32] Although, as Simon Dickie has usefully identified, the image of the eighteenth century as an time of increasing politeness and sensibility is not wholly accurate. His research in the archive of popular but largely forgotten comic texts of the period reveals the coexistence of pleasure in the suffering of others as well as the more rarefied pursuits more commonly associated with the era. Simon Dickie, *Cruelty and Laughter: Forgotten Comic Literature and the Unsentimental Eighteenth Century* (Chicago: University of Chicago Press, 2011).

[33] V.S. Pritchett, *George Meredith and English Comedy* (London: Chatto and Windus, 1970), p. 11.

[34] Moretti does not use 'serious' as a direct antonym to 'comic', but he does suggest that it 'means dark, cold, impassable, silent, heavy, solemn' and that there is a class element to the preponderance of this mode in the nineteenth century, implying that 'the middle has closed its ranks and uses its

in the writing of authors as apparently divergent as Jane Austen, Charles Dickens, George Eliot, Anthony Trollope and Oscar Wilde, and into the early twentieth century in Virginia Woolf,[35] Wyndham Lewis, Henry Green and Evelyn Waugh, as well as P.G. Wodehouse, of course, who may not be thought of as a formally innovative writer, but whose novels and stories stand as exemplars of the comic form. In the later twentieth century, writers of the 'angry' generation such as Kingsley Amis, William Cooper and Keith Waterhouse were often comic in their supposed anger, and a slightly later generation of women writers including Beryl Bainbridge, Fay Weldon and Margaret Drabble were both angry and comic in their own mordant ways. Migrant writers such as Sam Selvon, G.V. Desani and V.S. Naipaul brought levity as well as serious reflection to their representations of (post-)colonial and metropolitan life and the migrant experience, while David Lodge, Malcolm Bradbury and others published a run of comedies centring on life in academia and industry that were both minutely observed portrayals of their own seemingly narrow worlds and important studies of the post-war welfare state.[36] And the comic voice is not limited to realist fiction of the period but can also be read in more formally innovative work by writers such as B.S. Johnson, Brigid Brophy and Christine Brooke-Rose.[37] This is a necessarily brief summary of significant moments in the history of English comedy, but it aims to emphasize that the comic turn identified in this book is one of a series of comic turns, each of which speaks to its geographic and temporal specificity as well as a longer history of the form.[38]

To return to the comments that began this section, I am suspicious of Lodge's assertion that the comic novel is 'a very English, or at least British and Irish, kind of fiction, that does not always travel well'. Caveats about nomenclature

---

seriousness to distance itself from the "carnivalesque" noise of the labouring classes'. Franco Moretti, 'Serious Century', in *The Novel*, ed. Franco Moretti, 2 vols (Princeton, NJ: Princeton University Press, 2006), i, pp. 364–400 (pp. 369–70).

[35] As Judy Little and others have argued, humour plays an important role in Woolf's writing, and the fact that she is rarely discussed in these terms is representative of the marginalization of writing by women in critical studies of comedy. Judy Little, *Comedy and the Woman Writer: Woolf, Spark, and Feminism* (Lincoln, NE: University of Nebraska Press, 1983).

[36] James F. English, *Comic Transactions: Literature, Humor, and the Politics of Community in Twentieth-Century Britain* (Ithaca, NY: Cornell University Press, 1994), pp. 132–3.

[37] For a useful summary of comic fiction of this period with a focus on its class dynamics, see Philip Tew, 'Comedy, Class and Nation', in *The Oxford History of the Novel in English, vol. 7: British and Irish Fiction since 1940*, ed. Peter Boxall and Bryan Cheyette (Oxford: Oxford University Press, 2016), pp. 161–73.

[38] For summaries of the comic lineage in the English novel and readings of significant texts, see Glen Cavaliero, *The Alchemy of Laughter: Comedy in English Fiction* (Basingstoke: Macmillan, 2000); Manfred Pfister (ed.), *A History of English Laughter: Laughter from Beowulf to Beckett and Beyond* (Amsterdam: Rodopi, 2002); and Murray Roston, *The Comic Mode in English Literature: From the Middle Ages to Today* (London: Continuum, 2011).

aside, comedy is so imbricated with the history and development of the English novel that to deny the broader appeal of comic writing would be to deny the broader appeal of a huge swathe of literature. Indeed, Jonathan Coe, the subject of Chapter 1 and the author among those discussed here whose work is most self-consciously engaged with the vicissitudes of post-war regional and national English history, is also the writer with the largest non-Anglophone readership, to the extent that his work is more feted in Belgium, France and Italy than it is at home. At the same time, however, my primary focus is on English fiction. I am sceptical of generalizations about a 'national sense of humour', and questions of national identity are not my primary focus, but I am mindful of comedy's ability to work not only in universal, unifying ways – most obviously represented by shared laughter – but also in specific and sometimes divisive ways that require a tighter focus in order to understand, for example, the satirical precursors to which Coe's work is responding, the particular class dynamics of the relationship between characters and the authorial voice in Martin Amis's novels, or the cross-cultural encounters, understandings and misunderstandings found in the work of Zadie Smith.[39] The novelists whose work I discuss straddle several generations, from Martin Amis, Julian Barnes and Howard Jacobson, whose literary careers began in the 1970s and the early 1980s, and who, in the case of Amis and Barnes in particular, are associated with a lauded generation of writers that also includes Ian McEwan, Pat Barker, Kazuo Ishiguro and Salman Rushdie; to Jonathan Coe and Nicola Barker, who were first published in the late 1980s and the early 1990s; to Magnus Mills and Zadie Smith, whose work first appeared in the late 1990s and (just) into the 2000s, in the case of Smith.[40] Any sense of clear-cut generational divides is undermined by complicating factors such as the youthful starts of Amis and Smith and the relatively late starts of Jacobson and Mills, both of whom pursued other careers before they began publishing fiction. And while there are undoubted generational shifts and tendencies to be identified, for that I would direct readers to collections such as Peter Boxall and Bryan Cheyette's volume in *The Oxford History of the Novel in English* (2016), Robert L. Caserio and Clement Hawes's *The Cambridge History of the English Novel* (2012), or Berthold Schoene and Eileen Pollard's *British*

---

[39] For an insightful and provocative discussion of popular comedy and Englishness, see Andy Medhurst, *A National Joke: Popular Comedy and English Cultural Identities* (Abingdon: Routledge, 2007).

[40] As Berthold Schoene has noted, the publication of Smith's debut novel *White Teeth* (2000) 'was strategically delayed by her publishers to coincide with the ringing in of the new millennium'. Berthold Schoene, 'Twenty-First-Century Fiction', in *The Oxford History of the Novel in English, vol. 7: British and Irish Fiction since 1940*, ed. Peter Boxall and Bryan Cheyette (Oxford: Oxford University Press, 2016), pp. 549–63 (p. 549).

Literature in Transition, 1980–2000 (2019). My principal interest is in reading these authors' work as comic engagements with the contemporary, which is why I focus on novels published since 2000. The contemporary is a fluid construct, and I do not stick rigidly to this cut-off, preferring what the founding statement of the British Association for Contemporary Literary Studies describes as a 'rolling sense of the contemporary'.[41] At the same time, the choice of 2000 as the rough census date is not arbitrary and it follows the convention established in important recent interventions in contemporary literary studies such as Peter Boxall's *Twenty-First-Century Fiction* (2013) and *The Routledge Companion to Twenty-First Century Literary Fiction* (2019), edited by Daniel O'Gorman and Robert Eaglestone. It is significant that both of these volumes begin with a series of questions about the possibility of defining the contemporary and whether the twenty-first century can yet be thought of as a coherent literary period. As Michael North writes, 'Constant attempts to define the spirit of the age simply expose the fact that the age preceded its spirit, as the calendar precedes events,'[42] and I do not, therefore, seek to answer these questions about the precise nature and location of the contemporary, preferring to continue asking them and to consider what the study of comedy might add to these debates. *The Comic Turn in Contemporary British Fiction* is structured via a series of readings of authors, each of which takes a different approach to thinking about the nature of contemporary comedy and what it contributes to an understanding of contemporary literature and culture.

Chapter 1 examines the politics and political value of comedy via a reading of the novels of Jonathan Coe. It focuses on the role and efficacy of comic satire, examining Coe's work in light of his own re-evaluation of the form and his belief that contemporary satire has lost its bite. Coe has come to believe that, more often than not, satire reinforces existing views rather than holding the political establishment to account. In a 2013 essay for the *London Review of Books*, he reflects on the relationship between satirical comedy and the entrenchment of public cynicism about politicians, using the example of the English politician Boris Johnson – current UK prime minister, then the mayor of London – to argue that the bumbling, affable exterior he presents on topical television programmes such as *Have I Got News for You* is politically expedient and

---

[41] See the website of British Association for Contemporary Literary Studies (BACLS) at https://www.bacls.org/about/about/ (accessed 12 June 2019).

[42] Michael North, *What Is the Present?* (Princeton, NJ: Princeton University Press, 2018), p. 82. See also Amy Hungerford, 'On the Period Formerly Known as Contemporary', *American Literary History*, 20:1–2 (2008), 410–19.

allows him to conceal a more pernicious agenda: laughter replaces thought, and Johnson is exemplary of a phenomenon in which collective laughter has become a substitute for action. Coe's novels are frequently discussed as examples of satire,[43] and this is particularly true of *What a Carve Up!* (1994), the novel that made his name for its skewering of the free-market Thatcherite ideology of the 1980s and the 1990s. I trace the movement from *What a Carve Up!* to Coe's retrenchment from satire, reading his fiction alongside work from theorists such as Paolo Virno and Peter Sloterdijk to examine the political limitations as well as the potential of satire and other forms of comedy. Virno's work on the joke as a diagram of innovative action, for example, suggests one way in which humour might serve to question *éndoxa* (received opinion) and combat the pervading mood of cynicism in public life identified by Sloterdijk. In Coe's fiction, this speaks to English social and political life not only in the cutting satire of novels such as *What a Carve Up!* but also in the gentler comedy of *Expo 58* (2013), a novel whose long view of Anglo-European relations in some ways anticipates the national divisions that would be expressed in the UK's 2016 EU referendum and its aftermath; there is a tension throughout the novel, articulated through jokes, between the pull of continental Europe associated with modernity and ambition, and the pull of Britain represented by history and past glories. In a turn that now seems practically allegorical, Coe's protagonist chooses the easy consolations of the latter. The final section of the chapter discusses what I describe as Coe's 'metacomic' reflections on comedy in his novel *Number 11, or Tales that Witness Madness* (2015), a book that returns to the territory of *What a Carve Up!* but draws on the thinking expressed in his non-fiction writing to both perform comedy and reflect on its limitations. *Number 11* is a novel that incorporates a discussion of the nature of satirical humour in order to question its effectiveness, or rather to warn against mistaking mockery for critique or laughter for action.

Chapter 2 maintains a focus on the politics of comedy, but combines this with close analysis of literary style in order to discuss the relationship between style and ethics in the novels of Martin Amis. It begins with a discussion of Amis's claims for an ethics of style and considers what this means for the stylistics of comedy. Techniques such as bathos or its opposite, 'upgrading', are inherent to much comedy and are a notable feature of Amis's work, in which his famously 'high' style is frequently juxtaposed with the 'low' speech of his characters. Amis positions himself as part of an English comic lineage 'of writing about low events

---

[43] See, for example, Philip Tew (ed.), *Jonathan Coe: Contemporary British Satire* (London: Bloomsbury, 2018).

in a high style',[44] but the terms 'high' and 'low' bring with them a hierarchy that has important implications for his ethical claims. This chapter draws on work in narratology, humour theory and linguistics to analyse this hierarchy, arguing that Amis's comic style is often predicated on distinctions that fall along lines of social class. Techniques such as 'style shifting'[45] tacitly place readers on the side of Amis's eloquent middle- and upper-class characters and against his working-class characters, creating a troubling equivalence between linguistic value and moral worth. Comedy is often described in terms of laughing at versus laughing with, or of 'punching up' against those of higher status versus 'punching down' at those of lower status, and in Amis's novels, these relationships are indexed at the level of style; as Amis has himself written, 'style judges', and that judgement is frequently invited via the laughter that is directed towards his working-class characters and their demotic speech.

A different picture of the relationship between humour and society emerges in Chapter 3, which discusses the role of laughter in the novels of Zadie Smith. As I note earlier, laughter and comedy are not always synonymous, and Smith's fiction represents laughter's role as both a cohesive and a divisive force. This chapter focuses on laughter as affect, reading the nuances of its social and emotional roles in comic passages from Smith's novels as well as in textual representation of laughter. It begins with a discussion of James Wood's category of 'hysterical realism', which he applied to Smith's first novel *White Teeth* (2000) and the work of peers such as David Foster Wallace and Jonathan Franzen. I argue that Wood's description of an opposition between depth and shallowness fails to account for the more nuanced oscillation between modes of humour and modes of laughter that takes place in Smith's novels. This discussion of laughter's multiplicity continues in the second section of the chapter, which examines the kinship between laughter and tears, two affective responses that are too often treated as opposites but that share many commonalities as examples of what Helmuth Plessner describes as responses to 'boundary situations'.[46] Laughter also has the ability to cross other forms of boundary, and while it is important to acknowledge its role as a form of ridicule, it can also provide a way of establishing solidarity and understanding, however fleeting that may be. I explore this role in Smith's novels *NW* (2012) and *Swing Time* (2016), engaging with the work

---

[44] John Haffenden, *Novelists in Interview* (London: Methuen, 1985), p. 24.
[45] David Herman, *Story Logic: Problems and Possibilities of Narrative* (Lincoln, NE: University of Nebraska Press, [2002] 2004), pp. 197–8.
[46] Helmuth Plessner, *Laughing and Crying: A Study of the Limits of Human Behavior*, 3rd edn, trans. James Spencer Churchill and Marjorie Grene (Evanston, IL: Northwestern University Press, [1961] 1970), p. 144.

one of laughter's philosophical advocates, Georges Bataille, who argues for the significance of a unifying laughter of community and 'intense communication'.[47]

Theories of laughter, as well as theories of comedy and humour, are often predicated on the idea of surprise and on the pleasing cognitive shift that takes place when two incongruous concepts are juxtaposed. In many cases, this link between surprise and humour is persuasive, but how might one account for the comedy of repetition and the ways in which repetition can amplify rather than diminish amusement? Chapter 4 examines this question via a reading of the novels of Magnus Mills, whose comedies of working life describe contemporary systems of labour that are at once repetitive, funny and ultimately nightmarish. Mechanical repetition is central to Henri Bergson's thesis in the essay *Laughter* (1900), most famously expressed as *'Something mechanical encrusted on the living'*,[48] but whereas for Bergson the perception of machine-like, repetitive behaviour inspires the laughter of superiority that enforces societal norms, an alternative interpretation is also possible. I argue that like precursors such as Samuel Beckett and Flann O'Brien, Mills's obsessive repetitions serve to undermine rather than reinforce the systems and norms of behaviour he portrays. Works by Gilles Deleuze and Alenka Zupančič are instructive here because they offer ways to think not only about how repetition might be '*constitutive* of the comic genre as such' rather than an obstacle to its success[49] but also about how, in Deleuzian terms, this very repetition might serve to denaturalize the law in order 'to demonstrate its absurdity and provoke the very disorder that it is intended to prevent or to conjure'.[50] Mills's deadpan comedies conjure recognizable but off-kilter worlds and provoke comic laughter tinged with unease; they suggest that life, and particularly working life, is absurd and very possibly hellish.

That repetition should be funny may run contra to the presiding wisdom that comedy is predicated on surprise, but this should itself be no surprise. Such paradoxes are inherent to many forms of comedy, which often rely on the suspension of multiple, contradictory ideas or images. As I have already noted, this idea is central to the dominant theory of humour, incongruity theory, which posits that humour arises from the pleasing juxtaposition of seemingly incompatible ideas. Chapter 5 of *The Comic Turn in Contemporary British*

---

[47] Georges Bataille, *Inner Experience*, trans. Leslie Anne Boldt (Albany, NY: State University of New York Press, [1954] 1988), p. 95.
[48] Henri Bergson, 'Laughter: An Essay on the Meaning of the Comic' [1900], trans. Cloudesley Brereton and Fred Rothwell, in *Comedy*, ed. Wylie Sypher (New York: Doubleday, 1956), pp. 61–190 (p. 84).
[49] Alenka Zupančič, *The Odd One In: On Comedy* (Cambridge, MA: MIT Press, 2008), p. 149.
[50] Gilles Deleuze, *Masochism: Coldness and Cruelty*, trans. Jean McNeil (New York: Zone Books, [1967] 1989), p. 88.

Fiction examines comedy's propensity towards paradox and contradiction via a discussion of the novels of Nicola Barker, an author who has identified an abiding fascination with paradoxical states. It begins with a discussion of incongruity, identifying a strand of 'Pooterish' comedy in Barker's *Burley Cross Postbox Theft* (2010) that speaks to Schopenhauer's account of comic pedantry and the disjuncture between abstract ideas and lived experience. However, while incongruity theory may help account for aspects of Barker's humour, I argue not simply that incongruity *explains* humour, but rather that humour – the comic voice – is uniquely suited to the exploration of opposites at the centre of much comic writing and evident throughout Barker's work: that it *allows* it. In novels such as *The Cauliflower®* (2016), Barker explores the interplay of apparent opposites that can take place in comedy, and comic writing's ability to develop its own 'logic of the absurd'.[51] This examination of comedy's paradoxes continues into the next section of the chapter, which examines the categories of satire, the grotesque and the carnivalesque, and the claims that have been made for their radical potential versus the idea that they represent a licensed form of rebellion that ultimately serves hegemony. Finally, I discuss Barker's move away from satirical and carnivalesque modes and towards what Umberto Eco terms 'humour', in which emotion and empathy are brought into the field of the comic, and the feeling is one of empathy and unease rather than relief.[52] This speaks to contemporary debates about the transition from postmodern irony to post-postmodern sincerity, but again it is not a binary question of movement from one to the other: the modes of irony and sincerity coexist and overlap, and sincere engagement need not preclude irony. As this discussion of Barker's writing reveals, humour relies on opposites and paradox but is also itself paradoxical – it can inspire both ridicule and sympathy; it can liberate but also enforce norms; and it can be both ironic and sincere. As such, comedy is the medium best placed to explore such paradoxes.

Chapter 6 begins with a further paradox: the idea that comedy should be a space that is free from boundaries versus that idea that to tell jokes with complete impunity would mean there were no boundaries left to push and none of the frisson required for transgressive humour. Howard Jacobson is among those who have argued that comedy should be a space of total freedom, going so far as to defend comedy elsewhere dismissed as irredeemably racist and sexist. He

---

[51] See Jerry Palmer, *The Logic of the Absurd: On Film and Television Comedy* (London: BFI, 1987); and Jerry Palmer, *Taking Humour Seriously* (London: Routledge, 1994).
[52] Umberto Eco, 'The Frames of Comic "Freedom"', in *Carnival!* ed. Thomas A. Sebeok (Berlin: Mouton, 1984), pp. 1–9.

argues that laughter at taboo subjects provides an important function in releasing pent-up tensions that might otherwise be expressed in more destructive ways. Like Jonathan Coe, Jacobson is an author–critic who has written extensively about comedy, and this chapter reads his claims for the importance of a comedy without boundaries alongside his own provocative novels. It is a chapter about the ethics of comedy and the boundaries of comedy in several senses, including boundaries of offensiveness, boundaries of community and the right to tell jokes, boundaries of subject matter including the possibility of Holocaust comedy and finally the boundaries of possibility for satirical comedy in an age when the reality of public figures such as Nigel Farage, Boris Johnson and Donald Trump appears to outstrip satirists' capacity for invention. Throughout this chapter, I argue that boundaries are inherent to comedy but that these boundaries are not as simple as a list of proscribed or allowable topics. Rather, the boundaries between what is and is not acceptable – and indeed what is and is not deemed to be comic at all – rely on a negotiation between writer/performer and reader/audience, and always involve questions of situation and intention. Jacobson's fiction demonstrates an awareness of this fact that is less evident in his bombastic pronouncements about the value of comedy and the need for offence, expressed in non-fiction writing such as *Seriously Funny* (1997); his novels are undoubtedly provocative, but they also articulate the fact that comedy's boundaries are situational rather than structural and rely on a complex series of unspoken negotiations rather than a set of ethical absolutes.

The concluding chapter draws together a number of threads from earlier chapters to discuss Julian Barnes's *England, England* (1998) in the context of English identity and of the relationship between aesthetics and politics. Barnes's novel imagines the construction of a corporate, theme park version of England on the Isle of Wight, just off mainland England's south coast. The new park, named 'England, England', eventually supersedes the original country, which comes to be known as 'Old England' and finally 'Albion'. While England, England thrives, Albion reverts to a largely agrarian economy and slides into international irrelevance. The new economy of England, England is based on a performed version of Englishness, and the workers' embodiment of their characters speaks to Sianne Ngai's identification of a zany aesthetic that reflects the movement of affect and performance into the workplaces of post-Fordist economies. Although published over twenty years ago as I write, in this novel Barnes, himself a Francophile and committed European, also speaks to contemporary debates about Brexit, the devolution of the United Kingdom, and the position of England and the rest of the Britain on the world stage. *England,*

England is representative of the comic turn in the sense that it is part of the turn towards comedy identified throughout this book, but it is also representative of the secondary sense of 'turn' as a way of describing comic performance. It is also about England and about the fiction of Englishness. In these ways, it provides a fitting coda to *The Comic Turn in Contemporary English Fiction*.

Who's laughing now?

Robert Benchley's 1936 story 'Why We Laugh – Or Do We? (Let's Get This Thing Settled, Mr. Eastman)' is a response to Max Eastman's *Enjoyment of Laughter* (1936), a popular science book that attempts to explain the mechanics and meaning of jokes and laughter for a mass audience.[53] Benchley's story anticipates E.B. White's famous maxim that 'humor can be dissected, as a frog can, but the thing dies in the process and the innards are discouraging to any but the pure scientific mind',[54] reducing Eastman's pronouncements to absurdity and at the same time offering its own bravura comic performance. 'All laughter is merely a compensatory reflex to take the place of sneezing', Benchley writes, and 'what we really want to do is sneeze, but as that is not always possible, we laugh instead', adding that 'the old phrase "That is nothing to sneeze at" proves my point. What is obviously meant is "That is nothing to *laugh* at." The wonder is that nobody ever thought of this explanation of laughter before, with the evidence staring him in the face like that.' A series of ludicrous extrapolations follow, culminating in a list of 'five cardinal points' that must be in place in order for a joke to work:

1. The joke must be in a language we can understand.
2. It must be spoken loudly enough for us to hear it, or printed clearly enough for us to read it.
3. It must be about _some_thing. You can't just say, 'here's a good joke' and let it go at that. (You *can*, but don't wait for the laugh.)
4. It must deal with either frustration or accomplishment, inferiority or superiority, sense or nonsense, pleasantness or unpleasantness, or, at any

---

[53] Jon Michaud, 'Eighty-Five from the Archive: Robert Benchley', *New Yorker*, 16 February, 2010. Available online: https://www.newyorker.com/books/double-take/eighty-five-from-the-archive-robert-benchley (accessed 3 June 2019). As Benchley identifies, Eastman's book is a rich source of unintentional humour and begins with four laws of humour, beginning with the idea that 'things can be funny only when we are in fun' and including the cliché that being 'in fun' is a childlike state. Max Eastman, *Enjoyment of Laughter* (London: Hamish Hamilton, 1937), p. 19.

[54] Quoted in Mike Sacks, *Poking a Dead Frog: Conversations with Today's Top Comedy Writers* (New York: Penguin, 2014), p. xvii.

rate, with some emotion that can be analysed, otherwise how do we know when to laugh?
5. It must begin with the letter 'W'.[55]

Such lists of rules or conditions for the comic will be familiar not only to readers of Eastman's book but to readers of the numerous books on comedy and humour studies published before it and in the intervening decades. Chastened by Benchley's example, I will not offer my own account of the comic machinations of 'Why We Laugh—Or Do We?', but I will note that the approach he parodies is one that I have attempted to avoid. You will not find a series of rules or genre characteristics in the pages that follow, but you will, I hope, discover a series of new readings of significant contemporary writers and a series of new frameworks for thinking about the political, ethical, aesthetic and affective dimensions of comedy. And I make no apologies for killing the frog: critical studies of horror writing are not expected to be terrifying, and I have read enough books on comedy to realize that attempting to be funny in this context is nearly always a mistake.

---

[55] Robert Benchley, 'Why We Laugh – Or Do We? (Let's Get This Thing Settled, Mr. Eastman)', *New Yorker*, [2 January 1937] 16 February 2010. Available online: https://www.newyorker.com/magazine/1937/01/02/why-we-laugh-or-do-we (accessed 3 June 2019).

1

'Sinking giggling into the sea'?
Jonathan Coe and the politics of comedy

In a 2013 essay, the novelist and critic Jonathan Coe describes some of the difficulties inherent in defining the comic novel, suggesting that that 'for most British writers and critics, the comic novel is an elusive thing to define, even though it's meant to be something at which we excel'.[1] Yet Coe is plainly a writer of comedies. His early novels *The Accidental Woman* (1987), *A Touch of Love* (1989) and *The Dwarves of Death* (1990) demonstrate a mordant sense of humour amidst the more sombre prevailing tone,[2] but it was his fourth novel, *What a Carve Up!* (1994), which saw Coe turn to writing out-and-out comedy, fulfilling what he describes as a 'probably inevitable' trajectory towards the mode of political satire.[3] This trajectory began with an early obsession with comedy and shared laughter before developing into a belief in satire's political potential. It encompassed an MA dissertation on theories of comedy and a PhD thesis on narration in Henry Fielding's *Tom Jones* and other comic novels.[4] Coe's comedy draws from a significant range of reference points, including Fielding but also Samuel Becket,[5] B.S. Johnson (the subject of a prize-winning biography by Coe), David Nobbs[6] and many sources from popular culture, particularly British

---

[1] Jonathan Coe, '"Comic" Novels', in *Marginal Notes, Doubtful Statements: Non-Fiction, 1990–2013*, Kindle edn (London: Penguin, 2013).
[2] By 'tone', I mean what Sianne Ngai describes as 'a literary text's affective bearing, orientation, or "set toward" its audience and world', or the formal features that structure a text's 'affective "comportment"'. Ngai, *Ugly Feelings*, p. 43.
[3] Coe, 'The Paradox of Satire (I)', in *Marginal Notes*. Coe's move towards comedy and satire is my focus here, but this should not obscure the melancholic thread that runs throughout his work. See Joseph Brooker, 'Jonathan Coe's Stories of Sadness', in *Jonathan Coe: Contemporary British Satire*, ed. Philip Tew (London: Bloomsbury, 2018), pp. 35–50.
[4] See Jonathan Coe, 'Satire and Sympathy: Some Consequences of Intrusive Narration in *Tom Jones* and Other Comic Novels', PhD thesis, Warwick University, 1986.
[5] See, for example, the series of comparisons between Coe and Beckett made by Vanessa Guignery in *Jonathan Coe* (Basingstoke: Palgrave Macmillan, 2016).
[6] Coe has discussed on a number of occasions the inspiration he took from Nobbs, and the *Reginald Perrin* series in particular. Nobbs scripted a 2005 BBC Radio 4 adaptation of Coe's *What a Carve Up!* and Coe published a tribute following Nobbs's death in 2015. See Jonathan Coe, 'David Nobbs 1935–

sitcoms and films. Coe's novels combine self-referential tricksiness alongside a broader adherence to realism, delighting in intertextual and intermedial references, including within and between the storyworlds that he has himself created. They are varied in subject matter and tone, but they include clear points of intersection with English comic writers of the previous generation, including Nobbs (especially in work such as the Reginald Perrin-esque *The Terrible Privacy of Maxwell Sim* [2010]), Malcolm Bradbury (particularly in *Expo 58* [2013]), David Lodge and Kingsley Amis.[7] This is a tradition of which Coe, with his academic background and continuing work as an essayist, is well aware. Like Bradbury, who enjoyed parallel academic and creative writing careers, Coe is a writer who both writes comic fiction and maintains a scholarly interest in the nature of the comic, an interest reflected by a series of essays that describe Coe's changing relationship with comedy as a mode of writing and a mode of critique. These essays, and this chapter's discussion of Coe and comedy, take *What a Carve Up!* as their starting point.

What a Carve Up! is a comic tour de force, widely read as one of the defining satires of Thatcherism[8] and still probably Coe's best-known work. At once a Jacobean tragedy, a gothic horror, a *Carry On*-style farce, a story of personal love and loss, and a sweeping analysis of post-war British politics and culture, it was viewed on publication as 'one of the few pieces of genuinely political Post-Modern fiction around'[9] and 'a grand and intelligent novel, so full of accomplishment and pleasure',[10] and it has since been described as one of the defining novels of the era.[11] In an insightful reading, Pamela Thurschwell argues that *What a Carve Up!* and Coe's other novels set in the 1970s and the 1980s,

2015', Jonathan Coe Personal Website (2015), http://www.jonathancoewriter.com/blog.php/?p=475 (accessed 17 June 2019). In a 2015 podcast about Nobbs, Coe describes reading the first Reginald Perrin novel and Joseph Heller's *Catch-22* (1961) at age fourteen, and how they were fundamental to his realization that 'you can be funny and serious at the same time'. See Andy Miller and John Mitchinson, 'Episode 3 – David Nobbs' [podcast], *Backlisted Podcast*, 23 December 2015. Available online: https://soundcloud.com/backlistedpod/episode-3-david-nobbs (accessed 17 June 2019). Some intertextual references to Nobbs in Coe's own novels are discussed below.

[7] This list of male antecedents should not, however, obscure the parallel influence of women writers such as Rosamond Lehmann, Dorothy Richardson and May Sinclair, discovered by Coe via the Virago Modern Classics imprint. This influence is most evident in Coe's more muted and largely un-comic novel *The Rain Before It Falls* (2007), but in contrast to many of the comic writers with whom his work bears comparison, he has throughout his career written sympathetic and, to use E.M. Forster's terminology in *Aspects of the Novel* (1927), 'round' female characters. See 'Virago Modern Classics' and 'Two Novels by Rosamond Lehmann' in Coe, *Marginal Notes*.

[8] As John Su argues, *What a Carve Up!* is not about Margaret Thatcher or Thatcherism in a party-political sense. Instead, Coe casts awareness 'in personalized, almost metaphysical terms – Thatcherism is a zeitgeist more than a political ideology'. John Su, 'Beauty and the Beastly Prime Minister', *ELH*, 81:3 (2014), 1083–110 (p. 1091).

[9] Terry Eagleton, 'Theydunnit', review of *What a Carve Up! London Review of Books*, 28 April 1994, p. 12.

[10] Laurence O'Toole, 'A Right Carrion', review of *What a Carve Up! New Statesman*, 29 April 1994, p. 7.

[11] See Guignery, *Jonathan Coe* (pp. 157–63) for a valuable discussion of Coe's critical reception.

make us ask questions such as 'Who is responsible for the current state of Britain and the world?', 'Do individual desires stand a chance against the weight of historical forces?', 'What is the relationship between individual happiness and social misery?' They try and respond to these questions in local, painful (and sometimes painfully hilarious) ways. Frantically mixing genres and conventions, his books lead us towards the recognition of modern history as tragedy, but also towards the incredulous, shared laughter of those of us still in the audience (and on stage) for postmodernism's endless historical reruns: our second time farces.[12]

According to Thurschwell, the novel raises a series of questions and has a powerful critical role, referencing and recycling both popular and high culture as bitter farce in order 'to feed anger rather than defuse it'.[13] And for Paul Gilroy, *What a Carve Up!* inspires a similarly 'pointed, sometimes Swiftian laughter carefully and creatively orchestrated so as to employ the weapon of ridicule against particular varieties of greed, power and injustice'.[14] These readings underline the sense of 'unease and betrayal', as well as necessity, felt by Coe when he wrote the novel,[15] a feeling articulated by a reference to the state of political fiction as viewed from 1994 and embedded within the novel as a fictional book review written by the protagonist, Michael Owen: 'We stand badly in need of novels,' Owen writes, 'which show an understanding of the ideological hijack which has taken place so recently in this country, which can see its consequences in human terms and show the appropriate response lies not in sorrow and anger but in mad, incredulous laughter.'[16] Here, embedded in this much-quoted passage from the novel itself, is an argument for the political force of critical laughter that pre-empts many of the scholarly responses to *What a Carve Up!* It is an idea that goes back at least until Lord Shaftesbury's 'Essay on the Freedom of Wit and Humour' (1709)[17] and which more recently found influential expression in Mikhail Bakhtin's idea of the 'carnivalesque'.[18]

---

[12] Pamela Thurschwell, 'Genre, Repetition and History in Jonathan Coe', in *British Fiction Today*, ed. Philip Tew and Rod Mengham (London: Continuum, 2006), pp. 28–39 (p. 38).
[13] Ibid., p. 29.
[14] Paul Gilroy, 'The Closed Circle of Britain's Postcolonial Melancholia', in *The Literature of Melancholia: Early Modern to Postmodern*, ed. Martin Middeke and Christina Wald (Basingstoke: Palgrave Macmillan, 2011), pp. 187–204 (p. 199).
[15] Coe, '*What a Carve Up!*' in Marginal Notes.
[16] Jonathan Coe, *What a Carve Up!* (London: Penguin, [1994] 1995), p. 277.
[17] See Anthony Ashley Cooper, Third Earl of Shaftesbury, *Characteristics of Men, Manners, Opinions, Times* (Cambridge: Cambridge University Press, [1711] 1999), and particularly 'A letter concerning enthusiasm to my Lord *****' (pp. 2–28) and 'Sensus communis, an essay on the freedom of wit and humour in a letter to a friend' (pp. 29–69).
[18] Mikhail Bakhtin, *Rabelais and His World*, trans. Hélène Iswolsky (Bloomington, IN: Indiana University Press [1965] 1984). For a critique of Bakhtin's claims for the critical and ethical power

But although *What a Carve Up!* succeeds in inspiring this 'mad incredulous laughter', since its publication, and increasingly in recent years, Coe has expressed reservations about the political effectiveness of its humour, and indeed the political effectiveness of satire in general. First in a 2010 speech at La Milanesiana, an annual arts festival in Milan, and then in a 2013 article for the *London Review of Books*,[19] Coe reflected on his changing relationship with satire, concluding that he no longer shares his younger self's confidence in the power of satirical laughter. After the publication of *What a Carve Up!* he began to notice that 'everybody who disliked the book disliked because they did not agree with its politics. Everybody who did like the book liked it because they already agreed with everything that it said. In other words, my attempt to use laughter as an agent for change had failed completely.'[20] Satirical laughter, he argues, does not 'disrupt the established order' but rather cements allegiances among like-minded people:

> It brings about the very opposite of what the author was intending. It creates a space – a warm, safe, welcoming space – in which like-minded readers can gather together and share in comfortable laughter. The anger, the feelings of injustice which they might have been suffering beforehand, are gathered together, compressed, and transformed into bursts of delicious, exhilarating laughter, and after discharging them they feel relieved, content and satisfied. An impulse which might have translated into action is therefore rendered neutral and harmless. It's no wonder the rich and powerful have no objection to being mocked. They, at least, understand the paradox of satire. We write it in the hope of changing the world. But in fact, it is one of the most powerful weapons we have for preserving the status quo.[21]

On this view, satirical laughter is not a revolutionary force, it is not a way of holding the powerful to account, but is rather a way of cementing pre-existing beliefs and oppositions.[22] It may speak truth to power, but power does not have to listen.

---

of laughter, see Umberto Eco, 'The Comic and the Rule', in *Travels in Hyperreality: Essays*, trans. William Weaver (San Diego, CA: Harcourt Brace, 1983), pp. 269–79; and Eco, 'The Frames of Comic "Freedom"', pp. 1–9. This debate is discussed in greater detail in Chapter 5.

[19] Both interventions are published as a two-part discussion of 'The Paradox of Satire' in *Marginal Notes, Doubtful Statements*.

[20] Coe, 'The Paradox of Satire (I)'.

[21] Ibid.

[22] This idea that satire solidifies rather than challenges existing beliefs is borne out in recent research on viewers' responses to *The Colbert Report* (2005–14), in which the real-life Stephen Colbert played a right-wing talk show host, also called Stephen Colbert. A 2009 study reports that although the programme enjoyed popularity with both conservative and liberal audiences, conservatives were more likely to believe the stated beliefs of Colbert's character, while liberals were more likely to view

When Coe expanded on this thesis in an article for the *London Review of Books*, he did so in the context of what was ostensibly a review of the collected *bon mots* of the disgraced journalist, Conservative MP, former mayor of London and, at the time of writing, UK prime minister, Boris Johnson. The article, originally entitled 'Sinking Giggling into the Sea', discusses the British 'satire boom' of the 1950s and the 1960s, and its legacy in anti-establishment comedy, particularly the weekly satirical news quiz *Have I Got News for You*, which provided an early platform for Johnson to present his public persona of a bumbling, affable classicist who dabbles in politics: not the everyman persona affected by most contemporary politicians, but a harmless toff it is okay to like. Coe's reading focuses on an uncomfortable moment for Johnson when he is grilled by one of the regular team captains, Ian Hislop, on his role in a recorded telephone conversation with his friend Darius Guppy. Guppy asked Johnson to provide the address of a hostile journalist, the inference being that he planned to assault him.[23] During a squirm-inducing exchange between Hislop and Johnson, Paul Merton, the other regular team captain, chimes in with a punning joke that gets a big laugh from the audience: 'An uncomfortable situation is suddenly diffused: Johnson relaxes, the audience laughter gives him room to breathe and gather his thoughts. When he next speaks he is back on track again.' The difference between this and a later exchange on the same topic that took place on a more sober daytime news programme is that on *Have I Got News for You*, 'it was laughter, more than anything else, that let Johnson off the hook'.[24] What Coe

his statements as ironic and therefore critical of conservative attitudes. The authors conclude that while both conservatives and liberals 'know it is comedy and presumably watch it to be entertained, there are stark differences in how they see the comedy, who they think is being satirized, and how those differences polarize the electorate by reinforcing their own set of beliefs as valid and the opposing set of beliefs as laughable'. This research relies on a binary model of political belief, but it does lend further credence to the idea that satire may help retrench existing ideas. See Heather L. LaMarre, Kristen D. Landreville and Michael A. Beam, 'Political Ideology and the Motivation to See What You Want to See in *The Colbert Report*', *International Journal of Press/Politics*, 14:2 (2009), 212–31 (p. 226). One of the authors of this article, Heather L. LaMarre, features in an episode of Malcolm Gladwell's *Revisionist History* podcast on the topic of 'The Satire Paradox'. The podcast also features Coe, and Gladwell has suggested that Coe's *LRB* article on satire provided his inspiration for the episode. Malcolm Gladwell, 'The Satire Paradox' [podcast], *Revisionist History*. Available online: http://revisionisthistory.com/episodes/10-the-satire-paradox (accessed 17 June 2019). I am, however, sceptical about Gladwell's attitude towards humour more broadly, in part due to his misguided belief that laughter is too easy to come by ('the easiest thing in the world'), and that art which invokes tears is inherently superior. This overlooks the fact that laughter is a positive affective response that individuals are more likely to wish to invoke during everyday discourse. Making people upset and tearful is not as challenging as Gladwell suggests, but most actively seek to avoid it in most social situations. See Malcolm Gladwell, *Desert Island Discs*, 10 August 2015, BBC Radio 4. Available online: http://www.bbc.co.uk/programmes/b04d0xfx (accessed 17 June 2019).

[23] For an account of Johnson's involvement in this affair, see Heathcote Williams, *Boris Johnson: The Beast of Brexit*, 2nd edn (London: London Review of Books, 2019), pp. 36–46.

[24] Coe, 'The Paradox of Satire (II)'. For an excellent discussion of the post-war 'satire boom', which anticipates much of Coe's argument, see Stephen Wagg, 'You've Never Had It So Silly: The Politics

describes here is in many ways a version of a relief theory of laughter,[25] and Coe is unequivocal that it is laughter – as opposed to satire – that is the problem,[26] particularly as canny politicians such as Johnson are able to harness laughter to suit their own agendas:

> These days every politician is a laughing stock, and the laughter which occasionally used to illuminate the dark corners of the political world with dazzling, unexpected shafts of hilarity has become an unthinking reflex on our part, a tired, Pavlovian reaction to situations too difficult or too depressing to think about clearly. Johnson seems to know this: he appears to know that the laughter which surrounds him is a substitute for thought rather than its conduit, and that puts him at a wonderful advantage. If we are chuckling at him, we are not likely to be thinking too hard about his doggedly neo-liberal and pro-City agenda, let alone doing anything to counter it.[27]

The sagacity of Coe's essay has become increasingly apparent in subsequent years as Johnson has risen to the highest office in British politics, and in a 2019 follow-up piece, he notes that his diagnosis had been 'reasonably accurate' but did not go 'far enough': Johnson's 'only agenda is in fact to pursue power at all costs for his own personal gratification' and if he 'does have an ideology, it is even further to the right than many of us feared'.[28] To extend Coe's argument about the role of contemporary satire to his own *What a Carve Up!*, it can be argued that the laughter it invites at the expense of the Winshaws and their grotesqueries, and particularly at their finely orchestrated demises, serves a similar function to unthinking laughter at Boris Johnson and other politicians, acting as a cathartic release rather than an anger-inducing call to arms.

When, in a conceit borrowed from the 1961 film *What a Carve Up!*, a film with which Michael Owen is obsessed, the Winshaw siblings are summoned to

---

of British Satirical Comedy from *Beyond the Fringe* to *Spitting Image*', in *Come On Down? Popular Media Culture in Post-war Britain*, ed. Dominic Strinati and Stephen Wagg (London: Routledge, 1992), pp. 254–84. Wagg argues that 'the fruits of the "satire boom" have helped the satirists themselves and many western consumers shrug off any guilt they may have felt about enjoying themselves, simply by asserting the across-the-board absurdity of it all' (p. 281).

[25] Lord Shaftesbury, Herbert Spencer and Sigmund Freud have all posited a version of the relief theory of humour in which laughter acts as a pressure valve to release psychic energy. John Morreall's *Taking Laughter Seriously* (Albany, NY: State University of New York Press, 1983) and *Comic Relief: A Comprehensive Philosophy of Humor* (Chichester: Wiley-Blackwell, 2009) provide useful summaries of the relief theory and the other dominant theories of laughter, superiority and incongruity.

[26] For a discussion of the relationship between satire and humour, see Conal Condren, 'Satire and Definition', *Humor*, 25:4 (2012), 375–99.

[27] Coe, 'The Paradox of Satire (II)'.

[28] Jonathan Coe, 'How Bad Can It Get? Reflections on the State We're In', *London Review of Books*, 15 August 2019. Available online: https://www.lrb.co.uk/v41/n16/the-state-were-in/how-bad-can-it-get#coe (accessed 12 August 2019).

a gothic mansion and are killed one by one in a manner appropriate to their crimes, the scenes are orchestrated as set-up and punchline. Mark Winshaw, the unscrupulous arms dealer, is found as follows:

> The missing axe from the suit of armour, its blade red and sticky, had been left on top of the billiard table; and protruding hideously from the two pockets at the baulk end were Mark's severed limbs. To complete the macabre joke, a message had been scrawled in blood on the wall.
> It said: A FAREWELL TO ARMS![29]

Some theorists of satire and comedy would argue that this scene is inherently challenging. Most famously, Bakhtin's notion of the carnivalesque makes bold claims for the carnivalesque tradition that can bring about the (temporary) defeat 'of all that oppresses and restricts',[30] as does Northrop Frye who identifies 'militant irony' as characteristic of satire, whereby satirist and audience share common 'standards against which the grotesque and absurd are measured' and are in accord as to the appropriateness of an attack against a common target.[31] Writing in 1970, Muriel Spark argued that 'the only effective art of our particular time is the satirical, the harsh and the witty' because it persuades us 'to contemplate the ridiculous nature of reality before us, and [teaches] us to mock it'.[32] And more recently, Simon Critchley, quoting from Wittgenstein, has written about how satire 'transforms us into outlandish animals', producing 'a kind of shock effect that shakes us up and effects a critical change of perspective'.[33] Yet although the suspension of everyday norms and expectations associated with the carnivalesque and the exposure of folly associated with satire and mockery are useful touchstones for thinking about what Coe's comedy is doing here, it also true to say that such theories frequently overstate the revolutionary potential of comedy, or at least overlook some of its complexities.

For instance, rather than reinforcing the preceding critique of Thatcherite values, the series of grotesque and comic deaths that conclude *What a Carve Up!* may actually take some of the sting out of its tail. Using the structure of one influential family, Coe brilliantly animates the pernicious effects of free-market policies on almost every aspect of British political and cultural life, but

---

[29] Coe, *Carve Up*, p. 450.
[30] Bakhtin, *Rabelais*, p. 92.
[31] Northrop Frye, *Anatomy of Criticism: Four Essays* (Princeton: Princeton University Press, 1957), pp. 223–4.
[32] Muriel Spark, 'The Desegregation of Art', in *The Golden Fleece: Essays*, ed. Penelope Jardine (Manchester: Carcanet, 2014), pp. 26–30 (p. 30).
[33] Simon Critchley, *On Humour* (London: Routledge, 2002), pp. 34–5.

this family's painful demise at the conclusion is also a form of wish fulfilment,[34] a cathartic laugh that allows the reader to dismiss the Winshaws as mere caricatures or aberrations and to ignore the need to address the continuation of such attitudes and actions in the politicians and business leaders of our day. For Emma Parker, in these moments 'horror's subversive potential is diluted by humour', creating a 'conservative effect' whereby 'the defeat of Thatcherism is more a fun fantasy than a realistic political goal'. This is a persuasive reading, and although, as Parker further notes, *What a Carve Up!* does contain moments that serve to question 'the effectiveness of laughter as a subversive tool',[35] the cathartic, resigned laughter inspired by the Winshaws' deaths is surely what Coe argues against in his writing on satire and comedy: the idea that rather than reinforcing the political bite of satire, laughter can release tension, or even work in favour of those in authority. While Ian Gregson, for example, has argued for the power of caricature in challenging racial and gender stereotypes,[36] there is also an opposite potential to reinforce stereotypes or, in the case of satirical comedy, to substitute critical action with cathartic laughter.[37] If laughter can be a substitute for thought – even a way of preventing thought – and if it solidifies rather than challenges the status quo, it invites the question: can comic fiction be political and at the same time avoid appropriation by the establishment and the reaffirmation of polarizing positions?

In a further essay on the topic of comedy and laughter, Coe notes that 'satire and comedy are two quite different beasts – although many people insist on using the terms interchangeably – and no amount of rationalism or essay-writing can undermine my allegiance to comedy', going on to praise P.G. Wodehouse for his 'pure, unpolluted humour'. He concludes, 'More and more I feel that, just as all art aspires to the condition of music, all humour should really aspire to the condition of Wodehouse.'[38] Since *What a Carve Up*, Coe has published eight novels, a collection of short stories, a biography of B.S. Johnson

---

[34] Terry Eagleton makes this point in passing in his largely positive review of *What a Carve Up!* when he notes that the novel 'is fantastic wish-fulfilment, able to establish political justice only by a crafty shuffling of genres in which fairy tale is projected onto realpolitik'. See Eagleton, 'Theydunnit'.

[35] Emma Parker, 'A Comedy of Horrors: Thatcherism in *What a Carve Up!*, in *Jonathan Coe: Contemporary British Satire*, ed. Philip Tew (London: Bloomsbury, 2018), pp. 67–79 (p. 71).

[36] Ian Gregson, *Character and Satire in Postwar Fiction* (London: Continuum, 2006).

[37] As the political historian Steven Fielding has noted, much of the comedy referred to as satire would be more accurately described as anti-political comedy. Indeed, the 1980s comedy series *Yes Minister*, which propagated the idea that all politicians are liars and backstabbers, was actually a favourite of Margaret Thatcher, the prime minister at the time: 'It expressed her view that, as representative politics was a moral hazard, it should be replaced as far as possible by the market'. Steven Fielding, 'Comedy and Politics: The Great Debate', 29 September 2011. Available online: http://nottspolitics.org/2011/09/29/comedy-and-politics-the-great-debate/ (accessed 17 June 2019).

[38] Coe, '"Comic" Novels'.

and two children's books, none of which has returned to the satirical mode in the strictest sense. Yet in much of his work, Coe continues to engage with comedy as a political mode and to ask questions concerning the politics of comedy. Indeed, while it can be argued that there is a gently critical edge even in Wodehouse's depictions of an unchanging England,[39] Coe's fiction is more explicitly political. He is the author of a sequence of books that collectively examine the turbulent history of post-war Britain – with future volumes of a projected series entitled *Unrest* still to come – and has returned to writing about contemporary politics and society in a number of works since *What a Carve Up!*. The remainder of this chapter focuses on three of Coe's most recent novels, *The Terrible Privacy of Maxwell Sim*, *Expo 58* and *Number 11, or Tales that Witness Madness* (2015),[40] the latter of which is in many ways a follow-up to *What a Carve Up!*, to discuss the politics of comedy at the level of the joke and at the level of tone. It concludes with a discussion of metacomedy in *Number 11*, which offers Coe a way of practising satire, while at the same time questioning its ability to effect change.

Jokes and/as innovative action

Coe's move away from satirical modes of comedy could be viewed as a withdrawal from overtly political writing, but there is an opposite view that identifies the most readily recognizable unit of comedy, the joke, as inherently political, or at least destabilizing of orthodoxy. Taking Freud's taxonomy of jokes in *The Joke and Its Relation to the Unconscious* (1905) as his starting point, Paolo Virno argues that jokes are 'the *diagram* of innovative action'.[41] His essay 'Jokes and Innovative Action' focuses on the linguistic ambiguity of jokes, describing them as paradigmatic examples of creativity – modified verbal thought – in response to an emergency situation: 'jokes can offer us an adequate *empirical basis* for understanding the way in which linguistic animals give evidence of an unexpected deviation from their normal praxis.'[42] This is a version of the incongruity theory, the dominant theory of humour and laughter, which suggests that laughter is

---

[39] See, for example, Christopher Hitchens, 'Between Waugh and Wodehouse: Comedy and Conservatism', in *On Modern British Fiction*, ed. Zachary Leader (Oxford: Oxford University Press, 2002), pp. 45–59, and Peter L. Berger, *Redeeming Laughter: The Comic Element of Human Experience*, 2nd edn (Berlin: Walter de Gruyter, 2014), p. 146.

[40] I discuss *Middle England* (2018), at the time of writing Coe's most recent novel, in the concluding chapter.

[41] Paulo Virno, *Multitude: Between Innovation and Negation*, trans. Isabella Bertoletti, James Cascaito, and Andreas Casson (Los Angeles: Semiotext(e), 2008), p. 73.

[42] Ibid., p. 72.

generated by the pleasing juxtaposition of two normally incompatible elements. In the case of jokes, incongruity involves a linguistic juxtaposition that upsets normal patterns of thought or language, as in the stand-up comedian Ken Cheng's one-liner 'I'm not a fan of the new pound coin, but then again, I hate all change',[43] which riffs on dual meanings of the word 'change'. And although Virno misreads Freud's conclusions about the significance of incongruity in jokes,[44] he does provide a framework for thinking about jokes as undermining norms:

> As paradoxical as it may seem, the state of exception has its original place of residence in an activity that is only seemingly obvious, which Wittgenstein calls 'following a rule'. This implies, inversely, that every humble application of a norm always contains within itself a fragment of the 'state of exception'. Jokes bring this fragment to light.

Jokes therefore employ and embody norms and at the same time undermine those norms because 'the logical form of jokes consists of a deductive fallacy, or rather of an unmerited inference, or of an incorrect use of a semantic ambiguity'.[45] Virno's conclusion about the misapplication of semantic ambiguities and juxtaposition of incongruous elements works in parallel with the dominant interpretation of jokes in the linguistically orientated strand of humour studies, which identifies the opposition of two or more semantic scripts as fundamental to the operation of jokes.[46] But where Virno departs from this work, and where

---

[43] Since 2007, the British television channel Dave has presented an award to the best joke of the Edinburgh Fringe festival. Cheng's joke won the award in 2017. The inherent absurdity of the award aside, the annual shortlists provide abundant examples of linguistic incongruity in jokes, although the privileging of short-form one-liners, almost always based on puns, does the limit the possibilities for what a joke might be. For the 2017 shortlist, see BBC News, 'Pound Coin Gag Scoops Best Edinburgh Fringe Joke Award', 22 August 2017. Available online: https://www.bbc.co.uk/news/uk-scotland-40999000 (accessed 16 July 2019).

[44] Virno quotes Freud's summary of jokes as 'the coupling of dissimilars, the contrast of ideas, "the sense in nonsense", the sequence of bafflement and light dawning – bringing to light what is hidden – and the particular brevity in the joke', but neglects to note that Freud is summarizing the ideas of the novelist Jean Paul and the philosophers Theodor Vischer, Kino Fischer and Theodor Lipps, and that he goes on to suggest that these ideas are 'disjecta membra which we would wish to see integrated into an organic whole'. Freud's theory draws on these ideas, but ultimately develops a relief theory of humour in which laughter saves a degree of psychic energy. Here I quote from the 2002 Joyce Crick translation of Freud, whereas Virno's translators use the 1963 James Strachey translation. The sense is the same in both editions. See Virno, *Multitude: Between Innovation and Negation*, p. 79 and Sigmund Freud, *The Joke and Its Relation to the Unconscious*, trans. Joyce Crick (London: Penguin, [1905] 2002), p. 8.

[45] Virno, *Multitude: Between Innovation and Negation*, p. 74.

[46] In the Semantic Script Theory of Humour and its later revision as the General Theory of Verbal Humour, Victor Raskin and Salvatore Attardo suggest that jokes rely on an overlap between two or more opposing semantic scripts. For example, the earlier joke from Ken Cheng employs the scripts coins versus transformation. See Victor Raskin, *Semantic Mechanisms of Humor* (Dordrecht: D. Riedel, 1985) and Salvatore Attardo, *Linguistic Theories of Humor* (Berlin: Mouton de Gruyter, 1994).

his argument is of most relevance to this analysis of the political dimension of comedy, is in his discussion of the radical, transformative potential of jokes.

In the second part of 'Jokes and Innovative Action', Virno analyses jokes in relation to four categories taken from Aristotle's *Nicomachean Ethics*:

> a) *phrónesis*, or practical know-how; b) *orthós logos*, the discourse that enunciates the correct norm according to which action on one single case takes shape; c) the perception of *kairós*, of the proper moment for performing an action; d) *éndoxa*, that is, the opinions prevalent from time to time within a community of speakers.[47]

Of these, it is the joke's relationship to *éndoxa* that has the most significant critical role, both drawing on received opinion and the status quo and undermining them. The idea of a 'community of speakers' – Freud's third person – is important here because the joke requires shared understanding, but for Virno, the joke does not reinforce this understand and instead it 'refutes the same *éndoxa* from which it got its start. Or, better yet: it is a performative example of how that grammar of a form of life can be transformed.'[48] In a radically condensed form, the joke brings together heterogeneous and seemingly incompatible elements, undermining the foundations of the norms on which they are based. Virno largely eschews analysis of the content of jokes, focusing instead on their commonality as diagrams of creativity and innovative action that undermine *éndoxa*. On this view, jokes are inherently unstable and critical of conventional modes of thought. But while Virno follows much of Freud's method, he does not offer examples of joke work beyond those already offered by Freud. Therefore, while I agree with his conclusions about the radical potential of jokes, it is only by working through these ideas in relation to concrete examples that their linguistic innovation and latent political content can be examined. In response to Virno, Matthew Bevis suggests that this 'in turn can encourage reflection on whether we want to inhabit or resist that norm'.[49] And it is this type of reflection to which I will now turn in order to think not only about the politics of the joke in Coe's recent fiction but also about how we might think about the politics of comedy as a tonal as well as structural property that extends beyond individual jokes.

The Terrible Privacy of Maxwell Sim begins with four epigraphs that together summarize the mood and subject matter of the book. They are taken from Nicholas Tomalin and Ron Hall's book about Donald Crowhurst, whose life and

---

[47] Virno, *Multitude: Between Innovation and Negation*, p. 87.
[48] Ibid., p. 94.
[49] Matthew Bevis, *Comedy: A Very Short Introduction* (Oxford: Oxford University Press, 2013), p. 4.

tragic attempt to sail around the world single-handedly are mirrored by Coe's title character; from Alasdair Gray's novel *1982, Janine* (1984), in a passage describing the shrinking globe brought about by late capitalism; from David Nobbs's *The Fall and Rise of Reginald Perrin* (1975), in a typically pathos-laden passage about Reginald's legacy; and from a 1992 James Wood interview with Toni Morrison, from which the novel takes part of its title: 'Through words, she offers us her shaming revelations. Through words, she gives us her terrible privacy.'[50] Interior and exterior journeys, technology and the shrinking globe, the melancholy humour of life and the isolation of contemporary existence, these are the central themes of Coe's novel; and the epigraph from Nobbs, one of Coe's comic heroes, encapsulates the tragicomic tone of much of the book: 'One day I will die, and on my grave it will say, "Here lies Reginald Iolanthe Perrin; he didn't know the names of the flowers and the trees, but he did know the rhubarb crumble sales for Schleswig-Holstein."'[51] Reggie, the eternal malcontent, is here reflecting on his life and his knowledge of the business of Sunshine Desserts – the firm at which he works as a Sales Executive – against his lack of knowledge of the outside world, of the natural as opposed to the industrial; it has the structure of a joke but is also about mortality and isolation in an age of specialization. Moreover, although it does not conform to the structure of the punning joke that is the focus of much of Freud's – and Virno's – discussion, it does engage with and undercut similar oppositions to those identified by Virno. It opposes the, ahem, grave seriousness of a headstone and the intimations of mortality with the apparent triviality of the rhubarb crumble market in northern Germany, using 'but' as a hinge on which to hang two unequal aspects of character and knowledge: knowledge of the natural world versus knowledge of the international dessert market. The joke contains within it a discussion of hierarchies of value and questions of what is valued in a short-term, economic sense versus what is valued over the duration a lifetime, particularly at its end. Maxwell Sim is less of a malcontent than Reggie and more of an innocent abroad,[52] his naivety played off against the more knowing reader,

---

[50] James Wood, 'A Terrible Privacy', interview with Toni Morrison, *Guardian*, 18 April 1992, section Weekend, p. 5.

[51] This passage is taken from Reggie's speech at a conference held to celebrate International Fruit Year. He is there as a representative of his employer Sunshine Dessert and his speech is entitled 'Are We Getting Our Just Desserts?'. In an apparent nod to Jim Dixon's disastrous lecture on 'Merrie England' in Kingsley Amis's *Lucky Jim* (1954), Reggie gets drunk beforehand and uses the speech as an opportunity to rail against modern ills such as standardization and progress. Shortly afterwards, he fakes his own death. See David Nobbs, *The Fall and Rise of Reginald Perrin* (London: Mandarin, [1975] 1990), p. 153.

[52] Patricia Waugh describes Sim as suffering from a 'somatic weariness' and situates the novel as part of a neo-phenomenological turn in contemporary fiction, 'in which the dominant mood is depressive (though sometimes comic-depressive) rather than apocalyptic, manic or addictive'. Patricia Waugh, 'The Naturalistic Turn, the Syndrome, and the Rise of the Neo-Phenomenological Novel', in *Diseases*

and the jokes in the novel are tonally distinct from those in Nobbs's Perrin novels – gentler, and less wry and ironic. Nonetheless, it is possible to read the political back in to *Maxwell Sim*, a novel that is equally engaged with the absurdities of modern life and particularly the relationship between economic life and social life, between working relationships and interpersonal connections. Indeed, it is the title character Max's naivety that generates much of the humour and that opens up a series of questions about *éndoxa*.

In *Maxwell Sim*, Max meets a younger woman named Poppy, who invites him to a dinner party at her mother's house. Also at the party are Poppy's uncle Clive and a couple named Richard and Jocasta. Richard is an investment banker who has recently lost his job, and as he attempts to explain his role in the bank – he is an engineer by training – and the roles of the pure mathematicians and theoretical physicists who also work in its research department, Max becomes increasingly baffled:

> I was struggling to make a contribution to this discussion, and trying to think how a department of physicists and engineers could ever be of much use to a bank.
>
> 'So they were getting you to ... what, exactly? I suppose you were designing new ATM machines, and that sort of thing.'
>
> Jocasta laughed wildly when she heard this. Richard just said, 'Hardly,' and gave me one of the most condescending smiles I had ever seen.[53]

One reading of this passage would identify Max as the butt of the joke, citing his naivety in not understanding the complexities of modern banking, and his artlessness and incomprehension are indeed a running theme in the novel. Yet while it draws on this aspect of Max's character, the joke, and the discussion that follows, undermines any simple opposition between uncomprehending layman and knowledgeable banker. As Richard goes on to explain – or rather not to explain – the financial models developed by him and his team are almost unfathomably complicated. Having listed a series of jargon-laden products, he concludes that 'these things are best left to the people who understand them'.[54] Max questions whether the people selling these products understand what they are selling, and although his reference to his professional background in children's toys and toothbrushes elicits further laughter and disdain, he makes an uncomfortable and insightful point about the 2008 financial crisis that forms the

---

and *Disorders in Contemporary Fiction: The Syndrome Syndrome*, ed. T.J. Lustig and James Peacock (New York: Routledge, 2013), pp. 17–34 (pp. 23, 21).

[53] Jonathan Coe, *The Terrible Privacy of Maxwell Sim* (London: Penguin, 2010), pp. 111–12.

[54] Ibid., p. 113.

background to the novel: "'Surely anybody could see it was going to be a recipe for disaster. A salesman can't possibly sell something that he doesn't understand. And not just understand, but believe in.'"[55] As Virno suggests, then, this series of jokes both draws upon *éndoxa* and undermines the stability of a series of linguistic and ideological constructs. It scrutinizes the terms 'bank', 'engineer', and 'product', opposing the vernacular use of these terms with their use in the financial markets, not ultimately to ridicule Max's misunderstanding but to foreground the increasing levels of abstraction in the sector and the disastrous implications of this for the global economy and ultimately for individuals.[56] Max associates 'bank' with a bricks and mortar high street banks and engineers with machinery rather than complex financial models; similarly, 'products' are items like the eco-friendly toothbrushes he is ostensibly marketing, rather than financial products that few are equipped to understand and whose consequences most experts were unable to anticipate. The joke, then, builds on Clive's earlier observation that the financial markets represent "'an entire civilization built on … well, on air, really. That's all it is. Air.'"[57] As well as being one of the four elements around which the novel is structured, air is a key metaphor used to describe the nebulousness of late capitalism, whose absurdities Coe explores and exposes via the structure of a joke. The scene is not satirical precisely, but as Virno suggests of jokes in general, it 'pushes one single belief to the limit, to the point of extracting absurd and ridiculous consequences from it'.[58] It turns the joke not against Max, but against the systems that contributed to the financial crash, and although she does not discuss *Maxwell Sim*, the novel could profitably be considered as part of a genre of literature described by Katy Shaw as Crunch Lit, which 'employs fictional representations of real-life events to emphasize both the trauma of market dislocation and the impact of a breakdown in global economics on the life of ordinary individuals'.[59] Jokes, with their reliance on seemingly incompatible elements, may even provide the ideal medium not necessarily to understand the complexities of these systems but to denaturalize and scrutinize them.

Although the tone of Coe's next novel, *Expo 58*, is more broadly comic than that of *Maxwell Sim*, it also engages with moments of crisis in surprising ways. As

---

[55] Ibid.
[56] For a detailed discussion of *Maxwell Sim* in the context of the financial crisis and precarious labour, see Francesco Di Bernardo, 'A Terrible Precariousness: Financialization of Society and the Precariat in Jonathan Coe's *The Terrible Privacy of Maxwell Sim*', in *Jonathan Coe: Contemporary British Satire*, ed. Philip Tew (London: Bloomsbury, 2018), pp. 141–54.
[57] Coe, *Maxwell Sim*, p. 110.
[58] Virno, *Multitude: Between Innovation and Negation*, p. 94.
[59] Katy Shaw, *Crunch Lit* (London: Bloomsbury, 2015), p. 68.

the title suggests, *Expo 58* is set in 1958, and the Cold War tensions of the period provide an important backdrop; but more than this, the novel also explores the curious relationship between the UK and the rest of Europe. I first wrote a draft of this chapter in July 2016 when 52 per cent of the British electorate had recently voted to leave the European Union. Events will no doubt have moved on by the time it goes to press, but as I write this final draft, the UK is in a period of political limbo between the triggering of Article 50 and the agreement on what form, if any, the exit from the EU will take. Britain's future in Europe is again in the balance, and while Coe's novel does not predict these events, it does explore some of the suspicion and conflicted feelings that were part of the European project from the outset and that undermined its vision for European unity. Again, it is humour and the joke that serve to identify and challenge some of the paradoxical attitudes of the UK towards Europe as an idea and an identity. Though less structurally complex than many of his novels, Coe has described *Expo 58* as a multivalent work that

> can be read in a number of ways: as a traditional English 'comic novel' in the tradition of Henry Fielding, Michael Frayn and Kingsley Amis; as an *homage* to British comedy films of the 1930s, 40s and 50s; as a parody of Cold War spy fiction; and as the latest chapter in an interlocking network of novels and short stories which I have been writing for the last two decades.[60]

In a 2013 interview, Coe suggests that this is the closest he has come to writing a postmodern novel since *What a Carve Up!*,[61] primarily due to its allusiveness to other works of literature and film, including an array of characters taken from British cinema of the 1930s, the 1940s and the 1950s, and a series of in-jokes based on these films, as well as Ian Fleming's James Bond novels and other playfully invoked intertexts.[62] Yet although the novel is deeply allusive, it is structurally and tonally very different from *What a Carve Up!* and much closer to the English comic novels of Frayn and Amis noted earlier than to the corpus of texts conventionally described as postmodern. In fact, whether consciously or not, it is part of a lineage of 'innocent abroad' comic farces that can be traced through novels such as Evelyn Waugh's *Scoop* (1930), Beryl Bainbridge's *Winter Garden*

---

[60] Jonathan Coe, 'Expo 58', *Jonathan Coe Personal Website*, 2013, http://www.jonathancoewriter.com/books/expo58.html (accessed 16 August 2016).
[61] Waterstones, 'Jonathan Coe Discusses Expo 58' [video], YouTube (uploaded 29 August 2013), https://www.youtube.com/watch?v=E9e4eVLNC1I (accessed 16 August 2016).
[62] Guignery provides a fairly comprehensive summary of these allusions. See Guignery, *Jonathan Coe*, pp. 136–9.

(1980) and Malcolm Bradbury's *Rates of Exchange* (1983),[63] up to Frayn's *Skios* (2013) and Jesse Armstrong's *Love, Sex and Other Foreign Policy Goals* (2015). Like the protagonists of the Bainbridge and Bradbury novels, in *Expo 58*, Foley becomes the unwitting dupe in a plan to smuggle information, and in a further parallel with those novels, whose humour reflects Cold War anxieties, as the story develops, Foley's life becomes emblematic of a broader series of choices and conflicts: Britain or continental Europe; isolationism or integration; futurity or nostalgia.

Expo 58 is set around the titular expo, a World's Fair held in Brussels, with exhibitors from both sides of the Iron Curtain. The novel opens by quoting from the invitation letter sent to participating nations, stating the event's lofty ambition

> to facilitate a comparison of the multifarious activities of different peoples in the fields of thought, art, science, economic affairs and technology. Its method is to present an all-embracing view of the present achievements, spiritual or material, and the further aspirations of a rapidly changing world. Its final aim is to contribute to the development of a genuine unity of mankind, based upon respect for human personality.

The novel continues:

> History does not record how the British Secretary of State for Foreign Affairs reacted when he first read those impressive words. But Thomas's guess was that, seeing four years of stress, argument and expense ahead of him, he let the invitation slip from his fingers, put his hand to his forehead and muttered: 'Oh no ... Those bloody Belgians ...'[64]

Without wishing to generalize about a 'national sense of humour', on a superficial level, this is a classically English joke: a line that, tweaked a little, could be spoken by a Wodehouse character. Whereas the continental European sees a chance to demonstrate unity and a bright, technologically advanced future, the English politician sees only an administrative and logistical headache. And when Belgium later proposes *musique concrète* and compositions from Stockhausen and Xenakis as its musical contribution to the Expo, Britain proposes Elgar, Purcell and the 'usual suspects', with a military tattoo for 'contemporary music week'.[65] The joke draws on the opposition between British pragmatism and continental idealism, but it also undermines this opposition and has fun at the

---

[63] For a discussion of Bainbridge's and Bradbury's innocent abroad comedies, see Huw Marsh, *Beryl Bainbridge* (Tavistock: Northcote House, 2014), pp. 46–8.
[64] Jonathan Coe, *Expo 58* (London: Viking, 2013), p. 2.
[65] Ibid., p. 26.

expense of the largely staid and cynical British representatives, at the same time remaining alive to some of the eccentricities of the European project.

The central symbol of this contrast between continental European idealism and innovation and staid Britishness is the centrepiece of Britain's contribution to the Fair. As part of the Expo, Belgium built the Atomium, a 100-metre-tall monument to the atomic age modelled on the structure of an iron crystal and constructed in shiny aluminium, offering a panoramic view from the highest of its nine interlinked spheres. In contrast, one of the centrepieces of Britain's pavilion was a prefabricated pub named the Britannia, or as one character describes it, "'A little bit of Blighty transported over to boring old Bruxelles.'"[66] The pub was a relatively modern, light design, but it was bedecked with historic sailing paraphernalia in celebration of Britain's maritime history, striking an uneasy rapprochement between past and present; as the commemorative booklet describes it, the Britannia was 'modern if not advanced in style'.[67] Its subsequent history, documented in Coe's final chapter, is fascinating. The contents were reconstructed in the English port city of Dover in 1962, where they furnished a modern pub inspired by the original design, but after several changes of ownership and relaunches that tell a story of decline, it was eventually rebranded in 2005 as a topless dancing club. The landlady argued it was in keeping with Dover's position as the 'gateway to Europe'; "'I think people who would object to exotic dancing in Dover need to wake up,'" she told the *Dover Express*, "'it exists all over Europe, and in a lot of places around the UK.'"[68] The pub closed in 2008 and was demolished in 2011. There is a comic melancholy to the way in which these facts are introduced at the end of Coe's novel and a symbolic resonance in the creation and subsequent fate of a pub named Britannia, which was designed and built as a microcosm of Britain: the face it wished to present to the world. It speaks to a series of questions introduced in the opening pages of the novel, and which resonate throughout its length and beyond the 1950s setting:

> What did it mean to be British, in 1958? Nobody seemed to know. Britain was steeped in tradition, everybody agreed upon that: its traditions, its pageantry, its ceremony were admired and envied all over the world. At the same time it was mired in the past: scared of innovation, riddled with archaic class distinctions, in thrall to a secretive and untouchable establishment. Which way were you supposed to look, when defining Britishness? Forwards, or backwards?[69]

---

[66] Ibid., p. 49.
[67] *The Britannia Inn: Universal and International Exhibition, Brussels* (London: Whitbread, 1958), p. 4.
[68] Barry Smith and Paul Skelton, 'Britannia, 41 Townhall Street', *Dover Kent Archives*. Available online: http://www.dover-kent.com/Britannia-Townwall-Street.html (accessed 16 August 2016).
[69] Coe, *Expo*, p. 3.

Coe does not collapse the 1950s into the present, but this series of statements and questions do indicate the political dimension of the jokes in *Expo 58* and the novel's concern with national identity and transnational relationships. The paragraph quoted earlier begins with the sentence 'Brussels had livened things up a bit, that was certain',[70] and as any British reader would know, 'Brussels' has become an often pejorative metonym for 'Europe', which is itself a metonym for the European Union rather than geographical Europe, of which Britain is indisputably a part. *Expo 58*'s superficially 'light' comedy asks questions about Britain and its place in the word, both then and now.

Coe's twenty-first-century perspective on the 1950s allows him to develop a series of ironic jokes based on subsequent knowledge. At times, as when Foley agrees that his wife Sylvia should smoke while she was pregnant ('It was a stressful time for a woman, after all, and smoking did help her to relax'),[71] there is a hint of the what Mark Greif calls 'the genre of Now We Know Better',[72] in which past naiveties are mocked from a perspective of later knowledge, but mockery is not the predominant tone and the novel does not seek to shore up present certainties. Rather, much of the novel's humour uses Foley's experiences in Belgium to probe the relation between Britain and Europe, both in 1958 when the European Economic Community (EEC) was coming into existence and, by extension, in the 2010s when Coe wrote the novel. When Foley arrives at the Expo, his hostess, Anneke, identifies the striking building that has caught his attention: '"The American pavilion", Anneke explained. "And here is the Soviet one, right next door. Which," she added with a gleam in her eye, "is a typical example of the Belgian sense of humour."'[73] As well as drawing on – and questioning – British stereotypes about Belgian humourlessness, this reference to the juxtaposition between the pavilions emphasizes the charged historical dimension of this moment and the way in which the future direction of Europe and the world lay in the balance. When Foley unwittingly becomes implicated in international

---

[70] Ibid., p. 3.
[71] Ibid., p. 238.
[72] Mark Greif, 'You'll Love the Way It Makes You Feel', *London Review of Books*, 23 October 2008. Available online: https://www.lrb.co.uk/v30/n20/mark-greif/youll-love-the-way-it-makes-you-feel (accessed 23 July 2019). The context for Greif's identification of this genre is a discussion of the television series *Mad Men*, and what Greif perceives to be its smug pastiche of the social mores of the 1950s and the 1960s from a knowing future position. Coe sought to avoid this in *Expo 58*, describing it in an interview with Vanessa Guignery as 'just simple realism'. He notes that 'this is how people would have behaved, how they would have talked and if there is a kind of absurdity already in looking back at the manners and assumptions of 1958, that's a historical accident'. Vanessa Guignery, 'An Interview with Jonathan Coe – Looking Backwards and Forwards', *Études britanniques contemporaines*, 54 (2018). Available Online: https://journals.openedition.org/ebc/4396 (accessed 16 July 2019).
[73] Coe, *Expo*, p. 45.

espionage, the machinations are again comical – even farcical – and the plot involves messages smuggled in the salt sachets inside bags of Salt 'n' Shake crisps and a pair of secret service agents inspired by Charters and Caldicott, the comic Englishmen from Alfred Hitchcock's *The Lady Vanishes* (1938) and a series of later films. Ultimately, however, the tone becomes more melancholy and Foley is blackmailed, having been photographed in a compromising position with the hostess, Anneke. He faces a choice: continue to work for the secret service in exchange for their silence, and therefore continue in his unhappy marriage with his wife Sylvia, or allow his infidelity to be exposed and take a chance on his relationship with Anneke. He chooses the former and later laments that he thereby 'condemned [Sylvia], through vacillation, to a lifetime of unrest'.[74] Unrest is the title of Coe's sequence of novels charting the history post-war Britain, and its inclusion here, at the end of a sentence in the final paragraph of a chapter, is important. This is not a life of revolution, nor is it one of complete stagnation, but it is a life of unrest, uncertainty and unresolved questions. The novel is not an allegory in a simple sense, but Foley's choice is not only between heart and head. It is also a choice between the European promise represented by the Expo and the isolationism represented by the nostalgic view of Britain espoused at the outset of the novel by Foley's colleagues in the Civil Service. Coe is relatively unusual among English novelists in that he is very much a European novelist, more feted in continental Europe than he is at home,[75] and his success puts pay to the myth that humour does not travel. I also think that Europe and all it represents is an important context for this novel in particular. The jokes in *Expo 58* are integral to a profoundly political point, even though the tone may be closer to Wodehouse than to Swift. The tension between the pull of continental Europe, associated with modernity and ambition, and the pull of Britain, represented by history and past glories, is evident throughout the novel, and as Jean-Michel Ganteau astutely observes, the presiding feeling at the novel's conclusion is one of pathos, missed opportunities and a sense that

---

[74] Ibid., p. 250.
[75] Coe's fiction has a strong Continental European following, particularly in France and Italy. His novels have won more awards overseas than they have in the UK and he has been made *Officier de l'ordre des Arts et des Lettres* (Officer of the Order of Arts and Letters) by the French government. In a 2010 interview, Coe remarked that '"French sales [of his books] outstrip British by about four to one"' and that it is 'the same in Italy'. Paul Laity, 'A Life in Writing: Jonathan Coe', *Guardian*, 29 May 2010. Available online: https://www.theguardian.com/books/2010/may/29/life-writing-jonathan-coe (accessed 16 August 2016). See also Merritt Moseley, *Understanding Jonathan Coe* (Columbia, SC: University of South Carolina Press, 2016), pp. 4–5; and for a consideration of Coe's appeal to French readers and the translation of his fiction in relation to markers of social class, see Helena Chadderton, 'Translating Class in Jonathan Coe', *The Translator*, 23:3 (2017), 269–78.

'the future is always already beyond reach'.⁷⁶ As Virno's work suggests, jokes are not only jokes but rather models of innovative action, bringing together and holding in suspension multiple seemingly contradictory ideas in order to pose important questions about language and meaning. This analysis is borne out in my readings of these novels by Coe, whose scepticism of satire should not be read as a retrenchment from comedy's political potential. As Coe himself has argued, a joke can be 'a complex, multilayered thing, a way of conveying a complicated truth every bit as powerful as a political essay or piece of journalism'.⁷⁷

From satire to comedy

If, as I have argued, Coe's gentler post-*What a Carve Up!* comedy continues to evince an engagement with contemporary politics and to have a critical function, there remains a question over whether these comic narratives avoid the pitfalls that Coe associates with satire. To discuss this question, I will first consider what distinguishes satirical comedy from other forms of comedy, and how the move away from satirical comedy may or may not allow Coe to avoid creating 'laughter [as] a substitute for thought'. As Conal Condren argues in a 2012 essay, satire 'is unsuitable for an essentialist definition'; a degree of moral seriousness would seem to be implicit to the form, but this has been diminished by the tendency to collapse satire into humour and to defend offensive humour by arguing that it is 'only satire'. Once it is 'effectively consigned to the realm of the non-serious, satire can contract into really being only a joke'.⁷⁸ Condren qualifies this by noting that jokes are not *only* jokes, but his discussion of the topic emphasizes the difficulty of identifying a mode that no longer conforms to its original generic meaning or to subsequent interventions by figures such as Dryden and Pope, or more recently, Northrop Frye. Ian Gregson associates contemporary literary satire with caricature, arguing that that the preponderance of caricature in authors such as Philip Roth, Muriel Spark, Martin Amis and Will Self is 'symptomatic of a satirical attitude to the self which is tellingly characteristic of contemporary

---

[76] Jean-Michel Ganteau, 'Innocent Abroad: Jonathan Coe's Expo 58 and the Comedy of Forgiveness', in 'Focus on Comic Representations in Post-Millennial British and Irish Fiction', ed. Barbara Puschmann-Nalenz, special issue *Anglistik: International Journal of English Studies*, 27:1 (2016), 19–29 (p. 27).

[77] Jonathan Coe, 'Is Martin Amis Right? Or Will Jeremy Corbyn Have the Last Laugh?' *Guardian*, 30 October 2015. Available online: https://www.theguardian.com/books/2015/oct/30/martin-amis-jeremy-corbyn-humour-jonathan-coe (accessed 17 June 2019).

[78] Condren, 'Satire and Definition', pp. 396, 392.

culture' and of the postmodern in particular.[79] This is a useful intervention, and although it does not account for all of the forms categorized as contemporary satire, it does gesture towards a distinction that is identifiable in Coe's fiction. Asked whether his most recent novel, *Number 11*, which is a follow-up of sorts to *What a Carve Up!*, represents a return to satire after the gentler comedy of *Expo 58*, Coe suggests that the two novels are closer than superficial appearances may suggest:

> The OED definition of satire is 'the use of humour, irony, exaggeration or ridicule to expose people's stupidity or vices'. When it's put like that, maybe there isn't so much difference between the two books. You could read *Expo 58* as being a satire on indecisiveness and marital weakness. *Number 11* is a satire on greed, inequality, social media, reality TV and so on. So really there are only two differences: in tone (the satire in *Number 11* is more severe) and subject (the objects of satire in *Number 11* are social and political issues rather than personal qualities). To put it more simply: *Expo 58* is a gentle satire on human frailty; *Number 11* is a fierce satire on social injustice.[80]

Still maintaining that *Expo 58* contains social as well as personal critique, Coe's comments on tone are particularly apposite because it is the tonal quality of the more recent novels, more so than any formal features, that distinguishes them from the cynical satire with which Coe has lost faith.

This loss of faith finds parallels in Peter Sloterdijk's *Critique of Cynical Reason* (1983), which goes so far as to identify 'a universal, diffuse, cynicism' at large in modern culture, or what he defines as '*enlightened false consciousness*. It is that modernized, unhappy consciousness, on which enlightenment has laboured both successfully and in vain.'[81] As Andrea Huyssen puts it, for Sloterdijk 'cynicism is the dominant operating mode in contemporary culture, both on the personal and institution levels'.[82] This cynicism, on Sloterdijk's view, has ceased to have an effect; it is resigned and toothless, or 'sterile' as he puts it, and although it is 'truly the heir of the great *satirical* tradition, in which the motif of unmasking,

---

[79] Gregson, *Character and Satire*, p. 4.
[80] Guignery, *Jonathan Coe*, pp. 146-7. For a discussion of *Number 11* as a state-of-the-nation novel, see Caroline Lusin, 'The Condition of England Novel in the Twenty-First Century: Zadie Smith's *NW* (2012) and Jonathan Coe's *Number 11, or Tales That Witness Madness* (2015)', in *The British Novel in the Twenty-First Century: Cultural Concerns - Literary Developments - Model Interpretations*, ed. Vera Nünning and Ansgar Nünning (Trier: Wissenschaftlicher Verlag Trier, 2018), pp. 247-63.
[81] Peter Sloterdijk, *Critique of Cynical Reason*, trans. Michael Eldred (Minneapolis, MN: University of Minnesota Press, [1983] 1987), pp. 3, 5.
[82] Andreas Huyssen, 'Foreword: The Return of Diogenes as Postmodern Intellectual', in Peter Sloterdijk, *Critique of Cynical Reason*, trans. Michael Eldred (Minneapolis, MN: University of Minnesota Press, [1983] 1987), pp. ix–xxv (p. xi).

exposing, baring has served for aeons now as a weapon', modern ideology critique has 'cut itself off from the powerful traditions of laughter in satirical knowledge, which have their roots in ancient kynicism'.[83] The cynical laughter of modern satire is ineffectual because it is resigned and has 'given up its life as satire'. Sloterdijk calls for a return to the 'cheeky' kynical laughter of Diogenes, whose provocative gestures 'respectable thinking does now know how to deal with': 'Greek kynicism discovers the animal body in the human' and provokes 'a climate of satirical loosening up in which the powerful, together with their ideologist of domination, let go affectively – precisely under the onslaught of the critical affront by kynics'.[84] The proposed cure – the public pissing, shitting and masturbating of kynical defiance and animal laughter – may be very different from anything found in Coe's fiction, but Sloterdijk's diagnosis and loss of faith in contemporary satire is strikingly similar to Coe's. There is the same sense of a formerly biting satirical tradition becoming toothless, complacent and complicit. Coe's response to this loss of faith in cynical reason has been increasingly to move away from the caustic satire of *What a Carve Up!* and towards something altogether less aggressive and ironic.[85] This is particularly true in relation to characterization in Coe's fiction, and although *Number 11* is in some ways a return to the territory explored in *What a Carve Up!*, a tonal shift is evident in some important distinctions between the two novels.

As discussed at the outset of this chapter, *What a Carve Up!* portrays the wealthy Winshaw family as grotesques or caricatures, whose gruesome fates can be viewed as a form off cathartic retributive justice.[86] In *Number 11*, subtitled 'Tales that Witness Madness',[87] the Winshaw family reappear but in less tangible form, having largely been massacred in the earlier book. Michael Owen's history of the family, which he writes over the course of *What a Carve Up!*, is entitled

---

[83] Sloterdijk, *Critique*, p. 16.
[84] Ibid., pp. 16, 101, 103.
[85] As Peter L. Berger puts it, 'satire is the deliberate use of the comic for purposes of attack', and although I will argue that Coe's retreat from satire should not be read as a retrenchment from politics, there is less sense of attack, or 'militancy' in Northrop Frye's words, in his recent fiction. Berger, *Redeeming Laughter*, p. 146.
[86] This caricatural aspect of the Winshaws is emphasized by the cartoon portraits that preface each family member's section of the novel. These began as images for a set of promotional playing cards, but were then incorporated into the novel itself. Jonathan Coe, 'Winshaw Playing Cards', *Jonathan Coe Personal Website*, 2013, http://www.jonathancoewriter.com/books/winshawCards.html (accessed 17 June 2019).
[87] *Tales that Witness Madness* is a 1973 portmanteau horror film, directed by Freddie Francis. This is the first of a series of embedded references to horror films in the novel, which includes a character called Freddie Francis. It is also a continuation of the horror theme in *What a Carve Up!*, whose title is taken from a 1961 British comic horror film. *What a Whopper!* is a loose sequel to the film *What a Carve Up!* and is referenced throughout *Number 11*. It also provides the title for the final section of the novel.

The Winshaw Legacy, and this fictional book is referenced in *Number 11* and also suggests the novel's concern with the legacy of the ideology that the family represents.[88] There is a direct lineage from the earlier novel in characters such as Josephine Winshaw-Eaves, a vicious tabloid columnist and the daughter of Hilary Winshaw, and Helke Winshaw, Mark Winshaw's widow whose company now profits from the removal of the armaments her husband once sold, but there is less sense of an obvious or clearly identifiable target for *Number 11*'s humour. Rather, the Winshaws' true legacy is a series of apparently nebulous ideas that have real-world consequences. A portrait of Henry Winshaw hangs in the hall of Rachel's Oxford college, bearing the motto 'FREEDOM, COMPETITION, CHOICE', three abstract nouns that form the cornerstones of neoliberal ideology and whose more malign influence is traced by Coe. Of these interconnected concepts, choice is the most prominent throughout *Number 11*. For Roger, the husband of Rachel's university tutor Laura Harvey, choice is the enemy: '"He *hated* choice"', Laura tells Rachel, '"He loved the idea of trusting people to make decisions on his behalf. Not all of them. Just some. Just enough so that you were free to live other parts of your life the way that you wanted."'[89] Choice is symptomatic of the dismantling of the post-war consensus and the idea that a benevolent state should provide certain universal services for its citizens. The choice agenda is evident when Rachel asks her grandfather's doctor about a potentially lifesaving drug, Cetuximab, to treat his cancer of the colon and is told that it does not offer sufficient value for money to be prescribed via the National Health Service. There is the option to pay for it privately, but this choice is available only to the very wealthy because each year of life gained from taking the drug is estimated to cost £121,367. A choice is available, but it is a false choice that is out of reach for most. Coe's criticism of the choice agenda is also evident in the portrayal of the marketization of the ordnance clearance sector, in which war-torn countries can choose the most competitive tender to clear unexploded devices: Helke Winshaw's company Winshaw Clearance is shown to be ruthlessly efficient at securing contracts but less so at completing the work.[90]

---

[88] Livia, Rachel's friend and possible avenging beast from the depths of the Gunns' basement (see later), insists that Rachel borrow her copy of the book. When the police detectives Pilbeam and Capes later question Rachel, Pilbeam mentions the book as key to unravelling the mysterious disappearance of rich and powerful individuals linked to the Winshaw family. He is surprized to see that Rachel has a copy. Jonathan Coe, *Number 11, or Tales That Witness Madness* (London: Viking, 2015), pp. 315–16, 339.
[89] Coe, *Number 11*, p. 176.
[90] Winshaw Clearance's failure to complete the clearance of an area on the Marshall Islands leads to the death of the granddaughter of Faustina and Jules, the housekeeper and chauffeur for the family for whom Rachel works as a private tutor. Coe, *Number 11*, pp. 332–3.

Yet choice, or rather the critique of choice, also has an obverse side, as exemplified by Roger's quest for a lost film he watched as a child. Roger's pursuit of *The Crystal Garden*, which was broadcast due to a television scheduling mishap and which he saw just once, is less of a search for a lost film and more of a search for lost time, a lost time when his life was not complicated by the need to make decisions and when people would watch and listen to what broadcasters chose to transmit, abrogating certain choices to a quasi-parental establishment. The dangers of nostalgia are a recurrent theme in Coe's novels,[91] and in *Number 11* they are literalized when Roger is crushed to death under an avalanche of junk as he reaches for what he believes to be a canister containing the last remaining copy of the mythic film. Coe's mordant joke on the perils of obsession and nostalgia provides a warning against the idealization of a prelapsarian past before the 'FREEDOM, COMPETITION, CHOICE' agenda came to dominate political and social life. And at the same time the novel identifies the deleterious effects of choice as an ideological mantra.[92] Choice is the also the subject of the novel's final pages, narrated by Livia, originally from Bucharest and now working in London as a dog walker for the very rich. At the close of the novel, Livia says that she is also the vengeful, spider-like creature living in a tunnel in the eleventh story of the basement conversion beneath the house on Turngreet Road where Rachel works as a private tutor.[93] It is from here that Livia launches attacks on the wealthy and corrupt who stray into her path.[94] In the final sentences of the novel, she uses the language of choice to articulate her own agenda: 'You may feel pity for my victims. That is your choice. You may place your sympathies with them, or with me. That is your decision. In the end, I believe, we are all free to choose.'[95] *Free to Choose* is the title of a 1980 book and television series by the economists Milton and Rose Friedman, which advocates for the free market and laissez-faire economics. Milton Friedman in particular was one of the key thinkers behind neoliberal economic policy during the 1980s and

---

[91] See, for example, Michael Owen's attempts to recapture the past in *What a Carve Up!*, Benjamin Trotter's obsession with his schooldays, and particularly Cicely Boyd, in *The Closed Circle*, and Robert's equally obsessive unrequited love for Sarah in *The House of Sleep*.

[92] In another of the novel's subplots, Josephine Winshaw-Eaves pursues an aggressive agenda against social benefit claimants, intimating that poverty is a choice and reliance on state support an example of 'entitlement'. Coe, *Number 11*, p. 291.

[93] In a 2012 essay, Coe describes extravagant west London basement conversions as markers of 'hubris and excess', which are the subject of 'tales of mythical extravagance'. He equates them with the 'grand projectism' on the east London Olympic Park and concludes that 'many would argue that they are undermining the very spiritual and physical foundations on which London is built'. Coe, 'London', in *Marginal Notes*.

[94] The status of the creature is left ambiguous, and it may be a figment of Rachel's imagination. In the closing chapters of the novel it is implied that Rachel, like Michael Owen in *What a Carve Up!*, is the 'author' of the preceding narrative, or her 'memoir' as it is described. Coe, *Number 11*, p. 320.

[95] Coe, *Number 11*, p. 351.

beyond, and acted as an adviser to both Margaret Thatcher and Ronald Reagan. He believed that the trickle-down benefits of the free market were for all members of society, from the richest to the poorest. In this bitter joke at the end of *Number 11*, then, Coe turns this rhetoric of choice on its head, putting it into the mouth of a character who is justifying the murder of the wealthy according to the sentiment 'measure for measure, or the biter bit'.[96] This centralization and complication of the concept of choice suggests that the choice agenda – an agenda that promises equality but often represents a choice to the wealthy and enfranchised only – is itself a choice, and that, by extension, neoliberalism is an ideology and not the 'natural' state of affairs it is often presented to be. Coe's critique here is less linear than the satire of Thatcherism in *What a Carve Up!* but it is no less angry. *Number 11* is an angry novel and a funny novel, but the cynical reason of satirical humour is jettisoned in favour of something more downbeat and melancholic, yet still politically charged. Indeed, the politics of comedy and laughter itself is one of the subjects of the book, which scrutinizes the efficacy of the mocking satire found in the earlier novel and, as Coe has argued, in contemporary media more generally. One of the *Number 11*'s interlocking stories, 'The Winshaw Prize', is even prefaced by a warning about satire taken from William Cowper's 1785 poem 'The Task': 'Yet what can satire, either grave or gay? … / What vice has it subdued? whose heart reclaim'd / By rigour? or whom laughed into reform? / Alas! Leviathan is not so tamed'.[97] The story that follows is undoubtedly satirical, but it is also *about* satire, and is one of the ways on which Coe seeks to use the political potential of satirical comedy without succumbing to cynical resignation is via the interrogation of the form itself, or what I term 'metacomedy'.

Metacomedy

'The Winshaw Prize, or, Nathan Pilbeam's Breakthrough Case: A "Nate of the Station" Story' is the fourth of five interlinked sections that make up *Number 11*,

---

[96] Ibid.
[97] This section of Cowper's poem encompasses many of the challenges and contradictions of satire. The lines quoted by Coe are preceded by a satirical portrait of the English nobility's decadence and lack of masculine virtue, and are followed by a paean to religion and the pulpit as 'The most important and effectual guard, / Support and ornament of virtue's cause'. In the space of a few stanzas, Cowper moves from satire, to a discourse on the limitations of satire, to a statement about the true locus of truth and virtue. William Cowper, *The Task: A Poem in Six Books*, online edn (Ann Arbor, MI: University of Michigan Library, [1785] 2007), ii, pp. 57–62. Available online: http://quod.lib.umich.edu/cgi/t/text/text-idx?c=ecco;idno=004792652.0001.000 (accessed 17 June 2019). That Coe quotes the same passage from Cowper in his *London Review of Books* essay on satire is a further demonstration of the link between his critical reflections on comedy and his fiction writing. See Coe, 'The Paradox of Satire (II)'.

and as the full title suggests, it is a detective story of sorts. The Nate of the title is PC Nathan Pilbeam, a police officer who believes that 'every crime had to be seen in its social, political and cultural context' and whose investigations lead him through diverse areas of cultural theory and history: '"To solve an English crime, committed by an English Criminal, one must contemplate the condition of England itself"', he argues in an article for *Police* magazine.[98] Alongside his significantly less intelligent senior officer Detective Chief Inspector Gates,[99] Pilbeam investigates the death of two high-profile stand-up comedians, Mickey Parr and Ray Turnbull. Having initially suspected the newspaper editor Sir Peter Eaves of the murders, in revenge for the comedians' jokes at the expense of his daughter Hilary Winshaw-Eaves, Pilbeam ultimately realizes that the culprit is a blogger who writes under the name ChristieMalry2,[100] whose rage is aimed at laughter and its negative effect on public discourse:

> Every time we laugh at the venality of the corrupt politician, at the greed of a hedge fund manager, at the spurious outpourings of a rightwing [sic] columnist, we're letting them off the hook. The ANGER which we should feel towards these people, which might otherwise lead to ACTION, is released and dissipated in the form of LAUGHTER. ... Down with comedy, for fuck's sake! And on with the real struggle.[101]

Though expressed with less eloquence and more anger here, these sentiments echo Coe's own interventions on the topic of laughter and politics, discussed earlier, and Pilbeam's investigations draw upon many of the touchstones of

---

[98] Coe, *Number 11*, p. 185. Pilbeam's nickname 'Nate of the Station' is a clear pun on 'State of the Nation', the subject of Coe's 2012 essay '"State-of-the-Nation" Novels', collected in *Marginal Notes, Doubtful Statements*.

[99] The double act Pilbeam and Capes are a knowing reference to Chief Inspector Gate and Constable Barker, the detectives who investigate Reggie's 'death' in Nobbs's *The Fall and Rise of Reginald Perrin*. In Nobbs's novel, Barker studies criminology and cultivates an eccentric image, whereas Gate is very much of the old school. Their introduction is a superb piece of dry, comic parataxis: 'Chief Inspector Gate was a big, florid man whose habit was double whiskies. Constable Barker was a few inches shorter, and his hobby was detection. Chief Inspector Gate's qualifications were that he was six foot tall. Constable Barker's were nine "O" Levels and three "A" levels.' Nobbs, *Fall and Rise*, p. 185. The name Pilbeam is likely to be a reference to Nova Pilbeam, a 'forgotten' starlet who starred in two early Alfred Hitchcock films. *Expo 58* in particular is full of names taken from this era of film, including, as mentioned earlier, Radford and Wayne, detectives modelled on the characters Charters and Caldicott from *The Lady Vanishes*. Radford and Wayne are the surnames of the actors who played Charters and Caldicott in a series of British films of the 1930s and the 1940s, beginning with Hitchcock's *The Lady Vanishes* (1938).

[100] The blogger's name is a reference to B.S. Johnson's 1973 novel *Christie Malry's Own Double Entry*, in which the title character takes revenge for 'debits' perpetrated by society by instigating a series of 'credits', ranging to vandalism to poisoning and eventually bombing. Coe has written extensively about his interest in Johnson, including most notably in his biography *Like a Fiery Elephant: The Story of B.S. Johnson* (London: Picador, 2004) and the edition *Well Done God! Selected Prose and Drama of B.S. Johnson*, ed. Jonathan Coe, Philip Tew and Julia Jordan (London: Picador, 2013).

[101] Coe, *Number 11*, p. 205.

comedy and humour theory evoked by Coe in his non-fiction writing. Pilbeam has read the ancient theorists of humour as well as Hobbes, Kant, Kierkegaard, Bergson and Freud, up to Milan Kundera from whose *Testaments Betrayed* (1993) he quotes. Although Kundera is a believer in the good of humour and laughter, Coe reproduces his statement that satire is 'thesis art'; it is 'sure of its own truth, it ridicules what it determines to combat'.[102] Satire's certainty and its reliance on ridicule are central to Coe's own reservations about the form, and yet at the same time, these arguments appear in a book that is itself comic, and within the section of that book that is most overtly satirical. Coe describes the fact that '*Number 11* itself is not just a political comedy, but a book about political comedy', noting that 'if comedy itself was going to be one of the subjects of the book, it should also be woven into the fabric of the book'.[103]

'The Winshaw Prize' section of *Number 11* is set around the establishment of a prize established in memory of Roderick Winshaw, an art dealer who met his end along with most of his immediate family in *What a Carve Up!* The Prize is the reductio ad absurdum of prize culture, which, in an ouroboros-like perpetuation of the artistic awards cycle,[104] is presented annually to what is judged to be the best prize in the UK. It is the distillation of the Winshaws' belief in competition, and as the chair of the steering committee argues, '"a perfect poke in the eye to those sentimentalists who still believe that artistic creation is some sort of haven from competition"'.[105] This strand of the plot connects with the novel's broader critique of the neoliberal mantra 'FREEDOM, COMPETITION, CHOICE', applying it to the extension of market principles and values to artistic production, a satirical edge that is in many ways a continuation of Roderick's manipulation of the art market in *What a Carve Up!* – yet another example of the Winshaw legacy. Coe also continues the earlier novel's satirical depiction of the media in his portrait of Josephine Winshaw-Eaves, whose scurrilous clickbait stories show little regard for factual accuracy or consistency, focusing instead on generating controversy and baiting liberal opinion. To some extent, Josephine's journalism gestures to an earlier age of tabloid influence, but it also resonates with the work of contemporary journalists and media personalities such as Katie Hopkins, whose reputations rest on their ability to generate controversy via articles and

---

[102] Ibid., p. 203; Milan Kundera, *Testaments Betrayed: An Essay in Nine Parts*, trans. Linda Asher (New York: HarperCollins, [1993] 1995), p. 202.
[103] Guignery, 'An Interview with Jonathan Coe'.
[104] For an excellent discussion of cultural prizes, their significance, impact and cultural value, see James F. English, *The Economy of Prestige: Prizes, Awards, and the Circulation of Cultural Value* (Cambridge, MA: Harvard University Press, 2005).
[105] Coe, *Number 11*, p. 211.

commentary that are largely read, shared and commented upon online. The bitter but very funny exemplar of this model of journalism is Josephine's attempt to find a black, disabled lesbian who is living on social benefits, in order to prove that this straw man of lazy right-wing journalism actually exists. When she finds this person – or a person who can be cast in this role – her subsequent article on Alison Doubleday is an all-too-accurate parody of this form of discourse, whose real-world effects – Alison is later imprisoned for fraud – are of no concern to the author or publisher.

In 'The Winshaw Prize', then, the tone and tenor of the writing is much closer to the comic satire of *What a Carve Up!*,[106] yet at the same time one of the objects of this satire is comedy itself, particularly stand-up comedy, and particularly uninventive political stand-up comedy. Mickey Parr is first introduced in the second section of *Number 11*, 'The Comeback', where Val Doubleday watches him on a television panel show, making jokes about the iniquities of the banking system. Val cannot see the funny side and wonders why the audience are guffawing at his jokes about the continuation of bonuses even after the banks have failed: 'Why did it not make them angry and depressed?' she asks.[107] Parr then reappears in 'The Winshaw Prize', where he and another comedian, Ray Turnbull, are described as among dozens of other 'young, tousled, slightly overweight white men wearing loose brightly coloured shirts untucked at the trouser', posing on the covers of DVDs released in time for Christmas.[108] This thumbnail portrait will strike a chord with anyone who is familiar with the mainstream UK comedy scene of the early 2000s, as will Coe's description of 'audience members roaring with laughter at a series of unremarkable observations about gender roles or the minutiae of everyday social interaction'.[109] And although Coe is painting with broad brushstrokes here, there is a very specific critique of the laziness of certain types of 'political' comedy and its soporific effects, as expounded in the rants

---

[106] Even here, Coe notes that contemporary reality threatens the overwhelm the satirist's ability to invent, citing the example of his invention of the patently absurd Winshaw Prize and later discovery of the real-life 'Awards Awards' for best award of the year. Jonathan Coe, 'Will Satire Save Us in the Age of Trump?' *Guardian*, 6 January 2017. Available online: https://www.theguardian.com/books/2017/jan/06/jonathan-coe-will-satire-save-us-in-the-age-of-donald-trump?CMP=share_btn_link (accessed 16 July 2019). I return to the question of satire's role in the age of Trump at the end of Chapter 6.

[107] Coe, *Number 11*, p. 90.

[108] Ibid., p. 186.

[109] Ibid. This description is a recognizable portrait of a particular era of mainstream UK stand-up, but it is also bluntly satirical and does not account for the wide variety of innovative work that is performed under the umbrella term 'stand-up'. See, for example, Oliver Double, *Getting the Joke: The Inner Workings of Stand-Up Comedy*, 2nd edn (London: Bloomsbury, 2014), or Stuart Goldsmith's consistently excellent podcast *The Comedian's Comedian* available at http://www.comedianscomedian.com/ (accessed 23 August 2016).

of ChristieMalry2 and ultimately in his plot to murder comedians deemed to trivialize public discourse. *Number 11* is at once a satire against targets such as the cultural prize industry, the tabloid media and mainstream stand-up comedy, *and* a self-reflexive narrative about the shortcomings of comic satire. Although not often discussed in these terms, Coe's writing is frequently metafictional,[110] and it is predominantly comic. Here Coe combines these two elements to satirize aspects of contemporary culture while at the same time asking readers to reflect on the nature of satirical humour. In this way, *Number 11* retains the critical intent of *What a Carve Up!* but also seeks to avoid succumbing to cynical laughter and reason.

Number 11's metacomedy offers a further way to think about the relationship between comedy and politics in Coe's fiction, but by offering a commentary on satirical humour and at the same time practising satire, Coe could be accused of having his cake and eating it too, or even of undercutting any political commitment via irony. This is the paradox of self-reflexive narratives, which, it is frequently argued, demand a critical engagement from the reader. In fact, as Mark Currie argues in his introduction to *Metafiction* (1995), metafiction is a form that blurs the boundary between literature and commentary: 'A metafiction is not definitively a novel whose author is both a writer and a critic, but a novel which dramatizes the boundary between fiction and criticism.' Currie continues by suggesting that 'to unify metafictions under this definition requires a rather loose definition of "criticism",'[111] but it nevertheless introduces an overtly critical function into the fiction, a critical function that denaturalizes the narrative and asks the reader to scrutinize the conditions of their engagement with the text. Other critics, most notably Linda Hutcheon, have highlighted the political function of this critical function. In *Narcissistic Narrative* (1980), Hutcheon argues:

> The unsettled reader is forced to scrutinize his [*sic*] concepts of art as well as his life values. Often he must revise his understanding of what he reads so frequently that he comes to question the possibility of understanding. In doing so he might be freed from enslavement not only to the empirical, but also to his own set patterns of thought and imagination.[112]

---

[110] See the series of intertextual references to books and films discussed earlier in relation to David Nobbs and British cinema, for example. Or the ending of *Maxwell Sim*, in which Coe the author steps into the frame to tell Max that he is a fictional character. As Merritt Moseley argues, this metafictional aspect of Coe's writing is present from his earliest published novel, *The Accidental Woman*. Moseley, *Understanding Jonathan Coe*, pp. 10–11.

[111] Mark Currie, 'Introduction', in *Metafiction*, ed. Mark Currie (Harlow: Longman, 1995), pp. 1–18 (p. 3).

[112] Linda Hutcheon, *Narcissistic Narrative: The Metafictional Paradox* (Waterloo, ON: Wilfrid Laurier University Press, 1980), p. 139. See also, Linda Hutcheon, *The Politics of Postmodernism*, 2nd edn

On this view, metafiction has the potential to effect real-world change by demanding that readers question their assumptions, thereby altering 'set patterns of thought and imagination'. In *Reaganism, Thatcherism and the Social Novel*, Colin Hutchinson applies a similar logic to Coe's fiction, arguing that 'that the social novel ought to engage with issues in the "real" world, yet also indicate the problematic nature of the representation of such issues', and that the self-reflexive elements of *What a Carve Up!* mean that 'readers are obliged to interrogate the structuring of their own reality', a reality that lies beyond the purview of Coe's narrator Michael Owen.[113] I am more sceptical than Hutcheon and Hutchinson about the relationship between metafiction and real-world action, but I maintain that in *Number 11*, Coe's discourse on the nature of satire and laughter offers a way of retaining the bite and hard humour of satirical comedy while warning against the dangers of succumbing to a cynical mindset or assuming that laughter and mockery are themselves radical acts. In this continuation of Coe's comic exploration of post-war British culture and politics, comedy becomes both the mode and the subject of the fiction. The novel sees a partial return to the more overtly satirical territory of *What a Carve Up!*, while at the same time self-consciously reflecting on the nature of satirical humour in order to question its effectiveness, or rather to warn against mistaking mockery for critique or laughter for action.

In its exploration of the radical potential of jokes, its pursuit of political comedy that avoids cynical reason and its metacomic reflections on the nature of humour, Jonathan Coe's fiction demonstrates a commitment to the comic voice even as it probes the value of comedy and the fraught relationship between laughter and politics. This chapter has focused on three of Coe's most recent novels, but many of its arguments could be extended to his other post-*What a Carve Up!* work. In *The Rotters' Club* and its follow-up *The Closed Circle*, for example, Coe explores the dark underside of humour via wild, anarchic stunts of Harding, who goes from legendary schoolboy 'lord of misrule', to racist agitator and eventually to renouncer of humour.[114] Coe also explores the potential of comedy to unify disparate groups of people via shared laughter, as when in *The Rotters' Club* Benjamin Trotter watches the 1977 *Morecambe and Wise Show* Christmas special and feels a sense of 'oneness, ... a sense that the entire nation

---

(London: Routledge, 2002).
[113] Colin Hutchinson, *Reaganism, Thatcherism and the Social Novel* (Basingstoke: Palgrave Macmillan, 2008), p. 53.
[114] Jonathan Coe, *The Rotters' Club* (London: Penguin, [2001] 2002), p. 175.

was being briefly, fugitively drawn together in the divine act of laughter.[115] And *The House of Sleep* includes a number of jokes and comic set pieces that are at once wonderfully funny and deadly serious, for example when a set of misnumbered footnotes leads to a major libel case that bankrupts a magazine and comes close to ruining the career of the film critic Terry Worth.[116] In an interview conducted shortly after the publication of *The House of Sleep*, Coe describes a tension between high seriousness and low comedy in his writing and reading, and how 'combining comedy and seriousness is very important' to him.[117] This tension has proven productive, and while the tenor of the humour may have shifted somewhat since his most famous novel *What a Carve Up!* his fiction continues to demonstrate the mutual importance of seriousness to comedy and comedy to seriousness.

---

[115] Ibid., p. 274. *The Rotters' Club* does, however, contain a warning about generalizations on the universality of humour. When Benjamin tries to share his enthusiasm with Steve Richards, he discovers that Steve's family do not watch television on Christmas night and that he has '"never quite seen it, with those two."' Ibid., p. 282. Moreover, as Nick Hubble notes, the word 'briefly' can be read as an acknowledgement of the fact that 'any sense of a British common culture is already little more than an annual, albeit well-loved, pantomime' at this moment in history. Nick Hubble, 'What Became of the People We Used to Be? *The House of Sleep* (1997) and the 1970s Sitcom, *Whatever Happened to the Likely Lads?* (1973–5)', in *Jonathan Coe: Contemporary British Satire*, ed. Philip Tew (London: Bloomsbury, 2018), pp. 95–108 (p. 96).

[116] This set piece is a literary homage to the classic 1980 *Two Ronnies* sketch in which Ronnie Corbett appears on the television quiz show *Mastermind* with the specialist topic 'Answering the Question Before Last' and proceeds to do precisely that. The conceit leads to comic juxtapositions such as 'Q: What's the name of the directory that lists members of the peerage? A: A study of old fossils'. Ronnie Barker and Ronnie Corbett, 'Answering the Question before Last' [video], YouTube (recorded 1980, uploaded 18 December 2007), https://www.youtube.com/watch?v=y0C59pI_ypQ (accessed 17 June 2019).

[117] Michael Silverblatt, *Bookworm*, 'Jonathan Coe: *The House of Sleep*' [podcast], KCRW, 19 March 1998. Available online: http://www.kcrw.com/news-culture/shows/bookworm/jonathan-coe-the-house-of-sleep (accessed 17 June 2019).

2

'A grave disquisition'
Style, class and comedy in the novels of Martin Amis

The ethics of style

Martin Amis is known as a comic writer and as a stylist. When he first came to prominence, he was viewed as a part of a generation of English writers who looked beyond the country's borders for inspiration and broke free from the parochial slump into which the novel had fallen. As subsequent re-evaluations of this period have shown, this outline is simplistic,[1] but it is true that Amis looked to America and found the comic energy and bravura style of US-based writers such as Saul Bellow and Vladimir Nabokov energizing and inspirational.[2] And it is in relation to Bellow and Nabokov that he made a claim not only for the importance of style but also for an *ethics* of style. In a 1995 essay on Bellow's *The Adventures of Augie March* (1953), he notes that 'attentive readers will, I hope, have noticed that this is an extraordinarily *written* novel' and, after quoting examples of Bellow's stylish prose, concludes that this writteness should not be

---

[1] For critical re-evaluations of post-war British fiction see, for example, Andrzej Gąsiorek, *Post-War British Fiction: Realism and After* (London: Edward Arnold, 1995); Dominic Head, *The Cambridge Introduction to Modern British Fiction, 1950–2000* (Cambridge: Cambridge University Press, 2002); Lyndsey Stonebridge and Marina MacKay (eds), *British Fiction after Modernism: The Novel at Mid-Century* (Basingstoke: Palgrave Macmillan, 2007); Nick Bentley, *Radical Fictions: The English Novel in the 1950s* (Oxford: Peter Lang, 2007); Sebastian Groes, *British Fictions of the Sixties: The Making of the Swinging Decade* (London: Bloomsbury, 2009); and David James (ed.), *The Cambridge Companion to British Fiction since 1945* (Cambridge: Cambridge University Press, 2015). Much of this work responds to the view, perpetuated by influential accounts from critics such as Bernard Bergonzi and D.J. Taylor, that in the post-war period British fiction was, in Bergonzi's words, 'largely backward- and inward-looking, with rather little to say that can be instantly translated into universal statements about the human condition'. Bernard Bergonzi, *The Situation of the Novel*, 2nd edn (Basingstoke: Macmillan, 1979), p. 56. See also D.J. Taylor, *A Vain Conceit: British Fiction in the 1980s* (London: Bloomsbury, 1989).

[2] See, for example, Victoria N. Alexander, 'Between the Influences of Bellow and Nabokov', *Antioch Review* 52:4 (1994), 580–90. Nick Bentley lists Amis's influences as Swift, Dostoevsky, Bellow and Nabokov, and David James adds Joyce to the list. See Nick Bentley, *Martin Amis* (Tavistock: Northcote House, 2015), p. 4; and David James, '"Style Is Morality"? Aesthetics and Politics in the Amis Era', *Textual Practice*, 26:1 (2012), 11–25 (p. 16).

dismissed or diminished as superficial ornamentation. Rather, Amis continues, style is 'intrinsic to perception. We are fond of separating style and content (for the purposes of analysis and so on), but they aren't separable: they come from the same place. And style is morality. Style judges.'[3] Style judges. Style is intrinsic to and indivisible from content. According to Amis, the ideological, political, ethical or any other dimensions of the text are bound up with its style. He returns to this idea in the memoir *Experience* (2000), this time in a footnote recounting an argument with his father, Kingsley Amis, about a passage from Nabokov's *Lolita* (1955) that Amis *fils* particularly admires but Amis *père* dismisses as '"just style"'. Kingsley sees self-consciously stylish prose as '"diversionary stuff"', but Martin denies that conspicuous style is only so much garnish, returning to the idea that style is a form of ethics, this time with added emphasis: 'style *is* morality: morality detailed, configured, intensified. It's not in the mere narrative arrangement of good and bad that morality makes itself felt. It can be there in every sentence.'[4] On this view, morality inheres in the language of prose, at the level of the word, the sentence, the paragraph, as well as at the levels of characterization and plot. It is closely linked to Amis's mistrust of macro-level formal elegance and the shapely, neatly plotted narrative. As David James puts it in a 2012 essay, Amis is 'a master of the part rather than the whole'.[5]

James's essay '"Style is Morality"? Aesthetics and politics in the Amis era' focuses on the 1984 novel *Money* and explores the relationship between Amis's comments about style and writing and their significance for the reading of his novels, particularly in relation to the critical tendency to characterize *Money* as a quintessentially postmodern text:

> His respect for control perfectly matches his insistent rejection of style understood as purely ornamental. 'Style judges', he repeatedly claims. And the judgement is not simply diegetic, part of the plot; it is as applicable to Amis's own beliefs about form. Such beliefs remind us how important it is to regard Amis as a conscious artist, for whom there is nothing mysterious about style's deployment, even if he gives the impression of handling it so intuitively. While his convictions about the responsibilities of stylization exemplify an aesthetic seriousness that deeply complicates his affiliation with postmodernism, simply to ally Amis with other paradigms is equally tricky.[6]

---

[3] Martin Amis, 'The American Eagle', in *The War against Cliché: Essays and Reviews 1971–2000* (London: Vintage, [2001] 2002), pp. 447–69 (pp. 466–7).
[4] Martin Amis, *Experience* (London: Vintage, [2000] 2001), p. 121.
[5] James, '"Style Is Morality"?' p. 23.
[6] Ibid., p. 20.

This reading is particularly insightful for the connection it establishes between Amis's self-consciously 'high' style and his literary heritage, not only in relation to figures such as Bellow and Nabokov but also within a more localized tradition. There is a potential 'dissonance between the parochial and the cosmopolitan' in Amis's writing, and a tension between his claims for a carefully modulated ethics of style, readings of his work that focus on its innovations and transatlantic reach, and his own more modest claim that he belongs to an English comic tradition 'of writing about low events in a high style'.[7] This is a productive tension, and in the context of considering Amis as a specifically *comic* writer, it raises the question of how this modulation between 'high' and 'low' relates to humour in his work as well as to his claims about morality.

Amis's writing provides a point of comparison for Richard Robinson and Barry Shiels in their article 'The Violation of Style: Englishness in Edward St Aubyn's Patrick Melrose novels' (2016), which discusses style as a literary critical concept, focusing on questions of style, inheritance and Englishness in St Aubyn's pentalogy of Melrose novels. Robinson and Shiels return to Amis's comments about style and morality, noting that Amis's style 'sometimes raises critical suspicion. Neologistic, pornographic and plausibly modernist, his authorial voice continues to depend on the inherited mode of English satire – although that voice is also transatlantic, pointing to Amis's assimilation of an American alternative to "English" prose.' They find that for St Aubyn, in contrast with Amis, 'style is *immorality*'. Like James, Robinson and Shiels note both the distinctiveness of Amis's style and the way in which it moves between multiple registers, drawing on high culture and low life, transatlantic influences as well as a distinctively English comic and satirical tradition. James Wood describes this as Amis's 'partly Americanized yet English comic voice', which he views as the novelist's 'great achievement' because it led him 'part of the way out of the English verbal prison of the 1950s, 60s and 70s', a period during which, Wood argues, English fiction was largely moribund.[8] In the same essay, Wood is less enthusiastic about the direction Amis's fiction took

---

[7] Ibid., p. 23. Amis has positioned himself in an English tradition that runs from Henry Fielding to his own father. See Haffenden, *Novelists in Interview*, p. 24. Susanne Peters describes Amis's comedy as a type of 'anti-comedy' in which humour is suffused with menace. Susanne Peters, 'A Proletarian Comedy of Menace: Martin Amis's *Lionel Asbo*', in 'Focus on Comic Representations in Post-Millennial British and Irish Fiction', ed. Barbara Puschmann-Nalenz, special issue *Anglistik: International Journal of English Studies*, 27:1 (2016), 85–97.

[8] James Wood, 'Martin Amis: The English imprisonment', in *The Broken Estate: Essays on Literature and Belief* (London: Jonathan Cape, 1999), pp. 186–99 (p. 198). In this respect, Wood follows the critics noted earlier in his belief that British fiction largely slipped into parochialism and formal conservatism after the Second World War, only to be enlivened by American influences in the 1980s.

in *The Information* (1995) – of which more later – but again it is this sense of hybridity that distinguishes Amis as a stylist. And for Isabelle Zahar, it is precisely this multiplicity of styles which, in the depiction of *Money*'s narrator John Self, accounts for Amis's ethics of style by representing 'a consciousness with the number of styles it would need, to portray its vista on the world'.[9] The novel does not attempt verisimilitude in its representation of Self's voice, but rather employs the vocabulary, linguistic dexterity and multiplicity of registers necessary to give a sense of an inner life in all its complexity. Amis continues to be a divisive writer whose work elicits a range of contesting critical interpretations, yet there is consistent agreement about a number of aspects of his writing outlined earlier: that Amis is a distinctive stylist, that a defining feature of this style is its multiplicity (combining high and low, demotic and literary, and Anglo and American Englishes); that this stylistic multiplicity is often employed to comic effect; and, following Amis's own statements about the politics of style, that there is an ethical dimension to this stylistic virtuosity. Style *is* morality, form *is* content. Within these discussions, it tends to be the comic element that is marginalized in favour of other aspects of his work, and yet attention to this important element of his writing reveals how the interaction between a multiplicity of styles is fundamental to understanding the Amisian comic voice, and that understanding the Amisian comic voice is fundamental to understanding the relationship between ethics and style in his fiction, offering important insights into this relationship in comic writing more generally. More than this, the analysis of the comic voice in Amis's fiction helps to identify the need for a dialogue between literary studies, humour studies (including linguistic humour studies) and narrative theory, each of which offers significant insights that are too often examined independently of one another. This chapter explores style and comedy in Amis's recent fiction, arguing that the comic juxtaposition of – and movement between – radically different styles, or what Nick Bentley describes as 'a comedy of inappropriate stylistic juxtapositions',[10] becomes more pronounced in the later work and that the implicit hierarchy between high and low in these novels, particularly as it intersects with social class, raises significant questions about the ethics and politics of the comic voice.

---

[9] Isabelle Zahar, 'The Artist as Critic, Style as Ethics: Amis's American Stylists and Self's Stylisation', *Textual Practice*, 26:1 (2012), 27–42 (p. 39).

[10] Bentley, *Martin Amis*, p. 3.

High and low: Hierarchies of comic style

In *Money*, which remains Amis's most written-about novel, John Self, an English television advert director, narrates his misadventures in London and New York while attempting to produce his first feature film. From his opening lines describing a car 'sharking out of lane' as he is ferried in a taxi cab from JFK Airport to Manhattan 'still drunk and crazed and ghosted from the plane',[11] Self's voice bears the hallmarks of Amis's distinctive prose, a mixture of slang and more conventionally 'literary' language. It has sometimes been noted that this linguistic dexterity is not fully in keeping with Self's boorish persona,[12] but as Jeremy Scott argues, the interaction between 'the demotic (for the expression of reactions to the quotidian) and the hieratic (used for the narrator's capacity to aestheticize in response to the world around him)' can be read as 'a form of *unabashed* dialogism and a narrative discourse which could be read as containing within itself both the discourse of character and the discourse of author'.[13] There is no attempt on behalf of the author to disappear into the character, and the movement between authorial and characterological voices, as well as a number of other registers,[14] reveals the writtenness of the novel, and articulates aspects of Self's character and perceptions in ways that move beyond the character's own idiolect.[15] Moreover, despite his often grotesque attitudes and appetites, Self is not an entirely unsympathetic character and there is a degree of pathos in his characterization. Scott argues that 'this ambiguous (and ambivalent) attitude towards the author-narrator-character relationship is redolent of a defining quality of *disownment*', where towards the end of the novel, and particularly in the concluding italicized section, Self appears to achieve a form of 'quasi-

---

[11] Martin Amis, *Money* (London: Penguin, [1984] 2000), p. 1.
[12] Richard Todd, for example, argues that 'in devising a voice for John Self', Amis has 'quite explicitly chosen to use his own, a voice that is clearly recognizable from his own other published fiction'. Todd sees this as part of a 'self-conscious confrontation of the problem of solipsistic "closure"'. Richard Todd, 'The Intrusive Author in British Postmodernist Fiction: The Cases of Alasdair Gray and Martin Amis', in *Exploring Postmodernism*, ed. Matei Calinescu and Douwe Wessel Fokkema (Amsterdam: John Benjamins, 1990), pp. 123–38 (p. 135). Bentley is more circumspect, describing an 'unconvincing disparity between the nature of the man that Self appears to be and the powers of articulation he clearly has to convey his experience'. This use of an admirable style to describe problematic characteristics is viewed as part of a 'realism that eschews a straightforward opposition of commendable and reprehensible characters in fiction'. Bentley, *Martin Amis*, pp. 47–8.
[13] Jeremy Scott, *The Demotic Voice in Contemporary British Fiction* (Basingstoke: Palgrave Macmillan, 2009), pp. 157–8.
[14] Scott notes 'discourses ranging from the profane, the cosmopolitan, the urban, the millennial and apocalyptic, the erotic, to the lexis of sport, nursery rhymes and advertising jargon'. Ibid., p. 161.
[15] The presence of a prologue signed 'M.A.' as well as a number of other metafictional devices, most notably the appearance of a character named 'Martin Amis', further highlight the presence of the author and sense of the writtenness of Self's narration.

independence' from Martin Amis and his fictional doubles.[16] The narration is singularly Amisian, but it is never single, and in this sense, *Money* continues a tendency in Amis's earlier, predominantly first-person novels such as *The Rachel Papers* (1973) and *Success* (1978), in which a verbose and flamboyant authorial voice merges and interacts with character idiolects, eliciting a complex sense of agency and movement between sympathies via a series of nested voices-within-voices.[17] The novel that followed *Money*, however, marks a change that has persisted in most of Amis's later fiction. Whereas *Money* is largely narrated using a form of first-person *skaz*,[18] in *London Fields* (1988) and subsequent works, there is a greater proportion of third-person narration and more instances of authorial intrusion. Within the frame of *London Fields*, these intrusions are attributable to the narrator Samson Young, but as Scott notes, the 'overwhelming impression is of *narrator as author*, if not *the* author then his transparently disguised stand-in'.[19] This has a distancing effect, making the transitions between 'high' and 'low', demotic and hieratic, more marked, and introducing a sense of narratorial aloofness more closely aligned to the eighteenth-century English novels of Henry Fielding than the later Russian tradition of *skaz*. Whereas in *Money* the authorial and character voices are intertwined, articulating Self's thoughts using a lexis and tone that merges with the authorial voice, in *London Fields* and many subsequent Amis novels, there are marked transitions between the character and narrating voices and an implicit – or sometimes explicit – hierarchy between registers. If style is morality, increasingly these novels present an external perspective from which to judge the morality of characters' actions as well as their idiolects.

This clash between registers is a frequent source of humour in Amis's fiction,[20] as are the wry observations of his narrators, whose commentary on individuals

---

[16] Scott, *Demotic Voice*, pp. 163, 162.

[17] This movement is dramatized in *Success*, which traces the rise of the 'ordinary' Terry Service, and the decline of smooth-talking, handsome Gregory Riding. Martin Amis, *Success* (London: Penguin, [1978] 1985), p. 11.

[18] A term originating in early twentieth-century Russian formalist criticism, *skaz* 'is characterized by a personal narrator, a simple man of the people with restricted intellectual horizons and linguistic competence, addressing listeners from his own social milieu in a markedly oral speech'. Wolf Schmid, 'Skaz', in *The Living Handbook of Narratology*, ed. Peter Hühn et al. Available online: http://www.lhn.uni-hamburg.de/article/skaz (accessed 8 June 2017). As Monika Fludernik notes, it 'can be used to narrate both in a first- and in a third-person mode'. Monika Fludernik, *Towards a 'Natural' Narratology* (Abingdon: Routledge, 1996), p. 394n1. For a discussion of *skaz* in Amis's early fiction, see James Diedrick, *Understanding Martin Amis*, 2nd edn (Columbia, SC: University of South Carolina Press, 2004), pp. 24–6, 73.

[19] Scott, *Demotic Voice*, p. 169.

[20] M.A.K. Halliday and Ruqaiya Hassan define register as 'a configuration of meanings that are typically associated with a particular situational configuration of field, mode, and tenor'. It is the language associated with a particular situation or activity, and is distinct from, but often linked to, dialect, which is 'what you speak habitually, depending in principle on who you are; and that means where

and events runs parallel to the clichéd or inarticulate pronouncements of the other characters. For example, in *London Fields*, an account of a football match between the London-based teams Queens Park Rangers and West Ham United provides fertile ground for a detour into the language of sports punditry. The working-class Keith Talent recalls the previous Saturday's match to the upper-middle-class Guy Clinch, a fellow QPR supporter:

> Some of the light went out in Keith's eyes as he said, 'During the first half the Hammers probed down the left flank. Revelling in the space, the speed of Sylvester Drayon was always going to pose problems for the home side's number two. With scant minutes remaining before the half-time whistle, the black winger cut in on the left back and delivered a searching cross, converted by Lee Fredge, the East London striker, with inch-perfect precision. After the interval Rangers' fortunes revived as they exploited their superiority in the air. Bobby Bondavich's men offered stout resistance and the question remained: could the Blues translate the pressure they were exerting into goals?[21]

The passage continues for several further sentences, but this gives a flavour of Keith's account, its language familiar to anyone who has read, listened to or watched a sports report. It works as a comic interlude on a number of levels. Its style, at once prosaic and overburdened with unnecessary 'second-mention' adjectives – '*black* winger', '*East London* striker' – is incongruous in the context of a literary novel, particularly one that employs such an elevated register elsewhere, and it is also parodic in its too-perfect adherence to the clichés of the medium. Its sequence of journalistic tics could be taken from Flann O'Brien's 'Catechism of Cliché', a 'unique compendium of all that is nauseating in contemporary writing', which is structured in the question-and-answer format of Catholic catechism.[22] (Does a player ever run? No. He probes. And does he probe down the side of the pitch? No. He probes down the flank. And what is achieved by this probing? It poses problems. For the right-back? No. For the number two.) This change in register is clearly a swipe at the language of the game – part of Amis's 'War Against Cliché' – and the judgement that follows in

---

you come from, either geographically in the case of regional dialects, or socially in the case of social dialects'. M.A.K. Halliday and Ruqaiya Hassan, *Language, Context and Text: Aspects of Language in a Social-Semiotic Perspective*, 2nd edn (Oxford: Oxford University Press, 1989), pp. 38–9, 41.

[21] Martin Amis, *London Fields* (London: Vintage, [1989] 2003), p. 91.

[22] The Catechism of Cliché was an occasional feature in O'Brian's 'Cruiskeen Lawn' column, which ran in the *Irish Times* from 1939 until 1966 and was published under the name Myles na Gopaleen. A typical example reads: 'Is man ever hurt in a motor smash? No. He sustains an injury. Does such a man ever die from his injuries? No he succumbs to them.' Flann O'Brien (Myles na Gopaleen), *The Best of Myles: A Selection from the 'Cruiskeen Lawn'*, ed. Kevin O'Nolan (London: Picador, [1968] 1977), p. 202.

the novel is suitably withering: 'Keith's belated sigh of effort reminded Guy of the sound that Marmaduke would occasionally emit, after a rare success with some taxing formulation like *more chips* or *knife mine*.'[23] Marmaduke is Guy's infant son, and the inference is clear: Keith's language is similarly infantile. But this is not the only judgement, the only change in register, and several pages later the narrator, Samson Young, offers some commentary on the commentary:

> Keith's account of the football match. I've heard many such summaries from him – of boxing matches, snooker matches, and of course darts matches. At first I thought he just memorized sections of the tabloid sports pages. Absolutely wrong.
>
> Remember – he is modern, modern, despite the heels and the flares. When Keith goes to a football match, that misery of stringer's clichés *is what he actually sees*.[24]

Samson's summary offers a further, delayed punchline, combining at its end the unusual usage of 'misery' as a collective noun, with the colloquial but comparatively specialist 'stringer' instead of the more obvious 'journalist' or 'hack'. A contrast is set up between Keith's language and that of Amis's other characters, most notably the author–narrator Samson Young, and it is Keith who is found comically wanting having adopted the tabloid worldview as his own.

In the linguistic strand of comic theory, this mismatching is known as 'register humour', which Salvatore Attardo summarizes as 'humor caused by an incongruity originating in the clash between two registers'. Attardo's analysis is based on the 'script opposition theory' first developed by Victor Raskin, and which, in the case of register-based humour, emerges from the 'the concomitant (overlapping) activation of two or more scripts that weakly activate some scripts, among which there are at least two that are in a relationship of (local) antonymy'.[25] Two or more situational linguistic scripts collide, creating, in the example from *London Fields*, an incongruity between the register 'literary novel' and the register 'tabloid sports journalism', as well as a number of other sub-scripts – the scripts for 'sports analysis' and 'baby talk', for instance. Another example, which is shorter and conforms more closely to the structure of a joke, occurs in *London Fields* when Keith becomes concerned that on her trips to the

---

[23] Amis, *London Fields*, p. 91.
[24] Ibid., pp. 97–8.
[25] Attardo, *Linguistic Theories of Humor*, pp. 230, 252. See also Salvatore Attardo, *Humorous Texts: A Semantic and Pragmatic Analysis* (Berlin: Mouton de Gruyter, 2001), which largely repeats the analysis of Attardo's earlier work in respect to register humour.

library, his wife Kath has been reading the 'proper papers' rather than the usual tabloids:

> This touched a nerve in Keith (for he was very loyal to his tabloid, regarding its readers as one big family); but it also touched a chord. It was through the library that Kath had won Keith's heart. She had taught him how to read and write – easily the most intimate episode of his life. Oh, easily. The thought of it made tears gather behind his eyes, tears of shame and pride, tears of difficulty, of intimacy.
> 'Fuck off', said Keith equably – his usual way of registering casual disagreement.[26]

The register of tender reflection, of intimacy, is undercut by the baldly stated '"Fuck off"', which signally fails to articulate Keith's feelings. A further change in register, a further incongruity, then adds what stand-up comedians would call a 'topper' or a 'tag',[27] when the narrative voice returns to a more measured tone with the understated 'said Keith equably'. Bathos is one of Amis's core modes of comedy, a topic to which I will return , and his linguistic virtuosity lends itself to bathetic transitions; indeed, as well as his famous statement that his work fits into 'the English tradition of writing about low events in a high style', he also engages with an equally established tradition of moving between 'high' and 'low' modes to create a comic disjunction between registers.

Alan Partington identifies register humour as an 'underlying and recurrent' comic technique in P.G. Wodehouse's fiction and, as the examples from *London Fields* illustrate, the same can be argued for Amis. But Partington also notes that register is not limited to narrowly semantic significance; it is 'also a social and a psychological entity', relying on social agreement as to the appropriateness or otherwise of a particular register, as well individual recognition of that appropriateness.[28] Shifts between registers have significance beyond linguistic playfulness, and they rely on recognition and implied hierarchies of appropriateness, formality and value, as is suggested by the very designations 'high' and 'low'. Incongruities generated by register humour, therefore, encapsulate what Amis describes as an ethics of style, or in this case multiple styles, whose interrelation and interaction is comic precisely *because* of the judgement implied by their juxtaposition. To return to the football commentary passage from *London Fields*,

---

[26] Amis, *London Fields*, p. 105.
[27] These terms refer to further sub-punchline that adds to the punchline of the preceding joke.
[28] Alan Partington, 'From Wodehouse to the White House: A Corpus-Assisted Study of Play, Fantasy and Dramatic Incongruity in Comic Writing and Laughter-Talk', *Lodz Papers in Pragmatics*, 4:2 (2008), 189–213 (p. 194). See also Alan Partington, *The Linguistics of Laughter: A Corpus-Assisted Study of Laughter-Talk* (Abingdon: Routledge, 2006).

a further example on the subject of football, this time from Amis's journalism, provides a useful insight into the judgement behind the humour. In a review of Desmond Morris's *The Soccer Tribe* (1981), Amis digresses from his putative subject to discuss the language of football. He writes that 'it is curious that many of the automatic metaphors of football commentary, written and spoken, are connected with the idea of education. A thoughtful pass, a cultured back-heel. A football brain. Indeed, an educated right foot', before noting the contrast between this and the language of football as it is actually played and analysed: 'conceivably', he says, 'our football suffers from the dominance of its working-class ethos', comparing the English scene unfavourably with the rest of Northern Europe where 'they appear to have dispensed with the working classes altogether'. He concludes that 'it has been said that our footballers are paid too much money. Perhaps they should be paid in something else: book-tokens, lecture coupons, night-class dockets, culture vouchers', before relating an anecdote about an overheard conversation between a football manager, Malcolm Allison (Mal), and a footballer, Martin Chivers (Big Chiv): '"The more you learn, the more you know". / "This is it." / "This is it." / "The more you know, the more you learn." / "This is it."' And so on. The irony-laced conclusion is that 'Mal and Big Chiv weren't talking football. They were talking philosophy.'[29] In this non-fiction excursion into the language of football, Amis's humour is heavily reliant on register, but he also articulates a judgement that is implicit in Keith Talent's internalization and regurgitation of football cliché. A lack of style is associated with a lack of education – bad language is bad thought – and a lack of education is associated with social class. More than this, it is working-class language and ethos that are viewed as suspect in comparison with the erudition and conspicuous cultural capital of the other characters, narrators and indeed the author who frames the commentary on this language and ethos. The remainder of this chapter traces this complex relationship in Amis's recent fiction, identifying a nexus between humour, style, ethics and class, and arguing for the importance of understanding these relationships for an understanding of the workings and significance of comedy in fiction.

Comedy, class and style from *The Information* to *Lionel Asbo*

Amis's 1995 novel *The Information* had a troubled early life and became notorious more for extra-textual factors (Amis's split from his long-term agent,

---

[29] Martin Amis, 'Football Mad', in *War against Cliché*, pp. 345–50 (pp. 346–7).

Pat Kavanagh; the size of the advance secured by his new agent, Andrew Wylie; and his extensive and expensive dental work) than for anything in the book itself.[30] It is a novel about the travails of a writer, Richard Tull, and particularly his acrimonious friendship with Gwyn Barry, a much more successful writer. *The Information* is set largely in London and, like *Money* and *London Fields*, is about contemporary urban life and the interactions between different strata of society. It is a comedy, perhaps Amis's most out-and-out comic novel, and it describes a life in transition, and values and social codes that are also in transition. When Richard takes a vacuum cleaner to be repaired, his laboured description of the machine's many flaws elicits a strained interaction with the shop assistant, an episode that works as a set-up to the long-deferred punchline: 'Eventually, under TYPE OF MALFUNCTION, the young man wrote: NOT WORKING.' The conversation between the two also prompts a moment of reflection from Richard:

> Beyond them, in the street outside, the old divisions of social class and then race were giving way to the new divisions: good shoes versus bad shoes, good eyes as opposed to bad eyes (eyes that were clear, at one extreme, ranged against eyes that were far fierier than any tabasco), different preparedness for the forms that urban life was currently taking, here and now.[31]

Changes are underway, and one's adaptability to the urban environment trumps the old social stratifications of class and race. But it is equally significant that these changes take place 'Beyond them, in the street outside', because there is a parallel suggestion that Richard is not adapting to the new urban environment and remains within the old hierarchies. The shop assistant, who has been working in the same job 'longer than he should have', looks at Richard 'with pain and pre-weakened hostility', with eyes 'as dim and marginal as the lights of a car left on all night and well into the next morning'. The description of his eyes refers to the earlier 'good eyes' versus 'bad eyes' opposition, but something more is at play: 'What divided the two of them, in the shop, was words – which were universal (at least on this planet); the young man could look at Richard and be pretty sure

---

[30] See, for example, Charles Glass, 'It's Best to Roll with the Big Cats Forget the Jealous Snipers – If Amis Can Get £500,000 for His Novel He Deserves It', *Guardian*, 10 January 1995; Nicholas Lezard, 'Counting the Cost of Martin's Money', *Independent*, 11 January 1996; Sarah Lyall, 'Martin Amis's Big Deal Leaves Literati Fuming', *New York Times*, 31 January 1995. Available online: http://www.nytimes.com/books/98/02/01/home/amis-bigdeal.html (accessed 17 June 2019); and Mark Lawson, 'Molars, Money and Martyrdom', *Independent*, 14 March 1995. For a summary of this controversy, see Diedrick, *Understanding Martin Amis*, pp. 143–5, and for Amis's own account of the period, see Amis, *Experience*, pp. 247–9.

[31] Martin Amis, *The Information* (London: Flamingo, [1995] 1996), p. 50.

there were more where *they* came from.' Richard is a writer, a verbose writer with a superabundance of words at his disposal at that, but outside the particularities of his situation, it is again language that proves to be the biggest gulf between characters, and it is the clash of registers and levels of linguistic virtuosity that generates the humour, as well as the implicit judgement. The shop assistant's lack of felicity with words provides a joke ('TYPE OF MALFUNCTION ... NOT WORKING') but also something more fundamental; it is a marker of education and social class, and it is no coincidence that the paragraph that follows this interlude mentions a letter addressed to 'Richard Tull, M.A. (Oxon)', and includes a reference to Richard's story, a boost to his ego, that he 'had taken a formal first without ever lifting a pen'.[32]

In *The Information*, language, one's access to words, remains a fundamental source of social division as well as a fundamental source of Amis's humour. But language is also an index for other divisions, primarily associated with social class and cultural capital, and this relationship continues in Amis's subsequent writing, particularly in those novels set in contemporary society, or at least Amis's caricatured, dystopian versions of contemporary society. In *Transgressive Fiction* (2013), Robin Mookerjee argues that Amis has 'abandoned satire in his late work' and, like Evelyn Waugh 'has become less an arch humorist than a novelist of social retrospection, interrogating the ideas that got us here'.[33] Yet although this may be true of historical work such as *The House of Meetings* (2006), *The Zone of Interest* (2014) and to some extent in *The Pregnant Widow* (2010), many recognizable aspects of Amis's comic vision of contemporary society persist in the novels *Yellow Dog* (2003) and *Lionel Asbo: State of England* (2012), the latter of which would likely have been published too late for inclusion in Mookerjee's book. In *Yellow Dog*, a reference to Henry Fielding's fictional character Joseph Andrews, which is misunderstood as a reference to a real-life gangster of the same name, involves the actor and writer Xan Meo in a spiralling conspiracy involving the British monarchy, the tabloid press and the US pornography industry. A running theme in the novel is violence, and particularly sexualized male violence, a topic that was clearly on Amis's mind when he reported on his

---

[32] Ibid., pp. 50–1. For a discussion of the vacuum cleaner passage with a different emphasis, see John A. Dern, *Martians, Monsters and Madonna: Fiction and Form in the World of Martin Amis* (New York: Peter Lang, 2000), pp. 139–40. Dern views the scene as an example of the inability of Richard Tull, a 'marooned' modernist, accurately to convey information in a postmodernist world.

[33] Robin Mookerjee, *Transgressive Fiction: The New Satiric Tradition* (Basingstoke: Palgrave Macmillan, 2013), p. 170. *The House of Meetings*, *The Pregnant Widow* and *The Zone of Interest*, all contain comic elements that would reward further discussion but take place wholly or primarily in historical settings. The focus of this chapter is the novels set in reimagined versions of contemporary Britain and the United States.

research on the 'other' Hollywood of the California adult film industry for a 2001 *Guardian* article.[34] Similar concerns surface in *Lionel Asbo: State of England* (2012), a novel whose subtitle signals its lofty aims even while the subject matter – violence, criminality, celebrity and the tabloid press – are more firmly rooted in the quotidian. Lionel's surname derives from the acronym for Anti-Social Behaviour Order, a notorious measure introduced into British law in 1998, which was intended 'to protect the public from behaviour that causes or is likely to cause harassment, alarm or distress' and contains 'conditions prohibiting an individual from carrying out specific anti-social acts or (for example) from entering defined areas'.[35] Amis's Lionel views his series of ASBOs as a source of pride, and he changes his surname from Peppardine to Asbo because it '*has a nice ring to it*'.[36] He is a petty criminal who finds fame when he wins £139,999,999.50 on the National Lottery, and whose rise and eventual downfall is contrasted with his studious nephew Des Peppardine, who pursues education, family life and stability.

Although set in a highly exaggerated version of contemporary England, it is not hard to see parallels between characters and events in *Lionel Asbo* and real-life analogues, perhaps most evidently between Asbo and Michael Carroll, the self-styled 'King of Chavs'[37] who in 2002 became notorious after winning a National Lottery jackpot of nearly ten million pounds. The tabloid press made much of Carroll's criminal past and branded him the 'Lotto Lout' (the title of part two of *Lionel Asbo*) when he spent his money publicly and ostentatiously. The same press then delighted in the subsequent loss of his fortune and his return to working life in a biscuit factory. In a further parallel with tabloid news stories of the decade preceding its publication, Amis's novel also features a love interest known as 'Threnody', a glamour model with poetic ambitions who is rival to Danube, a character surely based on Jordan – now known by her birth name Katie Price – a former glamour model turned entrepreneur who has also published a series of bestselling autobiographies, novels and children's books. Price was for many years both courted and reviled by the press, her every action the subject of intense speculation. By the time *Lionel Asbo* was published, these

---

[34] Reproduced as Martin Amis, 'In Pornoland: Pussies Are Bullshit', in *The Rub of Time: Bellow, Nabokov, Hitchens and Other Pieces, 1994–2016* (London: Jonathan Cape, 2017), pp. 161–74.
[35] Crown Prosecution Service, 'Anti-Social Behaviour Orders on Conviction (ASBOs)', 2014. Available online: http://www.cps.gov.uk/legal/a_to_c/anti_social_behaviour_guidance/ (accessed 4 May 2017).
[36] Martin Amis, *Lionel Asbo: State of England* (London: Jonathan Cape, 2012), p. 27.
[37] As Owen Jones has noted, the term 'Chav' originates from the Romany word 'chavi', meaning child, but has spread into wider usage as a derogatory term for working-class youths. See Owen Jones, *Chavs: Demonization of the Working Class* (London: Verso, 2011).

knowing references to real-life people and events already looked dated, but they are emblematic of Amis's concern with satirizing tabloid sensationalism. Lionel and Threnody are grotesques, but as in all satire, they are grotesques anchored in a recognizable world. Moreover, they are grotesques who are invoked via Amis's customarily stylish prose, and again it is this style, and specifically Amis's negotiation of different stylistic registers, which is the source of much of the novel's humour, containing as it does numerous examples of what Bentley terms 'inverted free indirect discourse, in which the narrator presents characters in language from a register with a distinctly different social and cultural milieu to the one the characters inhabit'.[38] Take, for example, this passage from early in *Lionel Asbo*, in which Lionel educates his nephew, Des, on the finer points of English criminal law:

> There followed a grave debate, or a grave disquisition, on the difference between ABH and GBH – between Actual Bodily Harm and its sterner older brother, Grievous. Like many career delinquents, Lionel was up to PhD level on questions of criminal law. Criminal law, after all, was the third element in his vocational trinity, the other two being villainy and prison. When Lionel talked about the law (reaching for a kind of high style), Des always paid close attention. Criminal law was in any case much on his mind.
>
> 'In a nutshell, Des, in a nutshell, it's the difference between the first-aid kit and the casualty ward.'[39]

While the narrator holds forth with customary eloquence, preparing the ground for a 'grave disquisition' and suggesting that Lionel is 'reaching for a kind of high style' – note the modifying 'reaching for' and 'kind of' – what we get is a bathetic cliché followed by an analogy that cannot compete with the preceding 'sterner older brother' metaphor.

This passage on the legal distinction between actual and grievous bodily harm is a partial repetition from *Yellow Dog*, where Xan Meo's wife Russia reads from a newspaper report about her husband's attack and asks about the difference between the two types of assault. '"Uh," replies Meo, "extent of injury. Grievous is worse. Actual's bullshit."'[40] The word 'bullshit' becomes a symbol of the degradation of Meo's language, which happens in conjunction with his reversion to a more violent, atavistic state. 'Bullshit' is his judgement on many of the conventionally middle-class niceties he had come to enjoy before the assault

---

[38] Bentley, *Martin Amis*, pp. 115–16.
[39] Amis, *Lionel Asbo*, p. 17.
[40] Martin Amis, *Yellow Dog* (London: Vintage, [2003] 2004), p. 90.

that precipitated his personality change; the repetition of the word develops its own comic rhythm. During his recovery, Meo is not allowed to eat meat or to drink alcohol or coffee and is not happy with the alternatives. '"Tea", he tells Russia, "is bullshit", as is seafood: "What have I got to look forward to? This evening, before my meal, I'll drink a couple of glasses of near-beer. And if *beer* is bullshit, which it is, what's *near*-beer? It's not even bullshit. It's bullshit bullshit. And then what? A plate of bullshit. And yummy water."'[41] Bullshit takes on near philosophical significance for Meo, who is unhappy with his sons' lack of creativity when it comes to swearing: '"Boys, boys", he says after hearing them exchange a series of 'craps', "you've got to learn some new swearwords. Take crap, say. I mean bullshit actually means something. Something fairly complicated. Something like: rubbish intended to deceive. But crap. Crap just means crap. As a word, crap is *so* crap."'[42] Bullshit also provides a link to Amis's article about the increasingly violent world of contemporary pornography when, later in the novel, the porn actress Karla White – a pseudonym for Meo's niece, Cora Susan – explains the industry's historic 'overwhelming emphasis on male-female sodomy' to the tabloid journalist Clint Smoker: '"The rallying cry was Pussies Are Bullshit. They'd sign off with it on the phone: 'Pussies are bullshit!' One director said, 'With anal, the actress's personality comes out.'"'[43] This line is taken directly from Amis's *Guardian* article on the US adult movie industry, in which he reports that a high-profile porn actor, John Stagliano, told him that in contemporary porn, 'Pussies are bullshit'. 'Now', writes Amis, 'John was being obedient to the dictionary definition of "bullshit" which is nonsense intended to deceive', implying that vaginal sex is viewed as less authentic and more prone to deception than other forms of on-screen sex.[44] The anecdote about Stagliano's incongruous statement leads to the unedifying image of Amis, Ian McEwan, Salman Rushdie, Christopher Hitchens and Carol Blue at a conference on 'The Novel in Britain, 1950–2000', where '"Pussies are bullshit" became the (unofficial) conference slogan'. The group play a parlour game involving the substitution of the word 'pussy' with 'bullshit': 'What's New Bullshitcat. Bullshit in Boots. The Owl and the Bullshitcat' and so on.[45] In both *Yellow Dog* and the

---

[41] Ibid., p. 101.
[42] Ibid., p. 221.
[43] Ibid., p. 269. For a discussion of pornography as a facet of Amis's grotesque comic aesthetic, see Robert Duggan, *The Grotesque in Contemporary British Fiction* (Manchester: Manchester University Press, 2013), pp. 92–7.
[44] Amis, 'In Pornoland', p. 161.
[45] Revealingly, the version of the essay reproduced in Amis's collection *The Rub of Time* includes the reference to the running joke about the phrase 'pussies are bullshit' but omits the paragraph about the parlour game with his friends. See Martin Amis, 'In Pornoland', p. 174; and Martin Amis, 'A

preceding article, there is an underlying critique of the fetishization of male-female violence and a reflection on what this reveals about contemporary society,[46] but as so often in Amis's fiction, the comic treatment of this subject matter relies on implicit and explicit judgement of language, and particularly of language as an index of class and education. In *Yellow Dog*, the repetitious use of the bluntly effective bullshit has a bathetic function, punctuating the dialogue and often undercutting pretentious attitudes. It is also a metonym for a type of developmental reversion that, in Meo's case, is imbricated with his working-class origins and subsequent embourgeoisement, as when Russia invites their friends the Richardsons over for drinks and talk turns to the situation in Kashmir. Margot Richardson, emeritus professor of modern history at UCL, outlines the complex intersection of geopolitics and religion in the region and is met with a resolute response: "'Pakistan,' said Xan Meo, 'is bullshit.'" Russia, keen to contextualize her husband's behaviour, explains that "'The clinical term for it is *perseveration* … . When you have an accident like Xan's you can get hooked on certain words or ideas. We seem to have drawn 'bullshit'. … There's also a touch of *Witzelsucht*, or inappropriate humour.'"[47] The mention of *Witzelsucht* (a neurological condition associated with compulsive joking) draws the link between the repeated use of 'bullshit' and its role as a punchline, usually a contextually inappropriate punchline. Although Meo's personality change is described, in atavistic terms, as a regression to caveman-like impulses, there is also a strong sense in which, as Russia phrases it, he had 'escaped or evolved out of' his past, developing 'a set of rational contemporary attitudes' only to devolve,[48] rendering him both dangerous and comic.

Meo's interjections are further examples of the register-based humour discussed earlier, or what Scott describes as the complex 'intersection between the demotic and the hieratic' in Amis's fiction,[49] but also implicit in this interplay is a sense of judgement and hierarchy. Writing in 2007, Richard Bradford argues that Amis 'refuses to judge' his often unlikable protagonists and that he 'makes it difficult for the reader to do so by investing each with an energy, charisma,

---

Rough Trade' (Part Two), *Guardian*, 17 March 2001. Available online: https://www.theguardian.com/books/2001/mar/17/society.martinamis (accessed 17 June 2019).

[46] For a discussion of Amis's novel in the context of trauma and trauma theory, see Nick Bentley, 'Mind and Brain: The Representation of Trauma in Martin Amis' *Yellow Dog* and Ian McEwan's *Saturday*', in *Diseases and Disorders in Contemporary Fiction: The Syndrome Syndrome*, ed. T.J. Lustig and James Peacock (New York: Routledge, 2013), pp. 115–29.

[47] Amis, *Yellow Dog*, pp. 135–6.

[48] Ibid., p. 209.

[49] Scott, *Demotic Voice*, p. 159.

and often manic eloquence'.⁵⁰ Yet while this may be more true of work such as *Money*, it is less easy to sustain in the light of later work in which the *lack* of these positive attributes is often held up for ridicule. As Ben Masters argues, Amis's arguments for an ethics of style are concerned with how ethics 'might be felt at the level of the sentence, through style's precise and local "configurations"; how style "registers" its material',⁵¹ and such ethical judgements are apparent at the level of the sentence and in the movement between voices and registers, particularly where these transitions are untaken for comic effect. David Herman's work in narrative theory provides a valuable analytic framework here. In *Story Logic* (2002), Herman explores the concept of style shifting, which 'occurs when a speaker shifts, for example, from casual to formal speech or vice versa, shifting from, say *I wonder, do you happen to have any beer?* to *Give me a beer*'. Style, Herman notes, is frequently linked to social class and overlaps with dialect and register, cumulatively 'indexing the speaker's membership (or claim to membership) in a particular social group'.⁵² Applying this to a specifically literary context, his reading of Edith Wharton's *The House of Mirth* (1905) makes a case for the politics of style that is in many ways similar to Amis's own claims:

> Style in fiction is not just a device for characterization or a narratorial format but a way of encoding modes of alignment, opposition, and conflict operating at other levels of narrative structure as well. Style is content. More than this, however, Wharton's styles undermine the commonsensical idea that one selects from among various available styles to communicate who and what one is. Rather, her text shows that it is *by* communicating, *by* stylizing, that interlocutors take on a role as selves. Through verbal interaction participants become the centers of subjectivity that in turn help orient communicative behaviour. Content is style.

Style is content and content is style, and shifts between styles are important markers of characters' relative positions within the storyworld. But more than this, these shifts embody a degree of hierarchy because '*a reported utterance is evaluated more negatively the more it differs from the degree of formality, type of speech variety, and mode of situational appropriateness of the style in which the report is couched*'.⁵³ In *The House of Mirth*, Herman argues, these style shifts index class relations and serve to align the reader with the upper-class Lily Barth and against the working-class Mrs Haffen, as well as embedding a critique of gender

---

⁵⁰ Richard Bradford, *The Novel Now: Contemporary British Fiction* (Oxford: Blackwell, 2007), p. 38.
⁵¹ Ben Masters, *Novel Style: Ethics and Excess in Fiction since the 1960s* (Oxford: Oxford University Press, 2017), pp. 101–2.
⁵² Herman, *Story Logic*, pp. 197–8. Emphasis in original.
⁵³ Ibid., pp. 194, 201.

codes in Wharton's juxtaposition of 'masculine' and 'feminine' language. Beyond purely aesthetic considerations (if such an annexation can be imagined), style – and shifts between styles – has important implications for judgements about characters, and readers' relative evaluation of them. Herman's narratological work on style shifting, therefore, provides a valuable way to think about the link between Amis's comic stylistics (specifically register and style shifts as sources of humour) and his claims for an ethics of style as it pertains to the class dynamic presented in his fiction.

Crucially for this discussion, in Herman's work, the 'baseline narratorial style' against which relative deviations are judged is not a nebulous notion of 'standard' or 'literary' language, but rather the stylistic tendencies of the narrator, whose voice predominates and against whose language reported speech is measured and contrasted.[54] Social linguists describe this as the 'matrix language', which works in counterpoint to the 'embedded language' of the inserted speech,[55] and in Amis's fiction, the contrast between these elements is marked and is consistently exaggerated for comic effect, raising a series of questions about who is laughing and at whose expense the joke is being told. To take a further example from the dialogue between Lionel and Des quoted from earlier, one can see this style shifting at work when Des questions Lionel about an unprovoked assault in the Hobgoblin pub:

> 'And this Ross Knowles, Uncle Li. How long's he been in Diston General?' asked Des (referring to the worst hospital in England).
>
> 'Oy. Objection. That's prejudicial.'
>
> ...
>
> 'Why Prejudicial?'
>
> '"Hypothesis". *Hypoffesis*. "I give Ross Knowles a little tap in a fair fight, he comes out of the Hobgoblin – and walks under a truck."' Truck: pronounced truc-kuh (with a glottal stop on the terminal plosive). 'See? Prejudicial.'
>
> Des nodded. It was in fact strongly rumoured that Ross came out of the Hobgoblin on a stretcher.[56]

---

[54] Ibid., p. 201.
[55] See Peter Auer and Carol M. Eastman, 'Code-Switching', in *Society and Language Use*, ed. Jürgen Jaspers, Jef Verschueren and Jan-Ola Östman (Amsterdam: John Benjamins, 2010), pp. 84–112; and Barbara E. Bullock and Almeida Jacqueline Toribio, 'Themes in the Study of Code-switching', in *The Cambridge Handbook of Linguistic Code-switching*, ed. Barbara E. Bullock and Almeida Jacqueline Toribio (Cambridge: Cambridge University Press, 2009), pp. 1–18. Code-switching refers to shifts between languages in bilingual speakers, and as such is distinct from monolingual style shifting. However, the terminology of matrix language and embedded language provides a useful vocabulary for thinking about style shifting, and has been used by linguists in this context. See, for example, Paul Simpson, *Stylistics* (London: Routledge, 2004), pp. 106–8.
[56] Amis, *Lionel Asbo*, p. 17.

Amis's dialogue creates a clear disjunction between the narration (the matrix language, whose voice interjects) and the character Lionel (the embedded language), with the concluding 'strongly rumoured' providing a heavily ironic punchline. I have already discussed the role of bathos in Amis's humour, and here is an example of the reverse process, in which the humour emerges from the transition from a 'lower' register to a relatively 'higher' one,[57] a technique Partington terms 'upgrading'.[58] In the space of a few short lines, the passage shifts between multiple registers and styles, and as well as Des's and Lionel's spoken words, there is the interjection of a more distant, correcting narrator.[59] Lionel is not dismissed as a complete fool – however misguided, he does have some grasp of legal niceties – but his distance from the voice in which the speech is couched is associated, both inherently and explicitly, with language and with questions of class, particularly class as indexed by the comic possibilities of demotic speech. Rather than rendering Lionel's speech in an approximation of phonetic spelling, or what Leech and Short describe in their classic *Style in Fiction* (1981) as 'eye-dialect',[60] Amis's narrator becomes a judgemental grammarian, interjecting further to indicate how far Lionel diverges from Received Pronunciation.[61] The stylistic transition here is starker than the examples from *The House of Mirth* quoted by Herman, but the effect is strikingly similar, inviting judgement against Lionel not solely on the basis of his actions – actions that are, admittedly, cartoonishly appalling – but also according to his accent and relative infelicity with words. Masters astutely identifies this as a form of 'conflicted conservatism' manifested in 'a latent desire for overriding values and norms' that surface 'in Amis's often uneasy moments of authorial assertion'.[62] In many such moments

---

[57] Robert Duggan describes 'ironic reversal or inversion' as the 'trope that is probably most typical of Amis's fiction', and it is a trope that evident both at the level of the sentence and in the many Amis plots that involve a reversal of fortunes or, in the case of *Time's Arrow* (1991), a reversal of temporality. Duggan, *The Grotesque*, p. 110.

[58] Partington, *Linguistics of Laughter*, p. 76.

[59] There are parallels here with what James Wood describes as the 'comedy of correction' in which we laugh *at* rather than *with*. Wood opposes this to a more self-directed 'comedy of forgiveness', which he views as a more modern form. James Wood, 'Introduction: Comedy and the Irresponsible Self', in *The Irresponsible Self: On Laughter and the Novel* (London: Jonathan Cape, 2004), pp. 1–16.

[60] As Geoffrey Leech and Michael Short remind us, such writing is an example of 'EYE-DIALECT, where the impression of rendering non-standard speech by non-standard spelling is pure illusion'. Moreover, 'non-standard speech is typically associated with objects of comedy and satire: characters whom we see from the outside only'. Geoffrey Leech and Mick Short, *Style in Fiction*, 2nd edn (Harlow: Pearson, [1981] 2007), pp. 136–7.

[61] Two pages earlier, the narrator notes that Lionel 'pronounced "myth" *miff*. Full possessive pronouns – *you, their, my* – still made guest appearances in his English, and he didn't invariably defy grammatical number (*they was*, and so on). But his verbal prose and his accent were in steep decline.' Amis, *Lionel Asbo*, p. 15. Passages such as these establish a clear linkage between linguistic decline and other forms of decline, including societal and moral decline.

[62] Masters, *Novel Style*, p. 122.

of authorial assertion, Amis's fiction evinces a strong connection between style, judgement and class, and also between these elements and the specifically comic dimension of his writing, especially in the way in which style shifting via bathos or upgrading makes such variations laughable from a position of authority.

In the following example from *The Information*, a shift in styles denotes a comic mismatch between matrix and embedded language as well as between intention and articulation: as in *Lionel Asbo*, the 'lower' register carries with it clear associations with status and criminality. 13 is a character, a young black man whose real name is Bently:

> 13 drew in breath: he was about to give voice – and in the high style. His intention, plainly, was to speak not just for himself but for all men and all women, in all places and all times – to remind the human heart of what it had once known and now forgotten.
>
> 'The titheads', 13 began, 'is like a gang. The Old Bill', he went on, 'is like a gang. Hired by the government. When did it happen? It happened when they upped they pay. 1980 or whatever. They saying: it's gonna get rough. Unemployment is it. Riots or whatever. You keep a lid on it and we pay the extra. Where's the money come from? No worries. We'll *fine* the fuckers.'
>
> 'Who've you been talking to?'
>
> 'No one. Common sense.'[63]

This is a joke about high-minded concerns versus the inability to articulate them, but it is also a joke that, as with Lionel Asbo's 'grave disquisition' on the distinction between actual and grievous bodily harm, is set up using the ironic invocation of a 'high style'. In fact, it is set up with a heightened *demonstration* of Amis's high style in the overblown prose of the passage about reminding 'the human heart of what it had known and now forgotten' followed by 13's opening salvo about the 'titheads',[64] a further example of Amisian bathos. 13's speech is also framed with attributive phrases more usually found in journalism or academic prose ('13 began' and 'he went on'), punctuating his ungrammatical and fragmentary sentences to create further stylistic shifts. Moreover, the formulation 'he went on' is ironized by the fact that the words that follow are a precise repetition of the preceding sentence and not a continuation. It is

---

[63] Amis, *The Information*, p. 96.

[64] Never one to waste a snazzy phrase, this reference to 13's lofty ambitions is recycled from a 1982 essay on Saul Bellow, in which Amis argues that the 'High Style' has 'responsibilities' and 'attempts to speak for the whole of mankind, with suasion, to remind us of what we once knew and have since forgotten or stopped trying to regrasp'. In this less ironic form, it represents a further restatement of Amis's claims for the ethics of style. Martin Amis, *The Moronic Inferno and Other Visits to America* (Harmondsworth: Penguin, [1986] 1987), p. 5.

true that Amis's novel mocks people from all strata of society (later there is an extended riff on the difficulties of representing the linguistic tics of a character named Lady Demeter, who is related to the Queen),[65] but most often in these late novels, Amis's writing contains within it a high-low hierarchy that is emphasized through, and embedded within, stylistic shifts in his prose. Philip Tew views the inclusion of 'marginal' voices in *The Information* in positive terms, arguing that it and comparable novels by Will Self and others 'confront the epiphanic notions of transcendence and wish fulfilment conventionally associated with the literary' by 'drawing in underclass, ethnic, radically gendered, socially subversive and working-class subjects who articulate profoundly non-conventional senses of community and self via dialect, humour and profanity'.[66] I argue that, in contrast, the 'dialect, humour and profanity' of these characters are most often evident in negative opposition to the more elevated language and position of the predominating narrative voice. As Lawrence Driscoll puts it in reference to Amis's earlier fiction, while 'the working classes are satirized for their addiction to pornography, or drink or money or violence, these criticisms do not extend to the authorial voices in the novels'.[67] To this I would add that it is language itself that provides the most consistent index of the gulf between the stable position of the authorial voice and the laughable position of working-class characters in Amis's storyworlds; language is of course the vehicle of the humour, but it is also its target.

Returning to *Lionel Asbo*, Amis's jokes are not only at the expense of the title character and the philistinism represented by his particular attitudes and argot. In the opening pages of the novel, his nephew, Des, is implicitly mocked for the inconsistent spelling, punctuation and grammar in his letter to the tabloid agony aunt of the fictional paper the *Morning Lark*.[68] The letter is cathartic, a

---

[65] Ibid., pp. 256–7.
[66] Philip Tew, *The Contemporary British Novel*, 2nd edn (London: Continuum, 2007), p. 172.
[67] Lawrence Driscoll, *Evading Class in Contemporary British Literature* (New York: Palgrave Macmillan, 2009), p. 107. In *Evading Class*, Driscoll challenges what he views as a series 'evasions and erasures of class' in criticism on the contemporary British novel, particularly in criticism of a postmodern bent. In the section on Amis, he offers a reading of the 1996 short story 'State of England', which as its title suggests shares common themes with *Lionel Asbo*, as well as the other novels discussed here. Driscoll concludes that 'throughout Amis's fiction the working class (fat and stupid as always) are always running, desperate to keep up, while the narrative voice and the reader can stand idly at a safe distance laughing at this comical display of working-class powerlessness from a class that always seems to be on its last legs'. Ibid., p. 110. For a more sympathetic reading of the class politics in the story see Diedrick, *Understanding Martin Amis*, pp. 172–4.
[68] The *Morning Lark* is a fictional newspaper first introduced in *London Fields*, where it is Keith Talent's rag of choice. In *Yellow Dog*, Clint Smoker is its star reporter. A newspaper in name only, the *Lark* is surely modelled on the *The Daily Sport*, a now-defunct British tabloid specializing in softcore pornography, celebrity news and 'yellow journalism' (eye-catching, sensationalist stories with little or basis in fact).

way to express his angst about the affair he is having with his grandmother, and is not intended to be sent. Between excerpts such as '*The sex is fantastic and I think I'm in love. But ther'es one very serious complication and i'ts this; shes' my Gran!*', Amis's narrator provides context for Des's situation and describes his autodidactic pursuit of an education beyond that provided by his school Squeers Free, 'the worst school in England': 'The immediate goal, for Des, was to master the apostrophe. After that, the arcana of the colon and the semicolon, the hyphen, the dash, the slash.'[69] In these early sections, there is a marked transition between Des's spoken and written voices and that of the narrator; albeit less markedly than with Lionel, there is also a negative evaluation of Des's speech, to borrow Herman's terminology. Later sections of the novel are punctuated with excerpts from Des's imagined letters to Daphne, the agony aunt from the *Sun* newspaper, and a more thoughtful correspondent that the titillating Jennaveieve of the *Lark*. As with Kath's discovery of the 'proper papers' in *London Fields*, Des's transition to the *Sun* is one of the staging posts in his education, representing intellectual progression from the *Lark* for its inclusion of national and international news alongside gossip, scandal and female nudity. Des's letters to the paper demonstrate that he has indeed mastered the apostrophe, and his spoken and written language comes increasingly to coincide with that of the narrator. He eventually finds stability through marriage and through the birth of his daughter, Cilla, and he also finds employment as a crime reporter, first for the local *Diston Gazette* and then for the *Daily Mirror*, rival paper to the *Sun*. This progression leads to accusations from Lionel that he is a class traitor, and Des's movement from faltering, linguistically inept correspondent to professional writer takes place in tandem with his merging and eventual coincidence with the narrating voice. In the final third of the novel there are passages of free indirect style, as when Des goes to visit Lionel at his country estate in Essex:

> *The idiocy of rural life*. Who said that? Lenin? And is it idiocy, he asked himself (in his new editorial voice), or is it just innocence? What he sensed, in any case, was a bewildering deficit of urgency, of haste and purpose. And, somehow, a deficit of intelligence. For it was his obstinate belief that Town contained hidden force of mind – nearly all of it trapped or cross-purposed. And how will it go, he often wondered, when all of the brain-dead awaken? When all the Lionels decide to be intelligent? ... Meanwhile, here was Short Crendon and its pottering and pootering. I suppose I'm just a creature of the world city, he thought, and moved on.[70]

---

[69] Amis, *Lionel Asbo*, pp. 3–5.
[70] Ibid., p. 166.

An external perspective still intrudes here, as in the observation that Des is thinking 'in his new editorial voice', but the gap between the two has closed, and the narrator no longer stands at a distance from the character. The 'idiocy of rural life' and the following questions are clearly taken from Des's lexicon, and while he misattributes the line to Lenin rather than Marx, there is no sense of correction or judgement here. Similarly, his reflections on rural and urban life are much like those offered both tacitly and explicitly by the narrator throughout the novel. It is Lionel – one of the 'brain-dead' – who remains the butt of the joke and Des who is brought into linguistic and moral equivalence with the norms and judgements of the presiding narrative voice.

The ending of *Lionel Asbo* does suggest some form of hope or redemption – Des's daughter Cilla sings in imitation of 'the birds you could still sometimes hear, up on the thirty-third floor, so high above Diston Town'[71] – but throughout there is an evident discomfort and distaste for working-class speech and culture, as indexed thought style shifting and the relative positioning of the language and opinions of working-class characters: the debasement of English culture, a running theme, is seen to go hand in hand with the debasement of language. Amis deals in caricatures of course, but Joseph Brooker puts it well when he suggests that his tendency to 'return repeatedly to characters plainly different from himself – unlettered bruisers, abused floozies' – does not allow him to escape from himself and towards a recognition of alterity. Indeed, 'such monstrous and garish figures are a diversion from the difficulty of imaging life-sized, life-like people'.[72] The Other in Amis, and particularly the working-class Other, is repeatedly invoked as a comic foil, but not fully imagined or inhabited, and although this is not to suggest that the character Lionel Asbo should be seen as wholly emblematic of working-class people or culture – he is after all a violent criminal – it is to suggest that Amis's novel finds humour in the juxtaposition of Amis's famously 'high' style and forms of demotic speech. This juxtaposition has significant ethical implications because of the forms of hierarchy and judgement it introduces. As Herman suggests, 'styles invite reflection on how discourse is an instrument that can either work against or reinforce patterns of conflict',[73] and in *Lionel Asbo* and other examples of Amis's late fiction, this conflict between the narrating voice and the speech of the working-class characters is particularly marked. When applied to Amis's fiction, there is a clear indication not only

---

[71] Ibid., p. 276. This ending contains parallels with *Yellow Dog*, which concludes with an uncharacteristically gentle, even sentimental, evocation of the redemptive qualities of family life.
[72] Joseph Brooker, 'The Middle Years of Martin Amis', in *British Fiction Today*, ed. Phillip Tew and Rod Mengham (London: Continuum, 2006), pp. 3–14 (p. 11).
[73] Herman, *Story Logic*, p. 207.

of which style of language is grammatically correct but also of which style of language is *morally* correct. The suggestion is that the only way to remedy the moral failing of inarticulate and inelegant speech is through standardization via the conventional route of a university education, and that to express oneself otherwise is to be, well, laughable.

Here, then, is Amis's ethics of style in action. As Amis has suggested, 'style is not neutral; it gives moral directions';[74] it engenders alliances and sympathies, particularly in the transitions between styles. As comic theory recognizes, these transitional moments are also a fundamental source of humour, and Amis is a master of both bathos and its opposite 'upgrading': an attentiveness to style is fundamental to an understanding Amis's comedy. But the comic voice in Amis's recent fiction is predicated on class divisions as indexed by language. These comic techniques are not inherently reliant on a high-low class hierarchy,[75] but as Driscoll argues of Amis's earlier fiction, the target of humour tends be his working-class characters: 'it is them we are laughing at, while siding with the very stable positions that the novel provides',[76] a tendency that has only become more pronounced in recent work. And while I agree with Dominic Head's wariness about the critique of class bias in British fiction and the potential 'overestimation of what the novel can achieve',[77] it is significant that Amis's comedy embeds an equivalence, grounded in class difference, between bad language and bad morality, and that he enacts his ethics of style in prose that is in thrall to a caricatured version of working-class life, and particularly working-class masculinity. In Amis's words, 'style judges', and embedded in his humour is a consistent judgement against the values embodied by working-class diction, values that his narrators seem unable to view as anything other than worthy of ridicule.

---

[74] Haffenden, *Novelists in Interview*, p. 23.

[75] The novels of Irvine Welsh or James Kelman, for example, frequently subvert expectations in the opposite direction, shifting styles to demonstrate erudition or insights that challenge stereotypes. Paul Simpson notes this aspect of Welsh's style in a discussion of the courtroom scene in *Trainspotting* (1993), in which the narrator, Renton, is prompted to hold forth on the philosophy of Kierkegaard by a patronizing question from a magistrate who does not believe the books he stole from Waterstone's are for reading rather than to sell in order to buy heroin. Simpson, *Stylistics*, pp. 105–8.

[76] Driscoll, *Evading Class*, p. 102.

[77] Dominic Head, 'The Demise of Class Fiction', in *A Concise Companion to Contemporary British Fiction*, ed. James F. English (Oxford: Blackwell, 2006), pp. 229–47 (pp. 242–6).

3

'Talking about things we didn't want to talk about'

Zadie Smith and laughter

When Zadie Smith's first novel *White Teeth* was published in 2000, it was celebrated both domestically and internationally for its vibrancy and comic spirit.[1] Frank Kermode described the novel as 'comic, high-spirited, obscene in a long tradition, the multitudinous world as seen by a clear, happy eye', and for Kermode, the follow-up *The Autograph Man* (2002) was 'a new exhibition, somewhat different in tone, of the author's exceptional comic skills'.[2] The humour in Smith's third novel, *On Beauty* (2005), is more muted, but as its much-discussed dialogue with E.M. Forster suggests, the comic mode remained integral to her writing. In 2003, when she was working on *On Beauty*, Smith suggested that 'Forster ushered in a new era for the English comic novel'. Her conclusion that 'he allowed the English comic novel the possibility of a spiritual and bodily life, not simply to exist as an exquisitely worked game of social ethics but as a messy human concoction'[3] could be read as a mission statement for her own work-in-progress, with its complex intermingling of ethical and aesthetic ideals and messy or, to use the Forsterian term, 'muddled' actualities. And while the novel that followed *On Beauty*, *NW* (2012), has seldom been discussed in these terms, the comic lineage of Smith's fiction is apparent in many episodes even if the presiding tone is more sombre. Smith's most recent novel, *Swing Time* (2016), continues this complex engagement with the comic and with

---

[1] For a summary of the *White Teeth*'s critical reception, see Philip Tew, *Zadie Smith* (Basingstoke: Palgrave Macmillan, 2010), particularly pp. 118–35, and for a discussion of its international marketing and reception, see Katarzyna Jabukiak, 'Simulated Optimism: The International Marketing of *White Teeth*', in *Zadie Smith: Critical Essays*, ed. Tracey L. Walters (New York: Peter Lang, 2008), pp. 201–18.
[2] Frank Kermode, 'Here She Is', *London Review of Books*, 6 October 2005. Available online: https://www.lrb.co.uk/v27/n19/frank-kermode/here-she-is (accessed 9 July 2019).
[3] Zadie Smith, 'Love, Actually', *Guardian*, 1 November 2003. Available online: https://www.theguardian.com/books/2003/nov/01/classics.zadiesmith (accessed 9 July 2019).

laughter both *at* and *with* her characters. Although, as Smith acknowledges, her fiction has become discernibly less sunny and optimistic since *White Teeth*,[4] this signifies not a turning away from the comic but rather an engagement with different forms of comedy. Peter Childs and James Green put it well when they describe Smith as 'a comic novelist of serious moral intent',[5] and this modulation between humour and seriousness informs much of her writing. When reflecting on *NW* for a 2013 *Guardian* essay, Smith identified the influence, unconscious during the novel's composition, of Shakespeare's *Measure for Measure*, one of the so-called problem plays that mix comic and tragic modes. Problem plays, Smith suggests, 'seem closest to the mixed reality of our lives',[6] and it is perhaps this sense of mixed reality that has shaped her move from the kinetic humour of her early work to the tragicomedy of the more recent novels.[7]

Rather than examining comedy as a mode *en bloc*, this chapter traces these distinctive phases of Smith's career via a discussion of laughter. As I outline in more detail later, comedy and laughter are not synonymous, but they do have a strong affinity, and as the most common affective response to comedy, laughter is implicit in many of this book's discussions. Smith's novels are often comic, and they also demonstrate a distinctive engagement with the representation of laughter in its multiple forms, both comic and non-comic. This relationship is important to one of the most influential early critical formulations about Smith's fiction: James Wood's category of 'hysterical realism'. In a 2000 essay, Wood draws parallels between *White Teeth*-era Smith and peers such as David Foster Wallace and Jonathan Franzen, as well as an older generation of writers including Thomas Pynchon and Salman Rushdie. In addition to its primary meaning, associated with hysteria and emotional excess, in modern usage, the adjective 'hysterical' can of course be used to describe laughter, or the fact of being hilariously funny and inducing uncontrollable laughter in others; Wood's essay, as well as others reproduced in *The Irresponsible Self* (2004), suggests that this form of ungoverned, hilarious laughter is not his idea of fun and that he

---

[4] See Zadie Smith, 'On Optimism and Despair', in *Feel Free: Essays* (London: Hamish Hamilton, 2018), pp. 35–41.

[5] Peter Childs and James Green, *Aesthetics and Ethics in Twenty-First Century British Novels* (London: Bloomsbury, 2013), p. 55.

[6] Zadie Smith, 'Notes on *NW*', in *Feel Free: Essays* (London: Hamish Hamilton, 2018), pp. 248–50 (p. 249).

[7] Eva Ulrike Pirker describes this transition in spatial terms, noting that more recent work such as *NW* and the novella *The Embassy of Cambodia* (2013) 'mark Smith as an author who has moved away from humorous and ironic approaches to spaces determined by race-, gender- and class-related projections, and who explores the limitations that these pose for individuals'. See Eva Ulrike Pirker, 'Approaching Space: Zadie Smith's North London Fiction', *Journal of Postcolonial Writing*, 52:1 (2016), 64–76 (p. 72).

is scathing of those 'hysterical' writers whose work he deems superficial and playful for play's sake.[8] This argument, and the debate that followed, is the point of departure for this chapter, which begins by focusing on Smith's first novel and the ways in which laughter figures both in the much-discussed celebratory tone of *White Teeth* and, in the obverse to this, laughter as ridicule or mockery. It then goes on to consider laughter's affective dimension and Smith's portrayal of laughter as a borderline emotion, never far from its apparent antonym, tears. Finally, drawing on material from Freud and Bataille, it examines laughter as consolation, discussing Smith's representation of its bittersweet role in community building and reconciliation. Laughter is by its nature evanescent and highly personal, and my approach throughout is in line with that of Manfred Pfister's edited volume *A History of English Laughter* (2002), which engages with the 'traces of "textualised" laughter … both the laughter represented in the texts and the laughter they intend to raise'.[9] Smith is a writer with an abiding allegiance to comedy, whose work demonstrates a particular engagement with the representation of laughter in all its forms. As such, her fiction offers an evolving exploration of this textualized laughter, its relationship with humour and its multiple roles in social life.

What's so hysterical about hysterical realism?

Central to James Wood's writing in *The Irresponsible Self* is his identification of two distinct forms of comedy. There is an older form, associated with the Aristotelian idea of mocking laughter, which is accounted for in comic theory under the umbrella term 'superiority theory'.[10] And in contrast to this exists a more modern form, 'characterised by the mingling of emotions that Gogol famously called "laughter through tears"'. Both persist in modern fiction, but

---

[8] James Wood, 'Hysterical Realism', in *The Irresponsible Self: On Laughter and the Novel* (London: Jonathan Cape, 2004), pp. 167–83. For a nuanced critique of Wood's essay and its underlying assumptions, see Christopher Holmes, 'The Novel's Third Way: Zadie Smith's "Hysterical Realism"', in *Reading Zadie Smith: The First Decade and Beyond*, ed. Philip Tew (London: Bloomsbury, 2013), pp. 141–53.

[9] Manfred Pfister, 'Introduction: A History of English Laughter?' in *A History of English Laughter: Laughter from Beowulf to Beckett and Beyond*, ed. Manfred Pfister (Amsterdam: Rodopi, 2002), pp. v–x (p. vii). Alfie Bown also notes the importance of considering the 'laughter within a text (for instance, the laughter of characters)' from that of the reader or viewer. Bown, *In the Event of Laughter*, p. 36.

[10] Superiority theory is the most ancient theory of laughter and comedy, and it is traceable to Plato and Aristotle. Its basic premise is that humans laugh at that to which they feel superior in moral, intellectual or physical terms.

Wood's strong preference is for the latter, more melancholic type, 'a kind of tragic-comic stoicism which might best be called the comedy of forgiveness. This comedy can be distinguished – if a little roughly – from the comedy of correction. The latter is a way of laughing at; the former a way of laughing with.'[11] Comedies of correction are associated with laughing *at*, with mockery, caricature and scorn, whereas comedies of forgiveness, also termed comedies of irresponsibility, are associated with empathy, depth of characterization and laughing *with*. There is an implicit – and occasionally explicit – hierarchy at play here, in favour of the modernity and empathy associated with writers such as Chekhov, Henry Green, Svevo, Hamsun and, perhaps more surprisingly, V.S. Naipaul,[12] and against writers such as Evelyn Waugh, Muriel Spark and both Martin and Kingsley Amis. This preference is also at the heart of Wood's criticism of 'hysterical realism', a mode he associates not with the modernity of Freud's depth model of humour and the gentle self-mockery described in the essay 'Humour',[13] but with the 'vital simplicities' of Dickens.[14] Wood's criticism of Smith is tempered by his admiration for aspects of her writing,[15] but he finds her a 'frustrating writer' who is 'willing to let passages of [*White Teeth*] descend into cartoonishness and a kind of itchy, restless extremism', allowing her writing to move 'closer to the low "comic" style of a farceur like Tom Sharpe than it ought to be'.[16] It is this perceived unevenness that frustrates Wood, particularly as it relates to Smith's characterization and the novel's movement in and out of its characters' consciousnesses.[17] At times *White Teeth* employs a form of

---

[11] Wood, *Irresponsible Self*, pp. 3–4, 13.

[12] Wood refers to the early V.S. Naipaul of *A House for Mr Biswas* (1961), which for him demonstrates that 'comedy is not distance but proximity'. Wood, *Irresponsible Self*, p. 263. The same could be argued of Naipaul's first book *Miguel Street* (1959), which portrays the population of Port of Spain in Trinidad with a sympathetic humour at odds with his later spiky and combative reputation. I am grateful to Bill Schwarz for bringing *Miguel Street* to my attention.

[13] Freud's late essay 'Humour' posits self-effacing humour as a gentler form of the usually harsh, disciplinarian super-ego. 'It means', he concludes, '"Look! here is the world, which seems so dangerous! It is nothing but a game for children – just worth making a jest about!"' See Sigmund Freud, 'Humour' [1928], trans. Joan Rivier, in *The Standard Edition of the Complete Psychological Works of Sigmund Freud, Vol. 21: The Future of an Illusion, Civilization and its Discontents, and Other Works*, ed. James Strachey (London: Vintage, [1964] 2001), pp. 159–66 (p. 166).

[14] Wood, *Irresponsible Self*, p. 174.

[15] Wood's attitude to Smith appears to have softened with time, and although he has published full reviews of her more recent novels, in 2012, he cited *NW* as one of his books of the year, describing it as bursting 'with the imagined, lived, tragic-comic, polyphonic reality of London' and as 'the best novel she has yet written'. See James Wood, 'Books of the Year', *New Yorker*, 17 December 2012. Available online: https://www.newyorker.com/books/page-turner/books-of-the-year (accessed 9 July 2019).

[16] Wood, *Irresponsible Self*, pp. 179–80.

[17] Michael Dango describes this rapid jump-cutting between characters as an example of camp fiction, a form that aspires 'to a demographic ambition of bearing witness to all of the groups a global society could be said to include, and they find that one mode available for this ambition is camp collage, which knows how to traverse boundaries and contexts quickly, justifying itself along the way by the

indirect style and we are in her characters' heads, laughing in sympathy at their tragicomic limitations (good), and at other times we are outside, laughing at their failures from an exterior narratorial perspective that Wood aligns with Smith's own authorial position (bad). It is, Wood concludes, 'as if the novel were deciding at these moments whether to cast depths on its shallows, and deciding against'.[18]

The occasionally intrusive, information-packed narration in *White Teeth* is associated by Wood with the influence of post-war American fiction, though as Eva Knopp has argued, it could equally be associated with 'a particularly English comic tradition', the narrator's 'garrulous and digressive comments [being] highly reminiscent of the narrator of Lawrence Sterne's *Tristram Shandy*',[19] whose influence is strongly present in another of the 'hysterical realists', Salman Rushdie. Christopher Holmes traces Smith's response to Wood's criticism via her 2008 essay 'Two Paths for the Novel' and the earlier essay 'This is How it Feels to Me' (2001), a rawer piece that offers a more direct reply.[20] Holmes persuasively identifies two distinctive philosophies of the novel, borne out in Smith's and Wood's critical writing and, he argues, put into practice in Smith's fiction. Whereas Wood is nostalgic 'for the sympathetic character and the simply drawn scene', Smith views the novel 'as a series of unfinishable structures, formal work that has yet to be completed'. And while novels such as Tom McCarthy's *Remainder* (2005) – representative of one of the paths in 'Two Paths for the Novel', the other being Joseph O'Neill's *Netherland* (2008) – do not demonstrate the formal neatness or lyricism of the fiction favoured by Wood, the self-awareness, even auto-deconstruction of such fiction, 'frees the reader from the expectation that form has an analogue in "natural" ideas'.[21] The perceived unevenness of *White Teeth*'s characterization, then, is of a piece with Smith's later theorization of the novel form and with her critical responses to Wood's restrictive view of what a novel should be. Wood's division of comic texts into comedies of correction and comedies of forgiveness, and his denigration of certain forms of humour, denoted by the adjectives 'low' or 'shallow', limits the multiplicity of forms that laughter can take and offers a simplified version of Smith's fiction by

---

ferocity of its movement'. On this view, the superficiality that Wood diagnoses is a strategy employed to emphasize the interaction and distribution of bodies in a globalized world. See Michael Dango, 'Camp's Distribution: "Our" Aesthetic Category', *Social Text 131*, 35:2 (2017), 39–67 (p. 48).

[18] Wood, *Irresponsible Self*, p. 182.
[19] Eva Knopp, '"There Are No Jokes in Paradise": Humour as a Politics of Representation in Recent Texts and Films from the British Migratory Contact-Zone', in *Translation of Cultures*, ed. Petra Rüdiger and Konrad Gross (Amsterdam: Rodopi, 2009), pp. 59–74 (pp. 66–7).
[20] Holmes, 'The Novel's Third Way'.
[21] Ibid., pp. 152, 147, 146.

taking one form of laughter as synecdochic of her comic voice. Smith is, in fact, concerned with the very multiplicity of laughter, from her earliest novels to the tonally quite different later fiction. In 'This is How it Feels to Me', she responds directly to Wood's criticism of *White Teeth* and describes her aspirations at that moment in October 2001, a time overshadowed by the then very recent attacks of 11 September and the subsequent US-led invasion of Afghanistan. For her:

> It's all laughter in the dark – the title of a Nabokov novel and still the best term for the kind of writing I aspire to: not a division of head and heart, but the useful employment of both. And I could mention dozens of novels (I haven't been writing, but boy, I've been reading) that create a light in my head in between the news bulletins. Tolstoy's *The Death of Ivan Ilyich* – a miniaturist tale of a bourgeois man dying a bourgeois death – every time I read it, I find my world put under an intense, unforgiving microscope. But how does it work? I want to dismantle it as if it were a clock, as if it had parts, mechanisms. I wonder if Wood will take that question, then, as a replacement for my earlier one. Not: how does this world work? But: how is this book made? How can I do this?[22]

As Holmes suggests, Smith expresses her commitment to understanding the construction of fiction, its devices and mechanisms, and in addition articulates her aspiration towards 'laughter in the dark', a form of laughter that combines head and heart, intellect and emotion. In fact, laughter provides a framework to explore the possibilities of fiction and its ability to engage with multiple, seemingly contradictory viewpoints; it is less a question of choosing between depth and shallowness, forgiveness and correction, and more a question of representing laughter's many permutations and possibilities.

In the most sustained critical treatment of Smith's fiction so far, Philip Tew notes that *White Teeth* 'adapts several traditional forms', including 'the comic picaresque inter-fused with a family saga'. Later in the same study, he describes the novel as 'a post-Nietzschean "comédie humaine."'[23] This generic hybridity is one manifestation of the novel's much-discussed portrayal of multicultural London at the turn of the millennium, and is one source of what Wood sees as its unevenness in humour and characterization.[24] A passage, singled out as an

---

[22] Zadie Smith, 'This Is How It Feels to Me', *Guardian*, 13 October 2001. Available online: https://www.theguardian.com/books/2001/oct/13/fiction.afghanistan (accessed 9 July 2019).
[23] Tew, *Zadie Smith*, pp. 13, 51.
[24] As Bryan Cheyette notes, Wood's aesthetic critique is linked to Smith's subject matter: 'The excess of belonging of her *luftmenshen* – being simultaneously everywhere and nowhere – is critically related to the supposed unshaped verbosity of her written style, which is described as "excessively centripetal".' Bryan Cheyette, *Diasporas of the Mind: Jewish and Postcolonial Writing and the Nightmare of History* (New Haven, CT: Yale University Press, 2013), p. 263.

example of 'low' and linguistically 'thick-fingered' comedy, describes O'Connell's Pool House, the long-standing meeting place of old friends Samad and Archie. It is where they discuss 'everything from the meaning of Revelation to the prices of plumbers. And women. Hypothetical women', the discussion of whom Wood finds particularly unconvincing and inconsistent with what we have learnt about Samad to this point.[25] Inconsistency is the crux of Wood's dissatisfaction with *White Teeth* and with the other novels he identifies as examples of hysterical realism; as Lee Konstantinou summarizes, for Wood 'global implausibility disrupts the local pleasure one might take in a work of fiction that more judiciously doled out its unlikelihoods'. In short: 'hysterical realism's hysteria short-circuits its realism'.[26] Konstantinou continues by offering a persuasive critique of Wood's reading of both metafiction and of Smith and David Foster Wallace's relationship with postmodernism, but here I offer an alternative angle on this multiplicity of registers, which is that viewed from a different perspective, what Wood identifies as a flaw preventing the characters from seeming truly human can be seen as 'more real' than the depth model he values. This is not to suggest that Smith seeks a humanistic impression of fully rounded, knowable characters, but it is to suggest that in their multiplicity and discontinuity, her characters might offer an alternative view of reality and subjectivity. In contrast to the interior perspective elsewhere in the novel, in the O'Connell's passage, readers are positioned to laugh *at* the performative blokeishness of Samad and Archie's discussions, as well as the caricatured grimness and incongruity of their surroundings. Rather than a failing of authorial control, this is reflective of the nature of laughter. As Michael Billig notes in *Laughter and Ridicule* (2005),

> laughter does not possess a single rhetorical force even within the context of humour. It can be the laughter of hostile ridicule or the laughter of friendly appreciation: one can laugh with others and at others. As such, laughter can join people together and it can divide; and it can do both simultaneously when a group laughs together at others.[27]

Laughter has a force that needs to be understood pragmatically; its meaning is not consistent in either illocutionary or perlocutionary terms, and varies enormously according to company and context. Samad and Archie are, at this moment in the novel, about to make the disastrous decision to separate Samad's sons Millat

---

[25] Zadie Smith, *White Teeth* (London: Penguin, [2000] 2001), p. 183; Wood, *Irresponsible Self*, p. 180.
[26] Lee Konstantinou, *Cool Characters: Irony and American Fiction* (Cambridge, MA: Harvard University Press, 2016), p. 172.
[27] Billig, *Laughter and Ridicule*, p. 194.

and Magid, and that they arrive at this decision so flippantly, in the inauspicious surroundings of O'Connell's and following the advice of the oleaginous owner of the bar, Abdul-Mickey, is worthy of caricature in the context of a comic set piece. This does not obviate the tragicomedy of Samad's hubristic decision to send Magid to Bangladesh for a traditional religious education – only for him to return as an atheist in thrall to science – nor does it detract from the laughter in the dark at Samad's feeling that 'his sons had failed him' – the recognition of his self-deception combined with sympathy for his thwarted ambition[28] – but these contrasting forms of laughter represent the radically different forms of laughter that are possible at and with the same character. Agnes Heller rightly observes that 'laughter is a judgement' that can express both positive and negative values,[29] and that these forms of judgement, from hysterical mockery to resigned sympathy, coexist in *White Teeth* can be read not as an example of tonal unevenness, but as representative of laughter's many social manifestations.

However, while I maintain that rather than representing a failure of characterization, *White Teeth*'s portrayal of multiple registers of laughter is emblematic of Smith's engagement with the situational nature of laughter, some of the critical claims for the political significance of this laughter are harder to justify. The question of comedy's political efficacy is covered in greater detail in Chapter 1, but in the context of this discussion, it is notable that a number of critics have made strong claims for the powerful role of humour and laughter in *White Teeth*. For Helga Ramsey-Kurz, for example, *White Teeth*, along with Rushdie's *The Satanic Verses* and Hanif Kureishi's 'My Son the Fanatic', 'posit[s] humour both as a viable political stance and as a powerful, if not even as the only antidote to dogma',[30] while for Anna Wille, Smith employs mimicry as a strategy and 'a way of subverting colonialism by making it strange'.[31] And Phyllis Lassner invokes Mikhail Bakhtin's concepts of carnival and heteroglossia to argue that in *White Teeth*, 'Smith's carnival projects voices that in their intergenerational quarrels don't seem to hear each other, but the cacophony they produce effects a cultural transformation', concluding that 'what emerges is a cultural riot against

---

[28] Smith, *White Teeth*, p. 425.
[29] Agnes Heller, *Immortal Comedy: The Comic Phenomenon in Art, Literature, and Life* (Lanham, MD: Lexington Books, 2005), pp. 25–6.
[30] Helga Ramsey-Kurz, 'Humouring the Terrorists or the Terrorised? Militant Muslims in Salman Rushdie, Zadie Smith, and Hanif Kureishi', in *Cheeky Fictions: Laughter and the Postcolonial*, ed. Susanne Reichl and Mark Stein (Amsterdam: Rodopi, 2005), pp. 73–86 (p. 85).
[31] Anna Wille, '"Born and Bred, Almost": Mimicry as a Humorous Strategy in Zadie Smith's *White Teeth* and Hanif Kureishi's *The Buddha of Suburbia*', *Anglia*, 129:3–4 (2011), 448–68 (p. 458).

the English value of knowing one's place'.³² Ramsey-Kurz's position in particular demonstrates an occasional tendency in writing about comedy to make overly strong claims about what humour can achieve in social and political contexts. This is an inevitably retrospective, even revisionist view, coming after the terrorist attacks of 11 September 2001 and particularly the London bombings of 7 July 2005, but in contrast to these claims for the satirical force of Smith's comedy, her representation of the fictional Islamist group 'Keepers of the Eternal and Victorious Islamic Nation' (KEVIN) now seems like one of *White Teeth*'s missteps. KEVIN, as the comic acronym implies, is seen as a preposterous organization, whose leader, Brother Ibrāhīm ad-Din Shukhrallah, is a Wizard of Oz figure, inspiring loyalty and awe at a distance, but deeply unimpressive in person. Millat is KEVIN's 'big experiment', his militancy an act of rebellion inspired less by the Qu'ran and more by Martin Scorsese's 1990 gangster film *GoodFellas*,³³ and despite their violent intentions, his braggadocio and ineffectiveness are emblematic of the laughable nature of the group. Susie Thomas argues that in *White Teeth*, Islamic extremism 'is reduced to a *Carry on up the Khyber* farce', referring to the 7 July bombings when she concludes that 'now that KEVIN has come to King's Cross with his backpack, Smith's insight and understanding of contemporary issues seems hopelessly inadequate'.³⁴ While I am sceptical of Thomas's more scathing judgements on *White Teeth*,³⁵ her concerns about Smith's portrayal of KEVIN are a welcome corrective to the sweeping claims for the radical potential of laughter and mockery made elsewhere. It is not, as Ulrike Tancke summarizes in relation to a particular school of thought, 'that to portray an extremist group in anything but a serious light is insensitive or shows a lack of good taste',³⁶ but rather that to make such far-reaching claims for Smith's novel is first, to overstate the political potential of mockery, and second, to overestimate Smith's handling of this subject matter. It would be unfair to judge the novel in light of subsequent events, or to criticize Smith for not achieving the level of

---

[32] Phyllis Lassner, *Colonial Strangers: Women Writing the End of the British Empire* (New Brunswick, NJ: Rutgers University Press, 2004), p. 197.
[33] Smith, *White Teeth*, pp. 444–7.
[34] Susie Thomas, 'Zadie Smith's False Teeth: The Marketing of Multiculturalism', *Literary London*, 4:1 (2006). Available online: http://www.literarylondon.org/london-journal/march2006/thomas.html (accessed 9 July 2019).
[35] Thomas argues that *White Teeth* is derivative and that Smith's indebtedness to other writers such as Hanif Kureishi and Salman Rushdie has been 'papered over' by the 'publicity machine' surrounding the novel. Ibid.
[36] Ulrike Tancke, '*White Teeth* Reconsidered: Narrative Deception and Uncomfortable Truths', in *Reading Zadie Smith: The First Decade and Beyond*, ed. Philip Tew (London: Bloomsbury, 2013), pp. 27–38 (p. 34).

insight of a later text such as Chris Morris's *Four Lions* (2010),[37] but the KEVIN plotline, with its uncharacteristically monotone portrait of pettiness and self-interest, does not contain the requisite satirical bite to be effective as critique: satire requires an underpinning seriousness that is absent in this strand of the novel.

In her first novel, then, Smith represents the multiple forms of laughter in ways that are closer to its full social manifestations and changeability than is acknowledged by Wood's influential formulation hysterical realism. Laughter can be wry and self-deprecating, as Wood prefers, but it is not only that, and the variable tone of *White Teeth*, both in terms of the laughter it intends and the laughter it inspires, need not be viewed as a fatal inconsistency. However, it is wise to remain circumspect when making claims for laughter and mockery's radical or transformative potential, and *White Teeth*'s portrayal of the fictional terrorist organization KEVIN falls short of some of the stronger claims that have been made in its favour. It is not that laughter is necessarily ineffectual as critique, nor that terrorist groups should not be the subject of comedy, but rather that *White Teeth* dismisses KEVIN too lightly and does not allow the more empathetic response (laugher alongside and against, sometimes in the same moment) that characterizes Smith's writing elsewhere. In subsequent work, it is this very mixed-ness that characterizes her representation of laughter, including its affinity with seemingly antithetical affective responses such as tears.

Mixed emotions: Laughter and tears

In *Laughter: Notes on a Passion* (2010), Anca Párvulescu traces the movement from the seventeenth- and eighteenth-century term 'passions' to the modern term 'emotions', noting that laughter was included in discussions of the passions by thinkers such as Descartes, Hobbes and Spinoza, but that 'when the list of passions is sifted into a list of emotions, although most names of passions are retained, laughter is left behind'. 'Laughter does not become an emotion',

---

[37] *Four Lions* has not been entirely uncontroversial in its comic treatment of a hapless Islamist terrorist cell, but the detailed research that preceded production, an aspect of the film Morris was careful to emphasize during the media campaign, as well as the film's largely successful negotiation of the line between sympathy and demonization, means it has avoided many of the pitfalls that now make the KEVIN plotline of *White Teeth* seem such a misstep. For a consideration of Morris's comic depiction of terrorism, see Sharon Lockyer, '"Dad's Army Side to Terrorism": Chris Morris, *Four Lions* and Jihad Comedy', in *No Known Cure: The Comedy of Chris Morris*, ed. James Leggott and Jamie Sexton (London: BFI, 2013), pp. 197–211.

Parvulescu writes, 'and its surviving, civilized forms need to be explained as signs of other passions-turned-emotions, whether fear, cruelty, nervousness, or benevolence'.[38] Laughter is always displaced, a sign of something else, and as such we have an impoverished lexicon to describe it, a language that insists 'on imposing the same word ("laughter") on laughs that – ontologically, aesthetically, ethically – often find themselves at opposite ends of the laughing spectrum'. In the absence of a suitable lexicon, Parvulescu turns to description as a method for articulating the affective states encompassed by this single term: 'Description is an attempt to soften this [historical] injustice.'[39] The descriptive approach offers a way of exploring the subtleties of laughter that are too easily effaced by the single, blanket term available to English speakers, and which more often than not allies laughter with amusement. The novel provides a powerful demonstration of the efficacy of this descriptive approach, encompassing multiple variations in both the physical manifestations of laughter and its social and emotional motivations. Rita Felski speaks of literary texts as a form of knowledge, which 'do not just represent, but make newly present, significant shapes of social meaning';[40] and fiction's ability to describe laughter, to situate it in its social and psychological context, enables such knowledge about its complexity and multiplicity to emerge. Moreover, Smith's novels demonstrate a particular concern with the forms that laughter takes in both humorous and non-humorous contexts. As discussed earlier, *White Teeth* represents the varied social manifestations of laughter, inviting laughter both with and at her characters, and in subsequent novels, she continues this exploration of the meanings and functions of laughter, representing what Parvulescu describes as the ontological, aesthetic and ethical spectrum of laughter, including its association with mixed emotions and more stable states such as amusement or disdain.

The Autograph Man is less funny than *White Teeth*, but it is full of laughter. As Frank Kermode notes, in her second novel, Smith continues to be 'seriously comic about death, pain, faith'.[41] Its central character, Alex-Li Tandem begins and to some extent ends the novel emotionally isolated from those around him, obsessing over his niche interests of celebrity – particularly celebrity autographs, and particularly the autograph of the near-mythical movie star Kitty Alexander – and, following the comedian Lenny Bruce's extended riff on the topic,[42] the

---

[38] Parvulescu, *Laughter: Notes on a Passion*, p. 6.
[39] Ibid., p. 19.
[40] Rita Felski, *Uses of Literature* (Oxford: Blackwell, 2008), p. 104.
[41] Kermode, 'Here She Is'.
[42] An excerpt from Bruce's routine is included as an epigraph to the novel.

categorization of the world into Goyish things and Jewish things.[43] Alex is largely positioned at an ironic remove from the world, and his joking is one method of deflecting thought and attention from his emotional needs, primarily the unaddressed trauma surrounding his father's death. As Tew puts it, 'Alex follows a pleasure principle of sorts, which involves the radical avoidance of pain and suffering, including his failure to retrieve the memory of witnessing his father's death, an avoidance that means he cannot come to terms with this loss.'[44] This is reflected, Smith's novel suggests, in the numbing or distancing effect that Bergson viewed as vital to laughter's operation.[45] When Alex meets fellow philographer Honey Richardson,[46] the two light-heartedly discuss Honey's specialism in material relating to African-American actors. She tells Alex about the exoticization of Theda Bara, who was marketed as having been '"born in the shadow of the Sphinx"' and was '"supposed to be sex on legs"', but in reality was '"fat-faced with bad circulation. When her folks in Ohio heard she was born by the Nile, they were pretty damn surprised."' In response to Honey's droll, dead-pan humour, Alex laughs 'gleefully', and when she tells the story of Louise Beavers, who bulked up and faked a Southern accent to play the 'mammy' character in 'a dozen movies', he 'truly [begins] to enjoy himself'. Honey initially invites this laughter at the iniquities of Hollywood, but this changes when she turns her attention to Stephin Fetchit, who, in a reversal of actors such as Frances Gumm (Judy Garland), Archibald Leach (Cary Grant), or Phyllis Isley (Jennifer Jones), arrived in Hollywood with the majestic-sounding name Lincoln Theodore Monroe Perry, only to be rebranded with a prosaic, misspelled and implicitly servile stage name. With this, Honey, herself African-American, reflects that '"it's *tiring*, you know?"', a sigh of frustration that changes the mood: 'This thought seemed to take away her laughter. She stared despondently at her fingers.' Shared, ironic laughter builds between Honey and Alex, but then dwindles and dies when the distance between the individuals that Honey is discussing and her own situation breaks down. These actors' circumstances were fatiguing, but so is

---

[43] See Zadie Smith, *The Autograph Man* (London: Penguin, [2002] 2003), pp. 88–91.

[44] Philip Tew, 'Celebrity, Suburban Identity and Transatlantic Epiphanies: Reconsidering Zadie Smith's *The Autograph Man*', in *Reading Zadie Smith: The First Decade and Beyond*, ed. Philip Tew (London: Bloomsbury, 2013), pp. 53–68 (p. 57).

[45] For Bergson, 'laughter has no greater foe than emotion'. Bergson, 'Laughter: An Essay on the Meaning of the Comic', pp. 61–190 (p. 63). Agnes Heller agrees in her 2005 work *Immortal Comedy*, arguing that 'whatever the cause of mirth, neither sentiments, affects, or emotions are involved in its enjoyment'. Heller, *Immortal Comedy*, p. 10.

[46] Honey is both a collector and a celebrity of sorts, being loosely based on Estella Marie Thompson, better known as Divine Brown, a former sex worker who became famous in 1995 when she was arrested along with the actor Hugh Grant, having been found by the police giving him oral sex in his car in exchange for money.

hers, and her notoriety clearly has a racialized dimension, conforming to what Tracey L. Walters describes as the Jezebel stereotype.[47] Laughter is no longer possible once Honey recognizes the kinship between herself and those she is discussing, and once the required detachment is removed, she is left without appropriate words to express her feelings: "'Makes me want to throw up my hands and say MU! to the whole thing. MUUUU!'"[48] Alex is embarrassed at her display of emotion, which seems excessive and beyond his usual numbed range of expression. His recognition of Honey's pain prevents him from laughing it off.

Later in *The Autograph Man*, whose repeated structural and thematic references to Judaism and the Kabbalah are in many ways about the pursuit of interpersonal connection and the ability to live in the present,[49] Alex begins to lose some of his detachment from the life of the emotions, and again this is represented by a moment of laughter. He goes ice skating with Honey in New York and experiences an instance of pure joy:

> Alex felt something wet and brought his hand down from the air. On the crease of his lifeline, one of those unlikely snowflakes had landed, the size of a sweet. He watched it melt. Laughed. He laughed like a loon. Then the trees were kings in ermine, and every building was an achievement, and the sun was demanding the clouds move, and light made film stars of everyone, and Della's breasts became marvels, and the sky grew pink, and Sinatra was singing! Sinatra was making a list of the things he loved. A fireside. Potato chips. Good books.
>
> Conditions were favourable.[50]

This moment, albeit transitory like the snowflake, is exemplary of Alex's increasing openness and movement out of his private obsessions and into the world. And it is laughter, not gleeful, mocking or even comic laughter, but a laughter of abandon – 'like a loon' – that signifies Alex's mood and opens him up to the appreciation of his surroundings and his presence within them. It is *then*, after the laugh and the expressive release that it offers, that his surroundings change, or rather his appreciation of them changes, transforming trees into kings in ermine, and ordinary people into film stars. Kathleen Higgins describes

---

[47] Tracey L. Waters, 'Still Mammies and Hos: Stereotypical Images of Black Women in Zadie Smith's Novels', in *Zadie Smith: Critical Essays*, ed. Tracey L. Walters (New York: Peter Lang, 2008), pp. 123–39 (pp. 134–5).
[48] Smith, *Autograph Man*, p. 242.
[49] For a detailed discussion of the role of Judaism and its interrelation with questions of identity and performativity in *The Autograph Man*, see Sigrun Meinig, '"What's More Important Than a Gesture?": Jewishness and Cultural Performativity', in *Anglophone Jewish Literature*, ed. Axel Stähler (Abingdon: Routledge, 2007), pp. 65–75.
[50] Ibid., pp. 323–4.

laughter as a metaphorical 'gesture of sloughing off one skin and beginning to use another',[51] and here we see this in action, a temporary movement outside of Alex's old self and habits of mind. Laughter represents a feeling of heretofore uncharacteristic abandonment, representative of the abandonment that Helmuth Plessner associates with both laughter and crying: 'When a man [sic] laughs, he gives way to his own body and thus foregoes unity with it and control over it. With this capitulation as a unity of ensouled body and mind, he asserts himself as a person.'[52] Unselfconscious laughter, in contrast to the laughter of irony or mockery, demands a yielding of control over the body and is an expression of personhood, an apparent loss of agency that asserts, in Plessner's words, an individual's humanity. In the context of Smith's novel, Alex's spontaneous, public laughter represents a further stage in his coming to terms with loss and grief.

In the closing pages of *The Autograph Man*, Alex remembers another moment of laughter, this time involving his best friend Adam, and again it describes laughter as irrepressible and spontaneous. It takes place about a year after the death of Adam's father, Li-Jin, when Adam arrives at Alex's home, 'amused about something'. His smile is shocking as 'no one had dared smile in that house, not for a year, not since it happened', and yet Adam cannot repress his glee at the serendipitous sight of two people on the same train, one with a bike with a wheel missing and one with a wheel but no bike. There is no big punchline, but Adam's laughter is important and stays with Alex. Many years later, he recalls the effect it had on him and his mother Sarah:

> The radiance of the laugh came back to Alex now. The repeated dawn of the smile. He was thoughtful, Adam, and knew even then that one person's capacity for joy can pinch those people who can't manage it. Sarah and Alex, still shot-through, still heart-whacked by grief, could only look back at him blankly. Adam had tried hard to force that smile to lie flat, but it only rose again.[53]

Adam's laughter does not enact a miraculous transformation, but it does radiate, rising as at dawn, having an effect in its own way. Alex and Sarah are unable to join in, but it is not exclusionary and still pinches them, imparting a moment of sensation that is able to break through their 'heart-whacked' numbness. As with Alex's laughter at the ice rink, Adam's amusement forces him to yield control of

---

[51] Kathleen Marie Higgins, *Comic Relief: Nietzsche's Gay Science* (Oxford: Oxford University Press, 2000), p. 49.

[52] Plessner, *Laughing and Crying*, p. 142. Georges Bataille comes to a similar conclusion in his 1953 essay 'Un-knowing: Laughter and Tears', in which he also draws comparisons between laughter and tears, associating both with 'the sudden invasion of the unknown'. See Georges Bataille, 'Un-knowing: Laughter and Tears' [1953], trans. Anne Michelson, *October*, 36 (1985), 89–102 (p. 92).

[53] Smith, *Autograph Man*, pp. 373–4.

his body; once the laughter has passed, his smile rises up spontaneously, revealing his humanity, his thoughtfulness, even though Alex and Sarah are too dazed to respond. It is an example of laughter as what Lisa Trahair, discussing Bataille, describes as 'that powerless element over which consciousness has no power, that element that changes thought on the basis of its very passivity and inactuality';[54] it is uncontrollable and fleeting, but emotionally and philosophically significant. These and other representations of laughter in *The Autograph Man* are not grand or epiphanic, but Smith's descriptive attentiveness to the nuances and significance laughter address what Parvulescu calls the injustice of laughter's relegation to a secondary emotion, reducible to the denuded range of terms offered by the language. This relegation of laughter to secondary status is true of comic laughter, but applies to an even greater extent to its role outside of purely humorous contexts, or rather its ability to represent more than amusement or pleasure. Laughter is, according to Mary Douglas, 'a unique bodily eruption which is always taken to be a communication',[55] and this communicative aspect encompasses a considerable range of mixed and variable emotions, as well as a considerable range of communicative functions.

In *On Beauty*, the last so far of Smith's out-and-out comedies, there are many instances of humour-led laughter, but also a continuing engagement with laughter as a unique communicative behaviour that can signify more than a response to comic stimuli. Much has been written about the novel's dialogue with E.M. Forster's *Howard's End* (1910),[56] and like Forster, Smith is interested in the often-comic muddles of life and human interaction. These muddles are particularly pronounced in the relations between the Belsey and Kipps families, who, like the Schlegels and Wilcoxes in Forster's novel, are brought together under strained circumstances, and whose conversations are full of confusion and misunderstandings. When Kiki Belsey and Carlene Kipps meet, their

---

[54] Lisa Trahair, *The Comedy of Philosophy: Sense and Nonsense in Early Cinema Slapstick* (Albany, NY: State University of New York Press, 2007), p. 20.
[55] Mary Douglas, 'Do Dogs Laugh? A Cross-Cultural Approach to Body Symbolism', in *Implicit Meanings: Essays on Anthropology* (London: Routledge, [1975] 1993), pp. 83–9 (p. 86).
[56] For a discussion of the relationship between Smith's and Forster's novels, see, for example, Andrzej Gąsiorek, '"A Renewed Sense of Difficulty": E. M. Forster, Iris Murdoch and Zadie Smith on Ethics and Form', in *The Legacies of Modernism: Historicising Postwar and Contemporary Fiction*, ed. David James (Cambridge: Cambridge University Press, 2011), pp. 170–86; Ann Marie Adams, 'A Passage to Forster: Zadie Smith's Attempt to "Only Connect" to *Howards End*', *Critique*, 52:4 (2011), 377–99; Fiona Tolan, '"Painting While Rome Burns": Ethics and Aesthetics in Pat Barker's *Life Class* and Zadie Smith's *On Beauty*, *Tulsa Studies in Women's Literature*, 29:2 (2010), 375–93; and Catherine Lanone, 'Mediating Multi-Cultural Muddle: E. M. Forster Meets Zadie Smith', *Études anglaises*, 60:2 (2007), 185–97. And for critical commentary by Smith on Forster, see Smith, 'Love, Actually'; and Zadie Smith, 'E.M. Forster, Middle Manager', in *Changing My Mind: Occasional Essays* (London: Penguin, 2009), pp. 14–28.

conversation is punctuated by laughter, sometimes in accord but frequently at cross-purposes, as when they discuss Carlene's title, Lady Kipps, bestowed on her as a result of her husband's knighthood. Being called Lady Kipps, Carlene tells Kiki, 'feels like being dead already' and is not to be recommended. Kiki offers a light-hearted response, a mild joke at her own husband's expense:

> 'Carlene, I got to be honest with you, honey,' said Kiki, laughing, 'I don't think Howard's in any danger of a knighthood any time soon. Thanks for the warning, though.'
> 'You shouldn't make fun of your husband, dear,' came the urgent reply; 'you only make fun of yourself that way.'
> 'Oh, we make fun of each other,' said Kiki, still laughing but with the same sorrow she had felt when a hitherto perfectly nice cabbie began to tell her that all the Jews in the first tower had been warned beforehand or that you can't trust Mexicans not to steal the rug from under your feet or that more roads were built under Stalin …[57]

The laughter of bonhomie at her own joke quickly changes to the oxymoronic laughter of sorrow associated with strained politeness and here linked to Carlene's assertion that wives are, and implicitly that they *should* be, defined in relation to their husbands. The same response, laughter, expresses jocularity and sorrow in immediate succession, before reverting to a more affectionate mode when Carlene, herself laughing, compliments Kiki, telling her that she could tell from her face alone that she would like her: 'The silliness of this made Kiki laugh too.'[58]

These contrasting examples of laughter as expressions of amusement and sorrow gesture towards laughter's curious affinity with crying, which is evident in later passages of *On Beauty*. There is of course the expression 'crying with laughter', more properly but less elegantly expressed as 'eyes watering from laughter', but there is also the deeper relationship recognized by Plessner in *Laughing and Crying*. As already described in relation to *The Autograph Man*, laughter and crying require the same yielding of bodily control, but this tropism is not the end of their relationship. Rather, as Plessner argues, 'as reactions to a boundary situation they reveal typical common properties' because 'amusement and sorrow, pleasure and pain, are opposites too crude for the richness of life'.[59] Indeed, in these boundary situations, the division between laughter and crying

---

[57] Zadie Smith, *On Beauty* (London: Penguin, [2005] 2006), pp. 95–6.
[58] Ibid., p. 96.
[59] Plessner, *Laughing and Crying*, pp. 144, 152.

is not always clearly delineated, and either or both are possible in response to the same stimulus, as when Howard and Kiki argue following the revelation of Howard's affair with his colleague Claire Malcolm. Howard compounds Kiki's pain with an insensitive comment about her weight before attempting to regain the moral high ground:

> 'This is not the reason people have affairs, and I don't want to have this conversation on this level, I really don't. It's puerile. It's beneath you – it's beneath me.'
>
> 'There you go again. Howard, you should talk to your cock so the two of you are singing from the same hymn book. Your cock is beneath you. Literally.' Kiki laughed a little and then cried – childish, formless yelps that came up from her belly, relinquishing everything she had left.[60]

In this boundary situation, Kiki veers between laughter and tears, first laughing at her pun on the literal and figurative meanings of 'beneath you' and then bursting into tears, an act of 'relinquishing'. Freud draws connections between the letting go, the relinquishing, that takes place in both laughter and crying, describing them as examples of catharsis and arguing that each acts as a release valve for affect that would otherwise manifest itself in unhealthy ways.[61] Here, Kiki needs both methods, first joking about the situation, using humorous laughter as what Freud terms 'a means of withdrawing energy from the release of unpleasure already mobilized, and by discharging it, of transforming it into pleasure' and then dissolving into tears.[62] In Kiki's changing responses to this moment of heightened emotion, Smith's novel describes how laughter and tears are not opposites, but rather two possible reactions on a spectrum with multiple gradations in communicative and affective function. Later in *On Beauty*, Kiki and Howard are, possibly, on the verge of a reconciliation, and it is laughter that helps bring them together, though it cannot fully relieve Kiki of her underlying hurt. The scene revolves around Howard's retelling of his experience at a university dinner featuring a glee club performing acapella covers of pop music. This is a running joke in the novel wherein both Howard and Kiki find glee clubs toe-curlingly embarrassing, and are unable to maintain their composure in their presence (Kiki recalls offending the host of an event at Yale University by

---

[60] Smith, *On Beauty*, p. 207.
[61] For Freud's discussion of tears, see Sigmund Freud and Josef Breuer, 'On the Psychical Mechanism of Hysterical Phenomena: Preliminary Communication (1893)', in *The Standard Edition of the Complete Psychological Works of Sigmund Freud, Vol. 2: Studies On Hysteria*, ed. and trans. James Strachey (London: Vintage, [1955] 2001), pp. 1–18; and for his discussion of laughter, see Freud, *The Joke*, and Freud, 'Humour'.
[62] Freud, *The Joke*, p. 227.

'weeping tears' and having to leave the room). Howard says that the recent event was even worse the Yale fiasco and proceeds to imitate the group's rendition of a U2 song. Kiki lets out a 'big bellow of a laugh', eventually falling back on to the sofa cushions, 'everything on her wobbling'. But then the couple's son, Levi, interrupts their joking, asking them to keep the noise down. The spell is broken:

> 'Sorry!' whispered Howard. He sat down, picked up his glass and brought it to his mouth, still laughing, hoping to hold her, but at the same moment Kiki stood up, agitated, like a woman reminded of a task she hadn't completed. She was also still laughing, but not happily, and, as the laughter slowed, it became a kind of groan, and then a wispy sigh, and then nothing. She wiped her eyes.[63]

Howard seeks to 'hold' Kiki in the moment – suggesting the transitory nature of laughter, discussed in greater detail later – but it is too late, and her laughter slides through the scales from joyous abandonment to unhappy laughter, to a groan, to a sigh and finally to silence. In *On Beauty*, as across Smith's work, laughter is not a unitary thing, but rather a varied means of expression and act of communication that responds to and indicates a range of emotion, from hilarity to upset and many states in between. It also has important interpersonal and social functions, acting as a unifying as well as a potentially divisive force. This is the topic of the final section of this chapter.

Comedy and community

For David James, in common with a number of writers on Smith, *NW* marked a yet more decisive turn away from the 'hysterical' phase of Smith's writing.[64] Notable among these commentators was Philip Hensher, who suggested that *NW* 'is intensely funny in its disillusioned way, both laughing with its characters, and, sometimes in angry judgment, at them'.[65] This question of laughing 'with' versus laughing 'at' has been important throughout the preceding discussion of Smith's fiction and throughout the pages of this book, and it is the question that has

---

[63] Smith, *On Beauty*, pp. 351–3.
[64] David James, 'Worlded Localisms: Cosmopolitics Writ Small', in *Postmodernism, Literature and Race*, ed. Len Platt and Sara Upstone (Cambridge: Cambridge University Press, 2015), pp. 47–61 (p. 58).
[65] Philip Hensher, '*NW* by Zadie Smith: Review', *Telegraph*, 3 September 2012. Available online: http://www.telegraph.co.uk/culture/books/9508844/NW-by-Zadie-Smith-review.html (accessed 9 July 2019).

historically delineated the politics of joke work. As Hensher suggests, in Smith's novel, we are not given certainties or fixed positions, but rather a mutable sense of the comic tendencies and absurdities of people both individually and collectively. In *Comic Transactions* (1994), James English describes a form of postcolonial joke work that 'attempts to work *through* the crisis point toward a new laughter of community which would not celebrate a common identity, and a new politics of community which would not strive either to realize a common essence or to perform a common work'. He further suggests that it is the nature of such texts that they challenge such models of community as soon as they are set up, instead preferring what Georges Bataille describes as an evolving '"community of those who have no community"'.[66] While being careful to distinguish Smith's novel of cosmopolitan contemporary London from the specifically post-colonial context in which English discusses Salman Rushdie's *The Satanic Verses* (1988), *NW* shares a similar concern with the laughter of community, not only in the simple sense of bringing individuals together through shared joking but as a way of recognizing difference not as something to laugh at but, as English's work suggests, something to laugh through.[67]

NW principally centres on four characters living in the environs of the fictional Caldwell council estate in the real-life area of Willesden, north-west London: Leah Hanwell, treading water in an undemanding job allocating funding to charities; Natalie (formerly Keisha) Blake, Leah's childhood friend now a barrister apparently living the ideal bourgeois lifestyle; Nathan Bogle, a childhood crush of Natalie's who has fallen on difficult times; and Felix Cooper, a mechanic keen to put the problems of his past behind him. These characters' lives intersect to varying degrees and build a necessarily fragmentary picture of life in this corner of London. As in the novels of Martin Amis, discussed in the previous chapter, social class is an implicit concern of this novel, but it is viewed as a fluid thing, bound up with questions of ethnicity, education, experience, language and geography. As Lynn Wells argues, 'Smith challenges us to look beyond social narratives – whether racial, socioeconomic or gendered – to seek the hidden, complex lives of those around us, stories they long to tell and have

---

[66] James F. English, *Comic Transactions: Literature, Humor and the Politics of Community in Twentieth-Century Britain* (Ithaca, NY: Cornell University Press, 1994), pp. 236–7.
[67] For a fascinating discussion of questions of distance and proximity in *NW* from a different perspective, see Alice Bennett, *Contemporary Fictions of Attention: Reading and Distraction in the Twenty-First Century* (London: Bloomsbury, 2018), pp. 115–33. Bennett's chapter focuses on questions of ethics and identifies in *NW* a hesitations between two modes of ethical attention, a 'pragmatic boundedness' and a more radical Levinasian openness.

told.'⁶⁸ Wells's essay focuses on the power of secrets and, more importantly on the power of revealing the truth, and there is a similar power at work in the novel's humour and in its representation of laughter– in the telling of jokes as well as the telling of secrets.

In the 2008 essay 'Dead Man Laughing', Smith remembers her father and their shared love of comedy. She recalls how the English comedian Tony Hancock and his comic progeny 'served as a constant source of conversation between my father and me, a vital link between us when, classwise, and in every other wise, each year placed us further and further apart'; it is shared laughter and a shared sense of humour that neutralizes, at least temporarily, class and other divides. For Smith, 'it was a way of talking about things we didn't want to talk about'.⁶⁹ In *NW*, we see how this shared laughter works in both a partially negative sense – Leah's mother and Leah's partner Michel are sworn enemies, except in the delight they take in laughing at Leah's mistakes and foibles⁷⁰ – and as a way of talking about and talking through hidden or difficult topics. At one point, Felix goes to visit his father and afterwards falls into conversation with his father's neighbour Phil Barnes ('Barnesy'). It is the lightness, the back-and-forth humour of their conversation, which allows Phil to ask after Felix's brother Devon, who is serving time in prison for armed robbery. 'Phil was the only person on the estate who asked after Devon', we are told, and after a moment of reflection the two friends, one white and one black, one middle-aged and one in his early thirties, are soon joking: 'Laughter again, bent with laughter, hands on knees'.⁷¹ Here laughter does not dissipate the serious topic of their conversation, as is sometimes argued, but has rather allowed the conversation to take place. And although I agree with Tammy Amiel Houser's conclusion that many moments in the novel deny the possibility of empathy or fellow feeling between individuals,⁷² in passages such as the dialogue between Felix and Barnesy, there is the suggestion that laughter and a shared sense of humour can allow stories to be shared and conversations to take place across boundaries of age and ethnicity.

This and other episodes are at once comic (though not in the sense of conventional set-up and punchline jokes) and also about the relationship between laughter and community, its capacity both to bring people together

---

⁶⁸ Lynn Wells, 'The Right to a Secret: Zadie Smith's *NW*', in *Reading Zadie Smith: The First Decade and Beyond*, ed. Philip Tew (London: Bloomsbury, 2013), pp. 97–110 (pp. 110–11).
⁶⁹ Zadie Smith, 'Dead Man Laughing', in *Changing My Mind: Occasional Essays* (London: Penguin, 2009), pp. 237–52 (p. 239).
⁷⁰ Smith, *NW*, p. 18.
⁷¹ Ibid., pp. 114–15.
⁷² Tammy Amiel Houser, 'Zadie Smith's *NW*: Unsettling the Promise of Empathy', *Contemporary Literature*, 58:1 (2017), 116–48.

and push them apart. Later in *NW*, Felix travels to central London to buy a second-hand car and meets Tom Mercer, who is selling an old MG on behalf of his wealthy father. The two come from very different parts of London and they engage in often-awkward conversation as they negotiate on price. At one point, Felix, always seemingly in control of the situation, tells Tom

> 'No one's gonna pay six hundred for this. This one you won't be able to sell to no one but a mechanic, I promise you':
>
> Tom looked up, squinting.
> 'Good thing you're a mechanic then, isn't it?'
>
> There was something funny about the way he said it. Both men laughed: Felix in his big gulping way, Tom into his hand like a child.[73]

Laughter and, to use the British vernacular, the ability for both sides to take the piss out of one another, allows a degree of connection to develop, though it is only later that Tom recognizes this connection. When Felix offers Tom some heartfelt but clichéd self-help advice, Tom oversteps the tacit boundaries of their relationship and takes the joking too far:

> He nodded at Felix deeply, satirically, samurai-style. 'Thank you, Felix,' he said. 'I'll remember that. Best you that you can be. Personal equals eternal. You seem like a bloke who's got it all figured out.' He lifted his empty glass to clink against Felix's, but Felix was not impervious to irony and left his own glass where it was.[74]

On reflection, Tom realizes he has enjoyed Felix's over-familiarity and that his misjudgement has soured their joking relationship. Indeed, following this recognition, we get a passage, focalized through Tom, in which he takes stock of his life and the problems caused by his ironic detachment from events. The humour of the exchange between Felix and Tom is one primarily of awkwardness and misreadings, but in moments such as their shared joking and Tom's misjudged quip at Felix's expense, Smith's novel explores the importance and power of laughter as a social force that has the potential for both cohesion and division.[75]

---

[73] Ibid., p. 124.
[74] Ibid., p. 131.
[75] In *Cosmopolitanism in Twenty-First Century Fiction* (2017), Kristian Shaw discusses *NW*'s negotiation of questions of empathy and tolerance in the context of cosmopolitanism and Smith's representation of north-west London as a microcosm of transnational society. Kristian Shaw, *Cosmopolitanism in Twenty-First Century Fiction* (Basingstoke: Palgrave Macmillan, 2017), pp. 67–102.

To explain this relationship between laughter and community, Parvulescu turns to the philosophy of Georges Bataille. Bataille's insights on this topic are scattered throughout his work,[76] and Parvulescu argues that 'in contrast to what becomes his "reputation" in the wake of his work on erotism[77] and Foucault's translation of his notion of transgression, Bataille prefers a laughing orgy to a sexual orgy as a model for communication'. 'Bataille's laughter', she concludes, 'cannot be (or remain) a reactive laugh, the laughing *at* that excludes, closing the gates of community. In fact, as a state of communication, laughter displaces the very problematic of inclusion/exclusion on which the thought of community has been articulated.'[78] This is an important insight, and while I am sceptical about the extent of laughter's ability to traverse the inclusion/exclusion, at/with boundary on which so many models of community, as well as models of laughter, are based, it does gesture towards the state of unity that can be achieved through laughter, and which Smith describes in *NW* and elsewhere in her fiction.[79] Bataille likens this process to the confluence of water in a wave, and the passage in which he describes this process is worth quoting at length:

> If a group of people laugh at an absent-minded gesture, or at a sentence revealing an absurdity, there passes within them a current of intense communication. Each isolated existence emerges from itself by means of the image betraying the error of immutable isolation. It emerges from itself in a sort of easy flash; it opens itself at the same time to the contagion of a wave which rebounds, for those who laugh, together become like the waves of the sea – there no longer exists between them any partition as long as the laughter lasts; they are no more separate than are two waves, but their unity is as undefined, as precarious as that of the agitation of the waters.[80]

What is significant here is not only the contagion, the merging and cohesion that Bataille so values in laughter – and that Smith represents in the conversations between Barnesy and Felix, and Felix and Tom – but also the evanescent nature of this process. In this, one of Bataille's more sustained discussions of the topic,

---

[76] In addition to the passages from Bataille's work quoted elsewhere in this chapter, see also Georges Bataille, 'Attraction and Repulsion II: Social Structure' [1938], in *The College of Sociology, 1937–39*, ed. Denis Hollier, trans. Betsy Wing (Minneapolis: University of Minnesota Press, 1988 [1979]), pp. 113–24; and Georges Bataille, 'Laughter' [1944], trans. Bruce Boone, in *The Bataille Reader*, ed. Fred Botting and Scott Wilson (Oxford: Blackwell, 1997), pp. 59–63.
[77] 'Erotism' is a transliteration of the French 'L'erotisme'.
[78] Parvulescu, *Laughter*, pp. 89–91.
[79] In this sense, my reading of the novel is more hopeful than that of Caroline Lusin, for whom *NW* 'paints a bleak picture of a world in which the transgression of norms, the lack of perspectives and the failure of autonomous selves have become the status quo'. Lusin, 'The Condition of England Novel in the Twenty-First Century', pp. 247–63 (pp. 253–4).
[80] Bataille, *Inner Experience*, pp. 95–6.

the wave metaphor suggests a precarious, fleeting unity, bound to be dashed against the shore.[81] It is not, for all of the value Bataille places on laughter, a lasting form of community, an aspect of the phenomenon that is suggested by the changing tone of Felix and Tom's conversation, and in a passage from Smith's most recent novel, *Swing Time*.

Swing Time centres on the relationship between the unnamed narrator of the novel and her childhood friend, Tracey. It continues Smith's journey into more sombre territory but is punctuated by laughter in all its manifestations. In one pivotal scene, the narrator and Tracey are reunited after years of estrangement and they return to a pub in their childhood neighbourhood that has been gentrified in the intervening years. Aided by drink, the pair put any awkwardness behind them and enjoy themselves. The narrator describes 'reminiscing and laughing – laughing harder than I had in all three years of college – taking each other back to Miss Isabel's yellow shoes, to my mother's clay pit, to *The History of Dance*, through all of it, even things I never thought we would be able to laugh about together'.[82] To paraphrase Smith's recollection of her relationship with her father, joking and laughter provide a way of talking about things these estranged friends are otherwise unable to talk about, and the Bataillean waves of laughter unite them, carrying them along. But as Bataille goes on to suggest, this wave is a precarious thing, destined to crest and crash down. When the narrator asks after Tracey's absentee and possibly abusive father, the laughter stops, and the narrator recalls that Tracey's 'ever-expressive face turned pensive and took on that look of utter icy coldness I remembered so well from childhood'.[83] The distance between the two characters opens up once more. Here, laughter is represented as a powerful method of communication with the ability to develop understanding between individuals, but there is also a note of caution about its transformative potential that is typical of the multifaceted representation of laughter in Smith's novels.

---

[81] There is a striking contrast here between Bataille's metaphor of the wave and the extended wave metaphor that closes Henri Bergson's *Laughter*. Whereas for Bataille, the unification of waters in a wave represent a profound form of human communication and communion, for Bergson laughter is merely a manifestation of the 'form of [the] significant undulations beneath'. It represents, he concludes, 'a slight revolt on the surface of social life', and, like the brackish water left on the beach after the breaking of a wave, the philosopher of laughter 'may find that the substance is scanty, and the aftertaste bitter'. See Bergson, 'Laughter', pp. 189–90. Bataille was aware of Bergson's *Laughter*, and describes his experience of reading the essay in 'Un-knowing: Laughter and Tears'.

[82] Zadie Smith, *Swing Time* (London: Hamish Hamilton, 2016), p. 329.

[83] Ibid.

Bataille classifies laughter along with sexual behaviour as one of the 'two existing forms of perceptible human interattraction',[84] implying a bringing together and mutual attraction, and placing it at the centre rather than the periphery of human behaviour. However, the power of laughter exists in tandem with its fragility, a tension that Smith describes throughout her work and particularly in her most recent fiction, which is less comic than the early novels but no less concerned with laughter in its many forms. From her earlier 'hysterical' fiction to the more muted recent books, Smith is concerned with describing the multiplicity of laughter. Laughter often occurs in tandem with moments of humour but can equally express grief, sorrow, or other forms of conflicted emotions. It is not, in Smith's fiction, a unitary thing but both a positive and negative phenomenon, a method of mockery and an expression of fellow feeling. Finally, laughter provides a way of building community but without falling prey to the exaggerations of a wholly positivist view of its potential: it is a fragile and fleeting form of community but an important one nonetheless. The multivalence of this relationship is suggestive of the need to reclaim the study of laughter as a significant and critically generative field whose analysis provides an important new perspective on the affective dimension of literature and culture.

---

[84] Georges Bataille, 'Attraction and Repulsion I: Tropisms, Sexuality, Laughter and Tears' [1938], in *The College of Sociology, 1937–39*, ed. Denis Hollier, trans. Betsy Wing (Minneapolis: University of Minnesota Press, [1979] 1988), pp. 103–12 (p. 107).

4

'Like a monkey with a miniature cymbal'[1]
Magnus Mills and the comedy of repetition

Comedy, surprise and repetition

Discussions of the nature of comedy, and particularly the mechanics of humour, often emphasize the relationship between humour and surprise.[2] It is implicit in the notion of set-up and punchline, in which the joke-teller outmanoeuvres the audience before landing a surprise blow, and according to the novelist Will Self, it is vital to humour, which 'should be spontaneous, playful and inventive'. 'Nothing is funny twice', he argues, and duplication always has a weakening effect.[3] Novelty does undoubtedly play a role in many forms of the comic, and it is at the core of incongruity theory, the most widely accepted theory of humour, whose lineage stretches from contemporary theorists such as John Morreall, Victor Raskin and Salvatore Attardo back to the eighteenth and nineteenth centuries in the work of Kant and Schopenhauer. As I discuss in Chapter 2 in relation to Martin Amis's comedies of bathos, incongruity theories argue that humour involves the juxtaposition of two seemingly incompatible objects or ideas in a manner that is both surprising and pleasing. Subsequent iterations of this incongruity may continue to be pleasing, but the element of surprise will be lost along with the

---

[1] 'Over and over and over and over and over / Like a monkey with a miniature cymbal / The joy of repetition really is in you'. Hot Chip, 'Over and Over', in *The Warning* [Music Album] (UK: EMI, 2006).
[2] Isabel Ermida traces the notion of surprise as a constituent element of humour to Descartes and notes that this relationship has 'become established in present-day humor studies'. Isabel Ermida, *The Language of Comic Narratives: Humor Construction in Short Stories* (Berlin: Mouton de Gruyter, 2008), p. 18.
[3] Will Self, 'A Point of View: That Joke Isn't Funny Any More', *BBC News*, 22 August 2014. Available online: http://www.bbc.co.uk/news/magazine-28881335 (accessed 9 July 2019). Self has reiterated this point on a number of different occasions, identifying it as one of the reasons for his move away from the more expressly comic mode found in his earlier fiction. See Christine Fears, 'An Interview with Will Self', *The Literateur*, 6 February 2010. Available online: http://literateur.com/an-interview-with-will-self (accessed 9 July 2019). And for a repetition of the line 'nothing is ever funny twice', see Will Self, *Walking to Hollywood: Memories of before the Fall* (London: Bloomsbury, 2010), p. 50.

more explosive, spontaneous laughter elicited on the inaugural occasion.[4] As useful as these theories are for understanding humour in certain contexts, their dominance and the consequent assertion of the relationship between humour and surprise has arisen from the tendency of comedy and humour studies to focus on jokes at the expense of thinking about how humour works across a comic sequence or across the duration of a narrative. As Jeroen Vandaele has argued, there are significant differences between comic surprise and narrative surprise, as well as between jokes and comedy,[5] and to apply a model of humour based on jokes to all forms of comedy is to ignore the shifts in perspective and other structural devices that are possible in longer forms. In *The Odd One In* (2008), Alenka Zupančič makes a valuable distinction between the joke and the comic sequence, arguing that they represent distinct temporal experiences and contrasting the finality of jokes with the continuity of the comic sequence. Sequences, in contrast to jokes, do not rely on surprise, and construct humour via a paradoxical discontinuous repetition.[6] But given this distinction, how can one account for the comedy of repetition, particularly considering that so much thinking about comedy is predicated on the notion of surprise? And should repetition be considered a second-order form of humour that can only yield diminishing returns? This chapter addresses these questions, placing repetition rather than surprise at the centre of comic practice.

It is not universally true that repetition has been ignored in comedy and humour studies. Katarina Triezenberg, for example, has noted that repetition with variation can serve to magnify rather than diminish the humour in literary narrative,[7] while for Maurice Charney, 'repetition may be the single most important mechanism in comedy'.[8] For Mladen Dolar, it is comedy's propensity for reproduction and repletion that, contra Plato, makes it such a rich, productive and self-aware form of mimesis: 'Comedy is mimesis in action.'[9] And

---

[4] Brian Boyd notes the importance of surprise to fiction-making in general. Summarizing evolutionary perspectives on storytelling, he argues that 'even infants, like the rest of us, lose interest at mere repetition and suddenly look longer and harder at anything that strikes them as different', and therefore seek to incorporate elements of surprise in their stories from an early stage. Brian Boyd, *On the Origin of Stories: Evolution, Cognition, and Fiction* (Cambridge, MA: Harvard University Press, 2009), p. 184.

[5] Jeroen Vandaele, 'Narrative Humor (I): Enter Perspective', *Poetics Today*, 31:4 (2010), 721–85 (pp. 748–60, 775–7).

[6] Zupančič, *The Odd One In*, pp. 139–41.

[7] Katarina E. Triezenberg, 'Humor in Literature', in *The Primer of Humor Research*, ed. Victor Raskin (Berlin: Mouton de Gruyter, 2008), pp. 523–42 (p. 539). Salvatore Attardo has also noted the significance of repetition in both jokes and longer forms of comic narrative, a relationship which is 'a bit of a headache for [humour] theories based on surprise'. Attardo, *Humorous Texts*, pp. 85–6.

[8] Maurice Charney, *Comedy High and Low: An Introduction to the Experience of Comedy* (New York: Oxford University Press, 1978), p. 82.

[9] Mladen Dolar, 'The Comic Mimesis', *Critical Inquiry*, 43:2 (2017), 570–89, p. 588.

for Zupančič, comic repetition is not merely a technique but rather '*constitutive of the comic genre as such*'. Drawing on ideas from Deleuze, Nietzsche, Kierkegaard and Lacan, Zupančič argues that in contrast to tragedy, which relies on uniqueness and singularity, comedy 'thrives' on repetition and this repetition is inherent to its radical potential; comedy reproduces master-signifiers – the concepts fundamental to a subject's identity and understanding of the world – but destabilizes them through repetition. The very fact of repetition insists that no two events or utterances are identical because previous instances are always already contained in and acting upon subsequent iterations.[10] This emphasis on the relationship between comedy and repetition is not unique to Zupančič and is also present in Benjamin, Deleuze,[11] and at greater length in Bergson's classic essay *Laughter*. Bergson's conception of humour is fundamentally imbricated with the machine age in which he was writing and to the concept of *élan vital* at the centre of his philosophy, according to which laughter arises following the recognition of '*something mechanical encrusted on the living*' – when a person acts like a thing, as when one repeats a simple action like a factory machine or automaton.[12] Bergsonian laughter has a social, corrective function, restraining eccentricity and softening the 'mechanical elasticity' of the social body,[13] and although he and Zupančič are in agreement about the significance of the relationship between comedy and repetition, they arrive at opposite conclusions: whereas for Zupančič comedy's repetitions unsettle societal norms, for Bergson, they enforce them. Bergson's significance is further apparent in Michael North's *Machine-Age Comedy* (2009), which draws on Bergson's ideas, as well as those of Wyndham Lewis and others, in order to discuss twentieth-century comedies ranging from Disney cartoons and Chaplin films, to work by Duchamp, Beckett and Foster Wallace. North concludes that 'it is surely human repetitiousness that is at the heart of machine-age comedy'.[14] Throughout this important work, North identifies the interconnection not only between comedy and repetition, but also

---

[10] Ibid., pp. 149, 174, 177. As Gerard Genette points out in *Narrative Discourse* (1972), in linguistic terms no two occurrences are ever precisely the same, and '"repetition" is in fact a mental construction, which eliminates from each occurrence everything belonging to it that is peculiar to itself in order to preserve only what it shares with all the others of the same class'. Genette's classic study also offers a useful typology of narrative repetition. Gerard Genette, *Narrative Discourse: An Essay in Method*, trans. Jane E. Lewin (Ithaca, NY: Cornell University Press, [1972] 1980), pp. 113–17.

[11] See, for example, Walter Benjamin, 'Fate and Character' [1921], trans. Edmund Jephcott, in *Selected Writings, vol. 1: 1913–1926* (Cambridge, MA: Harvard University Press, 2004), pp. 201–6; and Gilles Deleuze, *Difference and Repetition*, trans. Paul Patton (London: Continuum, [1968] 2004), pp. 5–6.

[12] Bergson, 'Laughter', pp. 61–190 (p. 84).

[13] Ibid., pp. 64–5.

[14] Michael North, *Machine-Age Comedy* (Oxford: Oxford University Press, 2009), p. 199.

between comic repetition and the mechanization and human life in the modern age, an interconnection that is particularly strong in working life: as unlikely as the relationship may seem, it is often work that provides the situation and subject for comic narratives. Diverse examples include the factory in Chaplin's *Modern Times*, Watt's servitude in Beckett's *Watt* (1953), the office workers of the sitcom(s) *The Office* (UK, 2001–2003; US, 2005–2013) and novels such as Joshua Ferris's *Then We Came to the End* (2007) and Helen DeWitt's *Lightning Rods* (2011), or in the abundant genre of the comic campus novel. Comedy, repetition and work are fundamentally linked, and this chapter examines those links via a focus on the novels of Magnus Mills, a writer of peculiarly off-kilter comic worlds that are nevertheless grounded in recognizable versions of contemporary working life.

Magnus Mills

Mills's first novel, *The Restraint of Beasts* (1998), remains his best-known work, no doubt helped by a rare cover blurb from Thomas Pynchon and a Booker Prize nomination. It is the story of a high-tensile fence construction crew, sent south from their base in Scotland to a job on a farm in England. At the outset, the unnamed narrator is appointed foreman by the company boss, Donald, and charged with supervising Tam and Richie, laconic Scotsmen who Donald says "'can't go to England on their own.'"[15] This sets the pattern for subsequent Mills novels, most of which are narrated by an unnamed first-person narrator[16] and many of which are set in apparently mundane locales and workplaces. Since *The Restraint of Beasts*, he has published *All Quiet on the Orient Express* (1999), *The Scheme for Full Employment* (2003) and *The Maintenance of Headway* (2009), set in an out-of-season campsite, a distribution hub and on a bus network, respectively. There is also a parallel strand to Mills's fiction, inaugurated by *Three to See the King* (2001) and including *A Cruel Bird Came to the Nest and Looked In* (2011) and *The Field of the Cloth of Gold* (2015), which are more fantastical and gesture more firmly towards allegory. This chapter focuses mainly on the former group, though there is a continuity of tone across these books, all of which relay even the most unlikely or violent of scenarios in a deadpan, matter-of-fact voice, hinting at machinations the narrator is either unwilling or unable

---

[15] Magnus Mills, *The Restraint of Beasts* (London: Flamingo, 1998), p. 1.
[16] The exception to this is *Explorers of the New Century* (2005), which has an unnamed third-person narrator.

to articulate. There is also a degree of thematic continuity across Mills's work in its concern with structures of authority and group dynamics, whether among the employees of a London bus company, the officials of the imagined Empire of Greater Fallowfields or a group or vinyl record enthusiasts.

Journalism about Mills, particularly in the early years, has tended to focus on his parallel career as a London bus driver, a job he gave up after the success of *The Restraint of Beasts* only to return when he found that writing was only possible when he had 'no apparent spare time'.[17] To give too much weight to this admittedly unusual aspect of Mills's life would be a reductive move, but it is difficult to avoid the conclusion that it has informed the direction of his fiction, not simply in direct ways as in *The Maintenance of Headway*, a fictionalized account of life on the buses, or *The Restraint of Beasts*, which draws on Mills's experience as a fencing contractor.[18] Mills's novels are comedies *of* work; that is, they are about work in a fundamental sense, as both cornerstone of identity and mere economic necessity, as source of comradeship and conflict, as both vocation and trap. In this way they are distinct from workplace humour or portrayals of humour *at* work because for the most part Mills's characters are not intending to be funny.[19] The humour instead comes from situational absurdities and from his characters' stoical, deadpan reactions to outlandish occurrences.[20] His protagonists tend to be relatively low-status workers in manual industries, at odds with their managers and the organizational structures of the workplace. In this way, they differ from the performative workers discussed in the concluding chapter of this book in relation to *England, England* (1998) and are closer to the repetitive, mechanized labour that was central to theorists such as Bergson

---

[17] Magnus Mills, 'This Much I Know', *Observer*, 26 July 2009. Available online: https://www.theguardian.com/lifeandstyle/2009/jul/26/magnus-mills-this-much-i-know (accessed 9 July 2019).

[18] Magnus Mills, 'Small Talk', *Financial Times*, 30 September 2011. Available online: https://www.ft.com/content/047168ca-ea8a-11e0-b0f5-00144feab49a (accessed 9 July 2019).

[19] There is a significant body of work which endorses and/or studies workplace humour as a management tool. See, for example, John Morreall, *Humor Works* (Amherst, MA: HRD Press, 1997), Morreall's related Humorworks programme of seminars on using humour in the workplace (information available online: http://www.humorworks.com/index.php (accessed 9 July 2019)), and many of the essays in the collection *Humour, Work and Organization*, ed. Robert Westwood and Carl Rhodes (Abingdon: Routledge, 2007). This aspect of workplace humour is resolutely not a part of Mills's comic world, where bosses are amusing in their humourlessness. As the David Brent and Michael Scott characters demonstrate in the UK and US versions of *The Office*, managerial humour is often amusing for reasons other than those intended.

[20] For a thorough investigation of the nature of the absurd in fiction, see Neil Cornwell, *The Absurd in Literature* (Manchester: Manchester University Press, 2006). The term 'absurd' is used not to suggest that Mills's work belongs to the genre of the Theatre of the Absurd, but rather to identify a comic lineage from this mid-century movement, first identified by Martin Esslin in 1961. Eric Weitz, for example, identifies an absurdist tendency towards the grotesque, circular plots and equally circular dialogue, all of which are important in Mills's fiction. Eric Weitz, *The Cambridge Introduction to Comedy* (Cambridge: Cambridge University Press, 2009), pp. 145–60.

whose ideas are outlined earlier. Mills's comedies are reliant on the structural repetition emphasized by Zupančič, but they also represent repetition, in particular the repetitions of processes and systems of work and the repetitions of human thought and action inculcated by those same processes and systems. His fiction does not reduce working life to mindless, mechanical drudgery, but it is open to the absurdities of work and to the eccentricities of human behaviour it fosters. This discussion of his novels opens with an analysis of *The Restraint of Beasts* as a deadpan comedy of death and hard labour that is concerned with systems, authority and authoritarianism. It then discusses the representation of cyclical patterns of work and behaviour in two later novels, *The Scheme for Full Employment* and *The Maintenance of Headway*, whose comic repetitions serve to undermine the structures on which they rely. Finally, it returns to *The Restraint of Beasts*, discussing it alongside Mills's second novel, *All Quiet on the Orient Express*, to consider Mills's inheritance from writers such as Flann O'Brien and Samuel Beckett and the ways in which he departs from these models to create his own version of comic hell.

Deadpan; dead bodies: *The Restraint of Beasts*

The Restraint of Beasts begins *in media res* with the boss, Donald's, instruction to the unnamed narrator: 'I'm putting you in charge of Tam and Richie.'[21] Donald conducts his meetings in the manner of interrogations, controlling the temperature and layout of the room and keeping two hard chairs, 'slightly less than adult sized' on which visitors must perch.[22] Tam and Richie sit there discomforted like sulky schoolchildren as Donald admonishes them for sloppy workmanship on the fence of a client named Mr McCrindle. These opening pages introduce the dynamic of the relationship between the characters – tyrannical boss, reluctant foreman and sullen workers – and sets in motion the events that will define the plot, such as it is. It is unpromising material for comedy, but it is precisely this claustrophobia, repetitiveness and tension that generate much of the novel's humour. Having been reprimanded, Tam, Richie and the narrator return to Mr McCrindle's farm to repair his fence, but their visit takes a turn for the worse when Tam slips as he is tightening the final wire, sending the winch careening into Mr McCrindle's head: 'Mr McCrindle had a very surprised look

---

[21] Mills, *Restraint*, p. 1.
[22] Ibid., p. 7.

on his face. His eyes were wide open, but he was, apparently, dead.'[23] What follows does not conform to the logic of realist fiction, and is instead closer to what Jerry Palmer has described as the 'logic of the absurd'.[24] Rather than panicking or showing distress, the three workers treat Mr McCrindle's body as a problem to be solved, a mere object, a piece of industrial waste:

> After a long silence Richie said, 'What are we going to do with Mr McCrindle?'
> 'Well', I replied. 'I suppose we'd better bury him.'
> This was my first major decision as foreman.[25]

There is something of Joe Orton's *Loot* (1965) in the transformation of a human body into a thing, and the professional pride taken by the narrator in the masterfully worked final line is at odds with conventional logic and expectations. Any concern is reserved for Mr McCrindle's cows, the beasts that the fence is intended to restrain. 'On the way home a thought occurred to me', recalls the narrator:

> 'He was dead, wasn't he?'
> 'I'm sure he was,' said Richie.
> 'What about his cows?'
> 'They be alright.'[26]

The deadpan tone speaks to what Bergson would describe as 'the *absence of feeling* which usually accompanies laughter',[27] and this sets the template for Mills's next novel *All Quiet on the Orient Express* in which one of the characters, a milkman named Deakin, is drowned helping the narrator and his boss, Mr Parker, to fix a mooring buoy in a lake:

> 'Dear oh dear oh dear,' he said when I joined him. 'This would have to happen now, wouldn't it? Just when Deakin found a job he liked.'
> I gave no reply but simply shrugged and looked in the same direction.[28]

Again the reaction – '"Dear oh dear oh dear"' – is a bathetic understatement, and the characters immediately turn their minds to practical matters, principally the completion of Deakin's milk round: '"It's the least we can do under the

---

[23] Ibid., p. 32.
[24] See Palmer, *The Logic of the Absurd*; and Palmer, *Taking Humour Seriously*.
[25] Mills, *Restraint*, p. 34.
[26] Ibid., p. 37.
[27] Bergson, 'Laughter', p. 63. Bergson describes emotion as the 'foe' of laughter, but this only accounts for particular types of laughter. As I discuss in Chapter 3, laughter and emotion can coexist.
[28] Magnus Mills, *All Quiet on the Orient Express* (London: Bloomsbury, [1999] 2011), p. 230.

circumstances', says Mr Parker.[29] Deakin is barely mentioned later in the novel, nor does anybody give thought to recovering his body from the bottom of the lake.

The Bergsonian notion of treating people as objects does, in part, account for what it is that makes these deaths comic rather than tragic, but there is also a sense in Mills that the laughter of superiority, which for Bergson is directed at the machine-like person, is aimed less at the individual and more at the systems and structures of power within which they find themselves: that it is the peculiar effect of work itself that is the object of the humour. In *The Restraint of Beasts*, having finished Mr McCrindle's fence and taken care of the 'loose ends', the fencing crew travel to England to complete a large job for a farmer named Mr Perkins. Mr Perkins is absent for the majority of the time, and the narrator, Tam and Richie are left alone. They take a lucrative job moonlighting on a neighbouring farm, and when Mr Perkins eventually arrives to confront them, he finds himself on the wrong end of a fence post tossed blindly over a hedge:

> 'What are we going to do with him?' asked Tam.
> 'We'll have to bury him, I suppose.'[30]

This is an almost verbatim repetition of the dialogue following Mr McCrindle's death, as are the narrator's thoughts after the inevitable burial under a fence post:

> As we put the gear back in the truck a thought occurred to me.
> 'He was dead, wasn't he?'
> 'I'm sure he was,' said Tam.
> 'What about his sheep?'
> 'They'll be alright.'

Again, there is mordant humour to be found in the trio's disregard for Perkins's life, and this time their discussion is followed by the line, 'For some reason the conversation then came round to Mr McCrindle'.[31] It is as if McCrindle's violent death has already receded from their memories, but for readers, any comic surprise from the first iteration is lost. This feeling of déjà vu is reinforced after the similarly affectless response to the later death of Robert, Donald's business partner, who is struck by the head of a mallet that comes loose from its handle as the narrator is mid-swing. Donald is present on his occasion and witnesses Robert's death, but far from introducing an element of jeopardy or consequence,

---

[29] Ibid., p. 232.
[30] Mills, *Restraint*, p. 121.
[31] Ibid., p. 122.

responsibility for dealing with the situation merely moves up the hierarchy: "'What are we going to do with Robert?'" asks the narrator, "'We'll have to bury him'",[32] replies Donald. Work continues as normal, even as the body count rises. Why should this repetition of violence be comic? The incongruously deadpan reactions of the characters offer one explanation, though this does not account for the subsequent deaths and the identical, and now expected, reactions. Bergson's idea about the mechanical offers another. But is there a deeper, more structural affinity between comedy and repetition?

As noted in the introductory remarks to this chapter, Zupančič argues that it is comedy's tendency towards repetition that distinguishes it from its most obvious antonym, tragedy. Because tragedy is concerned with the singular fate of its protagonists (it is a 'work of sublimation, in the precise sense of elevating a singular subjective destiny to that place of the symbolic structure that represents its blind spot') it 'cannot stand textual, mechanical repetition', which would upset this sense of singularity. On the other hand, 'comedy not only stands it, but thrives on it'.[33] Repetition strips the event of its singularity,[34] a move that cannot be incorporated into the tragic narrative but which comedy, with its tendency towards universal situations and character types, uses as a form of amplification. Amplification is meant not in the sense of making the quotidian appear momentous but in the sense of moving from singularity to multiplicity, and from individuals to systems and structures. In *The Restraint of Beasts*, it is this repetition that makes the characters' deaths sufficiently quotidian as to appear comic, and such is the logic of repetition that more is more: a single death may be considered tragic, or may at least create a sense of jeopardy – what will happen when the boss or the police find out? – but the repetition of these accidents, and the complicity of all concerned, lends them a sense of mundanity, even inevitability. As Simon Critchley argues, 'comedy confronts us with the painful reality of death', but it does so 'badly, incompletely', without the transcendence of tragedy.[35] Moreover, it is this inevitability, this sense of prosaic repetition, which suggests a critical dimension to Mills's comedy. In *The Restraint of Beasts*, there is a developing sense that something violent inheres in the work of the fencing crew and that these industrial accidents are the norm, fostered and perhaps encouraged by Donald. After the job at Mr McCrindle's,

---

[32] Ibid., p. 144.
[33] Zupančič, *The Odd One In*, pp. 176, 174.
[34] This notion of the event is central to Judith Roof's conception of the comic in *The Comic Event*.
[35] Simon Critchley, 'Repetition, Repetition, Repetition: Richard Prince and the Three r's', in *Lacan, Psychoanalysis and Comedy*, ed. Patricia Gherovici and Manya Steinkoler (New York: Cambridge University Press, 2016), pp. 237–42 (p. 241).

Donald pointedly asks, "'Are you sure you finished him off properly?'", and subsequent events make it clear that his double meaning is intended. Donald has experience in this area and is unnervingly familiar with the most appropriate fence post under which to bury a body.[36] Towards the end of the book, events take a yet more sinister turn when the crew are commissioned to build a series of seven-feet-high pens for the mysterious Hall Brothers. The true purpose of these is unknown but potentially very macabre. There is a surprising absence of livestock in *The Restraint of Beasts*, a novel putatively about constructing high-tensile fences to contain farm animals, and the beasts of the title are perhaps not of the cloven-hoofed variety. In tandem with, and in fact as a result of, the comic machinations of the plot, the novel develops a challenging subtext about power, obedience and complicity.[37]

Mills has cited Primo Levi as an influence,[38] and although would be flippant to draw too close an analogy between events in *The Restraint of Beasts* and those experienced by Levi and recounted in his novels and memoirs, Mills's work demonstrates a comparable concern with both violence against individuals and with the structural violence associated with authoritarianism. This is akin to what Slavoj Žižek classifies in *Violence* (2008) as 'subjective' versus 'objective' violence, where subjective violence is violence as it is usually conceptualized, as violence against the subject or 'the perturbation of the "normal," peaceful state of things', and objective violence 'is precisely the violence inherent to this "normal" state of things', or the systemic violence inherent in social, political and economic structures.[39] Žižek's distinction between these two categories of violence suggests a further distinction between the humour of surprise and the

---

[36] Mills, *Restraint*, p. 77. After the narrator, Tam and Richie have killed Mr Perkins, they discuss where to bury him: 'we all agreed it was best to put him under the slamming post', the narrator recalls, 'although none of us could come up with a particular reason why this should be so'. Later, when the narrator kills Robert, Donald's business partner, and Richie is given responsibility for burying the body, Donald asks the narrator to remind him that "'it's best to put Robert under the slamming post rather than the hanging post'", though he cannot explain this preference either. Mills, *Restraint*, pp. 122, 144.

[37] There is an interesting parallel here with Mills's *Explorers of the New Century*, a novel that depicts a fantastical version of early twentieth-century polar exploration featuring talking mules. The polar party set out to reach the 'Agreed Furthest Point', taking the mules with them as beasts of burden. These 'beasts' are sentient beings whose lesser status is preserved by tracts such as *The Theory of Transportation* by F.E. Childish, which is a parody of imperialist, pseudo-scientific rhetoric about the 'white man's burden' as well the discourse surrounding the justification of slavery. An excerpt from Childish's (fictional) text refers to the 'inescapable burden' of the mules, which has existed since 'time immemorial'. Although the historical parallels are not sufficiently clear-cut for it to be considered allegory, Mills's novel is both a comic fantasy and an exploration of the iniquities of imperialism and racism. Magnus Mills, *Explorers of the New Century* (London: Bloomsbury, [2005] 2006), p. 106.

[38] Eleanor Mills, 'Don't Mention the Buses', *The Sunday Times*, 4 October 1998, section Features, p. 7.

[39] Slavoj Žižek, *Violence* (London: Profile, 2008), p. 2.

humour of repetition, wherein the inaugural irruption of violence represents the disturbance of the normal state of affairs, but subsequent iterations suggest the violence inherent in the structure of the normal. In *The Restraint of Beasts* individuals do meet violent ends, but they are also part of an economy that fosters or even encourages that violence. People are described as livestock, and the beasts of the title may in fact be the narrator, Tam and Richie. Donald's 'unfortunate turn of phrase' gives the narrator the feeling of 'being transported to some sort of penal colony or corrective camp, rather than merely going to undertake a commercial contract', and his reference to a penal colony clearly gestures towards Kafka's famous story.[40] By this point in the novel, Donald has already described his new electrified fencing as the '"final solution to the problem of the restraint of beasts"', and again the choice of wording is not accidental. Later, the Hall Brothers take over management responsibility for the fending crew, and when they are late for work John Hall tells his brother David: 'Take them to the pens … . That's the best place for them.'[41] Here Mills invokes the dehumanizing language of the Holocaust and the Soviet gulags, and for Theo Tait, who reviewed *The Restraint of Beasts* for the *London Review of Books*, it is at this point that the novel loses its way, unable to bear the weight of this heavy allegorical burden.[42] Yet this context remains ambiguous, and the true purpose of the Hall Brothers' pens is not finally revealed: the Brothers could be tyrannical but reputable businessmen, or they could be into something very much darker, even cannibalistic. It is this that has led Bo Pettersson to describe *The Restraint of Beasts* as an allegorical novel, albeit ambiguously so, for the way in which it examines the tendency of humans to act as beasts and for its depiction of the institutionalized violence that can incubate that beastliness.[43] The implication in Mills' fiction is not that there is a moral equivalence between these two poles, but that they each stem from the same authoritarian root. Looked at another way, it is the comic banality of the situations in Mills's fiction, the relatively

---

[40] Mills, *Restraint*, p. 183. Bo Pettersson observes that as well as the more literal meaning that the contractors are building fences to restrain beasts, 'Mills gradually extends the metaphor of Man is Beast, in two senses: (1) man is a beast that needs to be restrained for what he does to other humans, and (2) in restraining and incarcerating other humans, man acts in beastly ways.' He notes that the second of these two senses grows in strength as the novel progresses. Bo Pettersson, *How Literary Worlds Are Shaped: A Comparative Poetics of Literary Imagination* (Berlin: Walter de Gruyter, 2016), p. 171.

[41] Ibid., p. 190.

[42] Theo Tait, 'First one, then another, then another, then another after that', review of Magnus Mills, 'The Restraint of Beasts', *London Review of Books*, 26 November 1998. Available online: https://www.lrb.co.uk/v20/n23/theo-tait/first-one-then-another-then-another-then-another-after-that (accessed 9 July 2019).

[43] Pettersson, *How Literary Worlds Are Shaped*, p. 171.

low stakes, which enable him to broach such weighty topics. In a much later novel, *The Forensic Records Society* (2017), he imagines the factions that open up within a group of vinyl record enthusiasts after they form a society for the serious contemplation of music. Each member of the group has their own ideas about the correct way to listen to records, and again Mills returns to the familiar ground of tyranny and the merciless pursuit of perfection. Punning on the local and global meanings of 'society', the narrator is left wondering, 'Was it really beyond human capacity ... to create a society which didn't ultimately disintegrate through internal strife? Or collapse under the weight of its own laws? Or suffer damaging rivalries with other societies?'[44] Through the imbrication of these apparently banal tales of everyday work and of social life with much weightier subtexts about authority and domination, Mills relies on what might be thought of as examples of 'benign violation', Peter McGraw's explanation of humour in general,[45] doing so not to diminish the significance of historical totalitarianism but to identify its presence in the everyday. In no sense do these novels draw an equivalence between the tyranny of work and the tyranny of fascism or between the internal strife of a music appreciation society and the tendency towards entropy in society at large, but their comic treatment of these ideas allows Mills to explore correspondences and the ways in which the mundane coexists with the absurd or outlandish, and the ways in which pernicious structures of power inhere within everyday life.

Working to rule, ruling the workplace: *The Scheme for Full Employment* and *The Maintenance of Headway*

As Ian Sansom astutely observes in his review of Mills's 2011 novel *A Cruel Bird Came to the Nest and Looked In*, much of Mill's fiction has 'played basically the same delightful games and tunes around and about the nature of work, and about organizations, and about human systems'.[46] As we have seen, this is true of *The Restraint of Beasts*, but this concern with the nature of work, organizations and systems is yet more evident in *The Scheme for Full Employment* and *The Maintenance of Headway*. Mills places Huw Beynon's *Working for Ford* (1973) at

---

[44] Magnus Mills, *The Forensic Records Society* (London: Bloomsbury, 2017), p. 100.
[45] See McGraw and Warren, 'Benign Violations', 1141–9; and McGraw and Warner, *The Humor Code*.
[46] Ian Sansom, 'Review of Magnus Mills, *A Cruel Bird Came to the Nest and Looked In*', *Guardian*, 23 September 2011. Available online: https://www.theguardian.com/books/2011/sep/23/cruel-bird-nest-magnus-mills-review (accessed 9 July 2019).

the top of his list of favourite books,⁴⁷ and it is not hard to see why this influential work of sociology should occupy this position. *Working for Ford* draws on interviews with employees at the Ford car plant in Halewood, Merseyside, to examine the relationship between shop stewards and workers, discussing the lives of ordinary labourers in the context of an individual and a company that gave its name to a mode of industrial production and an ethos: Fordism.⁴⁸ Beynon's book speaks to Mills's approach to representing the workplace, his examination of its illogicality and paradoxes from the perspective of the put-upon worker, and the perniciousness of some forms of authority as well as the often thankless task of being in authority. Kafka is occasionally invoked as a point of comparison for Mills, and although it would be stretching the point to make too close an identification there is in Mills's work something of Kafka's nightmarish and blackly vision of modern life, as well as a shared inclination towards unnamed narrators. Kafka's 'The Great Wall of China' (1917), for example, with its unseen enemy from the north and absent, quasi-mythical emperor, surely informs the much smaller-scale constructions of *The Restraint of Beasts*, where fences are built for beasts that are never seen and whose bosses rule over their workers from a terrible distance.⁴⁹ And while Mills's debt to Kafka is most obvious in more fable-like novels such as *Three to See the King*, *Explorers of the New Century* and *A Cruel Bird Came to the Nest and Looked In*, in his representation of working environments pushed just beyond the bounds of realism, there is a similar concern with the absurdities and traps of everyday life, a combination of Kafkaesque dreamscape and Beynon-esque sociological scrutiny. Jean-Michel Rabaté's description of the comic function of abstraction in Kafka fits Mills well, and both authors' work has a tendency to reduce 'characters to marionettes, caricatures and robots that grotesquely enact ghastly and repetitive gestures', reducing them to their 'social function'.⁵⁰ In *The Scheme for Full Employment*, for example, Mills imagines a scheme that is at once absurd – employees drive vans between depots, transporting replacement parts for the same fleet of mechanically unreliable vans they are driving – and a microcosm of post-war British industrial relations. And in *The Maintenance of Headway*, a guiding principle introduced to regulate the frequency of buses becomes an insoluble paradox and a doctrinal matter for the employees of the bus company.

---

⁴⁷ Magnus Mills, 'My Favourite Books', *Guardian*, undated. Available Online: https://www.theguardian.com/books/top10s/top10/0,6109,99334,00.html (accessed 9 July 2019).
⁴⁸ Huw Beynon, *Working for Ford* (London: Allen Lane, 1973).
⁴⁹ Franz Kafka, 'The Great Wall of China', trans. Willa Muir and Edwin Muir, in *The Complete Short Stories*, ed. Nahum N. Glatzer (London: Vintage, 2005), pp. 253–66.
⁵⁰ Jean-Michel Rabaté, *Kafka L.O.L.*, Kindle edn (Macerata: Quodlibet, 2018), Chap. III.

Each of these novels evokes a working life of routine and repetition that is comic because of this repetition rather than despite it.

The Scheme for Full Employment begins with a reproduction of a route map and a 'Sample Duty' schedule for a typical day on The Scheme. A prologue strikes an elegiac tone that mourns the disintegration of this grand project, noting that 'if this had been any other country The Scheme would still be going today. In any other country it would have been regarded as a national treasure.' The narrator notes that the country's 'continental neighbours' adopted versions of The Scheme with 'unbounded success', but that it had been brought to its knees by 'us'.[51] Although the country is never named, it is clearly a version of England, and the story that unfolds is a version of post-war British industry and industrial strife, worker–boss relations and conflict over working patterns. The Scheme is predicated on circularity and repetition, a self-perpetuating system bound towards entropy. Ultimately, though, it is undermined by the human element. A conflict develops between the 'early swervers' and the 'flat dayers', with the former believing they are entitled to finish early (subject to being signed off by a lenient supervisor), and the latter believing that all employees should work their full eight-hour day. As the narrator explains, some workers build their entire working day around scheming for an early swerve: '"there's a difference between full employment and being fully employed"'.[52] Added to this is the controversy over the 'ten-off-the-eight', the ten minutes at the end of the working day that are officially allocated for locking up the vans and preparing to leave, but are in actuality seen as an entitlement to finish ten minutes early. Just before 4.20 pm every afternoon, the workers at the narrator's depot queue up to clock off, performing the same joke without fail. One of their number, Brian Tovey, clangs the bell and says '"goodnight"' as they wait impatiently for the hands to tick around and the bell to ring signalling the end of the day. Mills's typically affectless and nonplussed narrator relates these seemingly trivial controversies in detail, articulating both their farcicality and their increasing importance to elements among the workforce. As events escalate, these differences of opinion create factions with their own secret symbols: a figure 8 in a square for the flat-dayers and a 'g' with a long tail for the early-swervers (an imitation of the supervisor Gosling's signature, whose suspension for signing off early swerves is a flashpoint in the conflict). Moreover, a difference of opinion over whether the flat-dayers should claim the ten-off-the-eight causes a further split among their

---

[51] Magnus Mills, *The Scheme for Full Employment* (London: Harper Perennial, [2003] 2004), pp. v–vi.
[52] Ibid., p. 87.

number, and the utopian system of work starts to break down. The Scheme is 'on the verge of a schism'.[53]

Similarly religiose language inflects the later novel *The Maintenance of Headway*, which is in many ways a companion piece to *The Scheme for Full Employment*. Again, it is set in a workplace of routine and repetition, this time a bus garage. The unnamed narrator is a bus driver in an unnamed city that is clearly a version of London, who drives an unnamed bus route that bears a strong resemblance to the real-life number 3 bus route between Charing Cross ('the cross') and Crystal Palace ('the southern outpost'), and which includes London's busiest shopping street, Oxford Street ('the bejewelled thoroughfare').[54] A sense of repetition and circularity is emphasized from the outset, and the opening two chapters begin in precisely the same way, with an exchange between the narrator and a bus inspector, Breslin:

> 'There's no excuse for being early,' said Breslin.
>> 'No, I suppose not.'
>> 'None whatsoever.'
>> 'No.'
>> 'It is forbidden.'
>> 'Yes.'[55]

These exchanges set up the central plot point referred to in the title of the novel. Maintaining headway means to retain a fixed interval of time between buses in order to avoid the service becoming 'bunched', which would lead to multiple buses arriving at the same stop in quick succession followed by long gaps with no buses at all. What is in principle a simple idea proves to be a Sisyphean task, given the complexities of traffic and the vagaries of passengers. Nonetheless, as the narrator's colleague Edward explains, the maintenance of headway is a '"guiding principle"' of the service, '"held up as the one great truth by the Board of Transport. The officials are all indoctrinated with this central tenet. It's what they strive towards, and it's what makes men like Breslin believe they can perform miracles."'[56] As in *The Scheme for Full Employment*, there is humour in the bathetic interplay between the religiosity of the language associated with the work and the quotidian nature of the work itself: the characters invoke sacrosanct

---

[53] Ibid., p. 195.
[54] The place names in *The Maintenance of Headway* bring to mind those such as The Enchanted Ground and The Celestial City in John Bunyan's Christian allegory *The Pilgrim's Progress* (1678), a further example of the playful religious references that run through Mills's novel.
[55] Magnus Mills, *The Maintenance of Headway* (London: Bloomsbury, [2009] 2010), pp. 1, 14.
[56] Ibid., pp. 19–20.

ideology, righteousness, belief, the true path, prophesying, creed, heresy and a crusade.[57] There is also talk of a 'great schism' concerning the introduction of compulsory stops on bus routes, a link to the great schism about working hours in Mills's earlier novel. In this sense, *The Maintenance of Headway* offers a partial repetition of *The Scheme for Full Employment*, a repetition of a repetition, and throughout his work, Mills enjoys developing these echoes and allusions between books, a topic to which I will return later in this chapter. Here, the invocation of sacred language to describe mundane, secular matters is clearly introduced for comic effect, an interplay of registers as in the Martin Amis novels discussed in Chapter 2. But as with the depiction of industrial unrest in *The Scheme for Full Employment*, it also alludes to Mills's abiding concern with authority and the nature of work.

The use of religious language emphasizes Mills's preoccupation with work's centrality to human identity and behaviour, framing employment rules as a form of doctrine. Regulations that seem petty to outsiders in fact shape the manner in which persons spend the majority of their waking hours and may be adhered to or resisted with the same vehemence as religious edicts. In Mills's storyworlds, these edicts tend to be all for naught because of the messiness of the human element, and in *The Maintenance of Headway* this is articulated by Edward, the narrator's colleague and something of a sage on buses and the bus service:

> 'Buses will never change in this country,' [Edward] continued. 'They'll never get better and they'll never get worse: they'll simply remain the same forever. Oh, certain attempts have been made in the past to bring about improvements. The maintenance of headway was one such crusade, and there have been many others. Yet whatever measures are put in place, in this country they ultimately fail. True, you can calculate the movements of buses just as you can the motions of the stars and planets. What you cannot calculate, however, is the behaviour of people.'

Edward follows his speech with the question '"Shall I go on?"', to which the narrator answers '"You might as well .... Now you've started"', a verbal routine that punctuates the novel and which in this instance is followed by a litany detailing the types of people who disrupt the smooth and regular functioning of the service.[58] Edward's speech articulates many of the tensions at the centre of Mills's comedies of work, including the conflict between systems and persons and the essential stasis and repetition that abide in such systems. It is in examples

---

[57] Ibid., pp. 31, 114, 132, 133, 137, 142, 143, 150.
[58] Mills, *Maintenance*, p. 150.

such as this that the resemblance to Samuel Beckett is most marked: a linguistic repetition that signifies a systemic, even existential, stasis.

A Bergsonian reading of this repetition and circularity would emphasize its corrective nature through the representation of individuals acting in machine-like, inhuman ways;[59] on this view, laughter at repetition represents the enforcements of social norms because 'the truth is that a really living life should never repeat itself. Wherever there is repetition or complete similarity, we always suspect some mechanism at work behind the living.'[60] As Laura Salisbury puts it, it 'represents a disfiguring duration and of the human ... that should, for Bergson, be policed and corrected by laughter';[61] our laughter is the laughter of superiority intended to humiliate and enforce social norms. There is, however, a more radical interpretation that reads this comic repetition not as a way to reinforce social norms but rather as a way to undermine, or at least scrutinize, them, a possibility explored most prominently in the philosophy of Deleuze, and later in Zupančič. In *Difference and Repetition* (1968), for example, Deleuze argues that repetition is a form of 'transgression' that 'puts law into question': 'it denounces its nominal or general character in favour of a more profound and more artistic reality'.[62] Repetition overturns laws – it ascends 'upwards towards the principals' and challenges them through irony – or it descends downwards 'towards the consequences, to which one submits with a too-perfect attention to detail'. The second of these is the province of humour, which is demonstrated 'by absurdity and working to rule, but also in some forms of masochistic behaviour which mock by submission'; it is 'an art of consequences and descents, of suspensions and falls'.[63] Repetition is never identical because it is always transformed by the preceding event or series, and the very fact of repetition can therefore serve not to reinforce a particular law but rather to undermine it. Deleuze expands on these ideas in *Coldness and Cruelty* (1967), his study of Masoch, in which he describes the capacity of humour to reduce to the absurd: 'We all know ways of

---

[59] In *Machine-Age Comedy*, Michael North offers a parallel reading of Bergson's *Laughter* and Wyndham Lewis's theory of humour and laughter, developed throughout his writing career. Both rely on the identification an apparent contrast between human and machine-like behaviour, but their conclusions are radically different: 'in Lewis's case this laughter has no real corrective function, since human beings lack the power to change. Whereas for Bergson, laughter is to some extent redemptive, calling humanity back to its better, more flexible self, for Lewis, genuine, satiric laughter is bitterly tragic, since it exposes humanity's pretentions to be other than what it is'. North, *Machine-Age Comedy*, p. 118.
[60] Bergson, 'Laughter', p. 82.
[61] Laura Salisbury, *Samuel Beckett: Laughing Matters, Comic Timing* (Edinburgh: Edinburgh University Press, 2012), p. 124.
[62] Deleuze, *Difference and Repetition*, p. 3.
[63] Ibid., pp. 5–6.

twisting the law by excess of zeal. By scrupulously applying the law we are able to demonstrate its absurdity and provoke the very disorder that it is intended to prevent or to conjure.'[64] Here, the overly attentive adherence to and repetition of rules and laws is a form of mockery directed not at the subject's repetitive, mechanical behaviour but at the laws themselves. For Zupančič, whose Lacanian reading responds to and develops Deleuze's thoughts with a different emphasis, comic repetition has a similarly destabilizing effect:

> Master-Signifiers enter the scene of comedy not in order to have the last word, but in order to be repeated there (as well as subjected to other comic techniques). Their repetition is not simply their affirmation. An identical reaction (of a character) repeated ten times necessarily has its repercussions on the stability of the Master-Signifier involved. And the repercussions of this type of comic repetition usually point not in the direction of stabilizing the repeated position but, rather, in the position of shaking it.[65]

In other words, contra Bergson, comic repetition, whether Reginald Perrin's daily journey to work at Sunshine Deserts or Watt's obsessive recounting of the number of looks it takes for five committee members to make eye contact with one another, undermines the stability of received norms ('laws' in Deleuzian terminology), rendering them absurd. Neither Zupančič nor Deleuze are minded to discuss these ideas in applied terms, but in the aforementioned case of Reginald Perrin, the law in question might be the notion and desirability of a 'regular' job: Reggie is precisely eleven minutes late each day, and each day he feels bound to concoct an outlandish excuse to explain his delay.

In Mills's novels, the rules and routines of work described by his impassive narrators unfold with the absurd logic identified by Deleuze and Zupančič, and the rigid adherence to those rules has a cumulative effect that serves to expose their fragility. In *The Maintenance of Headway*, Edward describes those who follow the rules and go about their work without reflection as 'worker ants'. The narrator reasons that 'it would have suited the Board of Transport very well if all their employees were indeed worker ants'. Ultimately, though, the drivers are 'a mixed bunch', operating at such different speeds that they make the system almost impossible to regulate.[66] But that does not stop the supervisors from attempting to maintain the gold standard of consistent gaps between buses even though the efforts of one of the supervisors, Breslin, are described as '"a

---

[64] Deleuze, *Masochism*, p. 88.
[65] Zupančič, *Odd One In*, p. 177.
[66] Mils, *Maintenance*, p. 6.

form of alchemy'", doomed to fail.⁶⁷ Another supervisor, Greeves, develops his own highly convoluted method of adjustment, which involves offloading passengers and cutting out entire sections of the route to spread out the service, a strategy that puts the needs of passengers second to the overriding principle of maintaining headway. Greeves also has his own catchphrase: "'Right,'" he says, "'I'm going to adjust you and I'll tell you why'", wording he repeats each time he instructs a driver.⁶⁸ On one of these occasions, the narrator glances at his dashboard, 'where somebody had written the words I'LL TELL YOU WHY with a felt-tip pen'.⁶⁹ This phrase, 'I'll tell you why', is itself a repetition from another of Mills's favourite books, Charles Sale's *The Specialist* (1930), a monologue narrated by Lem Putt, who, in an 'age of specialization', is 'the champion privy builder of Sangamon County'. Putt, a man who takes pride in his work and describes his privies, their particular challenges and the refinements he has made to their design in comically close detail, always prefaces his advice to customers with the same phrase: "'I wouldn't do it, Elmer,'" I sez; "and I'll tell you why."'⁷⁰ But unlike Putt's expert advice about the ideal positioning of an outdoor lavatory, the advice of Greeves and the other officials is 'more likely than not to drop a spanner in the works, despite their best intentions'.⁷¹ Even Breslin, he of the refrain 'There's no excuse for being early', becomes disillusioned and admits that the maintenance of headway is 'impossible', that those who try to achieve it at all costs are 'upstarts' wishing to turn the bus routes into 'their own personal fiefdoms'.⁷² As Deleuze argues, then, in *The Maintenance of Headway*, the 'excess of zeal', the scrupulous application of laws, is enacted not in order to reinforce the law, but 'to demonstrate its absurdity and provoke the very disorder that it is intended to prevent or to conjure', shaking, in the words of Zupančič, the stability of the master-signifier by which the employers insist the workers should exist – its 'creed'. Indeed, this disruptive zeal finds parallels in forms of industrial action known in English as 'work to rule', but more pleasingly in Dutch as a 'punctuality strike' (*stiptheidsactie*),⁷³ where workers create disorder by sticking

---

⁶⁷ Ibid., p. 17.
⁶⁸ Ibid., pp. 20, 27, 125, 127.
⁶⁹ Ibid., p. 28.
⁷⁰ Charles Sale, *The Specialist* (London: Putnam and Co., 1930), pp. 9, 13, 17, 19, 22, 24. Sale's slim volume, based on his popular dramatic monologue, is an affectionate portrait of a man who is proud of the niche he has established in his working life. The author's preface to the volume describes how Putt was based on a real man who was 'just as sincere in his work as a great painter whose heart is in his canvas'.
⁷¹ Mills, *Maintenance*, p. 127.
⁷² Ibid., pp. 141–2.
⁷³ I am grateful to Matthias Somers for this reference.

rigidly to the letter of their contracts and by performing only their stipulated tasks and minimum working hours.

A similar pattern of industrial disruption develops in the more fanciful storyworld of *The Scheme for Full Employment*, although in this earlier novel, there is a stronger sense in which the machinations of the plot have an allegorical relationship with events in post-war British history and industrial relations.[74] As the conflict between flat-dayers and early-swervers escalates, the male-dominated workplace is disrupted by a new superintendent named Joyce. Joyce wastes no time in making her feelings about The Scheme clear: "'This Scheme's a complete sham,'" she tells the narrator, who replies that he sees it as the "'centrepin of [the] economic system'". "'Nonsense!'", she says:

> It's nothing more than a sideshow! A relic from some bygone age when people didn't know any better, dreamt up by do-gooders in their ivory towers. It's inefficient, expensive and wasteful, and what it needs is a thorough shake up. ... The depots should be put to proper commercial use, and the staff paid by results. Otherwise this entire outfit will go exactly the same way as all those other failed social experiments, like public transport, school dinners and municipal orchestras.[75]

As Leo Benedictus writes in his review of the novel, the 'analogy with Thatcherism ... is unavoidable',[76] and Joyce clearly represents a version of Margaret Thatcher and Thatcherite values about the value and desirability of free-market economics, a reference that is consolidated when the disputing parties request beer and sandwiches to sustain them during negotiations.[77] Benedictus is understandably sceptical of Mills's portrait of a 'glorious summer' of socialized employment

---

[74] Pettersson suggests that the 'speculative features' in *The Scheme for Full Employment* and *The Restraint of Beasts* indicate that they may take place in future versions of Britain. Pettersson, *How Literary Worlds Are Shaped*, p. 169. While I agree that *The Scheme for Full Employment* is indeed an 'allegorical fable' as Pettersson argues, it is a fable which is orientated more towards an alternative past than an imagined future.

[75] Mills, *Scheme*, p. 200.

[76] Leo Benedictus, 'Early Swerves', review of Magnus Mills, 'The Scheme for Full Employment', *London Review of Books*, 6 November 2003. Available online: https://www.lrb.co.uk/v25/n21/leo-benedictus/early-swerves (accessed 9 July 2019).

[77] In the 1970s and the 1980s, 'beer and sandwiches', a reference to the refreshments purportedly served during trade union meetings at Ten Downing Street, became emblematic of what was perceived to be an overly cosy relationship between the unions and Harold Wilson, prime minister under the Labour government that directly preceded Thatcher. Thatcher sought to break this relationship, an attitude often paraphrased with the soundbite 'No more beer and sandwiches at Number 10', though Thatcher did not phrase it in precisely those terms herself. See, for example, Margaret Thatcher, 'Speech to Conservative Party Conference', 12 October 1979. Available online: http://www.margaretthatcher.org/document/104147 (accessed 9 July 2019); and Margaret Thatcher, 'Speech to Parliamentary Press Gallery', 5 December 1979. Available online: http://www.margaretthatcher.org/document/104185 (accessed 9 July 2019).

brought to a shockingly swift halt due to the 'petty bickering, … inertia, and … stubbornness' of the workers. He views it as a simplification of period's history based on an unconvincing premise.[78] Towards the end of *The Scheme for Full Employment*, the narrator realizes that 'the future [belongs] to people like Joyce', and with seeming inevitability, an order to wind down The Scheme and sell its assets to private industry is not far behind. The signatory, Miss J. Meredith, is surely Joyce. But while there are clear parallels between the narratives of Mills's novels and the history of industrial relations in post-war Britain, and particularly the tensions between British industry and the destructive reforms of Thatcher's government, I think there is also a degree of ambivalence in the portrait. By repeating the events of this period, Mills does not so much reinforce their inevitability as emphasize their contingency. Their repetition in this allegorical form underscores the absurdities of hard-line positions on both sides – inertia and focus on pedantic details on the side of the workers, and ideology disguised as rational pragmatism on the side of the authorities – and suggests not that the triumph of market economics was inevitable but that it could always have been otherwise. Like Mills's more recent novel, *The Field of the Cloth of Gold*, which is an allegory of the settling and development of England set within the boundaries of a single field, the reduction of geopolitical forces to a human scale is suggestive of a nondeterministic model of history in which repetition emphasizes the possibility of variation.

Funny as hell: Beckett, O'Brien, Mills

As I have described throughout this chapter, comic repetition in Mills's novels inheres at the sentence level (repeated words and phrases), at the level of action (repeated events) and at the level of plot (structural parallels between texts as well as between plots and real-world events), but there is one further aspect of repetition that I would like to explore, a form of meta-repetition that links Mills's writing more closely still to that of precursors such as Beckett, and particularly to Flann O'Brien. In each of the novels discussed so far, there is the suggestion that it is not simply events that repeat themselves but also persons – persons who are part of a series and whose actions fit predefined roles. Early in *The Scheme for Full Employment*, for example, the narrator is unsettled when he sees another driver, Steve Moore, driving on an unauthorized route. He is further unsettled

---

[78] Benedictus, 'Early Swerves'.

when Steve ignores him and does not give the customary flash of his headlights or nod of recognition. Feeling snubbed, the narrator shouts '"Who does he think he is?"'[79] Later, when the narrator is himself asked to take on special duties in order to time the length of a new itinerary, it becomes clear that Steve Moore had been undertaking a similar task. Yet far from avoiding Steve's rudeness, the narrator repeats it. He begins by reciprocating the flashed headlights of his colleagues, but later comes to find 'their attentions rather irritating' because 'the vans that came plodding along on their daily round looked very ordinary, and their crews appeared hidebound and unadventurous. … Consequently, I soon stopped acknowledging oncoming vehicles, and pressed on as if I hadn't seen them.'[80] The narrator has become one of '"the chosen few"' and seems unaware that he is imitating the behaviour he found so infuriating in Steve.[81] The veneer of superiority covers his sense of comradery or fellow feeling, and later the hierarchy shifts yet again when Steve is promoted to superintendent. Now in charge of his own depot, he wastes no time asserting his authority by '"marching round checking on everything"', disrupting the previously relaxed pace enjoyed by the workers at the Eden Lacey depot.[82]

This sense of interchangeability and the replication of systems and structures of authority is also evident in *The Maintenance of Headway* in Jason's conversion from enthusiastic advocate of 'early running' to rule-enforcing inspector. At the beginning of the novel, he is described as taking an '"offensive" approach to other road users' and his first line is '"Fucking cunt"', directed at a car that gets in his way.[83] Jason's buses are usually empty as he accelerates past full bus stops to avoid the inconvenience of collecting passengers. Later, he becomes more elusive and is mentioned only in passing, before reappearing in the final pages:

> I was mildly surprised … when I reached the southern outpost and a figure appeared on the pavement, urgently flagging me down.
>   It was Jason. He was wearing the smart black uniform of a fully-fledged inspector of buses.
>   'You're early,' he said. 'Why's that?'[84]

---

[79] Mills, *Scheme*, p. 10.
[80] Ibid., pp. 109–10.
[81] Ibid., p. 106.
[82] Ibid., p. 245. Naturally, the dialogue between the narrator and Steve Moore repeats the same phrase from their earlier conversation about Steve's secondment. When the narrator asks why Steve was so secretive about his new role(s), he replies '"Didn't want to make anyone jealous, did I?"' Ibid., pp. 105, 244.
[83] Ibid., pp. 38–9.
[84] Ibid., p. 152.

In a repetition of the novel's opening lines, the narrator is warned for being early, but this time it is Jason and not Breslin doing the warning,[85] signalling Jason's move from rebel to enforcer and his integration into the system of work. Characters – persons – mould themselves to fit roles rather than the other way around, repeating the behaviour of their predecessors, however unlikely this conversion may seem. There is something mechanical about this, a suggestion that work enforces conformity through its prescribed roles and routines, and in Bergson's terminology, this is comic because it 'contrasts with the changing stream of life',[86] an idea that is taken to greater extremes in Mills's novels *All Quiet on the Orient Express* and *The Restraint of Beasts*, where the repetition of roles and events is still related to work but also contains a metaphysical element.

The plot of *All Quiet on the Orient Express* in some ways imitates that of the television drama *The Prisoner* (1967), or perhaps the more tonally similar sitcom *The League of Gentleman* (1999–2017). Both series feature characters who are trapped in fictional British villages populated by peculiar characters where shadowy schemes are underfoot; the motto on road signs for Royston Vasey, setting for *The League of Gentlemen*, reads 'Welcome to Royston Vasey – You'll Never Leave'. The narrator of *All Quiet on the Orient Express* is not subject to the same physical restraints as the unnamed man in *The Prisoner* or Benjamin Denton in *The League of Gentleman*, but his plans to journey overland to India, travelling much of the way on the railway referenced in the title, are thwarted by the series of odd jobs he is assigned by Mr Parker. Parker runs the campsite at which the narrator is staying and is the kingpin of his village. His opening line, '"I thought I'd better catch you before you go"' takes on an ominous double meaning as the narrator becomes overwhelmed with work,[87] initially with the small job of painting a fence and then with larger jobs such as painting a fleet of

---

[85] The word 'early' also brings to mind the phrase 'an early bath for Thompson', which recurs in several of Mills's novels. It first appears in *The Restraint of Beasts*, where it is the title of a (fictional) book by the (fictional) author A.D. Young, which Richie finds in the caravan and repeatedly tries and fails to read. It is then echoed in *The Maintenance of Headway*, not only in the repeated references to 'early swerves' but also in a slip of the tongue when a new recruit, Jonathan, mistakenly refers to an early swerve as an early bath. The phrase 'an early bath' has a vernacular meaning in football and refers to a player being sent off the pitch for misconduct, but in Mills it also has a more specific meaning which is only revealed in *The Maintenance of Headway*. After repeated attempts to tell the story of how a man named Thompson was unceremoniously sacked from his job, towards the end of the novel, the narrator finally succeeds in telling the story of how Thompson became so angry with the passengers on his bus that he drove it into the vehicle wash with them still inside and turned the wash on with the windows open: '"Hence the expression an early bath for Thompson."' This is a long-form joke within the novel, with a patient build-up towards the eventual payoff, and it is further enhanced with the knowledge of the even longer-form meta-joke that is taking place in tandem. Mills, *Scheme*, p. 70; Mills, *Maintenance*, p. 145.

[86] Bergson, 'Laughter', p. 119.

[87] Mills, *All Quiet*, p. 1.

rowing boats and taking on a milk delivery round and ice cream van following the death of Deakin, described earlier. Parker exerts a strange pull over the residents of the village, due in part to his famous temper that builds throughout the novel before exploding after a mix-up with the painting of the boats, a mix-up for which the narrator pays with the vintage motorbike that was his only means of escape.[88] For all of the humour in the narrator's tribulations with Parker and the residents of the village, including his period of exile from his favoured pub due to a no-show at a darts match, there is also a nightmarish quality to his predicament and a sense that his work there is part of an unchanging and predetermined plan. A short time into his extended stay at the farm, the narrator realizes that he has 'inadvertently become [Parker's] servant' and that his waking hours are now spent working at his whim for uncertain remuneration.[89] The narrator's only leisure time involves dashing to the Packhorse pub for a few pints before closing. There is also mention of the 'other lad' who used to work for Parker, and who turns up again at the end of the novel. A set of parallels with Deakin, whose path he is perhaps fated to follow,[90] begin to develop, and there is a strong suggestion that the narrator is the latest in a line of such visitors. This sense is reinforced when he sees half-a-dozen motorcycles lined up in Parker's shed – confiscated from his predecessors, perhaps – and when he plays darts with Parker's daughter Gail in the hay loft. She tells him she has done this '"Loads of times"' before, including with Marco, '"the one who was here before you"'.[91] As with the livestock metaphors in *The Restraint of Beasts*, Marco, Deakin and the narrator are referred to in depersonalized terms, emphasizing a sense of seriality and interchangeability. Drawing on Deleuze, J. Hillis, Miller distinguishes between two distinct forms of repetition, the Platonic, which 'is grounded in a solid archetypal model and is untouched by the effects of repetition', and the Nietzschean, which 'posits a world based on difference' in which things are 'unique, intrinsically different from every other thing'. The latter form is not grounded 'in some paradigm or archetype', and there is therefore 'something ghostly' and unsettling about its effects.[92] Miller does not make an absolute distinction between these two forms of repetition and goes on to discuss how each inheres in the other, but in this example from Mills it is the Nietzschean

---

[88] At one point the narrator does leave the village, only to be hampered by a deluge of rain that floods the engine of his motorbike. The rain clears almost the instant he returns to Parker's farm, suggesting even the natural environment is conspiring against him.
[89] Mills, *All Quiet*, p. 63.
[90] Ibid., pp. 99, 154.
[91] Ibid., pp. 145, 241–2.
[92] J. Hillis Miller, *Fiction and Repetition: Seven English Novels* (Oxford: Basil Blackwell, 1982), p. 6.

form that dominates. The eerie repetitions and near-repetitions of *All Quiet on the Orient Express* are unsettling as well as funny because they do not provide a clear origin, explanation or stable ground, and the narrator of the novel is haunted by a largely unnamed series of precursors whose roles and actions he is compelled to repeat.

These patterns of repetition and interchangeability operate across Mills's fiction and are part of what makes his work recognizably Millsian. This is not, however, to imply that Mills is sui generis, and his novels can be viewed as embodying repetition in one further, intertextual sense, something that is particularly evident in his engagement with two acknowledged influences, Samuel Beckett and Flann O'Brien. The pattern of repetition and entrapment in *All Quiet on the Orient Express* owes something to O'Brien's hell of eternal circularity, discussed later, but also to Beckett's *Watt* and what Steven Connor refers to as the novel's 'infinitely renewable' acts of repetition.[93] In Beckett's novel, Watt travels to the house of Mr Knott, who becomes his master. He is greeted at the house by Arsene, the outgoing servant. Arsene explains the order and sequence of servants who preceded him, a sequence of which it is implied Watt has become a part, and which will continue after him:

> There were three men in the house: the master, whom as well you know we call Mr Knott; a senior retainer named Vincent, I believe; and a junior, only in the sense that he was of more recent acquisition, named, if I am not mistaken, Walter. The first is here, in his bed, or at least in his room. But the second, I mean Vincent, is not here anymore, and the reason for that is this, that when I came in he went out, just as Vincent went out when I came in. And I, I mean Arsene, am not here any more either, and the reason for that is this, that when you came in I went out, just as when I came in Vincent went out and as Walter went out when Erskine came in.[94]

As Arsene puts it a little later in his monologue: 'the coming is in the shadow of the going and the going is in the shadow of the coming, that is the annoying part about it'. The only one who 'neither comes nor goes' is Mr Knott, the master.[95] As this brief passage illustrates, the language of *Watt* is more obsessively recursive than any found in Mills, but there are nevertheless strong echoes of

---

[93] Steven Connor, *Samuel Beckett: Repetition, Theory and Text*, rev edn (Aurora, CO: Davies Group, 2007), p. 35.
[94] Samuel Beckett, *Watt* (New York: Grove Press, [1953] 1994), p. 56.
[95] Ibid., p. 57. Knott's position may not, however, be as stable as it appears to Arsene, because in the Addenda to the novel, Arthur the gardener mentions the Knott *family*, leading Watt to realize that 'Mr Knott too was serial', perhaps part of an even larger sequence unknown to Watt and the other characters. Ibid., p. 253.

Beckettian repetition in *All Quiet on the Orient Express*'s description of a cycle of interchangeable workers around a still centre of authority. In both texts, this determinism is comic in its evocation of Bergsonian, machine-like passivity and unquestioning servility, but also Deleuzian in its scrupulous conformity to a predetermined hierarchy. Mr Knott in *Watt* and Mr Parker in *All Quiet on the Orient Express* are the stable centres, the sources of power and authority, while those around them are interchangeable, drone-like workers whose absolute subservience – masochism in the Deleuzian sense – is comic but also revealing of the underlying *doxa* of the boss-worker relationship and, in its most extreme form, even its hellishness. Like Watt, whose passivity 'allows him to bear the well-nigh intolerable intensity of ratiocination that is his life in Mr Knott's house',[96] the narrator of *All Quiet on the Orient Express* is resigned to his fate as one of a series, an interchangeable part of a pre-existing system that will continue after he has gone. It is only at the close of the novel that he – possibly – contemplates taking action, and it is not against his boss Mr Parker, but rather against the interloper Marco, who threatens to usurp him from his position. The final paragraph of the novel reads: 'I glanced towards the bothy, where Marco lay sleeping behind drawn curtains. Then I started the concrete mixer, and prepared a length of galvanized chain.'[97] Galvanized chain and concrete are constituent parts for a mooring buoy anchor, the implication being that Marco will meet the same fate as Deakin, who was dragged to the bottom of the lake and drowned. The narrator seeks not to resist Mr Parker but rather to defend his own lowly position in the hierarchy.

The murderous coda to *All Quiet on the Orient Express* is typical of Mills's noirish sensibility and the amoral worldviews of his trapped narrators, but in *The Restraint of Beasts*, he pushes the situation of his narrator further, implying that the novel might be set in a kind of hell. In this there are strong parallels with O'Brien's *The Third Policeman* (1967), a book Mills describes as having changed his life.[98] O'Brien wrote in a well-known letter of 1940 that *The Third Policeman* is set in 'a sort of hell' to which the main character has been consigned for murder; he is condemned to repeat the 'same terrible adventures' as if it were the first time. 'It is supposed to be very funny', O'Brien continues: when 'you are writing about the world of the dead – and the damned – where none of the rules and laws … holds good, there is any amount of scope for back-chat and funny cracks'.[99]

---

[96] Connor, *Samuel Beckett*, p. 189.
[97] Mills, *All Quiet*, p. 312.
[98] Mills, 'My Favourite Books'; and Mills, 'Small Talk'.
[99] Flann O'Brien, *The Third Policeman* (London: Harper Perennial, [1967] 2007), p. 207.

Elsewhere, he writes that 'Hell goes round and round. In shape it is circular and by nature it is interminable, repetitive and very nearly unendurable.'[100] On this view, hell is repetition and repetition is hell, but crucially, this hellish repetition is also *comic*. As we have seen, comic repetition is crucial to Mills's writing in several senses, and in these concluding paragraphs, I want to suggest that there is a further way in which repetition inheres in Mills's fiction and that it is linked to these hints from O'Brien.

After his prolonged sojourn in England, the narrator of *The Restraint of Beasts* returns to Scotland where he, Tam and Ritchie take stock of their fencing equipment: '"Right," I said when they'd finished [smoking]. "We'd better have a go at sorting out all this gear."' He describes the generally poor state of the equipment while Tam and Richie look on. They are finally spurred into action when Donald arrives, and begin tidying and returning their tools to the storeroom. The scene ends with Donald telling the three of them that they should take more care of their equipment but that they will have to leave it for the moment as he has received a '"serious phone call"' and needs to speak with them in his office.[101] This scene is unremarkable in itself, but it is notable that it is an exact repetition of a scene that took place some 150 pages earlier when the narrator first met Tam and Richie. Eight paragraphs, totalling more than 350 words are repeated verbatim, and as in the first iteration, the trio are taken into Donald's office to be reprimanded. On the first occasion, it had been Tam and Ritchie who were disciplined for allowing Mr McCrindle's fence to go slack, but on this second occasion, the narrator is also in trouble for the team's failure to keep Donald updated while they were away in England. Donald complains that their sudden return was '"like the retreat from Moscow"', repeating a line spoken by Mr Perkins shortly before he was fatally struck by a fence post,[102] and ultimately the narrator reflects that the 'post of foreman brought no benefits, only problems' and that 'it was beginning to seem like some sort of purgatory'.[103] His invocation of purgatory, combined with the repetition of the preceding passage, is one of several suggestions that that there may be a meta-plot at work, of which the narrator, like O'Brien's narrator, is unaware. When Donald later tells the narrator '"I don't ever expect you to leave"', he reflects that this is 'very

---

[100] Ibid.
[101] Mills, *Restraint*, pp. 153–4.
[102] Mills, *All Quiet*, p. 156. See Ibid., p. 120 for Mr Perkins' use of the same line.
[103] Ibid., p. 157. The narrator's disillusionment with his job as foreman finds a parallel in the example of the workers interviewed for Beynon's *Working for Ford*, discussed earlier, who 'were seen to suffer the abuses of management and the isolation of being between the firm and the lads'. Beynon, *Working for Ford*, p. 125.

reassuring',[104] ignoring the much darker undertone.[105] 'Welcome to Royston Vasey – You'll Never Leave'.

This sense of purgatorial repetition is heightened in final lines of *The Restraint of Beasts*, where the narrator finds himself being interrogated not by Donald but by Mr Hall, for whom he, Tam and Richie are building a series of suspiciously large holding pens. The scene is described in much the same terms as Donald's interrogations, and Mr Hall lists the '"trail of disappointed people"' they have left in their wake. When the narrator asks to which people he is referring, Mr Hall replies with the final line of the novel: '"Well … . Let's start with Mr McCrindle"'.[106] This phrase circles the story back round to the beginning, Donald's admonishment of Tam and Richie for Mr McCrindle's slack fence and Mr McCrindle's subsequent death. It is plainly also a reference to *The Third Policeman*, which concludes with the line '"Is it about a bicycle?"', repeating the question asked of the narrator when he enters the police station some one hundred pages earlier.[107] In both novels, the loop is closed at the end, suggesting their narrators are trapped in a repeating cycle. As Joseph Brooker identifies, the circularity of O'Brien's novel and of his imagined hell are neither perfect nor wholly consistent, an inconsistency that is 'perversely in keeping with the unfathomability of much that we encounter within it',[108] and this is a summary that could equally be applied to *The Restraint of Beasts*. The hellish, or at least purgatorial, repetition implied at the end of Mills's novel is not a perfect repetition of the events that have preceded it, but rather the narrator's final integration into a system of work and existence for which there is no end in sight. Bergson's formulation on laughter is useful here for his assertion that 'really living life should never repeat itself. Wherever there is repetition or complete similarity, we always suspect some mechanism at work behind the living.'[109] The mechanism at work in *The Third Policeman* is metaphysical and is related to damnation, and in *The Restraint of Beasts*, as with the other Mills novels discussed in this chapter, it is related to structures of authority and the repetitions of human labour. There is something hellish about the compulsive

---

[104] Mills, *All Quiet*, p. 169.
[105] Theo Tait notes a further parallel with Paul Auster's *The Music of Chance*, in which two characters are forced to build a stone wall in the middle of a field in order to pay a gambling debt they owe to a sinister and eccentric pair of millionaires. Like Mills's and O'Brien's novels, there is an absurdist element to the novel's repetitions and ellipses, but it is largely without their humour. Tait, 'First One, Then Another'.
[106] Mills, *Restraint*, p. 215.
[107] O'Brien, *Third Policeman*.
[108] Joseph Brooker, *Flann O'Brien* (Tavistock: Northcote House, 2004), pp. 51–2.
[109] Bergson, 'Laughter', p. 82.

repetitions of the narrator, Tam and Richie and of the hold that Donald and later Mr Hall have over them, but there is also something deeply comic and deeply human about it. Bergson's 'something mechanical encrusted on the living' goes some way to explaining this, but the effect is not corrective in the Bergsonian sense. Rather, Mills's novels of work are concerned with repetition as a method of reducing to the absurd.[110] In contrast to the Bergsonian opposition between the mechanical and the vital, they engage with what Zupančič refers to as the 'mutual implication' of automatism and the human spirit, or what Graham Matthews summarizes as the 'ways in which the mechanical is intrinsic to life and life embedded in the mechanical'.[111] The novels of Magnus Mill demonstrate the deep affinity between comedy and repetition at a structural, linguistic and thematic level. They develop comic capital from situations not far removed from reality, suggesting an existential dimension to their characters' entrapment in work, reproducing work's repetitions and structures of power not to affirm them nor precisely to dismantle them – this would be to overstate the possibilities of the comic – but to shake them, to expose their absurdities and to identify the comic possibilities within the quotidian.

---

[110] As Neil Cornwell has noted, repetition and the absurd are closely linked in the work of Kierkegaard, Nietzsche and others. Cornwell, *The Absurd in Literature*, p. 7.

[111] Zupančič, *The Odd One In*, pp. 120–1; Graham Matthews, *Ethics and Desire in the Wake of Postmodernism: Contemporary Satire* (London: Bloomsbury, 2012), p. 22. See also Dolar, 'The Comic Mimesis', p. 586.

5

'Simple high jinks'?
Nicola Barker and the comedy of paradox

During her 2017 Goldsmiths Prize interview, Nicola Barker described her 'great fascination' with paradox and contradiction in life and art, and how she sees these as the 'abiding themes' of her work. Specifically, she spoke about 'suffering and happiness' and how they are 'interwoven': 'you can't divide the two'.[1] This interest in seemingly paradoxical states exists in her fiction in parallel with a commitment to the comic in its many forms. Angela Carter and Martin Amis have been identified by critics and acknowledged by the author as strong influences on her comic style,[2] and Dickens is frequently identified as a more distant ancestor.[3] Like these precursors, Barker does not write books that can be neatly classified as 'comic novels', a category that, as I discuss in the Introduction, carries its own luridly coloured set of baggage, but from the earliest stories to the mordantly comic *H(A)PPY* (2017), Barker's fiction is funny: intentionally funny, and often wildly, exuberantly so.[4] Yet the fact that these novels are funny is more often than not passed over in discussions of her work, identified as a feature of

---

[1] Nicola Barker, 'The Goldsmiths Writers' Centre Presents Nicola Barker', interview at Goldsmiths, University of London, 24 January 2018.

[2] Susanna Rustin, 'A Life in Writing: Nicola Barker', *Guardian*, 1 May 2010. Available online: https://www.theguardian.com/books/2010/may/01/nicola-barker-life-in-writing (accessed 13 June 2019). Amis and Carter are mentioned on consecutive pages in Barker's novel *Reversed Forecast* (1994) via a passing reference to Amis's novel *Dead Babies* (1975) and a more sustained discussion of Carter's gender politics. Nicola Barker, *Reversed Forecast* (London: Faber and Faber, [1994] 1995), pp. 72–5.

[3] See, for example, Victor Sage, 'The Ambivalence of Laughter: The Development of Nicola Barker's Grotesque Realism', *Review of Contemporary Fiction*, 32:3 (2012), 87–97.

[4] Paul Dawson reads *Darkmans* (2007) as an example of 'pyrotechnic storytelling', which is 'typically humorous or satirical, employing a flourishing and expansive narrative voice, a garrulous conversational tone, to assert control over the events being narrated, eschewing the impersonality of analytic omniscience to the extent that the narrative voice often overshadows the characters being described or analysed'. This usefully encapsulates Barker's style and could apply to much of her fiction. See Paul Dawson, *The Return of the Omniscient Narrator* (Columbus, OH: Ohio State University Press, 2013), pp. 111–35. Richard Bradford has referred to Barker's 'flat unobtrusive prose' in the early stories, but her writing has become increasingly baroque, a change that is most starkly evident in the typographic experiments of *H(A)PPY*. See Richard Bradford, *The Novel Now* (Oxford: Blackwell, 2007), p. 55.

the writing but itself not a topic of sustained analysis. Comedy and humour are at the core of Barker's writing, and paradox and contradiction are at the core of her comic voice. They also play a central role in the comic mode more generally: paradox and contradiction are generative of comedy and this generative function is one of the reasons for the political and affective complexity of humour and comedy in general, as well as in Barker's fiction specifically.

Drawing upon and extending discussions from previous chapters about the politics of comedy and laughter (Coe, Amis and Smith) and humour's mutable and highly situational nature, this chapter discusses paradoxes and contradictions in Barker's fiction, focusing on a series of oppositions: first, on incongruity as a category of comedy that relies on ambiguity and paradoxical juxtapositioning; second, on the competing claims for political progressiveness versus conservatism found in the categories of the grotesque and the carnivalesque; and finally, on the relationship between Umberto Eco's categories of comedy and humour, as well as the roles of irony and sincerity, two modes that are often held in opposition to one another and that have become touchstones for debates about the relationship between postmodernism and what has come after. I begin with a discussion of *Burley Cross Postbox Theft* (2010) and *The Cauliflower*® (2016), before moving backwards to trace a line from Barker's earliest stories and novels (the work that speaks most directly to the aesthetic of the grotesque) to her most recent novels and the growing prominence of ideas of forgiveness and redemption. Throughout each period of her writing, Barker has maintained a commitment to the comic and an interest in states of paradox and contradiction; but more than this, these aspects of her work are interdependent: comedy both relies on and allows for paradox and contradiction and is perhaps the mode best placed to explore the paradox, contradiction and messiness of life.

Pooterism, pedantry and the logic of the absurd: Incongruity as comic practice

As I have already noted, Barker's novels resist easy classification as 'comic fiction', but it is also true to say that the farcical elements and prevailing lightness of tone in *Burley Cross Postbox Theft* bring it closest to what might be termed an out-and-out comic novel. It is here that that I will begin this discussion. *Burley Cross* depicts a particular type of eccentricity that is at once petty, Pooterish and, just beneath the surface, deeply weird. It is an epistolary novel, organized via the conceit that the eponymous post box, located in the fictional Yorkshire village of Burley Cross, has been burgled – its contents stolen and later recovered. The break-in is under investigation by local police, and the recovered letters are catalogued and presented as items of evidence. The opening letter is a memo from Sergeant Laurence Everill of Skipton Police, forwarding the evidence and passing responsibility for this 'savage, top-dollar dominatrix' of a case to his more junior colleague PC Roger Topping in nearby Ilkley.[5] Letters from local residents form the majority of the novel and are bookended by Everill's memo and concluding correspondence from Topping. The opening letter acknowledges that the volume of the recovered correspondence is unusual in these 'text and email-friendly times',[6] an oddity that requires a series of artful explanations including a particularly attractive Post Office worker, Nina Springhill, whose presence attracts admirers to her counter, and a computer virus that makes emailing temporarily impossible. The novel's setting in 2006 – on the cusp of the takeover of digital communication in Britain and the corresponding steep decline in conventional mail[7] – means that the conceit is not entirely implausible, but plausibility is not the organizing principle; rather, the epistolary form allows Barker to imagine the public and private personae of the residents of this fictional village, to expose their contradictions and deceits, and to reveal the hidden depths of marginalized individuals.

The adjective 'Pooterish' comes of course from George and Weedon Grossmith's *The Diary of a Nobody* (1892), and evokes a particularly self-important and provincial worldview concerned with minutiae and the quotidian rather than more elevated matters. Pooterism is apparent *avant la lettre* in characters such Samuel Pickwick in Dickens's *The Pickwick Papers* (1836) or the title characters in Flaubert's *Bouvard and Pécuchet* (1881), and subsequently in characters such Alan Partridge, Adrian Mole and Henry Farr in Nigel Williams's *The Wimbledon Poisoner* (1990), as well as directly in Keith Waterhouse's 1983 novel *Mrs Pooter's Diary*, which reimages the events of *Diary of a Nobody* from the perspective of Pooter's long-suffering wife Carrie. A unifying trait of these characters, and one from which Barker wrings a good deal of comic potential

---

[5] Nicola Barker, *Burley Cross Postbox Theft* (London: Fourth Estate, 2010), p. 4.
[6] Barker, *Burley Cross*, p. 20. Although postal correspondence is in decline, the use of the epistolary form in contemporary fiction is surprisingly common. Katharine Wilkinson explores the meaning and significance of this phenomenon in her doctoral research on 'The Persistence of Letters in Contemporary Fiction' (PhD, Queen Mary University of London, 2019).
[7] Statistics collected by the Royal Mail show that the total letters delivered annually in the UK peaked in 2004–2005 at over 20 billion. This figure dropped off sharply from 2006 onwards (Postal Museum, 2011). See Postal Museum website, 'Post Office Statistics: #11. Letters Delivered by the Royal Mail, 1920–2010', 2011. Available online: https://www.postalmuseum.org/discover/collections/statistics/ (accessed 22 February 2019).

in *Burley Cross*, is their tendency towards literal-mindedness and pedantry, as in Pooter's extended correspondence with *The Blackfriars Bi-weekly News* about the misspelling of his name among a lengthy list of attendees at a reception. According to the philosopher Agnes Heller, pedantry is one of the 'ten main vices' of comic drama, punishable by 'public laughter',[8] and the pedant is the butt of many jokes in *Burley Cross*, not least in Letter 1, from Burley Cross resident Jeremy Baverstock to Ms Linda Withycombe, an Environmental Health Technician at the local council. The letter, first published as 'For the Exclusive Attn of Ms Linda Withycombe' in *Granta* in 2009, details Baverstock's campaigning on a number of local issues, most prominently those *bêtes noires* of local politics: planning permission and dog fouling. It includes precisely one hundred footnotes and is a comic extrapolation the type of Nimbyism (Not-in-my-back-yard-ism) recognizable from local newspapers and single-issue campaign groups, which elevates grudges and self-interest to the level of life-or-death importance. As I have written elsewhere in relation to Barker's fiction, Nimbys are not unambiguously reactionary or self-interested,[9] but Baverstock is afforded less latitude than Beede in *Darkmans* (2007), another amateur historian and campaigner on local issues who is altogether more sympathetically portrayed.[10] Baverstock is particularly vociferous in sharing his opinions about 'Mrs Tirza Parry, widow', as she signs herself (occasionally misspelled as 'Mrs Tirza Parry, wi*n*dow', a mistake Baverstock is delighted to note).[11] His campaign centres on dog faeces and on Parry's habit of bagging up the mess left by other people's dogs and leaving the bags 'deposited on walls, branches and fence posts – apparently as a warning/admonishment to others less responsible than herself'. Baverstock takes against these 'bizarre activities' and, in his letter to Withycombe, refers at length to 'The Dogs Fouling Land Act, 1996' and the EnCams (now Keep Britain Tidy) leaflet *Dog Fouling and the Law*,[12] noting that he owns 'several copies of this useful booklet'. He also offers commentary on the '"signature"' bag used by Parry, and includes copious evidence, fastidiously

---

[8] Heller, *Immortal Comedy*, pp. 43, 190.
[9] See Huw Marsh, 'Nicola Barker's *Darkmans* and the "Vengeful Tsunami of History"', *Literary London*, 7:2 (2010). Available online: http://www.literarylondon.org/london-journal/september2009/marsh.html (accessed 29 January 2019).
[10] In this sense, Barker's cutting portrayal of Baverstock contrasts with the Grossmiths' Pooter, who is ultimately benign and well-intentioned. As Glen Cavaliero notes, Pooter is 'a good man, to be laughed with rather than laughed at'. Cavaliero, *The Alchemy of Laughter*, pp. 40–1.
[11] Barker, *Burley Cross*, p. 24.
[12] One of the delights of researching Barker's novels is that one finds oneself following in the author's footsteps like a behindling from the later Barker novel *Behindlings* (2002), searching for out-of-print pamphlets on dog fouling or similarly arcane topics, wondering if the documents quoted in the novel are genuine. The answer, as here, is usually 'yes'.

parenthesized and footnoted, relating to the context for the dispute and any earlier correspondence.[13] Baverstock's investigations culminate in the accusation that rather than collecting other dog owners' waste, Parry is in fact collecting her *own* dogs' excrement from her yard and liberally distributing it about the countryside. He speculates that this behaviour may be related to a sexual impulse or a grudge arising from an unresolved trauma, or perhaps, as his wife Shoshana suggests, drawing on knowledge gained during an abandoned correspondence course in child psychology, it is due to '"issues" during [Parry's] anal phase brought on by an overly strict and prohibitive potty-training regimen'. A series of minor local disputes and annoyances become, in Baverstock's telling, 'a complex web of problems',[14] and his pedantry is, as Heller suggests, punishable through laughter. It is not that Baverstock is portrayed as particularly malign, but it is clear that his concerns are misdirected and their scale out of proportion.

For Henri Bergson, pedantry 'is nothing else than art pretending to outdo nature', and as such represents a 'mechanical element introduced into nature'.[15] Using examples of pedantic debate from Molière's *Le Médecin malgré lui* (1666) and *Monsieur de Pourceaugnac* (1669), as well an anecdote about a philosopher who shut down a debate with the statement '"Experience is in the wrong"', Bergson suggests that pedantry represents what for him is the essential element of the comic, most famously expressed as '*something mechanical encrusted on the living*'.[16] As was discussed in more detail in the previous chapter in relation to Magnus Mills's novels, when humans act in machine-like or non-vital ways, they tip over into the realm of the comic, and the resulting laughter has a social, corrective function, encouraging them to step in line with collective norms. Bergson's formulation is an example of a superiority theory, the oldest theory of humour, traceable to Plato and Aristotle, and Baverstock's pseudo-scholarly pursuit of his own wild theories at the expense of common sense certainly speaks to Bergson's views on pedantry and corrective laughter. There is more than a degree of superiority in the laughter inspired by Baverstock's behaviour, and who could fail to raise a smile at the final (one-hundredth) footnote in his letter, where he hints at a shadowy conspiracy theory involving the Royal Horticultural Society? His book on the organization was, he claims, denied a publisher by a

---

[13] Barker, *Burley Cross*, pp. 30–3.
[14] Ibid., pp. 43–4.
[15] Bergson, 'Laughter', pp. 61–190 (pp. 91, 90).
[16] Ibid., p. 84.

cabal of high-profile figures including 'the Duchess of Windsor, Peter Sissons, and that queer little chap who owns Sainsbury – or possibly ASDA'.[17]

Yet viewed from another perspective, the pedantry of Baverstock and other characters in the *Burley Cross* correspondence could be read as an example not of superiority – or not only of superiority – but also of another, more modern account of humour: incongruity. This theory found its first expression in Immanuel Kant's *Critique of Judgement* (1790) and later, and of more relevance here, in Arthur Schopenhauer's *The World as Will and Representation* (1818–1819).[18] Incongruity theories posit that humour arises from the pleasing juxtaposition of seemingly incompatible concepts, as in the Simon Munnery one-liner 'Clowns divorce. Custardy battle', which brings together frivolity and gravity in one beautifully condensed and evocative joke.[19] Schopenhauer's particular version of the theory focuses on the difference between abstract ideas and lived reality, the juxtaposition of which is comic, or ludicrous as Schopenhauer prefers to call it, when ideas and reason are favoured over experience. An example would be the old joke about a driver stopped for speeding, who explains to the police officer that they are hurrying home because their brakes are faulty (to labour the point: abstract idea = 'less time on the road means less chance of an accident'; lived reality = 'speeding with faulty brakes means greater chance of a serious accident'). Schopenhauer is unintentionally comic in his own way, not least for his insistence in Volume 1 of *The World as Will* that his ideas are so self-evident that he does not need to provide examples, only to revisit the topic in Volume 2 with examples to satisfy the 'mental inertness' of his readers,[20] but his thoughts on pedantry as a form of incongruity are of particular value here. For Schopenhauer, pedantry is a type of folly arising 'from a man's having little confidence in his own understanding, and therefore not liking to leave things to its discretion, to recognize directly what is right in the particular case'. The pedant 'puts his [sic] understanding entirely under the guardianship of his reason' and therefore 'shows himself [sic] foolish, absurd and incompetent'.[21] In the case of Baverstock, this consists of twisting the fruits of his 'investigation' into ever more contorted shapes in order to portray Tirza Parry as a Machiavellian dog-shit distributor, or the Royal Horticultural Society as a low-rent Illuminati intent

---

[17] Barker, *Burley Cross*, p. 45.
[18] For useful summaries of the dominant theories of humour and laughter – superiority, relief and incongruity – see, for example, John Morreall, *Comic Relief: A Comprehensive Philosophy of Humour* (Chichester: Wiley-Blackwell, 2009).
[19] Simon Munnery, *And Nothing But* [Stand-up Comedy DVD] (UK: Go Faster Stripe, 2015).
[20] Arthur Schopenhauer, *The World as Will and Representation* [1818–19], trans. E.F.J. Payne, 2 vols (New York: Dover, 2000), ii, p. 92.
[21] Schopenhauer, *World as Will*, i, p. 60.

on suppressing the publication of his damning exposé. The humour in *Burley Cross*, then, demonstrates both Bergsonian superiority and Schopenhauerian incongruity in its depiction of Baverstock's pedantry; but wherever one places the emphasis, the judgement is clear: he is a harmless fool who is deserving of ridicule. The same is true for other characters in the novel, such as the translator, Rosannah Strum-Tadcastle, whose interventionist approach to translating one of the recovered letters from French into English overwhelms the text she is meant to be translating. There is something of Charles Kinbote from Vladimir Nabokov's *Pale Fire* (1962) in Strum-Tadcastle's focus on personal concerns at the expense of the work she is paid to perform. Her limitations as a translator are further emphasized by the fact that her heavily annotated translation of the letter is preceded by a version rendered into fluent and seemingly accurate vernacular English, heightening the incongruity between false reasoning and observable actuality.

Incongruity theory can, then, help to account for the humour in Barker's invocation of paradoxical states, but what I want to argue here is not simply that incongruity *explains* humour in Barker's fiction, but rather that humour – the comic voice – is uniquely suited to the exploration of opposites that is central to much comic writing and evident throughout Barker's work: that it *allows* it. At the heart of what Jerry Palmer terms comedy's 'logic of the absurd' is a propensity towards contradiction and the interplay of seemingly incompatible states that are 'simultaneously highly implausible and just a little bit plausible'.[22] The creation of plausible implausibility – or logical illogic – is part of how comedy functions at a structural level, and this structural propensity lends itself to the exploration of the incompatible elements that are a thematic and formal feature of Barker's work. At one point in *The Cauliflower**, for example, the narrator asks 'Is this book a farce, a comedy, a tragedy or a melodrama?'[23] It is all these things, and the point is that it does not ask us to choose between them. The novel explores the life of the nineteenth-century mystic Sri Ramakrishna, who remains enigmatic throughout – a combination of clown and guru. In the Western tradition, there are parallels with the figure of the wise or holy fool, who is free from the constraints of ordinary citizens and may be gross, and in some ways even stupid, but nonetheless has access to higher wisdom. As T.G.A. Nelson writes, in contrast to

---

[22] Palmer, *Taking Humour Seriously*, p. 96. For Palmer, jokes work via a bipartite structure, consisting of: '1. the sudden creation of a discrepancy, or incongruity, in the joke narrative; 2. a bifurcated process, which leads the listener to judge that the state of affairs portrayed is simultaneously highly implausible and just a little bit plausible.' Ibid. And for an earlier, more detailed description of Palmer's semiotic model, see Palmer, *The Logic of the Absurd*.

[23] Nicola Barker, *The Cauliflower** (London: William Heinemann, 2016), p. 126.

the merely foolish or idiotic character, 'there are many characteristics we would like to appropriate' from the wise or holy fool, and their '*angst* is one which we all experience from time to time'.[24] For Maurice Charney, the role of this figure can be yet more profound as they are able to act as a conduit for the divine: the gods may 'speak through their appointed fool, who is a mouthpiece for their dark and inscrutable wisdom, and who may actually be privy to their secrets'.[25] This comic figure embodies a series of oppositions between profundity and idiocy, spiritual otherworldliness and slapstick corporality, and without wishing to collapse the distinction between the Western tradition identified by Nelson and Charney and the Hindu tradition depicted in Barker's novel, there is a good deal of the holy fool in Barker's representation of Sri Ramakrishna, whose playfulness, comic pratfalls and otherworldly naivety are part of his method as a guru and figure of reverence. 'We were trained by him', a disciple, Narendra, recalls in one of the novel's many haiku, 'Without even knowing it – / Just through fun and games!',[26] and for every moment of more solemn profundity, there is a moment of absurdist bafflement or slapstick. 'A Chapter of Accidents', for example, lists a catalogue of pratfalls and comic scrapes caused by the unexpected onset of spiritual ecstasy, causing Sri Ramakrishna to topple over or go 'missing in action', only to be found oblivious, feet cut to ribbons, meditating under a thorny tree or tangled in a rosebush.[27] These moments are richly comic in the tradition of the otherworldly or naïve fool, but they are also examples of a profound faith that is all-consuming and overwhelming to the degree that, read another way, it could be considered damaging. The Chapter of Accidents is followed by another haiku: 'We call it a gift … / But when you think about it, / Isn't it a curse?',[28] suggesting the delicate balance between Sri Ramakrishna's gifts and the penalty he must pay for enlightenment. This relationship between gift and curse – the curse disguised as gift – is a common feature of tragedy and myth, but in Barker's rendering, it is part of the very human comedy of conflict and contradiction in which even the spiritually gifted fail, and fail again. To shift the emphasis again, one of the guru's

---

[24] T.G.A. Nelson, *Comedy: An Introduction to Comedy in Literature, Drama, and Cinema* (Oxford: Oxford University Press, 1990), p. 122. Jerry Palmer notes a further distinction, made by the medieval Christian church, between 'artificial' fools, who performed their foolishness in order to amuse, and 'natural' fools, who were genuinely mentally impaired or foolish in other ways. 'The positive senses of folly all derive from the concept of the natural fool', Palmer writes: 'a natural fool could be a holy innocent, or could inadvertently reveal the folly of the apparently wise, but the artificial fool was, for the Church, not to be condoned.' In Barker's telling, Sri Ramakrishna is firmly in the category of the natural fool. See Palmer, *Taking Humour Seriously*, p. 43.
[25] Charney, *Comedy High and Low*, pp. 173–4.
[26] Barker, *Cauliflower*, p. 185.
[27] Ibid., pp. 208–10.
[28] Ibid., p. 211.

grave regrets is the bathetic observation that his sudden trances prevent him from reaching the giraffe enclosure on visits to the zoo 'because the lion always brings to his mind the image of the goddess Durga', inducing a bout of ecstasy that curtails the trip.[29] Here, Barker's writing relies on a series of incongruities (wise manifestation of god on earth/childlike enjoyer of daytrip to the zoo; modest desire to see giraffes/godly intervention; gift of connection to God/curse of interference in everyday life). Importantly, however, these incongruities are not seen as incompatible or as problems to be overcome, but as of a piece, as representative of life's paradoxes and contradictions. *The Cauliflower®* constantly seesaws between moments of high comedy and a more conventionally serious tone, and even the guru's funeral has 'an atmosphere of farce about it'.[30] What this allows, and what tragedy, for example, is less able to articulate, is the suspension of opposites, or what Italo Calvino describes as comedy's ability to offer 'a way to escape from the limitations and one-sidedness of every representation and every judgement'.[31] In some ways, comedy is a binary form (it is either funny at the point of reception or not), but with the exception of some forms of satiric or didactic comedy, it is able to able to juxtapose opposites without hierarchy. In fact, it relies on this juxtaposition: both elements of the incongruity are mutually reliant and necessary, and there is no obvious division between vehicle and tenor.

According to the fictional letter from Laura Bartholomew included towards the end of *The Cauliflower®*, Sri Ramakrishna's conversation is 'weighted with great gems of spiritual enlightenment' but also leavened with mimicry, jokes and songs; in another chapter, it is presented as entirely appropriate that he can speak 'magical words' of advice to his followers while having each iteration of his name accompanied by the parping of a clown's horn.[32] Play and humour – a degree of lightness – are described as virtues in this novel, in contrast to the grave ways in which spiritualism and faith are often represented, and this interplay is part of the novel's exploration of binaries, or rather the fallacy of binaries: male and female, binding and releasing, Hinduism and Catholicism; modernity and antiquity, light and dark, and life and death. In Barker's 2019 novella *I Am Sovereign*, the narrator poses a pair of apparently contradictory questions about one of her characters, Avigail, before answering that Avigail is feeling 'both. At the same time. Because people are, by their very nature,

---

[29] Ibid., pp. 210–11.
[30] Ibid., p. 311.
[31] Italo Calvino, *The Literature Machine*, trans. Patrick Creagh (London: Secker and Warburg, [1980] 1987), p. 63.
[32] Ibid., pp. 291, 137.

contradictory. Because people are, by their very nature, paradoxical,[33] and this statement is in many ways a continuation of ideas explored in *The Cauliflower®*, a book that is interested in the ways in which Sri Ramakrishna's story 'somehow magically transcends the pair of opposites'. When Durga Charan Nag, one of Sri Ramakishna's devotees, is described as having led a 'crazy, stand-up comedy life',[34] it is not that the many accidents that befall him are simply laughable but that comedy is the form that best accounts for the combination of gravity and absurdity that made up his existence. This is an example of how Barker's comic voice is not ornamentation or a way to sugar the pill of more serious matters, but rather a method for exploring the paradoxes and contradictions at the centre of her writing.

'Is the fucking carnival in town or what?': Satire, the grotesque and the carnivalesque

Barker's comedy relies on contradiction, paradox and incongruity, and describes how these inhere in life, but critical writing on her work has tended to identify other models to account for the challenging humour in her work. Most often her fiction has been framed in terms of satire, and the linked categories of the grotesque and carnivalesque. These are not modes conventionally associated with contradiction and paradox, tending more towards critical and even didactic humour, but here Barker is ambivalent about their place and function, particularly in the later works. As I will go on to discuss, even as Barker's novels draw on elements of satire, the grotesque and the carnivalesque, they also reflect on the limitations of these modes and their potential to have the opposite effect to that claimed by advocates. Although Barker has been less explicit than Jonathan Coe in her commentary on this topic, there are parallels with Coe's increasingly ambivalent attitude towards satire's function and efficacy, a topic I address in Chapter 1. But before considering this ambivalence in more detail, I will first return to *Burley Cross Postbox Theft* to consider the harder edged humour that runs alongside its gentler portrayal of eccentricity as incongruity.

While *Burley Cross* does inspire laughter at foolish characters such as Jeremy Baverstock and Rosannah Strum-Tadcastle, it is a relatively gentle form of laughter at human folly and obsession. The more cutting, weaponized humour

---

[33] Nicola Barker, *I Am Sovereign* (London: William Heinemann, 2019), p. 198.
[34] Barker, *Cauliflower®*, pp. 119, 98.

of the novel is reserved for truly hypocritical figures such as Laurence Everill, the patronizing and compromised police sergeant who passes the postbox case to PC Topping at the outset of the novel, and perhaps most damningly for Baxter Thorndyke, local councillor and sender of multiple missives, each prefaced with 'A dispatch from the desk of: Baxter Thorndyke, Cllr'. Like Baverstock, Thorndyke is a pedant, particularly in his concern with the perceived threat to Burley Cross's manhole covers, detailed at length in letters to the local Member of Parliament and police (letters 11 and 12). He expresses his fear that 'plucky, ruthless and tenacious Chinese thieves' will target the manhole covers of Burley Cross, stealing them for their value as scrap metal, detailing his efforts to 'compile a permanent photographic record – an "unofficial archive", if you like – of all the manhole covers in Burley Cross (over ninety in total! Ninety-three, to be exact)'.[35] Manhole cover theft is not an entirely imaginary problem, and there are verified reports from the UK, China and elsewhere,[36] but Thorndyke's vociferousness and the scale of his suggested response puts him firmly in Schopenhauer's category of the 'foolish, absurd and incompetent' pedant. There is also more than a touch of racism and xenophobia in his references to the 'greedy, pitiless eyes' of the imagined thieves, or 'thieving Reds' as he describes them.[37] Thorndyke is characterized as a more poisonous type of fool, and the comedy of pedantry can also diagnose a more virulent malady.

Thorndyke is malicious in his pedantry and uses his campaigns to target individuals including the apparently harmless Basil Tunnicliffe, whose principle offence is that he has been awarded an OBE for his role in designing the wind turbine, thereby ruffling the feathers of the status-conscious Thorndyke. Thorndyke's broadside against Tunnicliffe takes the form of a lengthy response (Letter 9) to Tunnicliffe's letters to the local paper, the *Wharfedale Gazette*, about the environmental impact of consumerism during celebrations such as Valentine's Day, Mother's Day and Easter. Intending for his response to be published in the *Gazette*'s letters pages, Thorndyke concludes by asking:

---

[35] Barker, *Burley Cross*, pp. 148–9, 141.
[36] See, for example, Hugh Muir, 'Manhole Covers Vanish in the Night', *Guardian*, 25 October 2004. Available online: https://www.theguardian.com/uk/2004/oct/25/ukcrime.prisonsandprobation (accessed 22 August 2019); James Chapman, '50,000 Drain Covers Stolen "To Be Sold as Scrap in China and India"', *Daily Mail*, 14 August 2008. Available online: https://www.dailymail.co.uk/news/article-1044676/50-000-drain-covers-stolen-sold-scrap-China-India.html (accessed 22 August 2019); and Katy Lee, 'So Many Manhole Covers Are Stolen in China That One City Is Tracking Them with GPS', *Vox*, 22 March 2015. Available online: https://www.vox.com/2015/3/22/8267829/move-over-smart-watch-in-china-the-smart-manhole-cover-has-arrived (accessed 22 August 2019).
[37] Barker, *Burley Cross*, pp. 147, 149.

Am I *entirely* alone in wondering whether the only reason [Tunnicliffe] seems so determined to put a damper on all out High Days and Holidays is because (perish the thought!) the poor soul has so little to actively celebrate in his own life?

Has Mr Tunnicliffe OBE officially become 2006's greatest party-pooper because he has no party left of his own to poop?[38]

Thorndyke believes himself a great wit, and his letter, laced with repeated and revealing references to Tunnicliffe's OBE, is full of irony and barely concealed contempt, building to a crescendo that tacitly references the fact that Tunnicliffe is living alone in sheltered accommodation. Thorndyke's schadenfreude, which fits squarely into Tiffany Watt-Smith's category of the 'smug',[39] is clearly enjoyable and cathartic to him, as is his diminishment of Tunnicliffe's concerns via their pedantic reiteration, but there is no doubt where readers' sympathies are directed. Barker's depiction of this viciously idiotic pedantry is closer to what Northrop Frye classifies as Menippean satire, a genre that 'deals less with people as such than with mental attitudes' and includes 'pedants, bigots, cranks, parvenus, virtuosi, enthusiasts, rapacious and incompetent professional men of all kinds'. These vices are viewed 'as diseases of the intellect, as a kind of maddened pedantry which the *philosophus gloriosus* at once symbolizes and defines'.[40] For Frye, Menippean satire offers a harsher judgement on character types and patterns of thought than is offered by conventional novelistic discourse; it is a mode of 'exuberance', in which the satirist might overwhelm their 'pedantic targets with an avalanche of their own jargon'.[41] Jonathan Greenberg describes one of the main features of the Menippean novel as 'an intellectual or philosophical satire directed at an excessively systematic mind', the other features being a tendency towards metafiction and 'a critical attack on the bureaucratic and ideological institutions of modernity',[42] and although *Burley Cross* is not one of Barker's more conspicuously metafictional novels, it certainly conforms to Greenberg's other two criteria in its portrayal of institutions such as the police force, in its kinetic employment of jargon and in its representation of small-minded obsession. In the characterization of Thorndyke, *Burley Cross* moves from the gentler comedy

---

[38] Ibid., p. 134.
[39] Tiffany Watt-Smith, *Schadenfreude: The Joy of Another's Misfortune* (London: Profile, 2018), pp. 57–70.
[40] Northrop Frye, *Anatomy of Criticism: Four Essays* (Princeton, NJ: Princeton University Press, [1957] 2000), p. 309. Philosophus gloriosus translates as 'honoured philosopher' and is a stock character whose pedantry and rigidity of thought are the frequent subject of satire.
[41] Ibid., p. 311.
[42] Jonathan Greenberg, *The Cambridge Introduction to Satire* (Cambridge: Cambridge University Press, 2019), p. 213.

of foolishness and farce found in many of the other letters, including those from Baverstock and Strum-Tadcastle, and closer to bite and concern with morality found in the satirical mode.

In addition to his cruelty, Thorndyke is a hypocrite whose projected image as an upstanding citizen and moral arbiter contrasts with his private actions. Letter 14, a 'dispatch' from Thorndyke to his friend and fellow councillor Brian Brewster, details the 'Sex Hex', a spell requiring the careful preparation of a potion and the incantation 'COME TO ME!', followed by the name of one's object of desire. According to Thorndyke, who has, unbeknownst to his wife, used the Hex twelve times, it makes those who cast it unaccountably irresistible. One downside, he explains, is that after the 'astonishing' sex 'the Hex-ee will loathe you afterwards' and 'won't understand what it was that compelled them to initiate a random act of sex with you'. 'Who cares?' he reasons, 'You've got what you wanted so what the heck?'[43] There is noir humour in Thorndyke's callousness, including in the catalogue of disasters precipitated by the Hex – a Danish nurse who was struck by a car as she crossed the road in the Hex's grip, for example – but it is not humour at the victims' expense. Rather, it is Thorndyke the pedant, the little Englander and the morally compromised hypocrite, who is the object of laughter. The delayed punchline comes in a postscript to Letter 24, from Nina Springhill, the lusted-over Post Office worker, to her therapist Dr Bonner. Thorndyke has already mentioned Springhill in passing, referring to her as 'SEXY BRUNETTE IN THE POST OFFICE', and she is clearly the 'charming little Hex-ee' that he has 'lined up' for his next incantation.[44] But in Springhill's letter, we get the other side of the interaction. She describes feeling compelled to return the wallet that Thorndyke deliberately planted in the Post Office, and arriving at his home to find the front door wide open. She follows the sound of 'awful South American pan-pipey' music upstairs and finds Thorndyke in the bath, 'completely starkers, wearing this crown made out of ivy leaves (like something you might see at a really tacky yoga party) and holding a glass of what looked like champagne'. Despite the Hex, Nina fails to be charmed and takes his incantation of '"Pretty Post Office Girl, COME TO ME!"' as an invitation to hand back the wallet before turning on her heels and leaving as quickly as possible. She continues to feel 'tingly and light-headed and woozy' afterwards – perhaps there is something to the Hex's power – but the reversal of perspectives undermines Thorndyke's account of himself. On this view, he is not a lothario

---

[43] Barker, *Burley Cross*, pp. 159–60.
[44] Ibid., pp. 160–1.

made irresistible thanks to a magic spell, but an unattractive middle-aged man on his own in a bath with an ivy wreath on his head, attempting to lure a virtual stranger into his embrace and succeeding only in appearing 'really creepy'.[45]

Thorndyke is a comic type of the kind identified by Frye as representative of Menippean satire, and it is in Barker's representation of characters such as he that this apparently light, even flippant comedy of English rural life obtains its bite. As James Lever writes of *Burley Cross*, Barker's 'sensibility is starkly oppositional', and among her large cast of characters 'there are the bad guys (the middle classes) and the good (the marginal but rich-in-life)'.[46] The oppositional nature of this comedy has been discussed elsewhere in terms of the aesthetic of the grotesque,[47] a mode that celebrates freedom, and particularly bodily freedom: the way in which the grotesque, bulging, and protuberant body is transgressive of boundaries and always 'in the act of becoming', and which for Mikhail Bakhtin is linked to laughter and the comic. 'Wherever men laugh and curse, particularly in a familiar environment, their speech is filled with bodily images', writes Bakhtin in *Rabelais and His World* (1964).[48] Victor Sage argues that in Barker's earlier fiction, the grotesque represents a 'utopian drive towards freedom',[49] while for Sebastian Groes, the Rabelaisian element in Barker's *Clear* (2004) 'has a cathartic and revelatory function for society', the boisterousness and grotesquery of the crowd contrasting with the asceticism of David Blaine suspended high above in his Perspex box.[50] As Robert Duggan has discussed in the context of contemporary British fiction, the grotesque is a particularly challenging concept to define and it has been used to account for a 'seemingly open series' of artistic productions 'with very few common qualities apart from the perceived presence of the grotesque'; but for the purposes of the present discussion, I follow the Bakhtinian model, in which in contrast to the sealed, complete body of the classical figure, the body is represented as open, with the genitals and anus, rather than the face, constituting 'the key elements in

---

[45] Ibid., pp. 302–3.
[46] James Lever, 'Unshutuppable', review of Nicola Barker, *Burley Cross Postbox Theft*, *London Review of Books*, 9 September 2010. Available online: https://www.lrb.co.uk/v32/n17/james-lever/unshutuppable (accessed 1 February 2019).
[47] See, for example, Sage, 'The Ambivalence of Laughter'; Sebastian Groes, '"Please Don't Hate Me, Sensitive Girl Readers": Gender, Surveillance and Spectacle after 9/11 in Nicola Barker's *Clear*', in *Women's Fiction and Post-9/11 Contexts*, ed. Peter Childs, Claire Colebrook and Sebastian Groes (London: Lexington, 2015), pp. 159–77; and Len Platt, *Writing London and the Thames Estuary: 1576–2016* (Leiden: Brill, 2017), pp. 143–64.
[48] Mikhail Bakhtin, *Rabelais and His World*, trans. Hélène Iswolsky (Bloomington, IN: Indiana University Press, [1964] 1984), p. 317.
[49] Sage, 'The Ambivalence of Laughter', p. 94.
[50] Groes, '"Please Don't Hate Me, Sensitive Girl Readers"', p. 166.

human interrelations and existence'.[51] Barker's early fiction revels in this type of grotesquery, and her first collection of stories, *Love Your Enemies* (1993), features a character who attempts to revive a pulsing tumour removed from a beef carcass ('The Butcher's Apprentice') and another who develops a '"very natural and obvious relationship"' with her tapeworm ('Symbiosis: Class Cestoda').[52] The later story collection *Heading Inland* (1996) includes the tale of a foetus who is able to unzip his mother's belly and make his escape from her womb ('Inside Information') and a man whose organs are positioned back to front in his body ('Back to Front'); and characters in the novel *Small Holdings* (1995) have faces that are described as 'a vagina – all curls, all hair, with pink lips protruding and a small nose, labia-like, just above – a tender fold' and who consider frying and eating a piece of jellified nose blood.[53] Medve, the teenage narrator of *Five Miles from Outer Hope* (2000), takes particular delight in describing her own body and her feeling that she is '*unnatural*', over-sized from birth, with 'knees as wide as the skull of Neolithic man', eyes the colour of baby shit, a 'capacious anus' and a clitoris 'the approximate size of a Jersey Royal'.[54] Critics such as Mary Russo have rightly identified the gendered terms in which the grotesque is frequently evoked, and the way in which, as Margaret Miles succinctly describes it, the female grotesque is always defined against the male form, which is 'the perfectly formed, complete, and therefore normative body', in contrast to which 'women's bodies incorporate parts (like breasts, uterus, and vagina) and processes (like menstruation and pregnancy) that appeared grotesque to the authors and artists who represented women'.[55] And yet Medve, like most of Barker's characters, both female and male, is not ashamed of her body or self-declared freakishness, and instead delights in it, both in her addresses to the reader and in her interactions with other characters: the practical joke she plays on her antagonistic house guest La Roux, who is phobic about women's sexual organs, involves engineering a situation whereby he witnesses her pull a 'five inch, red-coloured, jelly-textured, thirty-seven-scraggy legged [plastic] centipede' from her vagina.[56] Moreover, Barker's writing does not tend to offer fixed ideals against which such characters

---

[51] Duggan, *The Grotesque in Contemporary British Fiction*, pp. 11, 22. See also Bakhtin, *Rabelais*, pp. 303–67 for his discussion of 'The grotesque image of the body'.
[52] Nicola Barker, *Love Your Enemies* (London: Faber and Faber, [1993] 1994), p. 77.
[53] Nicola Barker, *Small Holdings* (London: Faber and Faber, 1995), pp. 11, 85.
[54] Nicola Barker, *Five Miles from Outer Hope* (London: Faber and Faber, 2000), pp. 8, 12–13, 81.
[55] Margaret Miles, 'Carnal Abominations: The Female Body as Grotesque', in *The Grotesque in Art and Literature: Theological Reflections*, ed. James Luther Adams and Wilson Yates (Grand Rapids, MI: William B. Eerdmans, 1997), pp. 83–112 (p. 96). See also Mary Russo, *The Female Grotesque: Risk, Excess and Modernity* (New York: Routledge, 1994).
[56] Barker, *Five Miles*, p. 168.

are defined. Rather, Medve exists within a family of misfits, literally and figuratively separated from the straight world on an island, and when characters from the straight, normative world do impose it is they who are depicted as weird. As Lever suggests, Barker celebrates the 'marginal but rich-in-life' and is interested in upending hierarchies of taste and value.

In Bakhtin's thinking, this upending of hierarchies is inherent in the representation of the grotesque and is linked to his conception of both the carnivalesque and Menippean satire, a category discussed earlier in relation to Frye and *Burley Cross*. Bakhtin identifies Dostoevsky as writing in the lineage of Menippean satire, a form that became one of the 'main carriers and channels for the carnival sense of the world in Literature'.[57] The 'carnival sense', usually referred to as the carnivalesque, implies a literature of reversed norms, where paupers become kings and, as in the medieval carnival, the world is turned upside down for the day. Laughter is central to this upheaval, and is directed 'toward a shift of authorities and truths, a shift of world orders'.[58] In Barker's case, it tends to be directed towards the comfortable and complacent middle classes from the perspective of the marginal. As Bakhtin implies in his analysis of Dostoevsky, it is not that Barker is necessarily making a direct or conscious response to the Greek prose satires from which Menippean satire takes its name, but rather that a sense of riotous upheaval prevails, as in much of Angela Carter's writing.[59] It is apparent in Medve's triumphant resistance to norms, as well as in the comparable portrayal of Lily in the earlier novel *Wide Open* (1998), another teenager without 'any sense of restraint or delicacy'.[60] It is also there in the literal and metaphorical examples of opening up, becoming 'wide open', that run throughout that novel. Barker's comic grotesques celebrate this openness, despite the fact that the process of opening up can be frightening and chaotic.

---

[57] Mikhail Bakhtin, *Problems of Dostoevsky's Poetics*, trans. Caryl Emerson (Minneapolis, MN: University of Minnesota Press, [1963] 1984), p. 113.

[58] Ibid., p. 127.

[59] Writing about Barker's 2012 novel *The Yips*, Sarah Upstone argues that 'Barker's satirical style means that what might be substantial events in another novel are here swept aside in a swirling maelstrom of carnivalesque ludus' and that Barker's depiction of small-minded attitudes in the English town of Luton serves to perpetuate stereotypes rather than attempting to 'reshape them with an eye to the future'. While I take issue with some of Upstone's stronger pronouncements about Barker's political duty and I would argue that the novel demonstrates more affection for her characters than she allows, *The Yips* does feel less well-observed and less firmly situated in its locale than much of Barker's other work. Moreover, Upstone's evident frustration with the novel speaks to the politically ambiguous nature of satire, which is inherently anti-utopian. Sarah Upstone, 'Do Novels Tell Us How to Vote?' in *Brexit and Literature: Critical and Cultural Responses*, ed. Robert Eaglestone (Abingdon: Routledge, 2018), pp. 44–58 (pp. 50, 53).

[60] Nicola Barker, *Wide Open* (London: Faber and Faber, 1998), p. 50.

In *Reversed Forecast*, Sam, previously shut off from the world, comes to this realization:

> It felt to Sam as though her mind had opened up, like a flower. It was a strange and terrifying sensation. Usually her mind was closed, had one small door and a door-keeper who carefully selected the things that would be left out. But suddenly the door was wide open, and the supporting frames were cracking, crumbling, letting in more and more light, more and more air. And *people*.[61]

This process of opening up recurs in a bodily but also a psychological sense in Barker's fiction as a model for life that is 'strange and terrifying' but is nevertheless to be striven for. To return to the Bakhtinian conception of the grotesque, Barker's representation of the open and porous grotesque body is the opposite of the hermetically sealed and aesthetically perfect classical model, representative of life that is 'never finished, never completed' and always in a state of necessary upheaval.[62]

Grotesque imagery is less prevalent in Barker's later fiction, but it persists in *Burley Cross*, for example, in Everill's ungenerous description of Topping's appearance during childhood swimming lessons ('your soft belly bulging over the waistband like a generous slick of extra-thick UHT cream, the voluminous skin of your upper torso pulsing translucently'), or in Thorndyke's description of his adult form ('He's just as huge, forlorn elk, a tragic bison, lumbering about the place in that improbably gigantic pair of perpetually squeaking loafers of his like some heavily tranquillized mastodon.')[63] Moreover, it is a novel whose plot is predicated on carnivalesque upheaval, in which information intended to remain private is aired publicly, unsettling the usual distribution of knowledge and metaphorically revealing that the emperors – the Thorndykes and Everills of the community – have no clothes: that their apparent mastery is illusory and fleeting. It is no surprise that Topping, who is the subject of brickbats from the higher ranking and deeply condescending Everill in the opening pages of the novel, is given the last word and is able to offer his own, more artfully constructed series of ripostes. His memo to Everill, now promoted to Inspector, spins a convincing yarn to protect the real perpetrator of the Burley Cross Postbox Theft, before the penultimate letter from Topping to Wincey Hawkes, the hard-up landlady of the village pub, reveals the true story: he knows it was she who stole the letters but understands it was done out of desperation and he will not therefore pursue the

---

[61] Barker, *Reversed Forecast*, p. 185.
[62] Bakhtin, *Rabelais*, p. 317.
[63] Barker, *Burley Cross*, pp. 3, 139.

case. The lowly Police Constable has not only solved the crime but also controlled the outcome, misdirecting his superior officer and siding with the perpetrator who he should, according to the letter of the law (pun intended), be arresting.

But to return to Barker's abiding concern with paradox and contradiction, *Burley Cross* also contains an embedded critique of the revolutionary potential of carnivalesque upheaval, or rather of claims that overstate its transformative possibilities.[64] The document sandwiched between the memo to Everill and the letter to Wincey Hawkes draws attention to the limitations of the carnival and the challenge to authority it is often claimed to represent. It is a further memo from Topping, this time to his senior officer, Chief Inspector Iain Richardson, reporting that he has destroyed all evidence relating to PC Peter Richardson's dalliances in the local public lavatory. Peter is Iain's son, and Topping has been instructed to mount a cover-up, having been identified as 'one of the few people left on the force "stupid enough to care about the difference between right and wrong, but still sufficiently respectful to take direction from above – without even the remotest expectation of personal gain"'. Topping's irony-laced postscript notes that he is 'thinking of giving up all remaining shreds of my professional credibility for Lent' and asks: 'How about you, Chief Inspector? Just chocolate again, this year?'[65] Topping's moral code is trumped by loyalty to the police service, and he resignedly complies with authority. As Angela Carter concludes in 'In Pantoland', a story that for much of its length is a celebration of the gender fluidity and subversion of the British pantomime tradition, the carnival must end:

> As Umberto Eco once said, 'An everlasting carnival does not work.' You can't keep it up, you know; nobody ever could. The essence of the carnival, the festival, the Feast of Fools, is transience. It is here today and gone tomorrow, a release of tension not a reconstitution of order, a refreshment ... after which everything can go on again exactly as if nothing had happened.[66]

The carnival represents a *temporary* suspension of norms and exists on the understanding that life will return to normal once the festivities have ended. Carter here refers to Eco's essay 'The Frames of Comic "Freedom"' (1984), in

---

[64] Bakhtinian readings of contemporary authors were prevalent in the academy following the translation and subsequent rediscovery of his work in the mid-1980s. However, as Dominic Head notes somewhat wearily in relation to Angela Carter, there has been an occasional tendency to use authors 'to illuminate the theory, rather than vice versa' and to make sweeping claims in which the carnival is 'misappropriated as a model for the radical social challenge'. Head, *The Cambridge Introduction to Modern British Fiction, 1950–2000*, pp. 3–4, 104–5.

[65] Barker, *Burley Cross*, pp. 345–6.

[66] Angela Carter, *Burning Your Boats: Collected Short Stories* (London: Vintage, 1996), p. 389.

which he outlines the positive claims that have been made for comic carnival but concludes that 'carnival can only exist as an *authorized* transgression' and that 'comedy and carnival are not instances of real transgression: on the contrary they represent paramount examples of law enforcement'.[67] The law enforcement in Barker's novel involves, ironically, disregarding the law to comply with the wishes of authority, but Eco's point stands: by licensing transgression in the form of the carnival, its energy can be dissipated and its critique or challenge to authority can be reabsorbed by that same authority.

This simultaneous evocation and critique of the carnivalesque is described more explicitly in *Clear*, Barker's 2004 novel set around the spectacle of the magician David Blaine's 'Above the Below', in which he was suspended in a transparent box for forty-four days without food. The carnivalesque spirit that developed around the site of the performance on the banks of the River Thames next to Tower Bridge in London is evoked early in *Clear*, when the narrator, Adair Graham McKenny, describes the scene as 'getting all Dickensian again, all Rabelaisian'.[68] Rabelais is Bakhtin's exemplar of the carnival, and it is possible to argue, as Sebastian Groes does in the passage quoted earlier, that this communal spirit 'has a cathartic and revelatory function for society'.[69] At the end of the novel, as Blaine's performance comes to an end, there is a truly chaotic scene on Tower Bridge and surrounding areas, which causes Adair to ask, as he is swept up in the crowd, 'Has this bridge *ever* been so full of laughter and bustle?' At the same time, however, the grand dénouement, Blaine's emergence from the box, is subject to the control of commercial interests because 'tonight we're *ALL* to be held to ransom by the TV executives' who are broadcasting the spectacle and need to maximize their advertising revenue.[70] There is a genuinely celebratory mood, but Barker reminds us that the event is orchestrated from without and is not a free space of licence and abandon. Moreover, she applies a further caveat about the role of the carnival and public laughter, which is at the core of the novel's ambivalent attitude towards Blaine and what he means to the crowds of spectators. In reporting the Rabelaisian mood, Adair notes the antagonistic undercurrent that belies purely positivist notions about the value of public laugher: 'We're reconnecting to a long social *history* of public *spite* (and-credit where credit's due – public adoration)', he says.[71] This history of spite in humour

---

[67] Eco, 'The Frames of Comic "Freedom"', pp. 1–9 (p. 6). See also Umberto Eco, 'The Comic and the Rule' [1980], in *Faith in Fakes* (London: Vintage, 1995), pp. 269–78.
[68] Nicola Barker, *Clear* (London: Fourth Estate, 2004), p. 55.
[69] Groes, '"Please Don't Hate Me, Sensitive Girl Readers"', p. 166.
[70] Barker, *Clear*, p. 339.
[71] Ibid., p. 55.

and laughter is every bit as important as its more joyous aspect, and it is a history that has been recovered in work such as Simon Dickie's *Cruelty and Laughter* (2011), which reassess the gentility of the eighteenth century via a lost canon of popular comic literature, as well as in Michael Billig's *Laughter and Ridicule* (2005), whose central argument is that 'it is easy to praise humour for bringing people together in moments of pure, creative enjoyment. But it is not those sorts of moment that constitute the social core of humour, but, instead, it is the darker, less easily admired practice of ridicule.'[72] On this view, laughter is most often a form of ridicule and control rather than unification and celebration. This harsher undercurrent to laughter is also evident in *Darkmans* (2006), a novel written in parallel with *Clear*,[73] in the figure of John Scogin, a medieval court jester who returns as a spectre to the modern-day town of Ashford. Scogin is representative of a broader meditation on the return of and reconciliation with the past,[74] but the idea of a new medievalism also has a specifically comic dimension linked to spectacle and ridicule. Among the historical 'jests' recounted in the novel is the time when Scogin invited local beggars into his barn with the promise that he would distribute alms, only to lock them inside the barn and set fire to it before accusing them of arson. In *Scoggins Jests* (1626), a collection of the – possibly fictitious – jester's antics, this is described as both an amusing jape and as having a didactic function, using harsh ridicule to instil the message that Scogin should not be pestered for handouts: 'So some [beggars] ran through the fire in one place, and some in another, and durst not look behind them. Scogin cried, saying: tarry, w****sons and w****s, you have set my barn on fire, you shall be hanged every one! They fled for feare, and never durst come againe to Scogin's house for almes.'[75] That this should be related as a 'jest', or 'simple high jinks' as the character Winifred puts it in *Darkmans*,[76] might be shocking to modern readers, but Barker's novel suggest that despite a prevailing belief in increasing sensibility, refinement and the positive benefits of laughter, this form of mockery persists. Dickie argues that despite the dominant view of the mid-eighteenth century as the 'age of sensibility', 'Pity coexisted with indifference; sympathy

---

[72] Billig, *Laughter and Ridicule*, p. 2.
[73] Barker was so fascinated and enraged by the Blaine spectacle that she took a break from writing *Darkmans* in order to respond to it in the form of *Clear*. See, for example, Anthony Byrt, 'The World Cracked Open', *New Zealand Listener*, 19 January 2008. Available online: https://www.noted.co.nz/archive/listener-nz-2008/the-world-cracked-open/ (accessed 25 February 2019).
[74] For an extended discussion of this idea, see Marsh, 'Nicola Barker's *Darkmans*'.
[75] *The First and Best Part of Scoggins Jests. Full of Witty Mirth and Pleasant Shifts, done by him in France and other places: being a preservative against Melancholy* [1626], gathered by Andrew Boord, Doctor of Physicke, London, Printed for Francis Williams, in *Old English Jest-Books*, 3 vols, ed. W. Carew Hazlitt (London: Willis and Sotheran, 1864), pp. 37–161 (p. 100).
[76] Nicola Barker, *Darkmans* (London: Fourth Estate, 2006), p. 642.

was fleeting, unstable, and easily transformed into malice or delight',[77] and a similarly fraught relationship with modernity is apparent in *Darkmans*, which draws parallels between medieval spectacle and suggests that the cruelty and binarism of medieval judgement is apparent in the tabloid press.[78] The return and re-enactment of Scogin's jests throughout the novel is a reminder that this darker undercurrent to laughter and amusement continues alongside its more positive manifestations. In the opening pages, Kane catches a glimpse of Scogin in yellow jester's motley[79] and asks "'Is the fucking carnival in town or what?'":[80] it is, but the laughter of the carnival is a mutable, paradoxical thing, as likely to be cruel and divisive as affirming and unifying.

Returning to *Clear*, the novel offers a running discussion not only of the artistic merit and meaning of Blaine's performance but also of the public's reaction to it. The title of the novel is both a literal reference to the clear box in which Blaine lives and a reference to Blaine himself, who is seen as a void that people fill with their own meanings, anxieties and hopes. "'He's transparent. He's clear'", Adair's co-worker and love interest Bly says at one point, "'So when people look up at him they don't hate what *he* is. They project everything they're feeling on to him. They *vent* their hatred – their conformity, their rage, their poverty, their fear, their confusion – on to him.'"[81] There is a taxonomy of 'The Insiders vs. The Outsiders' (those who step inside the cordon surrounding Blaine versus those who remain outside), subdivided into sections on 'Eating', 'The Bridge' (Tower Bridge, from which vantage point people 'hurl their eggs and other consumables'), and 'The Haters', and an atmosphere of spite predominates. This is particularly true among the 'outsiders', where people eat conspicuously and performatively as Blaine starves, doing so 'with a real sense of vindictive *glee*'. The true outsiders, the haters, 'live *inside* a tabloid feeding frenzy, where everything's in bold and italics and capital letters'; their anger and mockery is described as a 'release button on society's pressure cooker',[82] language that speaks to the relief theory of humour discussed elsewhere in this book.[83] And although this laughter may be cathartic for some in the crowd, it is not a wholly, or even largely positive thing.

---

[77] Dickie, *Cruelty and Laughter*, p. 11.
[78] Barker, *Darkmans*, pp. 396–9.
[79] As Robert H. Hill notes *Tales of the Jesters*, which includes a chapter on Scogin that referred to in *Darkmans*, in the jester's clothing 'yellow predominated, for yellow was regarded as the fool's own colour'. Robert H. Hill, *Tales of the Jesters* (Edinburgh: W.M. Blackwood and Sons, 1934), p. 42.
[80] Barker, *Darkmans*, p. 25.
[81] Barker, *Clear*, p. 311.
[82] Ibid., pp. 56–64.
[83] In Chapter 1 on the cathartic effects of satire, for example, and in Chapter 6 on Howard Jacobson's theory about the benefits of laughter at racist jokes.

As Bly suggests in another of her monologues to Adair, Blaine is 'actually much more honest and individual and vulnerable and subversive than *they* [the haters] could *ever* be'; they are, she thinks, 'defining their mental toughness, their sacred individualism, their righteous *Englishness*' against this void into which people pour their admiration or scorn.[84] There is a certain national, even nationalist element to this, manifested in a reaction against the perceived pretentiousness and frustrating ambiguity of this performance by an American visitor, and it was a mood that was celebrated at the time, with broadsheet as well as tabloid media viewing it as a source of pride in 'our unstoppable British urge to ridicule and debunk him – our cocky, cockney lawlessness, our innate willingness to lampoon and pillory'.[85] Here, Barker's narrator paraphrases a *Guardian* column, in which Catherine Bennett celebrates the mockery of Blaine in a way that goes against the grain of the novel:[86] the predominant mood in *Clear* is not one of nationalistic pride but one of shame and embarrassment at the negativity shown towards an overseas guest. At one end, this is represented by detachment and aloof laughter at the silliness of the endeavour, and at the other it is expressed in jeering, open mockery and a modern form of the pillory.

Clear culminates in the spectacle of Blaine's release from the box, but there is a brief coda to Adair's narration that is worth quoting at length:

> The following morning, a Monday, I return for the last time to the scene of the crime. And when I get to the point on the bridge where I caught my first glimpse of him – that initial sighting, that seductive perspex glimmer – there's just this huge *hole* in the sky. Even the crane has gone. And when I get to the far end, where all the cars used to honk their horns at him, I see every other driver, turning and staring. I see their heads turn, one after the other. And all they see now are clouds and the tops of trees. And seagulls. But their heads *still* turn, and they look. Car after car. And it's a ballet of I Miss You David.
>
> A Symphony of He's Gone.[87]

As Eco and later Carter suggest, the carnival must and does end, and this peculiar transformative spectacle that brought out the best and worst in people has vanished within a day, leaving 'just this huge *hole* in the sky'. But the fact that the absence is registered, that the scene now seems incomplete,

---

[84] Barker, *Clear*, p. 118.
[85] Ibid., p. 67.
[86] Catherine Bennett, 'The Blaine Bashers Make Me Proud to Be British', *Guardian*, 11 September 2003. Available online: https://www.theguardian.com/uk/2003/sep/11/britishidentity.comment (accessed 7 February 2019).
[87] Barker, *Clear*, pp. 344–5.

suggests that something more lasting has occurred and that the carnival was not fully contained within those forty-four days of Blaine's performance. The passing motorists continue to turn their heads, and despite the foregoing spite and vitriol, the enduring feeling is one of melancholy and loss. We are again returned to Barker's preoccupation with paradox and contradiction. As with the evocation of opposites allowed by the comedy of pedantry and incongruity, Barker's treatment of the carnival and carnivalesque laughter both enables and relies upon the juxtaposition of paradoxical statements and states: on the one hand, it upsets convention and overturns social norms, but on the other hand, it can be negative and destructive; and while it can represent a powerful form of dissent, it is a temporary form of dissent whose very temporariness can reinforce the status quo. At the same time, something of the carnival endures: an intangible remainder that is felt rather than measured but is transformative in its own way. Barker's novels seesaw between these positions not as a means of abrogating commitment but as a reflection of the contradictions and paradoxes of laughter and comedy, and the ways in which these inherent qualities enable her to represent the contradictions and paradoxes of life.

Laughter and redemption: From comedy to humour

But if the carnival's importance is ultimately limited and its abiding effectiveness as action restricted, what, then, for the critical or political possibilities of comedy and of Barker's fiction specifically? In 'The Frames of Comic "Freedom"' Eco offers one possibility that speaks to the direction Barker's writing has taken in recent years. He argues that humour, as opposed to the comic, can avoid comedy's unwitting enforcement of the rule.[88] Drawing on Luigi Pirandello's essay *On Humour* (1908/1920),[89] Eco suggests that humour allows sentiment into the realm of laughter. He quotes Pirandello's example of an old woman who wears heavy makeup and dresses like a young girl (for the sake of balance, an old

---

[88] Here Eco offers a somewhat idiosyncratic distinction between comedy and humour, in which comedy is a more barbed, targeted form that works in the carnivalesque tradition, and humour is gentler and more reliant on empathy. More conventionally, comedy is used to describe the form that humour takes in works of art or jokes, for example, whereas humour is descriptive of the field of things that are funny, including unintentional humour.

[89] Pirandello's essay discusses the claims for classical comedy associated by Jean Paul Richter with 'gross jestings and vulgur satire' and modern humour, which inspires 'a laughter full of tolerance and sympathy'. Weighing up critical arguments that make claims for one or other of these modes, he leans towards the latter, arguing for a narrower conception of humour that is not necessarily tied to a particular period or national context. Luigi Pirandello, *On Humor*, trans. Antonio Illiano and Daniel P. Testa (Chapel Hill, NC: University of North Carolina Press, [1908/1920] 1960), p. 16.

man who dresses like a teenager and sports conspicuously dyed hair would work equally well): the carnivalesque comic would find her merely ridiculous, even grotesque, but a humorous treatment would sympathize with her and recognize that she is merely seeking to recapture her lost youth: 'One finds oneself halfway between tragedy and comedy', he concludes. Pirandello makes an important distinction between 'the beginning *perception of the opposite*', which is comic, and the 'shift to a *feeling of the opposite*', which is where humour resides.[90] Both the comic and humour rely on the play of opposites, but where the former relies on detached perception, the latter involves emotion and identification. For Eco, in humour 'there is still a sense of superiority but with a shade of tenderness', and in this way, it works from the inside, revealing our own limitations rather than offering an impossible (and temporary) freedom:

> Humour does not promise us liberation: on the contrary, it warns us about the impossibility of global liberation, reminding us of the presence of a law that we no longer have reason to obey. In doing so it undermines the law. It makes us feel the uneasiness of living under a law – any law.[91]

There are parallels here with what James Wood has described as the opposition between comedies of forgiveness and comedies of correction, discussed in greater detail in Chapter 3, or with Simon Critchley's view that true humour is self-effacing and involves the recognition that 'our wretchedness is our greatness',[92] but Eco politicizes these ideas, arguing that humour offers a more deeply felt and significant challenge to the law than carnivalesque comedy. In the context of Barker's fiction, the closing letters in *Burley Cross* offer a discernible shift between these modes and a transition towards what Eco and Pirandello would describe as humour. While Topping's letter to Wincey Hawkes is gently humorous, it is also full of pathos in its descriptions of Wincey's grief following the death of her husband, Duke, and the consequent hardships that led her to steal from the post box. It offers a degree of hope via Topping's references to the improving prospects of the pub, tempered with wistfulness for the slow passing of a certain way of village life. There is also subversion in Topping's decision to keep what he knows to himself: 'I know how to keep schtum. I know how to hold my tongue…' he writes, 'And I am holding it, Wincey. And I will continue to hold it – for your sake. For mine. For all our sakes.' Pointedly, this letter is written at

---

[90] Ibid., p. 113.
[91] Eco, 'Frames of Comic "Freedom"', p. 8.
[92] James Wood, *The Irresponsible Self: On Laughter and the Novel* (London: Jonathan Cape, 2004); Simon Critchley, *On Humour* (London and New York: Routledge, 2002), p. 111.

Easter time, and the end of the novel offers some hope of renewal and rebirth.[93] The final letter is in fact addressed to the aptly named Mrs Hope, Topping's administrative assistant, and is full of self-effacing humour as Topping wrangles with the auto-formatting options in the word processing programme he is using. 'What a clumsy oaf I am!' he writes,[94] but it is Topping, we are left feeling, who is the ethical centre of this novel and in whose humour we recognize the *'cold carnival'* described by Eco, which is more likely to be acknowledged with a smile than a riotous laugh.[95]

Burley Cross is a novel bookended by two distinctive forms of the comic and humour: Everill's verbose and grotesquely descriptive memo to Topping, and Topping's witty but more muted and melancholic memos and letters. In between, Barker has a good deal of fun with the comedy of pedantry, pettiness and small-mindedness, always siding with the underdog. These tonal transitions are typical of the stylistic and thematic range apparent throughout Barker's work, but the movement from hard, kinetic humour to something more muted is also representative of a broader shift in her writing. From the perspective of 2012, Victor Sage identifies *Five Miles from Outer Hope* (2000) as a breakthrough novel in the development of Barker's voice,[96] and recent work has continued this development. *In the Approaches* (2014), *The Cauliflower*® and even *H(A)PPY* are comic, at least in part, but there is less evidence of the grotesque humour with which Barker made her name, and a greater emphasis on forgiveness, redemption and empathy. She has retained her allegiance to comedy and the importance of scatological humour (*The Cauliflower*®, and *passim* throughout the novels) or laughter at physical misfortune (*In the Approaches*, and *passim* again), but these moments work in tandem with a greater emphasis on the importance of empathetic laughter and smiles. Such mixed modes of humour may not offer the same appearance of radicalism found in the carnival, but they instead give space for reflection on the absurdities of existence and of norms and rules of behaviour. Moreover, in *In the Approaches*, Barker literalizes this change via a series of metafictional conceits that reflect upon her earlier work and the forms that humour can take.

The plot of *In the Approaches* is typically non-linear and sprawling, an aspect of the book that is referenced during several metafictional asides. Briefly, it is

---

[93] According to Northrop Frye's schema, spring is also the season of comic mythos. See Frye, *Anatomy of Criticism*, pp. 163–87.
[94] Barker, *Burley Cross*, pp. 359–60.
[95] Eco, 'Frames of Comic "Freedom"', p. 8.
[96] Sage, 'The Ambivalence of Laughter', p. 94.

set in 1984 in the small coastal village of Pett Level in East Sussex, and centres on two characters, Miss Carla Hahn, a native of the village, and Mr Franklin D. Huff, a visitor whose connections to the place and its people are gradually revealed. Each of these characters has to reckon with events that took place over a decade earlier when the Cleary family moved to the cottage now occupied by Franklin. The Cleary's daughter, Orla, had developmental abnormalities caused by the drug thalidomide, and some religious devotees came to believe that she possessed miraculous, visionary powers. It is a novel that is about suffering, both in the context of Orla's suffering, which some believe brought her closer to the divine and a paradoxical form of bliss,[97] and in a more secular sense, in Carla and Franklin's reckoning with their pasts and with the love that develops between them. But it is also a comedy, even a romantic comedy, and it is concerned with the significance and variety of comic laughter, while at the same time reflecting on the type of comedy that Barker herself writes.

In the first of several interludes narrated by an otherwise peripheral character, Chapter 11 of *In the Approaches* is told from the perspective of Carla's ex-boyfriend Clifford Bickerton. Clifford is aware that he is a fictional character and begins by saying, 'I don't really understand why I'm becoming part of this story.' He does not see how he fits into the structure of the novel, which largely alternates between first-person accounts by Carla and Franklin, seeing himself as the 'spanner in the works' of the developing love-hate relationship between the main protagonists.[98] Like Caroline Rose, the protagonist of Muriel Spark's *The Comforters* (1957), who hears the sound of an author-figure typing her thoughts and actions into existence, Clifford is aware of an exterior presence shaping his words and deeds, and plotting his destiny. He is also aware of his own disposability and position in the characterological hierarchy: the 'cow Author', as he refers to Barker, 'is going to make me act totally out of character – rise to the occasion, give the smug, "cosmopolitan" arsehole [Franklin] what for – and then quickly kill me off'.[99] He counts himself fortunate that he survived his earlier tussle with an overly tight woollen jumper that cut off his circulation and left him looking as though he had been swallowed by a '"lambswool python"', and he

---

[97] The 'more difficult it was, the more blissful [Orla] became', Carla recalls at one point in a further example of Barker's interest in paradox. 'This was the great paradox. This was the strange mania. This was the deep mystery of Orla Nor Cleary.' Nicola Barker, *In the Approaches* (London: Fourth Estate, 2014), p. 280.

[98] Ibid., p. 83.

[99] Ibid., p. 89. See Alex Woloch, *The One vs. the Many: Minor Characters and the Space of the Protagonist in the Novel* (Princeton, NJ: Princeton University Press, 2003) for a fascinating discussion of the relationship between the form of the novel and the distribution of attention and space between characters.

has knowledge of Barker's oeuvre, comparing himself to hapless characters who have died from choking on a miniature pat of butter (*Wide Open*) or a sudden brain haemorrhage (*The Yips*).¹⁰⁰ This knowledge is metaleptic in the sense that it crosses an impossible boundary between the storyworld and the real world of the author, and it is also anachronistic because, as Clifford tells us, Barker did not begin writing fiction until 1987, after the date on which *In the Approaches* is set. Clifford is somehow aware of these impossibilities and acknowledges that it 'doesn't make any sense. It's ... it's unnatural, it's *supernatural*', yet he is able to reach a deal with the author that will free him from the mishaps and pratfalls that have so far been meted out as punishment for his rebellion: 'she will promise to leave me the hell alone (remember the dog bite? The swan attack?) just so long as I don't go sticking my giant hooter in anywhere that it isn't wanted.' In the same passage, he criticizes Barker's writing for its complex use of parentheses within parentheses, the affected, out of character literariness of his own vocabulary ('why would I – she – make me say these things, these arty-farty, stuck-up, *pretentious* things – shove words and ideas into my head and my mouth'), and the convolutedness of her plotting, suggesting that a '*real* writer' like Edna O'Brien would make a better job of it.¹⁰¹ There are similarities not only with Spark's *The Comforters* but also with another O'Brien, Flann O'Brien, whose *At Swim-Two-Birds* (1939) plays analogous games with character, agency and narrative levels, and which in many ways anticipates the later postmodernist texts that revived the innovations of the early novel to reflect on their own status as fiction.¹⁰² But if this is Barker's most postmodernist novel, then she arrived rather late to the party, in a period when most agree that postmodernism has receded to the point where it describes a historical period rather than a way of framing the present.¹⁰³ In the closing pages of this chapter, I want to argue that the self-reflexiveness and metafictional playfulness of *In the Approaches* in fact speaks not only to Barker's engagement with paradoxical and contradictory states and to the relationship between this and the comic voice in her fiction, but also to critical framings of the contemporary and what has come after postmodernism, in particular as it relates to a shift in the relationship between art and sincerity.

---

[100] Ibid., pp. 55, 89–90.
[101] Ibid., pp. 211–17.
[102] A clutch of titles published by Routledge in the late 1980s continue to be the defining accounts of this aspect of postmodernism. See Linda Hutcheon, *A Poetics of Postmodernism* (London: Routledge, 1988); Hutcheon, *The Politics of Postmodernism*; and Brian McHale, *Postmodernist Fiction* (London: Routledge, 1987).
[103] See, for example, *The Cambridge History of Postmodern Literature*, ed. Brian McHale and Len Platt (Cambridge: Cambridge University Press, 2016), whose existence indicates the posthumous nature of the postmodern.

One account of what defines the post-postmodern era identifies a renewed emphasis on sincerity in reaction to what was characterized as postmodernism's tendency towards irony. Irony, as Claire Colebrook writes, has a 'distancing function', predicated 'on a lost sense of the truly valuable or original' and representing a profound scepticism towards ideas of truth,[104] and as the character Martin Amis notes in Amis's novel *Money* (1984), '"the twentieth century is an ironic age – downward-looking"'.[105] But there has since been a discernible movement away from this ironic dominant, as twenty-first-century fiction seeks to explore new ways of accounting for knowledge and representing experience. Taking its lead from David Foster Wallace's 1993 essay 'E Unibus Plurum: Television and U.S. Fiction', critical writing about the 'new sincerity' identifies a group of authors including Wallace as well as Dave Eggers, Jonathan Franzen, Zadie Smith, George Saunders and others, who write in the wake of postmodernism but seek to escape what Wallace describes as the 'tyranny' of irony, with its slipperiness and negation of positive values, and to move towards forms of art that engage with belief rather than detachment and incredulity.[106] Rather than rehearsing a debate that has been discussed extensively elsewhere,[107] I want to emphasize one important aspect that is enacted in Barker's fiction, and which is particularly pertinent to this chapter's examination of the nexus between comedy and paradox. As Martin Eve notes in his essay 'Sincerity', 'it is never just a case of sincerity or irony and the two can co-exist'; in fact 'a delicate balance is always maintained in fiction between the use of irony and the desire to speak the truth about reality'.[108] Not all irony is comic irony, but there is a strong relationship between humour and irony, and Barker's centralization of the relationship between character and author in *In the Approaches* is a gesture that is both heavily ironic and concerned with belief and sincere expression.

---

[104] Claire Colebrook, *Irony* (London: Routledge, 2004), pp. 2–3.
[105] Martin Amis, *Money: A Suicide Note* (London: Penguin, [1984] 2000), p. 248.
[106] David Foster Wallace, 'E Unibus Plurum: Television and U.S. Fiction' [1993], in *A Supposedly Fun Thing I'll Never Do Again* (London: Abacus, 1998), pp. 21–82 (pp. 67–8).
[107] Martin Eve's essay 'Sincerity' includes an overview of critical work on what has come to be known as the 'new sincerity' as well as offering valuable insights of its own. See Martin Eve, 'Sincerity', in *The Routledge Companion to Twenty-First Century Literary Fiction*, ed. Daniel O'Gorman and Robert Eaglestone (Abingdon: Routledge, 2019), pp. 36–47. As Eve notes, his own contribution follows Adam Kelly, whose work is foundational in establishing and delineating the New Sincerity as a cultural mode, beginning with his essay 'David Foster Wallace and the New Sincerity', in *Consider David Foster Wallace*, ed. David Hering (Los Angeles: SSMG Press, 2010), pp. 131–46. The collection *Supplanting the Postmodern*, ed. David Rudrum and Nicholas Stavris (New York: Bloomsbury, 2015) includes an extensive selection of writing on the end of postmodernism and the new ways of framing the contemporary, as does *Metamodernism: Historicity, Affect and Depth after Postmodernism*, ed. Robin van den Akker, Alison Gibbons and Timotheus Vermuelen (London: Rowman and Littlefield, 2017).
[108] Eve, 'Sincerity', pp. 36, 45.

In one of Clifford's addresses to the author, he tells her: 'This is your story. But a man has his ... his *integrity* ... his ... his *pith*, and it's your job, your duty as "Author" ... to represent this fact in as honest – as *sincere* – a way as possible. Isn't it?'[109] His address to the implied author is precisely the type of flourish associated with postmodern irony and scepticism about fiction's truth value, but here it is articulated as request for a more sincere approach to characterization and a move away from treating characters as two-dimensional comic foils. It is an example of the type of fiction categorized by Lee Konstantinou as 'credulous metafiction', in which 'postmodern form is used to reject postmodern content' as a 'way to revive or reinvent the values, commitments and practices thought to be characteristic of life before [postmodernism's] debilitating onset'; David Foster Wallace's statement, quoted by Konstantinou, that he employs '"postmodern techniques", a "postmodern aesthetic"' in order '"to discuss or represent very old traditional human verities that have to do with spirituality and emotion and community and ideas"' is apposite here.[110] And while I agree with Konstantinou that sincerity is not necessarily the antonym to irony, as some writing on the topic has tended to assume,[111] it is a word that recurs in Barker's novel, as in Clifford's plea earlier, that she represent him in as sincere a way as possible, and which evokes precisely this tension between two poles or modes of engaging with the world. In Eco's terms, Clifford is asking that he not be treated as a comic character and that he is allowed the 'shade of tenderness' offered by humour. An ironic gesture is imbricated with a plea for sincerity, and this interplay of modes continues throughout the novel.

Clifford's plea to be treated with dignity could be read as a statement of intent by Barker, an indication that she will move away from the ironic authorial distance associated with the cutting, Menippean and often grotesque comedy found in much of her fiction and discussed earlier in this chapter, but the actuality is more complex than this. *In the Approaches* continues to delight in extended comic set pieces featuring, for example, Franklin's buttocks becoming 'sealed' following a ninety-mile walk, 'the copious blisters on either cheek' having 'been given the opportunity to dry and ... set into a fierce, crystalline glue'.[112] And Clifford continues cursing the 'Witch Author' for her cruelty and

---

[109] Barker, *In the Approaches*, p. 212.
[110] Lee Konstantinou, 'Four Faces of Postirony', in *Metamodernism: Historicity, Affect and Depth after Postmodernism*, ed. Robin van den Akker, Alison Gibbons and Timotheus Vermuelen (London: Rowman and Littlefield, 2017), pp. 87–102 (p. 93).
[111] Lee Konstantinou, *Cool Characters: Irony and American Fiction* (Cambridge, MA: Harvard University Press, 2016), p. 38.
[112] Ibid., p. 284.

control, as well as her repeated acts of revenge when he offers criticism or tries to assert his will. Finally, he begins haemorrhaging words from his nose, which join to form sentences that have appeared earlier in the novel, and as his lifeblood – his existence as text – leaves his body, he starts to lose language altogether and finally disappears from the pages.[113] Despite his protestations Clifford is, finally, nothing but text, but his interventions speak to a contrasting pull in Barker's fiction towards sincerity and even redemption for her characters. Barker – or rather her implied presence – retains detached, authorial control and does not show clemency towards Clifford, but his addresses to her and to the reader enacts a reckoning with the way in which he and other comic characters in her fiction are characterized: they are ironic, metafictional challenges to the notion of ironic detachment itself, or the type of fiction James Wood describes in relation to an earlier generation of writers as 'a comedy of apparent heartlessness, in which the novelist is always a knowing adjective ahead of his [sic] characters'.[114]

In the Approaches enacts a critique of aspects of Barker's own fiction, in particular laughter at the expense of her unfortunate characters, but at the same time continues to invite this form of laughter via the multiple, compounded physical and emotional blows dealt to those same characters. Although it was published too late for extended commentary here, this exploration of the relationship between author and characters continues in Barker's most recent work *I Am Sovereign* – pointedly and self-referentially described as a novella rather than a novel throughout its pages – which is set during the course of a twenty-minute house viewing in the Welsh seaside town on Llandudno. As the title suggests, it is about sovereignty and personal agency. It is also about the ethics of storytelling, and it contains a chapter about a character's resistance to being characterized: '*it is necessary at this point in the novella (henceforth referred to as I Am Sovereign)*', the chapters begins, '*to warn the reader that Nicola Barker (henceforth referred to as The Author) has been granted **absolutely no access** to the thoughts and feelings of the character Gyasi "Chance" Ebo*'.[115] Gyasi 'Chance' Ebo is a twenty-three-year-old Ethiopian professional carer with whom The Author does battle over subsequent pages before he is finally revised out of the main

---

[113] Clifford's disappearance is inevitable, and not only because he has already predicted his own demise. As Alex Woloch observes, the fate of minor characters have a structural purpose in what he terms the character-space and character-system of the novel: 'The minor character is always drowned out within the totality of the narrative; and what we remember about the character is never detached from how the text, for the most part, makes us forget him [sic].' Moreover, the significant of minor characters 'resides largely in the way that the character disappears, and in the tension or relief that results from this vanishing'. Woloch, *The One vs. the Many*, p. 38.

[114] Wood, *Irresponsible Self*, p. 283.

[115] Barker, *I Am Sovereign*, p. 149.

storyline, relegated to a passing reference in an earlier section. As with Clifford in *In the Approaches*, Barker has fun playing with levels of fictionality and with the relative levels of transparency and opacity afforded by her characters, but this is not purely a playful gesture. It is later implied that this resistance is related to The Author's trip to France, where she passed through the port of Calais. Previously her friend, also called Nicola, had told her, 'the entire area had been inhabited by young (for the most part) African men trying to find any means possible of crossing the Channel to Britain', but now the spaces behind the wire fences are 'blank, empty, liminal'; The Author recalls gazing at these non-places 'impassively' and asks 'Can it be any coincidence then, that only a couple of days later The Author began removing Gyasi 'Chance' Ebo from the narrative?' The Author, and by extension the author Nicola Barker, is unwilling, perhaps unable, to inhabit Ebo's consciousness, a move that occasions her to ask: 'Is The Author Truly Sovereign?'[116] The brittle ironic humour of Barker's game playing has something more vulnerable and empathetic at its heart, suggesting that characterization is bound up with questions of ethics and requires understanding and even love. The book ends with a description of Barker's characters crowded into her study, jostling for space as she writes its final pages. Those pages are imbued with a feeling of sorrow that this relationship must end: 'The Author loves them all so much, so very dearly, that she cannot bear to say goodbye to them, somehow.'[117] The Author is not as detached from characters and events as she initially appears, and the novella's mood alternates between ironic detachment and emotional engagement, posing questions about the ethics of representation and the necessity of empathy and understanding.

In the Approaches also develops a gentler, more heartfelt, more sincere form of comedy alongside its gleeful playfulness, showing that it is not a case of choosing between these modes, and that they are often interdependent: irony can represent a displacement of sincerity. Franklin and Carla's relationship is mutually antagonistic throughout the novel but is clearly built on a foundation of suppressed desire and eventually love. In the early portions of the novel, the interplay between these characters fits the classic romantic comedy mould of mockery, ironic badinage and affection disguised as contempt. Franklin recognizes this, but realizes it has an ambiguous and not altogether wholesome edge:

---

[116] Ibid., p. 205.
[117] Ibid., p. 209.

> Ah. She gets my sense of humour! Well that's refreshing. People sometimes struggle with it. I struggle with it myself, on occasion, Hmmn. Was I actually being funny, though? Or was I simply being rude? I must confess there is something about our dear Miss Hahn that brings out the spiteful in me, poor creature.[118]

The recognition of a shared sense of humour brings a feeling of identification, but it is also tinged with rudeness, spite and a desire to wound. Later, as he recalls Carla's vulnerability in response to another of his thoughtless acts, Franklin recognizes that his mockery has been a form of defence:

> Hadn't it always been this signal lack of feminine guile – of calculation – that had drawn me to Miss Hahn in the first instance? Or drawn me to mock her, more like? To satirize her mercilessly? Because I was such an ignorant fool? So proud? So haughty? So terrified of … of … ? Of *here*? Of *here*? Of being *here*, feeling *this*, this miserable love?[119]

Mockery and irony can, Franklin recognizes, be ways of distancing oneself emotionally and temporally – a way of not being *here*, in the present but of standing at a distance and observing. Following this recognition, he is finally able to profess his love for Carla. What follows is a chapter told from Carla's perspective, with occasional interjections from Franklin, in which she attempts to justify her behaviour by telling the story of what actually happened between her, Orla, and Orla's parents. It is not the complete story – as Clifford has earlier noted, Barker does not offer linear or comfortably resolved plots[120] – but it is the most Carla is able to achieve with a story that 'could never … be conclusively told'. The chapter ends with a literalization of Carla's love, rendered as a beam of light emanating from her chest, representing the '"most terrible … most burning … most … most devastating *love*"' that she now feels; her confession breaks through the carapace within which her emotions had been contained, allowing a sincere connection with Franklin.[121] Yet even here, Barker shows how this sincere connection between her characters is not absolute, and Carla's confession is followed by Franklin's more measured response in which he says that he is 'intensely fond' of Carla 'insofar as [he is] capable of … you know, anything approaching sincere human feeling', reasoning that he is in fact '"in love"' with her. The quotation marks denote his scepticism about the concept

---

[118] Barker, *In the Approaches*, p. 121.
[119] Ibid., p. 461.
[120] Ibid., p. 214.
[121] Ibid., p. 490.

love, but he goes further than this and professes that the preceding chapter was 'sheer torture' because Carla's description of events 'was so *woefully inadequate*':

> I mean all that pointless, interior *gumph*! All that endless self-examination! All that ludicrous self-excoriation when the action – the real *action* – [is] outside her, on this porch, in this place, in this moment ...[122]

Franklin makes a bathetic return to irony following Carla's heartfelt confession, but it is an ironic response that calls not for distance and coolness but for a connection with the present moment. It is also a reminder that the modes of irony and sincerity coexist and overlap – that sincere engagement need not preclude irony and vice versa. Franklin's sincere love for Carla exists in the context of his profoundly pragmatic, often ironic disposition.

Barker's recent fiction demonstrates a growing engagement with sincerity and belief in contrast to the more ironic inflection in her earlier work, not only in *In the Approaches* but also in *The Cauliflower®*'s exploration of faith, and Mira A's pursuit of feeling in *H(A)PPY*. But it also reflects on the fact that the concept of a post-ironic age is true only in the sense that it comes after a period in which an ironic worldview was dominant.[123] It is 'post' only in the way that postmodernism represented both a response to and continuation of aspects of modernism rather than a complete rupture; as Konstantinou notes, 'Postironists don't advocate a simple return to sincerity – they're not anti-ironists – but rather wish to preserve postmodernism's critical insights (in various domains) while overcoming its disturbing dimensions.'[124] To return to the quotation with which I began, this interplay between irony and sincerity is demonstrative of the interest in paradox and contradiction that is central to Barker's work and to her comic voice. Comedy invites this exploration of paradox via its reliance on incongruity, discussed earlier in the context of pedantry and the transcendence of opposites, but Barker also centralizes a further series of paradoxes that are central to an

---

[122] Ibid., p. 491.
[123] In an already famous article, Timotheus Vermeulen and Robin van den Akker argue that 'new generations of artists increasingly abandon the aesthetic precepts of deconstruction, parataxis, and pastiche in favour of *aesth-ethical* notions of reconstruction, myth, and metaxis. These trends and tendencies can no longer be explained in terms of the postmodern. They express a (often guarded) hopefulness and (at times feigned) sincerity that hint at another structure of feeling, intimating another discourse.' It should be noted, however, that one of the epigraphs to the essay is taken from a 2010 *New Yorker* article by Jerry Saltz, which argues contemporary artists 'grasp that they can be ironic and sincere at the same time, and they are making art from this compound-complex state of mind'. In other words, a desire for sincerity does not necessitate the wholesale abandonment of irony. Timotheus Vermeulen and Robin van den Akker, 'Notes on Metamodernism', *Journal of Aesthetics and Culture*, 2 (2010), 1–14 (p. 2). The authors return to this topic in their introduction to the collection *Metamodernism*.
[124] Konstantinou, 'Four Faces of Postirony', p. 88.

understanding of what comedy is and what it does, showing how it can subvert social norms while also reinforcing them, and how it can be both sincere and sceptically ironic at the same time.

Rabbit-duck/Duck-rabbit

In Barker's 2002 novel *Behindlings*, the enigmatic Wesley, a character whose legend is built on tales told in Barker's earlier short story collection *Heading Inland*,[125] sets a series of riddles to be solved by his followers, his Behindlings. One of them inspires particularly extended analysis and debate:

> Rabbit-duck?
>   Duck-rabbit!
>   Ludwig? Ludwag!
>   Catch me out, honey,
>   And I'll catch you at it[126]

This riddle refers to the duck-rabbit image that Ludwig Wittgenstein uses in *Philosophical Investigations* (1953) to discuss ambiguities in visual perception: the duck-rabbit is a line drawing that can be interpreted as either a duck or a rabbit, via which Wittgenstein illustrates the concept of aspect seeing, or the ways in which a single image can be viewed in multiple ways.[127] But Barker's riddle also enacts this multiplicity by combining the references to Wittgenstein with terminology from the sport of cricket, in which a batter can be 'caught out' by a member of the fielding team, and to be 'out for a duck' means to lose one's wicket without scoring a run. 'Rabbit' is also a term of abuse in cricket, meaning an incompetent batter who is invariably out for few or no runs, as well as meaning a batter who is frequently out to the same bowler: he or she is the bowler's 'rabbit', or more commonly their 'bunny'. The meanings of these terms are multiple and co-existent, as they are in all puns,[128] and they are both philosophically significant – Barker notes that Wittgenstein's duck-rabbit example is a refutation of Platonic ideals – and a joke: 'Wittgenstein was a bit of wag – see?', explains Jo, 'Ludwig-

---

[125] As Richard Bradford and others have noted, Wesley's name and the quasi-religious zeal with which people are attracted to him invite parallels with John Wesley, the eighteenth-century Protestant dissenter. Bradford, *The Novel Now*, pp. 55–6.
[126] Nicola Barker, *Behindlings* (London: Flamingo, 2002), p. 177.
[127] Ludwig Wittgenstein, *Philosophical Investigations*, 3rd edn (Oxford: Blackwell, [1953] 1968), pp. 194–207.
[128] For an exhaustive and insightful account of the history and meaning of puns, see Walter Redfern, *Puns: More Senses Than One*, 2nd edn (London: Penguin, [1984] 2000).

Ludwag – and a wag means a joker'.[129] Although Wittgenstein was not a noted wag or joker, he did famously acknowledge the potential of jokes in his much-quoted statement that 'a serious and good philosophical work could be written that would consist entirely of *jokes*',[130] and to think of it in these terms, Wesley's riddle is emblematic of Barker's philosophy of comedy. Just as Wittgenstein's duck-rabbit can be seen alternately as a duck or a rabbit and is both of these things at the same time, Barker's comedies are a method for exploring the nature of opposites and the fallacy of seeing things as mutually exclusive alternatives. *I Am Sovereign* states this baldly, at the same time acknowledging the challenges of sustaining such openness to contestation:

> It's so *wearying* when everything is being perpetually challenged and contested like this, though, isn't it?
> But shouldn't fiction strive to echo life (where everything is constantly being challenged and contested)?
> Or is fiction merely a soothing balm, a soft breeze, a quiet confirmation, a temporary release?
> Why should it be either/or?
> Can't fiction be exquisitely paradoxical?[131]

These exquisite paradoxes are at the centre of Barker's work, and the comic voice allows her to explore them without becoming wearisome. Her comedies rely on the interplay of levity and seriousness, demonstrating humour's reliance on opposites and paradox, but also showing how humour is itself paradoxical: how it can inspire both ridicule and sympathy, how it can it can liberate but also enforce norms, and how it can be both ironic and sincere at the same time.

---

[129] Barker, *Behindlings*, pp. 176–7.
[130] Norman Malcolm, *Ludwig Wittgenstein: A Memoir*, 2nd edn (Oxford: Oxford University Press, [1958] 2001), pp. 27–8.
[131] Barker, *I Am Sovereign*, pp. 201–2.

6

'No drawing of lines'
Howard Jacobson and the boundaries of the comic

When Howard Jacobson's *The Finkler Question* (2010) was awarded the 2010 Booker Prize, it was hailed as an overdue vindication of comedy's literary status and was widely seen as the 'first comic novel' to win the prize,[1] or in one formulation, the first 'unashamedly' comic novel to win.[2] Leaving aside the question of what a *shamefully* comic novel might look like, the repetition of variations of the phrase 'first comic novel to win the prize in its 42-year history' across multiple international press outlets suggests the origins of this headline lie with Booker, an organization highly skilled at marketing itself and its prize winners.[3] While this claim to uniqueness is false and ignores previous winners such as Kingsley Amis's *The Old Devils* (1986) or DBC Pierre's *Vernon God Little* (2003), as well as novels such as Salman Rushdie's *Midnight's Children* (1981), J.G. Farrell's *The Siege of Krishnapur* (1973) and Penelope Lively's *Offshore* (1979), which have strong comic elements, *The Finkler Question*'s win did succeed in inspiring a debate about the role and status of humour in fiction.[4] Although

---

[1] See, for example, Anita Singh, 'Man Booker Prize: Howard Jacobson Is Surprise Winner', *Telegraph*, 12 October 2010. Available online: https://www.telegraph.co.uk/culture/books/booker-prize/8060132/Man-Booker-Prize-Howard-Jacobson-is-surprise-winner.html (accessed 29 April 2019); BBC News, 'Howard Jacobson Wins Booker Prize', 12 October 2010. Available online: https://www.bbc.co.uk/news/entertainment-arts-11526278 (accessed 29 April 2019); and Paul Hackett, 'Howard Jacobson Wins Man Booker for Comic Novel', *Globe and Mail*, 12 October 2010. Available online: https://www.theglobeandmail.com/arts/books-and-media/howard-jacobson-wins-man-booker-for-comic-novel/article4328936/ (accessed 29 April 2019).

[2] Mark Brown, 'Howard Jacobson Wins Booker Prize 2010 for *The Finkler Question*', *Guardian*, 12 October 2010. Available online: https://www.theguardian.com/books/2010/oct/12/howard-jacobson-the-finkler-question-booker (accessed 29 April 2019).

[3] For an in-depth and enlightening discussion of the relationship between the Booker Prize and media controversy, see English, *The Economy of Prestige: Prizes, Awards, and the Circulation of Cultural Value*, pp. 197–216.

[4] In a piece written for the *Guardian* books blog, Sam Jordison thoroughly debunks claims for *The Finkler Question*'s unique status, suggesting that the very first winner of the prize, P.H. Newby's *Something to Answer For* (1968), was a comic novel and that there have been a number of other examples among subsequent winners. Sam Jordison, 'Booker Prize Disdains Comedy? What a Joke',

Jacobson did not himself stake a claim for his novel's singularity in the roster of Booker winners, he did take the opportunity to lament the critical status of comic fiction and to make a claim for the centrality of comedy to the novel genre. He has reservations about the terms 'comic novel' and 'comic novelist' (reservations I share and that are discussed in the Introduction to this book), and in an essay published in the *Guardian* shortly after the announcement of the award, he writes that comedy and the novel are so entwined that 'talk of the comic novel is tautologous'. According to Jacobson, contemporary literary culture has 'created a false division between laughter and thought, between comedy and seriousness, between the exhilaration that the great novels offer when they are at their funniest, and whatever else it is we now think we want from literature'. He begins the piece with the statement '"show me a novel that's not comic and I'll show you a novel that's not doing its job"', and while he acknowledges that he is exaggerating, the essay that follows is an impassioned argument for the importance of comedy and its denigration in a culture that values an erroneous equivalence between seriousness and humourlessness.[5] It is a hyperbolic essay, but Jacobson is a hyperbolic writer, and the type of comedy he most values is replete with exaggeration and is often obscene, grotesque or otherwise challenging to delicate sensibilities. He admires the humane insights of George Eliot's *Middlemarch* (1871–2) and calls it 'one of the greatest novels ever written', but is drawn to the 'deeper disquiet' caused by Dickens's comedies. Other touchstones are Dostoevsky, Cervantes, Kafka, Joseph Roth, Henry Miller and Rabelais, all of whom inspire laughter but do not offer easy consolation. A notable omission from this list of writers is Jacobson himself, and it is into this lineage that he tacitly situates not only *The Finkler Question* but also his body of work, beginning with the ribald campus comedy *Coming from Behind* (1983).

In a much-quoted aphorism that he traces to an off-the-cuff remark made during an interview at the Hay Festival (and repeated many times since), Jacobson has distanced himself from comparisons with American-Jewish writers such as Philip Roth, instead describing himself as 'the Jewish Jane Austen'.[6] It is a witty and useful rebuff to lazy comparisons, but it is also misleading. Jacobson studied under F.R. Leavis at Downing College,

---

Guardian, 14 October 2010. Available online: https://www.theguardian.com/books/booksblog/2010/oct/14/booker-prize-disdains-comedy-joke (accessed 29 April 2019).

[5] Jacobson, 'Howard Jacobson on Taking Comic Novels Seriously'.

[6] Mireille Silcoff, 'Booker Prize Winner Howard Jacobson on Zionism, English Literature and Why Serious Stuff Is Better Than Froth', *National Post*, 29 October 2010. Available online: https://nationalpost.com/afterword/mireille-silcoff-booker-prize-winner-howard-jacobson-on-zionism-english-literature-and-why-serious-stuff-is-better-than-froth (accessed 21 March 2019).

Cambridge, and is understandably keen to place himself within Leavis's 'great tradition'.[7] But although Austen's masterful control of perspective and close examination of social mores and familial relationships are undoubtedly an influence on Jacobson as on so much Anglophone writing, the predominant style and subject matter of his work is worlds away from Austen, particularly in its comic moments.[8] In fact, in the book and accompanying television series *Seriously Funny* (1997), Jacobson makes a forceful claim for the importance of a different mode of comedy, a comedy that reminds us that 'we resemble beasts more closely than we resemble gods, and that we make great fools of ourselves the moment we forget it'; a comedy that 'scratches and jeers at us from quite some other place and from quite some other time'.[9] This is much closer to antecedents such as Henry Fielding or Tobias Smollett, or to later writers such as Dickens and indeed Roth, than it is to Austen, and in this book-length study of the history and significance of comedy and laughter, Jacobson traces an alternative lineage that skirts Austen but takes in the bawdy, often priapic humour of Greek Old Comedy, the clowning traditions of the Native American Hopi Tribe, the grotesquery of Rabelais and Dickens, and a strand of English stand-up comedy represented by figures such as Bernard Manning and Roy 'Chubby' Brown, whose jokes approach and often overstep boundaries into misogyny and racism. The overarching argument is that 'there can be no drawing of lines with comedy' – that comedy has a restorative power and that no topic is beyond its reach.[10] Jacobson's hyperbole throughout *Seriously Funny* mimics that of the comedies whose importance he extols, and it is clear that he is making a claim not only for the type of comedy that he values but also

---

[7] In a 2011 lecture at Downing College, later published in the *Telegraph*, Jacobson reflected on the combination of intimidation and admiration he felt studying under Leavis and how that admiration has continued into the present. Howard Jacobson, 'On Being Taught by FR Leavis', *Telegraph*, 23 April 2011. Available online: https://www.telegraph.co.uk/culture/books/8466388/Howard-Jacobson-on-being-taught-by-FRLeavis.html (accessed 29 April 2019).

[8] In this sense, I differ from Christopher Houswitschka, whose reading of *The Finkler Question* argues that like Austen, 'Jacobson achieves comedy and humour mainly by shifting focalization' and does not use 'any obvious rhetorical features such as hyperbole'. While shifts in focalization do have a part to play in the novel's humour, Jacobson also makes frequent use of hyperbole, from the opening page when the accident-prone Julian Treslove imagines 'real and present dangers' such as lamp posts and trees 'splintering his shins', cars mounting the pavement 'leaving him lying in a pile of torn tissue and mangled bones', and sharp objects falling from scaffolding and piercing his skull. Christopher Houswitschka, '"Show me a novel that's not comic …:" Howard Jacobson's *The Finkler Question*', in 'Focus on Comic Representations in Post-Millennial British and Irish Fiction', ed. Barbara Puschmann-Nalenz, special issue *Anglistik: International Journal of English Studies*, 27:1 (2016), 45–59 (p. 57); Howard Jacobson, *The Finkler Question* (London: Bloomsbury, [2010] 2011), p. 3.

[9] Howard Jacobson, *Seriously Funny: From the Ridiculous to the Sublime* (London: Viking, 1997), pp. 2, 8.

[10] Ibid., pp. 36–7.

for the type of comedy he writes. Like Jonathan Coe, whose views on satire and the efficacy of political comedy are discussed in Chapter 1, Jacobson is a practitioner-critic with strong opinions on comedy that stand in complex and sometimes contradictory relation to his fiction. This chapter engages with Jacobson's claims for the importance of comedy in the novel, and particularly for comedy that is free from boundaries, using these as the starting point for a discussion not only of Jacobson's fiction but also of broader questions concerning the relationship between comic licence and offensiveness. It begins by considering examples of humour that rely on racist or sexist stereotypes, analysing the situational factors that affect their reception and interpretation as well as the disjuncture between Jacobson's stated opinions and his comic practice. Aspects of this discussion continue into the second and third sections, which focus on Jewish humour, the identity politics of joke telling, and particularly Jacobson's treatment of traumatic personal and world-historical histories, most notably the legacy of the Holocaust, which raises questions about the limitations as well as the possibilities of the comic. Finally, I consider Jacobson's 2017 novel *Pussy*, a satire of Donald Trump's rise to power, exploring whether contemporary geopolitics offer a rich seam of comic possibilities, or whether their extremity and unpredictability are in some ways beyond satire, a comic *cul-de-sac*. Each of these areas represents a potential limit or boundary for comedy, but as I will go on to discuss, while boundaries are in a number of ways necessary for comedy they are related not to interdictions about content but are contingent on the triangular relationship between author/comedian, their subject matter and the audience, as well as on the perceived intention behind the humour.

Lancing the boil: *Zoo Time, Coming from Behind* and the necessity of offence

In many ways, Jacobson's 2012 novel *Zoo Time* develops the ideas he expressed in interviews and journalism following *The Finkler Question*'s Booker Prize win. It is narrated by a writer, Guy Ableman, who after early success finds himself struggling in a culture where reading is devalued, particularly the reading of what is contentiously known as 'literary' or 'quality' fiction, and yet more particularly the reading of 'literary' or 'quality' fiction that is comic. Ableman is not quite an analogue of Jacobson, but their bibliographies share some parallels in their work's frank, comic depictions of heterosexual relationships and their authors' scepticism of plot, which is both a running theme in Jacobson's novels and a quality of the novels themselves.[11] Ableman also shares some of Jacobson's dissatisfaction with the literary marketplace,[12] and at one point compares the role of the modern author, who is expected to perform at literary festivals and other events, with that of a stand-up comedian, an observation that inspires him to evaluate his career:

> A plain logic demanded we ask ourselves this question: if we wanted to play the comedian why didn't we just call ourselves comedians and dispense with the vestigial bookishness? We were finished, anyway. Comedians had taken over. The best of the stand-ups worked from scripts that might as well have been short satiric novels; they saw as novelists saw, they enjoyed the rhythm of the language, they deployed exaggeration and bathos as we did, they excoriated, they surprised, they caught laughter on the wing, in the moment it threatened to tumble into terror. They were predictable and complacent and self-righteous, too, but then who wasn't? What is more, they had a slavish following. Where had all the readers gone? Wasn't it obvious? They were watching stand-up comedy.[13]

Ableman is right about the rise in the profile and significance of stand-up comedians in English cultural life,[14] but at the same time, he employs the same exaggeration he identifies as a quality of both stand-up comedy and fiction writing. Jacobson's hero Dickens was a hugely prolific and successful public performer and it is debatable whether readership is truly in decline;[15] what

---

[11] The narrator of *Kalooki Nights* (2006), for example, laments that it is 'All anyone was interested in – fucking plot!', and in *The Making of Henry* (2004), plot is described as 'nothing more than the way things turn out, a mere arbitrary intrusion into the game of life, causing the pieces to be shifted right enough, and some even to be swept from the board altogether, but not affecting the overall shape of the contest'. Jacobson values characterization over any conventional sense of plot. Howard Jacobson, *Kalooki Nights* (London: Vintage, [2006] 2007), p. 310; Howard Jacobson, *The Making of Henry* (London: Vintage, [2004] 2005), p. 268.

[12] For example, in a 2018 essay originally written for the BBC, Jacobson worried about the 'infinite distractions of the Jumpin' Jack Flash screen, so deceptively alluring compared to the nun-like stillness of the page, whose black marks you can neither scroll through nor delete' and expressed his concern for the future of literary fiction. Howard Jacobson, 'Why the Novel Matters', *Times Literary Supplement*, 4 July 2018. Available online: https://www.the-tls.co.uk/articles/public/importance-fiction-modern-times-jacobson/ (accessed 29 April 2019).

[13] Howard Jacobson, *Zoo Time* (London: Bloomsbury, [2012] 2013), p. 87.

[14] On the growth of growth of stand-up comedy and the comedy industry see, for example, Sam Friedman, *Comedy and Distinction: The Cultural Capital of a 'Good' Sense of Humour* (Abingdon: Routledge, 2014), pp. 22–5.

[15] A 2017 Arts Council England report does suggest that the market for 'literary fiction' has fallen over the past decade. However, authors' claims that 'not enough people are reading books' usually equate to 'not enough people are reading *my* books'. As Katy Shaw argues in response to Will Self's equally dire prognostications about the novel, the novel is a highly adaptable form that can be seen to 'exist in a permanent state of imminent demise and doom' but that nevertheless 'continues to adapt, ingest and shape-shift, remaining relevant to each generation of readers – and writers'. See Arts Council England, *Literature in the 21st Century: Understanding Models of Support for Literary Fiction*, 15 December 2017. Available online: https://www.artscouncil.org.uk/publication/literature-21st-c

Ableman is really moving towards is not a discussion of the decline of the novel but rather a discussion of his anxiety about the relationship between comedy and the novel. 'Funny might be ruling the world', he continues, but 'as far as the novel went, it was a dead letter. You can't have funny where you have sacred, and someone somewhere had left the windows of the novel open for the sacred to spirit itself in on broken wings.' Ableman believes that the novel has become a space for piety and sacred reverence, squeezing out the profane humour offered by stand-up. He recalls an editor who 'had never found a novel funny, riotous or Rabelaisian in his life' and concludes that 'no publisher with a business brain allowed the word "funny" to appear on a book jacket',[16] echoing Jacobson's own statements.[17] The adjective 'Rabelaisian' is important because it is not wit or pithy *bon mots* that are seen to have been squeezed out of the novel, but rather a more robust comic spirit. *Zoo Time* ends with Ableman finding new success with a series of sentimental novels about the virtues of women, beginning with *The Good Woman*, a novel that contains 'no sex, except by intimation – on pain of death no *squish-squish* – and no jokes'. He compares his writing to pornography because both share a quality whereby 'a single laugh and the trance is broken': jokes are not possible in this new mode of writing, and *The Good Woman* is 'the pornography of the sentimental'.[18] There is a sense of defeatism in the concluding pages, as though the fun police have finally caught up with our hero Ableman, and this mood is both telling of the perceived status of comedy in contemporary fiction and ironic, given that *Zoo Time* is the bawdy, comic follow-up to *The Finkler Question*, the less bawdy but still undeniably comic novel that won Jacobson one of the world's largest and most prestigious literary prizes and brought his work to new audiences.

Jacobson's commentary on the marginalization of comic voices, then, is reflective less of his own marginalization than of his perception that a particular type of comedy has been unfairly denigrated. Given his view that comedy is concerned with the bestial nature of humanity, it is no accident that the title of his novel is *Zoo Time* and that his narrator's first novel is *Who Gives a Monkey's?* Men, in particular, often figure as simian characters in Jacobson's work, driven by animalistic urges and cocking a snook at conventional sensibilities. In *Seriously*

---

entury-understanding-models-support-literary-fiction (accessed 29 April 2019); and Katy Shaw, 'Will Self: Why His Report on the Death of the Novel Is (still) Premature', *Independent*, 20 April 2018. Available online: https://www.independent.co.uk/arts-entertainment/books/will-self-repor t-death-novel-is-still-premature-literature-a8289716.html (accessed 29 April 2019).

[16] Jacobson, *Zoo Time*, pp. 87–8.
[17] Jacobson, 'Howard Jacobson on Taking Comic Novels Seriously'.
[18] Jacobson, *Zoo Time*, p. 366.

Funny, Jacobson has no time for 'humourless little shits' who take offence at jokes and are themselves often the butt of humour,[19] but he also goes further and defends humour that has been accused of racism and sexism, arguing that it has an important social function. More than fifteen years before he depicted stand-up comedy as a new locus for former readers of fiction, Jacobson devoted a significant section of his book on comedy to defending comedians' right to cause offence, or rather to the foolishness of taking offence at comic discourse. Ever the contrarian, Jacobson mounts a defence not of controversies emerging from the alternative comedy scene that had by 1997 become the mainstream of English comedy,[20] but rather of club comedians such as Bernard Manning, Jim Davidson and Roy 'Chubby' Brown, against whom many of the alternative comedians of the 1970s, the 1980s and the 1990s were reacting. In *A National Joke* (2007), Andy Medhurst mounts a more nuanced defence of aspects of Brown's act than is managed by Jacobson,[21] but is less sympathetic to Manning and Davidson, finding them exemplary of 'closed, unitary and change-resistant versions of Englishness'; they are 'ideologically irredeemable'.[22] And yet it is Manning whose significance, even importance, Jacobson is particularly keen to defend. Manning enjoyed mainstream television success in the 1970s via his appearance on *The Comedians*, a primetime British television show that showcased the almost exclusively male club comedians of the time. The show, and Manning himself, later fell out of favour and he became what the comedian Stewart Lee describes as 'the liberal press's chief old-school whipping boy'.[23] From the 1980s onwards, Manning's brand of comedy, which was characterized by a series of discrete jokes with little narrative or linkage and which often relied on gender or racial stereotypes, was considered virtually unbroadcastable, but Manning continued to find regular and lucrative work, most famously at his own Embassy Club in Manchester. This is where Jacobson finds him in *Seriously Funny*, in which he recalls an atmosphere of 'communal purgation' where 'the busloads of mauve-collared drinking men who are [Manning's] friends laugh

---

[19] Jacobson, *Seriously Funny*, p. 16.
[20] For a discussion of the rise of alternative comedy in Britain, see Oliver Double, *Getting the Joke: The Inner Workings of Stand-Up Comedy*, 2nd edn (London: Bloomsbury, 2014), pp. 42–7.
[21] Medhurst acknowledge the many troubling aspects of Brown's act, including his homophobic and xenophobic jokes, but argues that he is the 'most significant English male comedian of the past quarter-century' for offering a working-class perspective that speaks to a working-class audience, for his resistance to homogeneity, for his continuation of a lineage of bad behaviour in English comedy and for his material's ability to bring into focus questions of belonging. Medhurst, *A National Joke*, pp. 187, 200–1.
[22] Ibid., pp. 54, 191.
[23] Stewart Lee, *How I Escaped My Certain Fate: The Life and Deaths of a Stand-Up Comedian* (London: Faber and Faber, 2010), p. 3n.

uproariously' at the obscenities and ugliness emanating from the stage. 'The cliché has it that this is comedy operating as a safety valve',[24] Jacobson notes, but he prefers a more bodily image: 'Comedy in a club like Bernard Manning's lances the boil. It enables the pus to run' and as such is a service that should be available on the National Health Service. However, he goes on to note that at the point at which he is writing, Manning is in trouble for 'saying black a few too many times to an audience of almost exclusively white off-duty policemen'.[25] Jacobson is uncharacteristically coy here, perhaps because it does not help his argument to set down Manning actual words at a 1995 charity dinner for police detectives. The epithets were considerably stronger than Jacobson implies. As Jane Littlewood and Michael Pickering write, a covertly recorded video revealed that Manning 'referred throughout to "niggers" and "coons"' and 'talked of feeling "like a fucking spot on a domino" when he visited Bradford', a city with a large South Asian population. He also singled out the only black police officer in the audience, asking 'if he considered "having a night out with nice people" preferable to "'swinging through the fucking trees"'.[26]

As I have advanced throughout this book, an understanding of context is vital to an understanding comedy, but it is hard to imagine a context that would make Manning's lines anything other than bigotry with the thinnest veneer of humour, and the fact that they were addressed to an audience of police officers compounds the matter. It also is noteworthy that in his defence of Manning, Jacobson does not consider that shared laughter might reinforce rather than defuse prejudice, suggesting tacit acceptance and agreement. Alfie Bown notes laughter's potential to 'create and reinforce prejudice' among groups.[27] And while it may have a role in lancing the metaphorical boil and releasing built-up pressure, does it not also have the potential to rub dirt into the consequent wound, incubating a secondary infection? This is not to argue that topics such as ethnicity and gender should be off limits for comedy, but it is to identify a peculiar blind spot in Jacobson's argument. Michael Redfern has suggested that he would 'ban prohibition' against humour, arguing that 'trying to restrict the field of humour is equivalent

---

[24] This is a version of the 'relief theory' of humour, which has its roots in the eighteenth century and whose most famous exponent was Sigmund Freud. Simply put, this theory suggests that laughter allows the venting of nervous energies that would otherwise express itself in other, more damaging ways.

[25] Jacobson, *Seriously Funny*, pp. 31–2.

[26] Jane Littlewood and Michael Pickering, 'Heard the One about the White Middle-class Heterosexual Father-in-law? Gender, Ethnicity and Political Correctness in Comedy', in *Because I Tell a Joke or Two: Comedy, Politics and Social Difference*, ed. Stephen Wagg (London: Routledge, 1998), pp. 291–312 (pp. 299–300).

[27] Bown, *In the Event of Laughter*, p. 9.

to refusing to talk about all aspects of human experience'.[28] I agree, but humour's rhetorical power cannot be accounted for by a list of proscribed or allowable topics and instead 'retains an ambivalence which means that allegations of offence are widely contested, leading to questions of intention and context in a manner that would be unnecessary if rules of conversation and propriety were followed'.[29] As Helen Davies and Sarah Ilott argue here, it is vital to consider questions of context and intention when examining the distinction between comedy that treads the line between acceptability and offensiveness, and that which blunders across the line into targeted bigotry or even hate speech. There is a significant difference in both intention and audience between black comedians such as Richard Pryor or Dave Chappelle making copious use of racial epithets and stereotypes about black people in their acts and a white performer such as Bernard Manning or Jim Davidson making copious use of those same epithets and stereotypes: one is reflecting on themselves and their own experiences to an audience who may share or at least recognize those experiences, and the other is creating a division between, on the one hand, themselves and the audience and, on the other hand, the group at whose expense the joke is being told. However lightly it is dismissed by Jacobson, this division is particularly marked when the audience are a group of senior police officers whose relationship with minority communities in Britain has been historically uneasy or even hostile. As Michael Ross puts it: 'Jacobson does not consider that hearing the unsayable said publicly might conceivably encourage police officers to do the undoable when on duty in tense, racially mixed neighbourhoods.'[30]

Nonetheless, however bombastic he is in his non-fiction writing on humour, Jacobson's fiction often demonstrates greater insight into the politics of joke work; and while his humour is certainly not safe or middle-of-the-road, his writing does recognize the difference between the potential to cause offence that is inherent in all humour and the reproduction and reinforcement of intolerance or harmful stereotypes. His first novel, *Coming from Behind*, is a campus novel set at the fictional Wrottesley Polytechnic, a heightened version of Wolverhampton Polytechnic (now the University of Wolverhampton) where Jacobson taught in the 1970s. One strand of the plot features Kevin Dainty, captain of the local

---

[28] Michael Redfern, *French Laughter: Literary Humour from Diderot to Tournier* (Oxford: Oxford University Press 2008), pp. 176–7.
[29] Helen Davies and Sarah Ilott, 'Mocking the Weak? Contexts, Theories, Politics', in *Comedy and the Politics of Representation: Mocking the Weak?* (Basingstoke: Palgrave Macmillan, 2018), pp. 1–24 (pp. 5–6).
[30] Michael Ross, *Race Riots: Comedy and Ethnicity in Modern British Fiction* (Montreal and Kingston: McGill-Queen's University Press, 2006), p. 15.

football club Wrottesley Wranglers, who has written a novel entitled *Scoring*. The Polytechnic's senior management are hoping for an endorsement of the novel by a member of the English faculty in order to help secure Dainty as a governor and assist their plans to twin the institution with the football club and share resources. Sefton Goldberg, the protagonist of *Coming from Behind*, is charged with reading *Scoring*, with the strong suggestion that he should like it and report favourably. Goldberg is predictably acid in his judgement, blaming Dickens for inventing the idea that Londoners are all 'sentimental warmints [sic], coves and dodgers, as energetic as a tugboat and as home loving as Toodle, fly and artful, but not nat'rally wicious [sic]'. That the line 'Naterally Wicious' is used by a Dickens character from Kent to the south-east of London is apparently immaterial:[31] Kevin Dainty is a Londoner, and once Goldberg realizes this, he can see what type of novel it will be: 'there was only one novel a Londoner could write', he reflects. And yet, when Goldberg actually reads *Scoring* 'there were a couple of small surprises'.[32] Rather than the 'expected aphoristic market-stall holder', the hero's best friend is an 'aphoristic West-Indian cab driver', a difference that changes the dynamic of the relationship when this friend shares a one-night stand with the hero's wife Elaine. Goldberg speculates that as a result of this change, when Elaine and the hero are finally reunited, she is unable to confess to the affair:

> Sefton thought it was shrewd of Kevin Dainty to have calculated what his hero could and couldn't cope with, and shrewd of Elaine to have calculated likewise. The Jewish stallholder, a temporary consolation rather than a rival, would not have been too impossibly difficult for the most jealous of husbands to manage mentally, now that Jews were making themselves sexually harmless and going in for having heard of Christ, compassion, and interpersonal human relationships. … But a West Indian cab-driver putting out the light is an altogether darker proposition. A husband might shudder and draw the line at that.[33]

Here Jacobson makes comic capital out of stereotypes, using them to speculate on the relative acceptability of being cuckolded by one or other ethnic or religious group. He invokes the toxic stereotype of the sexually potent and feared black Other, but the difference from the jokes of Manning and his ilk is that

---

[31] The phrase is taken from *Great Expectations* and is spoken by Mr Hubble the wheelwright. It refers to Hubble's views on the natural disposition of children and is addressed to Pip and an audience of assenting adults. Charles Dickens, *Great Expectations* (Oxford: Oxford University Press, [1861] 2008), p. 24.
[32] Howard Jacobson, *Coming from Behind* (London: Abacus, [1983] 1986), p. 145.
[33] Ibid., pp. 146–7.

it is also told against the Jewish Goldberg, who offers the counter-stereotype of the sexually unthreatening 'benign and philosophical' Jew. This is dangerous territory because, as Michael Ross notes, one's own position as part of a minority group does not provide a free pass for racialized humour, nor is there any necessary equivalence between groups and situations.[34] Moreover, the political valency of these stereotypes is quite distinct and I would not wish to draw a direct correspondence between them: Sefton/Jacobson are clearly in a position of authority here. The passage about the 'darker proposition' represented by the stereotype of the sexually potent black male was written during the era of the uprisings in areas such Brixton in London and Toxteth in Liverpool, when black communities erupted in response to their disproportionate targeting by police; it was also a time when comedians such as Manning continued to have mainstream outlets for jokes told against those same groups. Nevertheless, in this passage from *Coming from Behind*, the stereotype does not provide the final punchline. Rather, Goldberg's reflections lead to a sigh and an ironic lament:

> There had been a time when his race, too, had occasioned phallic terror in the minds of English gentiles. It would be nice to bring a bit of that back. He, for one, had been far too accommodating. Hiding and stooping and apologising and being grateful. It was time to reassert himself.[35]

By reflecting on the changing role of Jewish masculinity – and by extension black masculinity – in the English imaginary, this passage from *Coming from Behind* emphasizes the historically contingent nature of stereotypes and the way in which they can accrete around different groups at different moments in history, enacting what Bown describes as the ability of jokes not only to 'powerfully impose and construct nationalisms, identities and genders' but also to 'undo and unsecure these things by showing how contingent they are'.[36] Goldberg's desire to reclaim 'phallic terror' for his own purposes, as well as the way in which the novel skirts the boundaries of taste throughout, mean that this is not an example the safe, conciliatory comedy of which Jacobson is so dismissive, but nor is it humour that relies solely on the reproduction and reinforcement of damaging stereotypes. Boundaries are not set by subject matter but rather by addressivity and intention, and while I am sceptical about the glee with which Jacobson reproduces racist tropes as well his arguments for the legitimacy of doing so,

---

[34] Ross, *Race Riots*, p. 16.
[35] Jacobson, *Coming from Behind*, p. 147.
[36] Bown, *In the Event of Laughter*, p. 62.

Coming from Behind is a novel that also reflects on the conditional nature of those same tropes.

Jacobson's blunt argument in *Seriously Funny* for a comedy without boundaries, and his defence of nakedly prejudice-filled comedy is not, then, entirely reflective of the humour in his own fiction, which may revel in the 'coarse laughter' he prizes but which is more inclined to invite laughter *about* stereotypes rather than *against* the subjects of those stereotypes. But there is also a more fundamental relationship between comedy and boundaries, however notional those boundaries may be. As Sharon Lockyer and Michael Pickering note, boundaries are in fact necessary to humour:

> Paradoxically, making offensive jokes about others with total impunity would mean that there are no boundaries to push any more. This would lead to the defeat of humour, which is subject to our ability to choose. Humour is only possible because certain boundaries, rules and taboos exist in the first place.[37]

On this view, Jacobson's imagined free space of total comic licence would negate the possibility of comedy, or at least negate the possibility of comedy that has any kind of bite. As Lockyer and Pickering suggest, choice and the potential to offend are essential components in humour that pushes boundaries, and taking offence at a joke is not always a marker of being a 'humourless little shit'. Laura Salisbury puts it well when she writes that the 'transgressive pleasure experienced within the comic world would never be felt if the limit was absolutely impermeable; but equally there would be no frisson, no pleasure to be gained from stepping outside of the law if that law was not felt, at least momentarily, to be constructively real'.[38] In other words, comedy and particularly challenging or transgressive comedy, requires the presence of the very boundaries it seeks to challenge, a relationship that is tacitly acknowledged by Jacobson when he discusses Trevor Griffiths's play *Comedians* (1976). *Comedians* is set in an evening class for would-be stand-up comedians and later at a working men's club where the performers have the opportunity to try out their material in the hope of impressing a comedy booker. It is about the rhetoric of comedy and the rhetoric of prejudice, and Jacobson focuses on a passage in which the tutor of the class, an old professional comedian named Eddie Waters, expresses a series of anti-Semitic slurs, quoting Hitler and concluding that the Jewish people are

---

[37] Sharon Lockyer and Michael Pickering, 'Introduction: The Ethics and Aesthetics of Humour and Comedy', in *Beyond a Joke: The Limits of Humour*, 2nd edn, ed. Sharon Lockyer and Michael Pickering (Basingstoke: Palgrave Macmillan, 2009), pp. 1–26 (p. 16).

[38] Salisbury, *Samuel Beckett*, p. 20.

'Scarcely human. Grubs'.[39] For Jacobson, this passage fails not because it invokes offensive stereotypes but because Griffith's writing 'is inept as a parody of racist comedy'. He makes a valid point about Griffith's own apparently unthinkingly stereotypical stage directions when he introduces the '*fat, Manchester Jewish*', cigar-smoking Sammy Samuels,[40] but he also skirts over the reaction to Waters's diatribe, which is greeted with '*Uneasy laughter, dying fast*'. A further series of slurs against groups including 'negroes', workers and women is then followed by '*Silence. Coughing. Shuffling of feet*'.[41] The point is that this is a failed routine that relies on shock and naked prejudice and that is presented by Waters as an ugly lesson in stereotypes, the attitudes that lie behind them and his own warped view of what comedy should be. It is a deliberately inept parody of racist comedy, and cannot be considered a failure on Griffith's part on those terms. *Comedians* stages a series of conflicts concerning the role and possibilities of comedy, and as Terry Eagleton argues it 'does not seek to resolve the conflicts it portrays'.[42] Jerry Palmer notes of the depiction of sexist humour in *Comedians* that there is a difference between attempted jokes that are naked in their hostility and jokes that invoke stereotypes but succeed due to 'the absurdity of the situation evoked in the punch line'. I am not convinced that the fact that 'many women' laugh at the joke Palmer cites is sufficient proof of his proposition – the joke involves an imagined encounter between the comedian Gethin Price's wife and an orangutan – but he makes an important observation when he notes that the same joke delivered at the same time could both feed the hatred of a misogynist in the audience and be more innocently enjoyed by others whose laughter 'would not necessarily imply anything other than the perception of the absurdity of the situation'.[43] While putatively critiquing Griffiths's crude, unfunny depiction of anti-Semitic humour, then, Jacobson in fact reinforces the idea that it is not particular topics that are off limits (even in the context of Griffiths's play) but rather something more complex, which emerges from the nexus between performer and audience and which concerns not simply subject matter and whether material conforms to the structure of a joke but also the vital question of perceived intention. As Peter Berger notes in a discussion of Jewish humour and the pejorative versus

---

[39] Trevor Griffiths, *Comedians* (London: Faber and Faber, 1976), p. 19.
[40] Ibid., p. 9.
[41] Ibid., p. 19.
[42] Terry Eagleton, *Humour* (Newhaven, CT: Yale University Press, 2019), p. 155.
[43] Palmer, *The Logic of the Absurd*, p. 18. Another explanation for the audience's apparent amusement may be what Steven Gimbel calls the 'smash and grab' of shock comedy, in which laughter is 'generated by strong sudden emotions, by surprise or pleasure at the breaking of social norms', and which is often followed by a sharp intake of breath. Steven Gimbel, *Isn't That Clever: A Philosophical Account of Humor and Comedy* (New York: Routledge, 2018), p. 83.

celebratory use of the 'shrewd businessman' stereotype: 'it is not just a question of *how* jokes are told, but by *whom* and *when*!'[44] Following his discussion of *Comedians*, Jacobson notes in parentheses that 'I, a Jew, feel far more threatened by those who would wipe out ethnic jokes than by those who unthinkingly make them',[45] a comment that pinpoints a significant aspect of the debate about the boundaries of comedy: the censorship of particular topics for comedy is a straw man and its success depends instead on the fragile relationship between joke teller and joke receiver. Jacobson's own novels are evidence of this, having made comedy out of Jewish identity and history, including its very darkest and most harrowing episodes. It is to this topic that I turn next.

'Jew know why'?: *The Finkler Question*, Jewish jokes and the politics of joke-telling communities

Returning to his quip about being the 'Jewish Jane Austen' as opposed to the 'British Philip Roth', Jacobson's desire to instate himself in a British, or rather English, lineage is understandable not only due to his background as a Leavisite but also because British-Jewish fiction has so often been overshadowed by its American cousin. In his short essay on British-Jewish literature for *The Routledge Encyclopedia of Jewish Writers of the Twentieth Century*, Bryan Cheyette notes that 'there exists a commonplace perception, despite a good deal of evidence to the contrary, that Jewish writers in Britain do not exist'.[46] Cheyette and numerous other scholars have shown this perception to be demonstrably false, but it offers a further context for Jacobson's desire to distance himself from Roth. This desire is particularly marked in Jacobson's case given what Nadia Valman describes as his 'abiding preoccupation with masculinity, as the central subject of the British-Jewish novel', a preoccupation that 'belies his aspiration, as a comic writer, to be considered the "Jewish Jane Austen" rather than the "British Philip Roth"'.[47] Jacobson's north Manchester is markedly different from Roth's Newark, and it is not that he emulates Roth as such,[48] but the two writers do share elements of both

---

[44] Berger, *Redeeming Laughter*, p. 84.
[45] Jacobson, *Seriously Funny*, p. 35.
[46] Bryan Cheyette, 'British-Jewish Literature', in *The Routledge Encyclopedia of Jewish Writers of the Twentieth Century*, ed. Sorrel Kerbel (New York: Routledge, 2010), pp. 7–10 (p. 7).
[47] Nadia Valman, 'Jewish Fictions', in *The Oxford History of the Novel in English, vol. 7: British and Irish Fiction since 1940*, ed. Peter Boxall and Bryan Cheyette (Oxford: Oxford University Press, 2016), pp. 347–67 (p. 359).
[48] Indeed, speaking from an American perspective, Jeremy Dauber writes of *The Finkler Question* that the 'spiralling, traumatic conclusion, shrouded and shot through all about with fundamental concern

subject matter and sensibility. And the line from Roth's *Sabbath's Theater* (1995) that Jacobson quotes approvingly in *Seriously Funny* – 'For a pure sense of being tumultuously alive, you can't beat the nasty side of existence'[49] – is revealing of a shared interest in finding humour in the seedier, more uncomfortable, aspects of life. Valman goes on to quote Jacobson's assertion that the 'voice of the Jewish novel ... emulates that of the Hebrew prophets: "When you think of the Jewish novel, you think of the patriarchal voice, the voice of demanding, the buttonholing voice"', arguing that Jacobson's central preoccupations are 'the heroic drama of men engaged in Oedipal struggle with their fathers, and in competition with other men, processes that are profoundly impaired by the legacy of the Holocaust and Jewish assimilation'.[50] This is a valuable summary of the territory around British-Jewish identity and masculinity to which Jacobson's comedy is attuned, and to which he goes in the moments of nastiness, trauma or controversy suggested by the Roth quotation and examined at length in *Seriously Funny*. But equally important is Valman's statement earlier in her essay that 'it is only comedy, therefore, that can reach into the murk of confusion and prohibition produced by a traumatic inheritance'.[51] There are parallels here with Terrence Des Pres's important essay 'Holocaust Laughter', in which he argues that 'in the realm of art, a comic response is more resilient, more effectively in revolt against terror and the sources of terror than a response that is solemn or tragic',[52] and both Valman and Des Pres offer positions that are subtly different from Jacobson's more blunt statements. They suggest not that anything is allowable in comedy, but rather that comedy *can allow anything* – it can, in Freud's terminology, be 'tendentious',[53] offering ways to discuss challenging topics that are not possible via other forms of discourse. In this respect, Jacobson's comedies are part of a lineage of Jewish comedy that makes laughter out of pain and suffering without making light of them.

The Finkler Question, for example, is a novel concerned with Jewish identity within and between individuals, as well as from without as it is understood by

---

about the possibilities and prospects for an Anglo-Jewish community, seems impossibly alien to an American context'. Jeremy Dauber, *Jewish Comedy (A Serious History)* (New York: Norton, [2017] 2018), p. 41.
[49] Philip Roth, *Sabbath's Theater* (London: Vintage, [1995] 1996), p. 247; quoted in Jacobson, *Seriously Funny*, p. 119.
[50] Valman, 'Jewish Fictions', p. 359.
[51] Ibid., p. 358.
[52] Terrence Des Pres, 'Holocaust Laughter', in *Writing into the World: Essays 1973-1987* (Harmondsworth: Penguin, 1981), pp. 277–86 (pp. 281–2).
[53] Freud makes a distinction between innocuous jokes in which 'the joke is an end in itself and serves no particular purpose', and tendentious jokes that put themselves 'in the service of such a purpose'. Freud, *The Joke and Its Relation to the Unconscious*, p. 87.

non-Jews. This external perspective is primarily provided by Julian Treslove who idealizes the Jewish faith and culture of his friends Sam Finkler and Libor Sevcik. Treslove wishes to be Jewish, and the novel contains many jokes about his anxieties and longings, his feelings of exclusion and his projection of those feelings onto his friends. Early in the novel, there is a flashback to a school holiday during which a fortune teller predicts that Treslove will fall in love with a woman named Juno. When he asks Finkler whether he knows anybody named Juno, Finkler responds with a pun: '"J'you know Juno?" Finkler replied, making inexplicable J noises between his teeth.' But Treslove does not get the joke and Finkler has to write it down to demonstrate the wordplay: '*D'Jew know Jewno?*'[54] Still Treslove fails to see the funny side and Finkler tells him that he would not understand even if he were to explain it to him; it becomes a question of identity and background. '"Non-Jews don't find it hilarious to see the word Non-Jew,"' Treslove says. '"We aren't amazed by the written fact of our identity."' To this Finkler replies, '"And Jew know why that is?"' Treslove's frustrated response is to tell Finkler '"Go Fuck yourself."' The conversion concludes with Finkler's question "And that's non-Jew humour, is it?"', outsmarting Treslove again. 'Finkler' becomes Treslove's private synonym for all Jews, and when he reflects that 'he would never be clever in a Finklerish way. *D'Jew know Jewno* ... . He'd never be able to come up with anything like that',[55] he is referring both to his friend and to a particular quick-wittedness he associates with a specifically Jewish sense of humour. Later, when Treslove starts a relationship with Libor's niece Hephzibah, whose friends sometimes refer to her as Juno, Treslove tries a version of Finkler's joke on her – '"D'Jew say Juno?"'[56] The attempt falls flat, as do his later efforts to mimic Hephzibah's comic intonations. When he tells her that the roof to his world collapsed when they met, Hephzibah replies '"I'm the roof now!"' and Treslove is enraptured, believing 'his heart would break with love for her' because 'She was so Jewish. ... *That* was what it was to be a Jewess. ... A Jewess was a woman who made even punctuation funny.' But when he tries to reciprocate with a reversal of the same phrase, he cannot make the joke land: 'He threw in everything he had – a shrug, a "so", a "now" and an extra exclamation mark. "So I'm not the roof now!!"' And yet

---

[54] This joke is itself a reference to a scene in Woody Allen's 1977 film comedy *Annie Hall* (1977), in which Allen's paranoid character Alvy Singer believes he hears an associate answer his question 'Did You Eat Yet?' with '"No, D'Jew?"' *Annie Hall*, [Film] dir. Woody Allen (USA: United Artists, 1977).
[55] Jacobson, *Finkler Question*, pp. 19–21. Ruth Gilbert notes that 'the joke in *The Finkler Question* is that, although Jewishness is the focus of extreme and even obsessive interest, it cannot quite be spoken', hence Treslove's use of his private word 'Finkler'. Ruth Gilbert, *Writing Jewish: Contemporary British-Jewish Literature* (Basingstoke: Palgrave Macmillan, 2013), p. 11.
[56] Jacobson, *Finkler Question*, p. 161.

still she didn't laugh. He couldn't tell if she was annoyed with him for trying. Or maybe it was just that Finkler jokes didn't work in the negative. It sounded funny enough to him. *So, I'm not the roof now!!* But it could have been that Finklers only permitted other Finklers to tell Finkler jokes.[57]

Treslove and his obsessive Philosemitism are the butt of a series of jokes here, but this is also a sequence about joking itself, its ability to include or exclude, and the contested notion that there is a specifically Jewish sense of humour. Jacobson pokes fun at Treslove's essentialist notions of Jewish identity, but at the same time, the novel suggests that there is such a thing as uniquely, or at least characteristically, Jewish comedy and that not everybody has the right or ability to produce it.

In *Jewish Comedy (A Serious History)* (2017), Jeremy Dauber explores many of the historical and contemporary permutations and possibilities of Jewish comedy, but he is clear from the outset that *'Jewish humor has to be produced by Jews'*:[58] there are identifiable tropes, topics and even intonations in Jewish humour, but it is created in a specific cultural and religious context that is not replicable by non-Jews. This is what Jacobson identifies in Treslove's frustrated and floundering attempts at humour in *The Finkler Question* – that is, the significance of joke-telling communities and their often unspoken rules, an idea that again runs contra to Jacobson's arguments about total comic licence. The practice of comedy is bound up with questions of identity and community, and although Treslove is a comparatively innocuous presence in the novel, his attitude towards his Jewish friends and later his lover is clearly held up as an example of simplistic and unhealthy idealization. But *The Finkler Question* also makes finer-grained distinctions about subject matter, inclusion and exclusion, which move away from a binary distinction between Jewish and non-Jewish humour. During the course of the novel, Treslove's friend Sam Finkler, a popular philosopher, becomes a member and later de facto leader of a group named ASHamed Jews, made up of media personalities and other public figures who are ashamed of aspects of their Jewishness, particularly as it pertains to Zionism and the Israel-Palestine conflict. This group is a thinly veiled satirical portrait of the real-life organization Independent Jewish Voices, one of whose founders Jacobson has engaged in public and acrimonious dispute.[59] Its portrayal in *The*

---

[57] Ibid., pp. 192–3.
[58] Dauber, *Jewish Comedy*, p. xii.
[59] In 2009, one of the founders of Independent Jewish Voices, Jacqueline Rose, wrote a piece for the *Guardian* newspaper that was critical of Jacobson's accusation that Caryl Churchill's play *Seven Jewish Children* (2009) is anti-Semitic. Rose is an associate director on the play, and her response elicited a reply from Jacobson, who reiterated his accusation. Rose again responded to address

Finkler Question provides a vehicle for some of the arguments he was rehearsing in journalism throughout the novel's composition. During a discussion of the semantics of the name ASHamed Jews and the makeup of the group's membership, Jacobson's narrator notes that the name ASHamed Zionists was rejected because it implied its members had once been Zionists. However,

> To be an ASHamed Jew did not require that you had been knowingly Jewish all your life. Indeed, one among them only found out he was Jewish at all during the course of making a television programme in which he was confronted on camera with *who he really was*. In the final frame of the film he was disclosed weeping before a memorial in Auschwitz to dead ancestors who until that moment he had never known he'd had. 'It could explain where I get my comic genius from,' he told an interviewer for a newspaper, though by then he had renegotiated his new allegiance. Born a Jew on a Monday, he had signed up to be an ASHamed Jew by Wednesday and was seen chanting 'We are all Hezbollah' outside the Israeli Embassy on the following Saturday.[60]

For Ruth R. Wisse this passage 'spears Holocaust exploitation – that by now perennial target of Jewish satire – and the Jew's floundering sense of identity in a declining culture attracted to fanatics who are secure in their cause'; it does so not by satirizing 'British elites per se', but rather by targeting 'the craven Jewish complicity with them'.[61] It is not clear from Wisse's commentary who those 'elites' might be, and in my reading of the passage, the focus is more specific and localized. I will go on to talk in greater detail about Jacobson's treatment of the Holocaust in a comic context, but for the moment, I want to place the emphasis on the unnamed comedian's reference to the origins of his '"comic genius"' and what the novel suggests about the right to tell jokes. Wisse argues that the comedian is a 'know-nothing' who 'claims the license, as his birthright, to exploit for comedy what other Jews have been paying for with their

---

Jacobson's misrepresentation of her position. For Jacobson's initial article, see Howard Jacobson, 'Let's See the "Criticism" of Israel for What It Really Is', *Independent*, 18 February 2009. Available online: https://www.independent.co.uk/voices/commentators/howard-jacobson/howard-jacobson-letrsquos-see-the-criticism-of-israel-for-what-it-really-is-1624827.html (accessed 10 April 2019), and for Rose's response and links to subsequent correspondence, see Jacqueline Rose, 'Why Howard Jacobson Is Wrong', *Guardian*, 24 February 2009. Available online: https://www.theguardian.com/commentisfree/2009/feb/23/howard-jacobson-antisemitism-caryl-churchill (accessed 10 April 2019). For a discussion of this debate in the context of Jacobson's novel, see Ned Curthoys, 'Howard Jacobson's *The Finkler Question* as Holocaust Pedagogy', *Holocaust Studies*, 19:3 (2013), 1–24.

[60] Jacobson, *Finkler Question*, p. 167.
[61] Ruth R. Wisse, *No Joke: Making Jewish Humour* (Princeton, NJ: Princeton University Press, 2013), p. 241. Ned Curthoys is critical of *The Finkler Question* for the very same manoeuvre, arguing that it 'affiliates itself with a Zionist identity politics disdainful of independent or anti-Zionist Jews who are perceived to undermine the Jewish State's symbolic capital as the rightful heir to Holocaust memory'. See Curthoys, '*The Finkler Question* as Holocaust Pedagogy', p. 2.

lives',[62] again suggesting that the ability to make jokes about a topic is distinct from having the right to make jokes about it. However, while the comedian's attribution of his comic genius to his newly discovered heritage is itself absurd in its essentialism, this passage also reinforces another form of essentialism that brackets off Holocaust trauma or the taking of a position on the Israel-Palestine conflict as the preserve of those who have earned it through both heritage and lived experience. This raises the question of who has the right to speak – or to feel – and who is in a position to make judgements about those rights. Moreover, Jacobson's strident assertions about the right to tell jokes and his belief that no topic should be off the table do not extend to his own largely unexamined and conservative positions on Jewish identity and politics, beliefs that erupt in the narrative via thoroughly un-comic moments such as Finkler's disturbing fantasy of sexual violence and murder against Tamara Krausz, a fellow member of ASHamed Jews who Finkler loathes seemingly because she is a woman who has the audacity to hold strong opinions and express them publicly. Jacobson's own politics remain a blind spot in his comic view of the world. In *The Finkler Question*, the right to make jokes has to be both *learned* and *earned*, and the stand-up comedian's Soloman Grundy-esque conversion followed by disavowal fits neither of these criteria.[63] While attempting to satirize essentialist notions about what it means to be Jewish, the novel fails to identify its own aporia and instead reproduces via its depiction of Jewish joking a further series essentialist criteria for who has the right to be seen as authentically Jewish.

A further strand of *The Finkler Question*'s plot involves Hephzibah's work for a new museum of Anglo-Jewish culture in the London district of St John's Wood, and the attempts by anti-Semites to prevent this from happening. Hephzibah is clear that it is not to be a Holocaust museum, but she is weighed down by 'the wild proliferation of conspiracy theory' and is forced to engage with those who tell her, 'Shut up about your fucking Holocaust … or we will deny it ever happened.' The very fact of the Holocaust has, she feels, 'become negotiable', and when she runs into her ex-husband Ben, he relates a 'hellish tale about his sleeping with a Holocaust denier and negotiating numbers in return for favours. He'd come down a million if she'd do this to him, but would want a million put back in return for doing that to her.' Hephzibah says she does not believe him,

---

[62] Wisse, *No Joke*, p. 167.
[63] In *Roots Schmoots*, Jacobson traces his own journey in pursuit of his Jewish roots, describing in the Introduction his passage from not feeling Jewish at all to feeling 'so exclusively Jewish that [he] barely had room to know anything else'. Howard Jacobson, *Roots Schmoots: Journeys among Jews* (Woodstock, NY: Overlook Press, 1994), p. 6.

but it is unclear whether his story is a fabrication. The back-and-forth of their discussion treads a fine line between the gravely serious and the gravely comic, and when Ben makes a comparison between himself and the '"list man"' Oscar Schindler, joking that the difference is that unlike Schindler Ben is '"saving those already exterminated"', Hephzibah tells him, '"That could be the foulest joke, no, those could be the foulest *two* jokes, I've ever heard."' Ben argues he was attempting to reform this unnamed Holocaust denier, and he and Hephzibah continue to riff on the idea:

> 'And did you?'
> 'Did I what?'
> 'Reform her.'
> 'No, but I got her up to 3 million.'
> 'What did you have to do for that?'
> 'Don't ask.'

Despite describing Ben's jokes as the '"foulest"' she has heard, Hephzibah realizes that they *are* jokes and is shocked but not offended. She also recognizes that Ben, who is Jewish, is joking not in order to endorse Holocaust denial but in order to extend and undermine its twisted logic in diminishing or denying non-negotiable facts. Again, an understanding of intentionality and of the subject positions of joke tellers is vital here because, *pace* Jacobson's own comments in *Seriously Funny*, the same words delivered by a different individual can have a wholly different meaning. And yet Hephzibah also understands that although Ben intends no malice, standards of acceptability are not universal, recalling that that 'She didn't tell her bosses the Ben story. You never knew what a Jew was or was not going to find funny.'[64] There are those for whom certain subjects remain beyond a joke, and although it goes against the representation of Jewish humour and jokes elsewhere in the novel, this punchline is indicative of the fact that the boundaries of humour do not follow strict delineations of religion, ethnicity or other forms of individual or collective identity.

'Not *only* funny': *Kalooki Nights* and Holocaust comedy

The idea that certain subjects lie beyond the boundaries of humour is brought into sharp relief when it comes to humour about the Holocaust and anti-Semitism,

---

[64] Jacobson, *Finkler Question*, pp. 352–4.

and yet Jacobson has traversed this border country not only in *The Finkler Question* but also elsewhere in his work, most notably in *Kalooki Nights*, about which he has written that 'the more tragic the themes – in this case massacre, murder, derangement (and, of course, taking oneself too seriously or not seriously enough) – the more obliged I feel as a novelist to mine the comedy in them'.[65] *Kalooki Nights* is narrated by Max Glickman, a comic-book artist whose north Manchester childhood and adolescence share similarities with Jacobson's background and with the milieu described in some of his earlier fiction. Max has enjoyed moderate professional success, but his passion project, a comic-book history of the Jewish people entitled *Five Thousand Years of Bitterness*, was met with indifference when it was published in 1976, a victim Glickman believes of resurgent Jewish pride following Operation Entebbe, when Israeli forces rescued hostages held captive in Uganda following the hijacking of a flight from Tel Aviv. This show of strength demonstrated that that the Jewish people 'took no shit', and Max reasons that 'people who take no shit don't have to go around making jokes about themselves': 'Jokes are the refuge of the *Untermenschen*', meaning that his brand of embittered comedy fell out of style.[66] He has already noted that he is 'the fruit of Five Thousand Years of Bitterness' and as such is also 'heir to Five Thousand Years of Jokes',[67] and throughout the novel jokes and comedy are represented as the refuge and revenge of the downtrodden, a necessary corrective to victimhood. As Aída Díaz Bild notes, quoting a 2001 article by Jacobson on Jewish comedy, the 'masochist knows how to turn defeat into victory and this explains why self-derision "leaves us not at all humiliated but invigorated"'.[68] There are parallels here with the Deleuzian concept of masochism discussed in Chapter 5 of this book in relation to Magnus Mills's comedies of repetition,[69] but also with a specifically Jewish form of joking, identified by Devorah Baum as 'taking pride in one's difference *and* feeling ashamed at the same time'.[70] This is different from the shame imagined by Jacobson via the ASHamed Jews plotline in *The*

---

[65] Howard Jacobson, '*Guardian* Book Club Week Three: Howard Jacobson on Writing Kalooki Nights', *Guardian*, 2 October 2010. Available online: https://www.theguardian.com/books/2010/oct/02/book-club-howard-jacobson-kalooki (accessed 15 April 2019).
[66] Jacobson, *Kalooki Nights*, pp. 166–7.
[67] Ibid., p. 47.
[68] Aída Díaz Bild, '*Kalooki Nights* or the Sacred Duty to Remember the Holocaust', *Holocaust Studies*, 23:3 (2018), 265–86 (p. 278).
[69] Valman argues that in 'claiming this history of subjugation and physical vulnerability for their own erotic purposes, Jacobson suggests, Max and Manny invert the hierarchy of power', a reading that shares parallels with the Deleuzian view of masochism as resistance rather than simple enjoyment of pain. Valman, 'Jewish Fictions', p. 357.
[70] Devorah Baum, *The Jewish Joke: An Essay with Examples (Less Essay, More Examples)* (London: Profile, 2017), p. 13.

Finkler Question because it is a self-directed 'being at odds with oneself' rather than an outwardly directed, politicized shame. In this sense, it is closer to Freud's suggestion in the essay 'Humour' that laughter at oneself can offer a gentler form of prohibition than is customary from the 'severe master', the superego.[71] Both Baum and Jacobson acknowledge Freud's earlier analysis of joking against 'one's own people', which in contrast to jokes told by outsiders relies on knowledge of 'their real faults and how they are related to their good points'. This allows the joke teller a share in the humour and helps foster the 'subjective conditions for the joke-work that are otherwise difficult to set up'. Freud suspects it is unique to Jews 'that a people should make fun of its own nature to such an extent' and notes that this form of self-mockery is 'particularly favourable to the tendentious joke'.[72] *Kalooki Nights* contains multiple examples of both these forms of humour – the self-mockery identified by Jacobson, Baum, Freud and others as characteristic of Jewish comedy and the tendentious, challenging humour that this allows.[73]

In fact, *Kalooki Nights* pushes the masochism inherent in self-mockery to extremes by making humour out of sexual masochism in the context of the Holocaust. Max's co-author of the early drafts of *Five Thousand Years of Bitterness* is his childhood friend Manny Washinksky, with whom he first embarks on his 'blasphemous' project.[74] It is also Manny who first introduces Max to the *Scourge of the Swastika* (1954), Lord Russell of Liverpool's account of Nazi war crimes, a book that awakens Max to the recent past and his 'solemn destiny'; Max acknowledges that he was 'born safely, at a lucky time and in an unthreatening part of the world', but there is 'no refuge from the dead'.[75] The *Scourge of the Swastika* is a book that is referred to in Jacobson's earlier work, passingly in *The Mighty Walzer* (1999)[76] and at greater length in *Peeping Tom* (1984), where the narrator, Barney Fugelman, is lent a copy by his friend Monty

---

[71] Freud, Sigmund, 'Humour' [1928], trans. Joan Rivier, in *The Standard Edition of the Complete Psychological Works of Sigmund Freud, Vol. 21: The Future of an Illusion, Civilization and Its Discontents, and Other Works*, ed. James Strachey (London: Vintage, [1964] 2001), pp. 159–66 (p. 166).

[72] Freud, *The Joke*, pp. 108–9.

[73] For Homi K. Bhabha, who draws on the Freudian analysis of jokes, this form of joke work allows the formation of a 'self-critical community', which resists the 'regulative and rebarbative function of an orthodox tradition that polices jesters and banishes poets'. Homi K. Bhabha, 'Foreword: Joking Aside: The Idea of a Self-Critical Community', in *Modernity, Culture and 'the Jew'*, ed. Bryan Cheyette and Laura Marcus (Cambridge: Polity, 1998), pp. xv–xx (p. xix).

[74] Jacobson, *Kalooki Nights*, p. 39.

[75] Ibid., p. 5.

[76] After losing his fingers in a freak accident, Aishky Mistofsky, a player at the narrator Oliver Walzer's ping-pong club, tells Oliver that the end of his ping-pong career will allow him more time for reading and asks if he knows *The Scourge of Swastika*. Howard Jacobson, *The Mighty Walzer* (London: Vintage, [1999] 2000), p. 181.

Frankel, a character who shares many similarities with Manny Washinsky.[77] The surreptitious nature of this passing of knowledge is suggestive of the fact at this point in history, it was not simply a question of the Holocaust being beyond a joke but of it being unspeakable. There is a double movement taking place in these novels, and a double conception of the limits of discourse, in which Jacobson's humour provokes the sensibilities of the time in which he is writing via the representation of a period when it was less a question of whether the Holocaust was a proper subject for comedy and more a question of whether it could be spoken about at all. In both *Peeping Tom* and *Kalooki Nights*, *The Scourge of the Swastika* provides elicit knowledge, but typically of Jacobson's fiction, it also carries an erotic charge. In *Kalooki Nights*, the copy of Russell's book that Manny lends to Max does not contain the harrowing photographs it originally included, but these are later supplied by the local gardener, Errol Tobias, for whom Max works as an assistant. By unspoken agreement, Max's payment for his work is ceremoniously to be shown the images, one at a time, an experience that has such an effect on him that he claims to be able to recall them many years later in the precise order in which they were revealed. The photographs of Ilse Koch, wife of Karl-Otto Koch the commandant at the Buchenwald concentration camp, make a particular impression, as does that of a naked Jewish woman being humiliated by Nazi guards. The nexus of degradation, humiliation and eroticism make for some unsettling comedy throughout the novel. As Díaz Bild notes, the most extreme versions of this are projected onto the story, told in parts throughout the book, of Mendel (Hebrew for Max), a fictional prisoner at Buchenwald who Koch demands should draw her, one body part at a time, but erase each picture once at the end of the day; should Mendel become aroused, she will beat him. This strand of the novel is part of Jacobson's strategy throughout *Kalooki Nights* to 'subvert any pious approach to the Holocaust by exploiting its erotic possibilities',[78] and there is humour in the interactions between Mendel and Koch, notably when the conversation turns to satire. Like Max, Mendel is a caricaturist:

'Is it Jewish, this satire of yours, Jew?'

'It is, Frau Koch. Satire is written into our natures. Nietzsche believed we invented democracy out of a satiric impulse, as a refusal of aristocrats and heroes.'

---

[77] Monty/Manny are orphaned in both novels. In *Peeping Tom*, Monty's mother dies and his father commits suicide shortly after, and in *Kalooki Nights*, Manny murders his parents in a grotesque re-enactment of the death camp gas chambers. Both characters also have an obsession with morbidity and have facts and figures about war and death at their fingertips.

[78] Díaz Bild, '*Kalooki Nights* or the Sacred Duty to Remember the Holocaust', p. 275.

> ... 'So are all Jews satiric?'
> 'Only the clever ones, Frau Koch.'
> 'I thought you were all clever.'
> 'We are, Frau Koch.'[79]

This is an example of the humour of the *untermensch* that Max values, in which Mendel at least temporarily gains the upper hand. But it is also more uncomfortable than a simple reversal of authority because there is a flirtatious element to the conversation, a projection of the fantasies developed during Max's adolescence. Andrzej Gąsiorek describes *Kalooki Nights* as a novel that 'turns on the question of guilt', suggesting 'that condemning the Nazi regime for its crimes is easy, whereas admitting that one might share some impulses with those who perpetrated them is frighteningly difficult'.[80] In these moments, writes Ruth Gilbert, we 'are forced to consider the relationship between power and sex, history and fantasy, desire and displacement, that inform many representations of gendered Jewishness'.[81] It is in this interplay between disgust, eroticism, shame and humour that the novel creates its most challenging comedy. Like Barney in *Peeping Tom*, who dreams of 'women with names like Mad Olga who ripped open their uniforms and showed their breasts to their victims before castrating them',[82] Max's erotic life has developed around one of the least socially acceptable of foci, and it is here that Jacobson offers the form of humour that his character Max – as well as Jacobson himself – values, a form that may not make one laugh and is '"not *only* funny"' but '"horribly depressing as well"'.[83] In a much-quoted line from the novel, Max recalls being unable to find a publisher for a cartoon that played on the phrase 'Never again' – an injunction frequently invoked to emphasize the necessity of remembering the horrors of the past. 'Hard to get people to laugh at the Holocaust,'[84] he reasons, and the suggestion throughout the book is that this difficulty is important.[85] Max values the work of James Thurber, but is not sure that the word 'humour' is sufficient to account for what

---

[79] Jacobson, *Kalooki Nights*, p. 360.
[80] Andrzej Gąsiorek, 'Michael Chabon, Howard Jacobson, and Post-Holocaust Fiction', *Contemporary Literature*, 53:4 (2012), 875–903 (p. 892).
[81] Gilbert, *Writing Jewish*, p. 110.
[82] Howard Jacobson, *Peeping Tom* (London: Penguin, [1984] 1993), p. 48.
[83] Jacobson, *Kalooki Nights*, p. 358.
[84] Ibid., p. 119.
[85] There is an important distinction here between Jacobson's novel, which depicts Max's post-war generation and the 'in-between generation' of Max's parents who were not directly affected by the Holocaust and were 'too old to want to know the gory details', and the well-documented examples of laughter in the dark from those who were persecuted and used humour as a coping mechanism. Ibid., p. 117. For discussions of humour during the Holocaust, see, for example, Wisse, *No Joke*, pp. 143–81; Dauber, *Jewish Comedy*, 28–34; and Morreall, *Comic Relief*, pp. 119–24.

makes it funny: '"What makes Thurber funny"', he explains to an American editor, '"is that you smell death in every sentence he wrote and despair in every line he drew."'[86] Despair, desperation and laughter are seen as interdependent and as every bit as appropriate and necessary a response to tragedy as solemn memorialization. It is this that allows the novel, as David Brauner has argued, 'simultaneously to interrogate seriously the effect of the legacy of the Holocaust on a generation of Jews who were insulated from any direct contact with it and comically to deconstruct that legacy, to parody the way in which the Holocaust has been fetishized'.[87]

In *Kalooki Nights*, this humour manifests not only in Max's projected fantasies but also in his relationships in the present. One of the novel's repeated comic motifs involves Max's attraction to women with umlauts or diareses in their names, a marker of his masochistic attraction to domination by stereotypically Teutonic women who are hostile to his Jewishness. Principal among these are his wives Zoë and Chloë. He describes Zoë as 'Hitlerian' and as his 'flaxen *Übermadchen*', and says she is embittered against Jewish people having been rejected by a previously friendly neighbourhood family once she reached puberty: '"The minute I became a woman, in their eyes, I became filth,"' she tells Max, '"That's why … I am in love with you. … Because they deprived me of my right to love Jews."' Max's family warn him that she will call him a '"dirty Jew"' and accuse him of killing Christ, but he is defiant and denies at least some of their prognostications: 'Zoë never did accuse me of killing Christ. But "dirty Jew", yes, or at least "Jew" with the dirty – meaning heated, meaning tumultuous, meaning unrefreshed and unrefreshable – implied'. The reason for his attraction, he explains, is that 'in the fairy stories which Jewish men tell themselves, the princesses are always Gentile' and, consequently, he views it as his mission 'to warm back into life the chilly universe of Shiksehs'. Later, as their relationship breaks down, Zoë decides that Max looks *too* Jewish and should perhaps consider having a nose job, and yet he continues in the relationship, first, because he feels apologetic about her childhood trauma; second, because he was 'brought up to be sorry for any woman … who was married to me – a Jew with the stinking waters of Novoropissik in his veins'; and third, because her suggestion stirs something in him: 'You can get sick of looking like a Jew. And you can get sick of being looked at like a Jew as well.'[88] Again, Jacobson returns

---

[86] Jacobson, *Kalooki Nights*, p. 57.
[87] David Brauner, 'Fetishizing the Holocaust: Comedy and Transatlantic Connections in Howard Jacobson's *Kalooki Nights*', *European Judaism*, 47:2 (2014), 21–9 (p. 25).
[88] Jacobson, *Kalooki Nights*, pp. 24–7.

to oppositions between Jews and gentiles, reproducing dangerous stereotypes to explore their comic possibilities, in this instance suggesting that Max may be at least partially complicit in Zoë's bigotry and racialized hostility. That he leaves this possibility open creates a degree of uncomfortable ambiguity and, yes, despair at the apparent reciprocation between anti-Semitic prejudice and masochistic desire. Efraim Sicher and Linda Weinhouse have identified Jacobson as part of 'a new generation of Jews "with attitude"', who have 'challenged the long-standing apologetic position of the Anglo-Jewish establishment' by 'acting out the stereotype in parodies of the Jew who has internalized racialized typecasting, yet masochistically wishes to be part of an "Englishness" that defines itself as excluding Jews'.[89] And this attitude is evident in this example of Jacobson's comedy that lances the boil and allows the pus to run. But in Max's interactions with Zoë, as well as with his first wife Chloë, there is also a parallel discussion that indicates a more complex position and a different relationship between boundaries and the significance of the comic

Max's relationship with Zoë repeats many of the patterns already established with his first wife Chloë, but when he recalls his relationship with Chloë, there is a third person in the relationship – Chloë's mother Helène, to whom he has grown attached 'in an equilibrium-of-detestation sort of way'. Max despises Helène's 'cutesie genteel Gentile' ways, and she hates everything about him. In particular, he loathes her use of punning aphorisms such as her habit saying she is going '"up the little wooden hill to Bedfordshire"' when going upstairs to bed. Max is unable to sleep until he can 'match [his] mother-in-law's wooden hill to Bedfordshire with some odious genteel Gentile punning cosiness of [his] own'. Finally, he has a moment of inspiration, and following a card game in which his wife and mother-in-law have speculated on his genetic predisposition to 'genius level' triviality and the Jewish people's natural affinity with accountancy, or 'stockings and shares' as Helène puns, he seizes his moment, and 'espying her heading in the direction of retirement with a volume of G.K. Chesterton in her hand', he calls out '"Off up the little wooden hill to Buchenwald, are we?"' His wit is not well received:

> Chloë was outraged. 'Max!'
> 'What?'
> 'How dare you talk to my mother like that!'
> 'Like what?'

---

[89] Efraim Sicher and Linda Weinhouse, *Under Postcolonial Eyes: Figuring the 'Jew' in Contemporary British Writing* (Lincoln, NE: University of Nebraska Press, 2010), p. 202.

'How dare you wish my mother in a concentration camp!'
'Book,' I said. '*Book*enwald, for fuck's sake.'
'Leave it,' Helène shouted down. 'He spent his formative years in Dewsbury, remember.'
'Jewsbury!' I shouted back. 'Did you just say Jewsbury?'
But she'd won again. I knew that. She was mistress of the gazeteer of the British Isles, to whatever end of phobia and whimsy, and that was that.[90]

The cry of '"Jewsbury"' anticipates the 'D'Jew know' joke discussed earlier, but it comes too late and Max has already been defeated in this joking contest. He goes too far and openly articulates what has previously been hidden behind gentility and politeness; he has made a misjudgement. His interactions with Helène again rely on a series of archetypal relationships and juxtapositions (between husband and mother-in-law, Jew and gentile, and working class and middle class), but these oppositions work to suggest the situational complexities of joking, in which prejudice can be cloaked in politeness and layers of irony, here represented by the low-level hum of anti-Semitism that will not quite openly declare itself.

Later in the novel, Max describes a similar battle, this time after he has beaten Chloë and Helène at both Monopoly and Scrabble and has made a self-effacing reference to his lack of physical prowess as a gesture of consolation. '"It really is no cost to you, admitting you're all coward-cowardy-custards in your bodies"', Helène tells him, '"when it's really only the brainbox you value."' What follows is a contemptuous discussion of Jewish intellectualism, in which hermeneutics is rendered as 'Hymie Neutics' and Chloë and Helène speculate over whether Victor Frankenstein is '"one of yours"'. When Max notes that he doubts Frankenstein made any money out his creation, Helène answers with, '"Well, money, I have to say, was the last thing on *our* minds, wasn't it, Chlo?"' at once repeating an anti-Semitic slur and laying responsibility for it at Max's feet. He curses himself for 'falling on her chintzy fist and knocking [himself] out yet again'.[91] And when Max buys a Volkswagen, a car Chloë insists they should choose despite its historical associations with Nazism, Helène gives him a toy rabbi to hang in the window. He wonders how she came by this trinket and reasons that it cannot have been expensive:

'I'm as tight as you people are,' she winked at me one day. 'Only I'm a tightey-whitey, whereas you're …'
She couldn't think of anything.

---

[90] Jacobson, *Kalooki Nights*, pp. 82–4.
[91] Ibid., pp. 297–8.

'A meany-sheeny,' I came back, quick as a flash.

How did she do that? How was she able to lure me into being rude about myself? It was an astonishing gift. She could make you say the vilest things in the hope of saying them before she did.[92]

Max has won the contest of wits by arriving at a pun 'quick as a flash', but it is a pyrrhic victory claimed because he is unable to stop himself from showing off. His engagement with Helène runs the risk of legitimizing her prejudice and reveals the extent to which these stereotypes have been internalized by Max. As Baum notes, Jewish jokes told by non-Jews can 'sound suspiciously similar to anti-Semitic ones' and even when told by Jews the difference between a Jewish joke and an anti-Semitic joke can be slippery because 'some Jewish jokes seem to manifest an internalized anti-Semitism'.[93] *Kalooki Nights* is, among other things, a novel about these distinctions and about the right to tell jokes, as well as the wrongs of telling jokes, and it is significant that Max's cartoons are collected by anti-Semites who 'show them on websites much visited by extremists with too much time on their hands'[94] – stripped of context their meaning can be divorced from the intent. A final example illustrates this relationship, and it again involves one of Max's ex-wives and a Volkswagen. '"How many Jews can you get into a Volkswagen Beetle?"' Zoë asks Max, demonstrating how she is 'nothing if not humorous'. '"None"', he says, neglecting to tell her that he had owned one when he was married to Chloë, because '"no Jew would get into a Volkswagen Beetle"'. Zoë is irritated by his answer and asks '"Why won't you let anyone tell a joke?"' and so with heavy irony Max resolves not to 'ruin a hilarious joke' and invites her to tell it again. The punchline is '"One thousand and four. Two in the front, two in the back, and one thousand in the ashtray"', a punchline he does not condemn outright but that does cause him to wonder whether it would be amusing to a Holocaust denier.[95] Jacobson gives two punchlines to the same set up here, and the milder, funnier first punchline throws the second, merely offensive one, into relief. Both follow a classic joke structure of set-up and reveal and both rely on awareness of a traumatic history, but Max's punchline is told from the inside in order to demonstrate wit – and yes, perhaps out of a sense of ownership, as Zoë points out – and the other is told from the outside to shock and wound. That this exchange takes place just after the couple have made love takes us back to Max's masochistic streak and his queasy complicity in Zoë's enmity, but it also

---

[92] Ibid., p. 158.
[93] Baum, *The Jewish Joke*, pp. 39–42.
[94] Jacobson, *Kalooki Nights*, p. 272.
[95] Ibid., pp. 136–7.

suggests that a boundless, anything-goes approach to humour may be desirable in a theoretical sense but that the pragmatic reality is quite different.

In his persuasive consideration of *Kalooki Nights* alongside Michael Chabon's *The Amazing Adventures of Kavalier and Clay* (2000), Andrzej Gąsiorek comes to a similar conclusion via a different route. Focusing on Ekphrasis and the relationship between Max's cartoons and the novel's treatment of satire, humour and the memory of the Holocaust, Gąsiorek concludes that despite Max's claims for the power and necessity of mockery and grotesque satire, Jacobson 'displays a psychological penetration that is at odds with the aesthetic that Glickman promotes in his defense of satire and also systematically exposes Glickman's emotional obtuseness'. There is, he argues, 'a distinction to be made between the text in which this fictional protagonist speaks and his descriptions of satire: *Kalooki Nights* is not a cartoon but a psychologically astute novel that exposes the limits of satire and explores the troubled personality of its first-person narrator'.[96] While I would question the assumption that satire cannot be psychologically astute, I agree with Gąsiorek's conclusion that the novel's tone and Max's growing recognition of the limitations of caricature go against his bombastic and exaggerated pronouncements about the necessity of 'ceaseless mockery'.[97] Moreover, as I have argued throughout this chapter, there is a further distinction to be made between Jacobson's extra-textual pronouncements about the need for comedy to be a boundless space of plenitude and offence, and the implicit, and frequently explicit, exploration of precisely those boundaries that takes place in the novels. *Kalooki Nights* and much of Jacobson's other work takes readers to uncomfortable places and dares them to laugh, but it is also aware of the subtleties of intent and addresses that separate a self-effacing Jewish joke from an anti-Semitic joke, or a joke that evokes stereotypes from one that reinforces them. Whether Jacobson's comedies succeed in walking this line will always be a matter of judgement – and I have identified some points at which they veer from this line – but to deny its existence and attempt to work entirely without boundaries would lead to the failure of comedy rather than its triumph.

---

[96] Gąsiorek, 'Post-Holocaust Fiction', pp. 893, 897.
[97] This quotation is taken from a conversation between Max and Manny about the role and nature of art, in which Max is particularly sceptical of abstract expressionism and the appeal of Jewish artists such as Mark Rothko to non-Jews. According to Max, such art offers idealized, even sentimentalized images of the transcendent soul which are akin to conventional, representational forms of idolatry: 'Abstraction doesn't solve it, Manny. Abstraction's a con. Only ridicule solves it. Only mockery keeps you the right side of idolatry.' Jacobson, *Kalooki Nights*, pp. 264, 267. This is a further example of Jacobson's reiteration and refinement of ideas on humour and mockery introduced in *Seriously Funny*, in which he argues that abstract and conceptualist art is never funny because comedy relies on plenitude and hyperbole rather than reduction. Jacobson, *Seriously Funny*, pp. 80–1.

Comedy Trumped? *Pussy* and the challenge for contemporary satire

At the time of writing, however, some are arguing that satirical comedies such as Jacobson's most recent novel *Pussy* face an existential threat not from censorship or readerly sensitivities, but from the pace and direction of current events. The title *Pussy* is taken from Donald Trump's boast, recorded in 2005 and leaked in the run-up to the 2016 presidential election, that his celebrity makes him a 'magnet' to beautiful women and that he cannot resist kissing them: 'And when you're a star, they let you do it. You can do anything. Grab 'em by the pussy. You can do anything.'[98] The novel is a *roman-à-clef* in which Trump is rendered as Prince Fracassus, the petulant, Twitter-addicted heir to a fortune who develops ambitions to become 'Prime Mover' of his nation, known as the Republics. There are clear echoes of Jonathan Swift's satires throughout and particularly in its setting in a world that is fantastical and at the same time recognizable to its readership as just a few steps removed from our own. Jacobson wrote the novel out of a sense of 'raging indignation' at Trump's election and 'at great speed, not wanting to iron anything out. Haste was part of it. A feeling of impetuosity. An unseemly rush of passion that time and care would have falsified.' It is a novel he describes as relying on derision, 'but underlying it a perplexing question that derision cannot answer. How does such a thing come about? What creates the climate? How do the "people" – that suddenly cherished entity, invoked by every rogue in Washington and Whitehall – fill the space occupied by nothingness with the ghost of their wish-fulfilment?'[99] Derision is not sufficient to the task of understanding the politics of Trump, he suggests, and the novel's epigraph from Swift's essay 'Thoughts on Various Subjects' (1706) indicates that Jacobson may also have doubts about the didactic possibilities of his work: 'How is it possible to expect that mankind will take advice, when they will not so much as take warning?'[100] I began this book with a chapter on the possibilities and limitations

---

[98] David A. Fahrenthold, 'Trump Recorded Having Extremely Lewd Conversation about Women in 2005', *Washington Post*, 8 October 2016. Available online: https://www.washingtonpost.com/politics/trump-recorded-having-extremely-lewd-conversation-about-women-in-2005/2016/10/07/3b9ce776-8cb4-11e6-bf8a-3d26847eeed4_story.html?noredirect=on&utm_term=.7bfa10a4e7c1 (accessed 25 April 2019).

[99] Howard Jacobson, 'Howard Jacobson on Why He Wrote *Pussy*, a Furious Dedication to Trump', *Penguin Books*, 12 April 2017. Available online: https://www.penguin.co.uk/articles/2017/howard-jacobson-on-pussy/ (accessed 26 April 2019).

[100] Jonathan Swift, 'Thoughts on Various Subjects', in *The Battle of the Books and Other Short Pieces* (London: Cassell, 1886). Available online: http://www.gutenberg.org/files/623/623-h/623-h.htm (accessed 26 April 2019).

of contemporary satire, focusing on the extent to which is has become complicit with the politics and politicians it seeks to hold to account. But while this question remains pertinent to satires of Trump, the impediments to effective satire have become yet more extreme: events increasingly appear to outstrip artists' ability to invent.

Although Jacobson argues that derision was not his primary aim in writing *Pussy*, it is a novel that is full of derisive and often only lightly fictionalized depictions of Trump and the debasement of culture and politics he is seen to represent. The tone is set by the cover image of the first edition, a cartoon by Chris Riddell of Trump as a man-baby, wearing a nappy and clutching a naked Barbie-style doll, which provides a reminder of Max's profession in *Kalooki Nights* but gives little sense that Jacobson is attempting to analyse the limitations of the caricature mode as he did in the earlier book. In a chapter entitled 'In which language is discerned to go backwards', for example, a young Fracussus is asked by one of his tutors, Dr Cobalt, to provide synonyms for the word 'woman'; he manages 'girl', but then goes straight to 'prostitute'. When Cobalt asks him for synonyms for 'prostitute', he manages 'whore, then tart, then hooker' and his tutor notes that he has more words for prostitute than he does for woman: '"I want to ask you something"', she says, '"Why can't you think of a woman without thinking of a prostitute?"' Fracussus loses his temper and accuses her of playing a crooked game. '*Crooked?*' Cobalt wonders, her thoughts focalized through the third-person narrator, 'That was a surprise. Didn't you have to understand the concept of straight before you could understand the concept of crooked?'[101] The word 'crooked' is a reference to Trump's repeated description of his 2016 presidential election opponent Hillary Clinton as 'Crooked Hillary', and there is plenty of evidence for the real-life Trump's associative connections between women and financial transactions. The difficulty, however, is that whereas Swift and Pope would scandalize their audiences and skirt the bounds of legality with their portraits of public figures, there is little to add when a presidential candidate has been heard bragging about grabbing women by their genitals and been elected to office nonetheless, or when their accusations of crookedness are such a flagrant attempt at deflecting attention from their own affairs. Moreover, Fracussus's misogyny is not so far removed from many of Jacobson's other protagonists, whose backstories and attitudes are often strikingly similar to Jacobson's own and with whom readers are invited to sympathize. A further set of difficulties are presented by Fracussus's exaggerations about the scale of his

---

[101] Howard Jacobson, *Pussy* (London: Jonathan Cape, 2017), pp. 28–31

riches and his omission of any mention of his wealthy father in order to present himself 'as a phenomenon of self-generation': there may be pleasure in seeing this laid out on the page with scorn and derision, but these aspects of Trump's self-mythology are true and well-documented.[102] Indeed, many aspects of the Trump campaign and presidency have gone beyond what Jacobson depicts in *Pussy* in both scale and absurdity, and yet it has made little impact on either Trump's core supporters or his opponents, who have if anything become more entrenched in their respective positions. Satire is a form that relies on exaggeration and hyperbole for its effect, but in *Pussy*, Jacobson may have found the limits of comedy not by joking about subjects that are conventionally considered beyond humour but by joking about a subject whose extremity and brazenness put him out of reach.[103]

Since Trump's candidacy and election, dozens of articles have been published declaring either the necessity of satire as a mode of redress and understanding[104] or the impossibility of satire in the era of Trump,[105] and one of the most perceptive of these references Jacobson's *Pussy* in the context of a more extended discussion of Mark Doten's novel *Trump Sky Alpha* (2019). Ben Greenman's 'Is

---

[102] See, for example, David A. Fahrenthold and Jonathan O'Connell, 'How Donald Trump Inflated His Net Worth to Lenders and Investors', *Washington Post*, 28 March 2019. Available online: https://www.washingtonpost.com/graphics/2019/politics/trump-statements-of-financial-condition/?utm_term=.3be0102388d6 (accessed 26 April 2019); and David Barstow, Susanne Craig and Russ Buettner, 'Trump Engaged in Suspect Tax Schemes as He Reaped Riches from His Father', *New York Times*, 2 October 2018. Available online: https://www.nytimes.com/interactive/2018/10/02/us/politics/donald-trump-tax-schemes-fred-trump.html?module=inline (accessed 26 April 2019).

[103] In 2017, Jonathan Coe returned to the question of satire's role in contemporary society discussed in Chapter 2 in order to reflect on the possibility of satire in the age of Trump. He concludes that 'perhaps such epoch-defining events [as Trump and the Brexit vote] are best portrayed not in satirical terms but through the lens of magic realism'. Coe, 'Will Satire Save Us in the Age of Trump?' *Guardian*, 6 January 2017. Available online: https://www.theguardian.com/books/2017/jan/06/jonathan-coe-will-satire-save-us-in-the-age-of-donald-trump?CMP=share_btn_link (accessed 16 July 2019).

[104] See, for example, Josephine Tovey, 'Satire Is a Pointed Weapon in the Age of Trump', *Sydney Morning Herald*, 8 February 2017. Available online: https://www.smh.com.au/opinion/satire-is-a-pointed-weapon-in-the-age-of-trump-20170208-gu808r.html (accessed 26 April 2019); Anne Karpf, 'Satire Won't Rid Us of Trump, But It Will Make Us Feel Better', *Guardian*, 26 December 2016. Available online: https://www.theguardian.com/commentisfree/2016/dec/26/satire-donald-trump-bigotry-prejudice-humour-escapism (accessed 26 April 2019); and Sophia A. McClennen, 'Hitting Trump Where It Hurts: The Satire Troops Take Up Comedy Arms against Donald Trump', *Salon*, 11 February 2017. Available online: https://www.salon.com/2017/02/11/hitting-trump-where-it-hurts-the-satire-troops-take-up-comedy-arms-against-donald-trump/ (accessed 26 April 2019).

[105] See, for example, David Sanderson, 'Rise of Trump Makes Satire Unnecessary, Says Armando Iannucci', *The Times*, 1 October 2018. Available online: https://www.thetimes.co.uk/article/rise-of-trump-makes-satire-unnecessary-says-armando-iannucci-vpdncxr9f (accessed 26 April 2019); Seán Moncrieff, 'Welcome to the Death of Satire', *Irish Times*, 19 January 2019. Available online: https://www.irishtimes.com/life-and-style/people/se%C3%A1n-moncrieff-welcome-to-the-death-of-satire-1.3751287 (accessed 26 April 2019); and William Cook, 'Have Donald Trump and Brexit Killed Off the Dark Art of Political Satire?' *Independent*, 18 January 2018. Available online: https://www.independent.co.uk/news/long_reads/donald-trump-satire-politics-late-shows-us-president-paradox-john-oliver-stephen-colbert-a8165401.html (accessed 26 April 2019).

Satire Possible in the Age of Trump?' (2019) rehearses many of pro- and anti-satire arguments and concludes that 'Doten's novel is both an illustration of how Trump and Trumpism have hamstrung public discourse and a set of instructions for untying ourselves: Remain vigilant. Remain skeptical. Question everything. Even the satires.'[106] *Trump Sky Alpha* is an extraordinary book that is funny in parts but that is also about humour and its role in contemporary discourse. It is largely set in a post-apocalyptic United States, the result of Trump's hubristic detonation of the country's nuclear arsenal. There are pitch-perfect renditions of Trump's speech patterns, but also a palpable sense of Trump's power and the potentially devastating effects of exercising that power. The central character in the novel is Rachel, a journalist who is commissioned by a re-launched version of *The New York Times* to write a piece on 'Internet humour at the end of the world' and whose research in an archive salvaged from the internet before the world went offline reveals that

> the internet's record of its own destruction – and that of the greater part of life and civilization – is given in part through jokes, many of them familiar, though often modified, mutating. *People are making jokes like there's no tomorrow*, for instance, is an old joke already available in multiple image macros.[107]

By reflecting on the ineffectualness of these jokes, and by extension the role that humour has played in shaping and enabling Trump's presidency, Doten does not fully escape satire's double binds,[108] but he does avoid the sense of merely reiterating what is already known that is a feature of novels such as *Pussy* as well as the many Trump parodies on programmes such as *Saturday Night Live*. It is not that I disagree with Judith Roof's assertion that in an American context 'the comic has become one of the only means of trenchant political and social

---

[106] Ben Greenman, 'Is Satire Possible in the Age of Trump?' *New York Times*, 8 March 2019. Available online: https://www.nytimes.com/2019/03/08/books/review/mark-doten-trump-sky-alpha.html?smid=tw-nytbooks&smtyp=cur (accessed 26 April 2019).

[107] Mark Doten, *Trump Sky Alpha* (Minneapolis, MN: Graywolf Press, 2019), p. 86. Jeff Loveness's story 'This is the Political Satire That Finally Stops Trump' is an interesting companion piece to Doten's novel for its wry acknowledgement of the proliferation of anti-Trump comic internet memes and their apparent ineffectualness. The narrator announces that he has 'brought an end to the terror of President Trump by utilizing the greatest power of all: Comedy', specifically by tweeting a photo of Trump's face superimposed onto that of the *Star Wars* character Jabba the Hutt. It then imagines a series of outlandish scenarios in which first Trump and then Vladimir Putin recognize the devastating power of the tweet and see the error of their ways. It ends with the narrator viewing his work framed in the Smithsonian Museum as a father looks on and tells his son, '"Yes. That's him. That's the man who saved America."' Jeff Loveness, 'This Is the Political Satire that Finally Stops Trump', *McSweeney's*, 23 January 2017. Available online: https://www.mcsweeneys.net/articles/this-is-the-political-satire-that-finally-stops-trump (accessed 12 July 2019).

[108] See Chapters 1 and 5 for discussions of comedy and self-reflexivity.

commentary still available',[109] but I am more circumspect about the forms such commentary can take while avoiding the entrenchment of existing positions and patterns of thought. Without wishing to overstate the possibilities of satire, it is important to note that in order to continue to be a viable and powerful medium, satirical comedy has to reckon with its own imbrication within the processes it satirizes and to think beyond the mere reproduction or allegorizing of the status quo. In this sense, *Pussy* again demonstrates both the presence and the fluidity of comedy's boundaries, the difference being that much of Jacobson's other work interrogates these boundaries whereas the failings of *Pussy* merely serve to identify them. Jacobson is concerned in both his fiction and non-fiction writing with the boundaries of comedy, arguing for the necessity of comedy without limits that can and should be able to tackle any subject. However, as I have argued throughout this chapter, his pronouncements on the topic go against the exploration of the limits of comedy enacted in work such as *The Finkler Question* and *Kalooki Nights*. These novels retain the ability to shock and offend, but are also concerned with the specificity and contingent appropriateness of jokes and humour, in which boundaries are not defined by subject matter but by a complex negotiation of the relationship between writer, material, audience and perceived intention. *Pussy* demonstrates the presence of boundaries in another sense, and it is hamstrung not by proscriptions about comic subject matter and acceptability but by the limitations of Jacobson's own range and the ability of real-world events to outstrip his inventive capabilities. Comic writing has always found ways to respond to contemporary events in inventive and confrontational ways, but *Pussy* demonstrates the fragility of this relationship – whereas Swift scandalized, Jacobson merely inspires the laughter of bitter recognition.

---

[109] Roof, *The Comic Event*, p. 35.

Conclusion

The comic turn in contemporary English fiction

In Chapter 1 of *The Comic Turn in Contemporary English Fiction*, I discussed the political role of comedy in the context of Jonathan Coe's argument that rather than holding the establishment to account, contemporary satire may inculcate a cynical worldview, meaning that mockery becomes a substitute for action. Central to this discussion is a perception that politicians such as the former mayor of London and current prime minister of the UK Boris Johnson have learned to perform a version of benign affability that enables them to hide their true ambitions and escape closer scrutiny. Who could forget the image of Johnson stuck in mid-air on a zip-line during a publicity stunt, trousers hoisted above his ankles, clutching a Union Flag in each hand as he gurned like a naughty schoolboy? Or reclaiming ping-pong as 'whiff-whaff' and reminding the world that the game was invented 'on the dining tables of England', all the while gurning like a naughty schoolboy? Or gurning like a naughty schoolboy as he defended a false claim about the UK's financial contribution to the European Union? Or when he held a kipper aloft while gurning like a naughty schoolboy and intoning about the restrictiveness of EU red tape, continuing the manufactured Euroscepticism his early journalism did so much to incubate?[1] These moments are of a piece and are demonstrative of the way in which Johnson's constructed character of affable eccentricity extends beyond PR opportunities and is employed in order to afford him a degree of latitude when it comes to political blunders or outright deceptions. Self-deprecation, he is on record as saying '"is a very cunning device"' that plays on the public belief that politicians are '"a bunch of

---

[1] In the early 1990s, Johnson's sensationalist Eurosceptic reports from Brussels for the *Telegraph* newspaper did much to solidify the British stereotype of the European Union (at that point still the European Community) as an bureaucracy intent on seizing greater power and imposing unnecessarily restrictive laws about, for example, the curvature of bananas or the standardization of condom sizes. See Jennifer Rankin and Jim Waterson, 'How Boris Johnson's Brussels-bashing Stories Shaped British Politics', *Guardian*, 14 July 2019. Available online: https://www.theguardian.com/politics/2019/jul/14/boris-johnson-brussels-bashing-stories-shaped-politics (accessed 30 July 2019).

shysters".[2] It is significant that the examples of Johnson's behaviour I list concern nationalism and national identity, because his public persona is an amplification of a particular type of sub-Wodehousian dishevelled upper-class Englishness based on scripted gaffes and artfully untucked shirts.[3] It is a performance of a persona and a performance of Englishness. Two of these examples also relate to his promotion of the 2012 Olympic Games in London during his time as the mayor, but they run contrary to the opening ceremony of the Games themselves, which offered a quite different version of national identity. Titled *Isles of Wonder*, the ceremony demonstrated pride in Britain's heritage as exemplified by institutions such as the National Health Service; it was equally performative, but largely avoided flag-waving nationalism, and as Michael McKinnie notes in a 2016 article, 'in the United Kingdom media commentators almost universally applauded *Isles of Wonder*, regardless of their own political leanings or those of the outlets in which their work appeared'.[4] It was a moment that brought much of the population together in admiration and pride, a performance of Britishness (rather than Englishness) that was unifying rather than divisive. It was also a weird, eccentric spectacle – 'bonkers' was the adjective most commonly used to describe it.[5] Jonathan Coe captures this moment in a pivotal passage from his novel *Middle England* (2018), the third part of the sequence begun with *The Rotters' Club* (2001) and continued in *The Closed Circle* (2004). The passage moves between multiple households and multiple characters, showing how they are each moved by aspects of the ceremony and what it represents. The journalist Doug Anderton feels the stirrings of a new emotion that he has not felt before, 'having grown up in a household where all expressions of patriotism had been considered suspect':

> national pride. Yes, why not come straight out and admit it, at this moment he felt proud, proud to be British, proud to be part of a nation which had not only achieved such great things but could now celebrate them with such confidence and irony and lack of self-importance.

---

[2] Quoted in Williams, *Boris Johnson*, p. 11.
[3] See, for example, Paul Waugh, 'The Donald Trump and Boris Johnson Show: UK and US Braced for the New "Special Relationship"', *Huffington Post*, 1 June 2019. Available online: https://www.huffingtonpost.co.uk/entry/donald-trump-and-boris-johnson-will-blond-ambition-be-enough-to-forge-a-new-special-relationship_uk_5cf292dbe4b0e346ce7ef269 (accessed 14 June 2019); and Matt Charlton, 'How Satire Gave Boris Johnson His Persona', *Vice*, 20 August 2018. Available online: https://www.vice.com/en_uk/article/8xb7vv/how-satire-gave-boris-johnson-his-persona (accessed 13 June 2019).
[4] Michael McKinnie, 'Olympian Performance: The Cultural Economics of the Opening Ceremony of London 2012', *Public*, 53 (2016), 49–57 (p. 49).
[5] Ibid., p. 50.

After the ceremony, Doug's friend Benjamin Trotter is left with a feeling of contentment: 'England felt like a calm and settled place tonight: a country at ease with itself. The thought that so many millions of disparate people had been united, drawn together by a television broadcast, made him think of his childhood again, and made him smile.'[6] Benjamin's contentment is partly founded on nostalgia – the scene is a knowing reference to the *The Rotters' Club* and his sense of national 'oneness' during the 1977 *Morecambe and Wise Show* Christmas special[7] – but Coe is not critical of this nostalgic impulse and it is represented as a moment of genuine fellow feeling. Crucially, the ceremony is also suffused with humour, a move which Coe argues enabled British viewers to see a 'resonant, complex vision of [their] own national identity without resorting to cliché'.[8] The feelings it inspires do not, however, last. The next scene takes place two years later and the opening ceremony already feels '"like a long time ago"': two of Coe's characters, Sophie and Sohan, stand on the viewing platform of London's Shard skyscraper, surveying a city dominated by similarly conspicuous shiny monuments to capital, built and owned by foreign investors while the rest of the country is in the grip of punitive austerity measures imposed by the Conservative government.[9] As McKinnie concludes, the experience of the Olympic opening ceremony is one 'that is increasingly unavailable to us outside the confines of the performance. In the real world, the economic antagonism that *Isles of Wonder* stages may be equally – or even more – conspicuous, but there austerity has the upper hand.'[10] In contrast to Johnson's rebarbative performance of affability and eccentric Englishness, then, Danny Boyle's *Isles of Wonder* offers a progressive view of national history and identity across classes and nations, but its staging of nationhood has since been undermined by the growing inequality and the social and political divisions that have opened up over subsequent years. Performance, and performed identity, is at the core of both of these examples, and so is humour in all of its complexity. As Coe has argued, the 2012 ceremony shows how humour could allow British viewers to experience pride without reporting to jingoism, while the success of Johnson's 'artfully shambolic' persona, on the other hand, shows how that the nation's pride in its sense of humour can have negative consequences as well: 'We pride

---

[6] Jonathan Coe, *Middle England* (London: Viking, 2018), pp. 132, 139.
[7] Jonathan Coe, *The Rotters' Club* (London: Penguin, [2001] 2002), p. 274. This moment is discussed in Chapter 1.
[8] Jonathan Coe, 'How Brexit Broke Britain', *Time*, 6 June 2019. Available online: https://time.com/560 1982/how-brexit-broke-britain/ (accessed 7 June 2019).
[9] Ibid., p. 146.
[10] McKinnie, 'Olympian Performance', p. 56.

ourselves on our sense of humor, but have rarely stopped to think how often we use it to avoid thinking seriously about things.'[11] In this concluding chapter I return to the idea of the 'comic turn' as a form of performance, and analyse the relationship between performance, labour and questions of English national identity in Julian Barnes's satirical novel *England, England* (1998).

Selling the past as the future: Nationhood, work and performance in Julian Barnes's *England, England*

England, England imagines the construction of a miniature version of England on the Isle of Wight, an island of 147 square miles just off the south coast near the city of Southampton. 'England, England' is the vision of the fictional industrialist Jack Pitman, who sees it as an opportunity to attract 'Top Dollar and Long Yen' from overseas visitors by consolidating all of England's major tourist attractions into a single space. It is a version of England based on a mythologized past and a picture postcard version of the present; as one of Sir Jack's project consultants announces: '"We must sell our past to other nations as their future!"'[12] There are several extant accounts of the novel's depiction of Englishness in relation to (absent) multiculturalism, questions of heritage and Jean Baudrillard's category of the hyperreal,[13] but here I develop on this work by focusing the novel's comic depiction of performance and the relationship between performance, national identity and contemporary patterns of work. Focusing on the second of the three sections that make up what Nick Bentley has aptly described as a 'hybrid' novel,[14] I engage with Sianne Ngai's work on the category of the 'zany', which brings together a number of ideas about the politics, performativity, affect and aesthetics of comedy that have been important throughout this book.

Just as the *Isles of Wonder* opening ceremony traced a lineage from pastoral Britain to industrial Britain to a post-industrial Britain represented by popular culture, so the world of the England, England holiday resort draws on folk

---

[11] Coe, 'How Brexit Broke Britain'. There are striking parallels here with Wyndham Lewis's argument in 'The English Sense of Humour' that English people's pride in their sense of humour represents a *'philosopic rot'* that impairs 'the will to act'. Wyndham Lewis, 'The English Sense of Humour', *Spectator*, 15 June 1934, pp. 915–16 (p. 915).
[12] Julian Barnes, *England, England* (London: Picador, [1998] 1999), p. 40.
[13] See, for example, Nick Bentley, 'Re-writing Englishness: Imagining the Nation in Julian Barnes's *England, England* and Zadie Smith's *White Teeth*', *Textual Practice*, 21:3 (2007), 483–504; Jong-Seok Kim, '"Getting History Wrong": The Heritage/Enterprise Couplet in Julian Barnes's *England, England*', *Critique*, 58:5 (2017), 587–99; and Peter Childs, *Julian Barnes* (Manchester: Manchester University Press, 2011), pp. 108–25.
[14] Bentley, 'Re-writing Englishness', p. 493.

memory of pastoral and industrial England from the perspective of a post-industrial, service-led economy. In Barnes's novel, this is less about knowledge and more about feeling, as Sir Jack's 'Concept Developer' Jeff describes to the project's official historian, Dr Max: "'Well, the point of *our* history – and I stress the our – will be to make our guests, those buying what is for the moment referred to as Quality Leisure, *feel better*.'" When Max questions the meaning of 'better', Jeff replies by saying that the emphasis should be on the verb: "'Feel. We want then to *feel* less ignorant.'"[15] Feeling and appearances trump historical accuracy, and this emphasis on emotional engagement extends not only to the park's visitors but also to its workers. The economy of England, England harks back to England's productive industries but is not itself based on production. Rather, it is a more extreme version of the post-industrial economy found on the mainland (what comes to be known as 'Old England' and later 'Anglia'), in which workers provide services to cater for the desires of visitors and to make the experience *feel* authentic. Sianne Ngai's *Our Aesthetic Categories* (2012) offers a valuable way to think about this in the context of broader socioeconomic and aesthetic shifts that have taken place in the late-twentieth and early twenty-first centuries. Ngai identifies three under-examined and marginal aesthetic categories that are nevertheless 'the ones in our current repertoire best suited to grasping how aesthetic experience has been transformed by the hypercommodified, information-saturated, performance-driven conditions of late capitalism'. The zany, the cute and the interesting relate to categories of production, circulation and consumption, respectively, and as such represent an aesthetic suited to our times. There is much to be said about Ngai's rich and rewarding text, but the topic of most interest here is her discussion of the zany, an aesthetic linked to the move towards a post-Fordist service economy in which the affective requirements of the workplace begin to trouble the distinction between work and play: 'Zaniness is the only aesthetic category in our contemporary repertoire explicitly about this politically ambiguous intersection between cultural and occupational performance, acting and service, playing and labouring.' Zaniness, as represented by the obsessive role-playing of the eponymous character in Jim Carrey's *The Cable Guy* (1996), for example, represents how workers are no longer required merely to work, but also to perform: it 'evokes the performance of affective labor'.[16] Building on work by Jon McKenzie, Luc Boltanski and Eve

---

[15] Barnes, *England, England*, p. 70.
[16] Sianne Ngai, *Our Aesthetic Categories: Zany, Cute, Interesting* (Cambridge, MA: Harvard University Press, 2012), pp. 1, 182, 201–2, 7.

Chiapello, and others,[17] Ngai's work helps to suggest some ways in which Barnes's comic depiction of an imagined near-future dystopia emerges from a cultural and economic movement towards feeling as commodity and performance as a mode of work.

In Barnes's novel, the visitor experience of England, England is designed as a holistic performance, in which the lines between work and leisure are blurred. But during the planning process, the Project Manager, Mark, notes a potential problem with the proposal that those who perform in the agricultural dioramas by day should interact with visitors in the pub by night, thereby 'foregrounding the background'. Mark notes:

> You're asking some guy who's worked in a sock factory or something to stand around all day threshing and then go down the pub and instead of talking about sex and football with his mates as he wants to, you're going to make him work even harder at being a yokel with visitors who are, dare I whisper it, quite possibly a little more intelligent, and fragrant, than our trusty employee.

It is the equivalent, he says, of the actors at a play leaving the stage and shaking hands with the audience afterwards, '"like, hey, were only figments of your imagination up there but now we're showing how we're flesh and blood the same as you"'.[18] He is concerned that the park's workers will have to maintain verisimilitude and perform at all times or else risk breaking the illusion and marring the visitor experience. Subsequent events show that he need not have worried. Rather than breaking character and spoiling the illusion, Martha, the central protagonist of the novel, who usurps Sir Jack and takes over the running of the park, finds that her workers overcommit to their roles. Such is the success of England, England that it declares independence from the mainland, and within a few months, some of the island's cast 'could no longer be addressed as Pitco employees, only as the characters they were paid to inhabit'. Agricultural workers, for example, are 'increasingly reluctant to use company accommodation', preferring to 'sleep in their tumbledown cottages'. Although this move has the potential to develop into 'mere sentimental indiscipline', it may also prove to have benefits for the company in terms of reduced housing costs. Less ambiguously problematic, however, is the decision of the fake smugglers in the three 'smugglers' villages' on the island actually to begin smuggling,

---

[17] See John McKenzie, *Perform or Else: From Discipline to Performance* (London: Routledge, 2001); and Luc Boltanksi and Eve Chiapello, *The New Spirit of Capitalism*, trans. Gregory Elliott (London: Verso, [1999] 2007).

[18] Barnes, *England, England*, pp. 110–11.

inhabiting their roles by bringing illicit goods to the island. This is a challenge for Martha and the project, but rather than discreetly firing them, she incorporates their actions into the island's economy, staging a dawn raid 'lit by flaming torches with rough fill-in from floodlights' to be witnessed by three hundred paying customers. The smugglers are then allocated new roles as criminals: justice becomes 'job retraining' and the ringleaders will 'sit in the stocks and be pelted with rotten fruit, while others [will] tread the grain wheel and append their signatures to the resulting convict loaves'.[19] Once their corporate fines have been paid, they will be quietly deported. In this world, performance becomes work and work becomes performance, and as Ngai suggests of the zany aesthetic, the workers are required both to emotionally invest in their roles and to adapt their performances to meet their changing circumstances.

Barnes's portrayal of an imagined England is absurd in the extremes to which the premise is taken, but its absurdity diagnoses a relationship between labour and performance that requires 'radical fluidity and thus incessant performing in one's self presentation to others'. Invoking Bergson's definition of comedy as mechanization, Ngai asks whether 'if the rigidity of others is what makes us laugh, can an absolutely elastic subject – one who is nothing but a series of adjustments and adaptations to one situation after another – be genuinely funny?' The answer in Barnes's novel is 'yes', and in the smugglers' over-commitment to their roles and Martha's attempts to manage them we see the 'stressed-out, even desperate quality that immediately sets [the zany] apart from its more lighthearted comedic cousins, the goofy or silly'.[20] This mood also spreads to other characters on the island, where 'Robin Hood' begins to act as an actual outlaw, poaching livestock from the Animal Heritage Park, and 'Samuel Johnson' increasingly comes to resemble his historical namesake. Whereas it was intended that he would offer 'Johnsonian soliloquy, repartee among co-evals, and cross-epoch bonding between the Good Doctor and his modern guests' at the Dining Experience in a mock-up of Ye Olde Cheshire Cheese pub, Martha receives complaints about the actor's 'rank smell', poor table manners, irritability and many unnerving tics. The actor changes his name to Samuel Johnson, and comes to share Johnson's bouts of melancholy and way with aphorisms, even when he is not performing for guests. Martha reminds him that they want him to '*be* "Dr Johnson"', meaning the wit who exists in the popular imagination, but he is already too firmly embedded in the performance. Colin Hutchinson

---

[19] Ibid., pp. 198–202.
[20] Ngai, *Our Aesthetic Categories*, pp. 208, 174. 185.

suggests that in acting against the wishes of the island's corporate management, Johnson, Robin Hood and the other misbehaving characters demonstrate how 'some form of reality will always emerge in order to challenge or to defer the authority of any attempt to articulate and control',[21] but I argue that their 'acting out' is in fact a foreseeable consequence of late capitalism and its facility to demand that workers adapt their performances and are reintegrated into the system of work. Barnes's representation of performative labour does not have the gendered dimension identified by Ngai, but it does suggest the same stressed-out quality she identifies in the zany aesthetic and the same blurring of boundaries between work and leisure. For a moment Martha seems to recognize this and thinks she may have found a 'kindred spirit' in Johnson, hinting at the degree of performance involved in her own role and professional demeanour, though she quickly returns to problem-solving mode:

> Should they hire a new Johnson? Or rethink the whole Dining Experience with a different host? An evening with Oscar Wilde? Obvious dangers there. Noel Coward? Much the same problem. Bernard Shaw? Oh, the well-known nudist and vegetarian. What if he started imposing all that on the dinner table? Hadn't Old England produced any wits who were ... *sound*?[22]

Barnes is surely aware that both Wilde and Bernard Shaw are Irish by birth, and this elision is a further joke about the nature of national myths and the instability of notions of Englishness. Not only are there no examples of literary wits who are sufficiently benign to please the paying guests, but two of the individuals on the three-person shortlist are not unproblematically English. Returning to the ideas with which I opened this chapter, in *England, England*, performance, the *comic turns*, of the actors are not only about the nature of contemporary work and individual identity, but also about the nature of national identity.

The final section of *England, England*, titled 'Anglia' after the name given to mainland England once it has reverted to an agrarian economy, strikes an apparently nostalgic air. It describes Martha's return to what is now a rural backwater, a world of village fetes, horse-drawn transport, 'family evenings round the wireless and dialling "O" for Operator'.[23] It is also a country isolated from its resurgent British neighbours and from continental Europe. Like the England, England project, Anglia is a version of England that never existed, and Martha notes that the revival of old ways cannot properly be described as

---

[21] Hutchinson, *Reaganism, Thatcherism and the Social Novel*, p. 123.
[22] Barnes, *England, England*, pp. 207–13.
[23] Ibid., p. 253.

nostalgia because much of what is recreated existed before she was born; it is, perhaps, 'nostalgia of a truer kind: not for what you knew, or thought you had known, as a child, but for what you could never have known'.[24] Moreover, it is a world based on a common agreement not to shatter the illusion of authenticity. 'Jez Harris', who cuts the grass in the churchyard with a scythe and dispenses wisdom about the natural world while clad in a 'countryman's outfit of his own devising, all pockets and straps and sudden tucks', was until relatively recently Jack Oshinsky from Milwaukee. Jack has reinvented himself to 'play the yokel whenever some anthropologist, travel writer or linguistic theoretician would turn up inadequately disguised as a tourist'.[25] In this sense I disagree with John Su's conclusion that 'when *England, England* is describing the future of Great Britain, it can do so only by self-consciously recycling pastoral tropes of rural Englishness'.[26] Su makes a number persuasive points about the novel's relationship with Thatcherism, and Barnes's presentation of Albion as the only alternative to the naked marketization of England, England; but in my view, Barnes is more sceptical than Su allows and does not attempt to imagine such an alternative. Rather, as Hutchinson argues, Barnes's use of parody 'distances the novel from any unambiguous assertion that the revival of national identity is a suitable antidote to the ills of contemporary capitalism'.[27] The suggestion is not that once the hyperreal world of England, England takes primacy 'Old England' re-establishes a form of authentic, bucolic living and being; rather, both versions represent the post-Fordist movement of performance and affective labour into the economy of work. This again returns the conversation to questions of satire's role as purely negative critique, but *England, England* is an important text for the links it identifies between social and economic transitions, and questions of heritage and national identity, the creation of which may be performative and based on the simplifications of folk memory, but whose existence comes to have lasting, real-world effects.

Vanessa Guignery has identified parallels between *England, England* and Jonathan Coe's *Expo 58* (2013), a novel discussed further in Chapter 1, for their

---

[24] Ibid., p. 260. There are parallels here with Svetlana Boym's distinction between restorative and reflective forms of nostalgia. For Boym, restorative nostalgia 'puts the emphasis on *nostos* and proposes to rebuild the lost home and patch up the memory gaps', whereas reflective nostalgia 'dwells in *algia*, in longing and loss, the imperfect process of remembrance'; in both cases there is desire for the past, but reflective nostalgia acknowledges both the impossibility of its recovery and the partial nature of its existence in memory. Svetlana Boym, *The Future of Nostalgia* (New York: Basic Books, 2001), p. 41.

[25] Barnes, *England, England*, pp. 242–3.

[26] Su, 'Beauty and the Beastly Prime Minister', 1083–110 (p. 1091).

[27] Hutchinson, *Reaganism, Thatcherism and the Social Novel*, p. 127.

common interrogation of national identity via the presentation of 'make-believe' worlds;[28] both novels are about England's past and about the role of that past in the future, and both examine the pull between globalism and parochialism. The questions raised by these books feel especially pertinent as I write these concluding remarks during the period between the UK's 2016 EU membership referendum and triggering of Article 50 to leave the Union, and whatever comes next. Published almost twenty years apart, these novels feel contemporary and speak to the 'rolling sense' of the present discussion in the Introduction. They also address a sense of imminent or actual crisis through comedy, which is not to say that they make light of real-world concerns or seek to diminish their significance, but is to argue that they address them via a register that is distinct from 'serious' modes, offering a valuable alternative perspective. As Ngai concludes in relation to the zany aesthetic, 'the zany is not just funny but angry',[29] and the comic zaniness of *England, England* expresses anger and frustration at the iniquities of contemporary working life and the disingenuous manipulation of national memory and identity for the benefit of a small group of individuals. As well as speaking to the comic turn in contemporary English fiction discussed throughout this book, Barnes's novel is therefore about the performative meaning of 'comic turn' and about the notion of Englishness as a category. My discussion of it engages with questions of politics, affect, aesthetics, history, ethics and identity, and in that sense it offers a microcosm of this book as whole, which is concerned with comedy's multiple manifestations and multiplicity of meanings. Focusing on comedy offers a new vocabulary for thinking about contemporary English fiction and a different perspective on existing frameworks, bringing work from fields including literary studies, narrative theory, philosophy, linguistics, humour studies and comedy studies into dialogue around the family resemblances that define the comic. An understanding of the comic turn in contemporary fiction must entail a turn towards other disciplines and the resources they offer in order to explore comedy not as an adjunct to the serious work of literature but as a site of rich possibilities for the understanding of fiction and the contemporary moment.

[28] Guignery, *Jonathan Coe*, p. 136.
[29] Ngai, *Our Aesthetic Categories*, p. 218.

Bibliography

Adams, Ann Marie, 'A Passage to Forster: Zadie Smith's Attempt to "Only Connect" to *Howards End*', *Critique*, 52:4 (2011), 377–99.
Adorno, Theodor W. and Benjamin, Walter, *The Complete Correspondence 1928–1940*, ed. Henri Lonitz, trans. Nicholas Walker (Cambridge: Polity, 1999).
Adorno, Theodor W. and Horkheimer, Max, *Dialectic of Enlightenment: Philosophical Fragments*, ed. Gunzelin Schmid Noerr, trans. Edmund Jephcott (Stanford, CA: Stanford University Press, 2002).
Ahmed, Sara, *The Cultural Politics of Emotion*, 2nd edn (Edinburgh: Edinburgh University Press, 2014).
Alexander, Victoria N., 'Between the Influences of Bellow and Nabokov', *Antioch Review*, 52:4 (1994), 580–90.
Amis, Kingsley, *Lucky Jim* (London: Penguin, [1954] 1992).
Amis, Martin, *The Rachel Papers* (London: Penguin, [1973] 1984).
Amis, Martin, *Success* (London: Penguin, [1978] 1985).
Amis, Martin, *The Moronic Inferno and Other Visits to America* (Harmondsworth: Penguin, [1986] 1987).
Amis, Martin, *Time's Arrow* (London: Penguin, [1991] 1992).
Amis, Martin, *The Information* (London: Flamingo, [1995] 1996).
Amis, Martin, *Money* (London: Penguin, [1984] 2000).
Amis, Martin, *Experience* (London: Vintage, [2000] 2001).
Amis, Martin, *The War against Cliché: Essays and Reviews 1971–2000* (London: Vintage, [2001] 2002).
Amis, Martin, 'A Rough Trade' (Part Two), *Guardian*, 17 March 2001. Available online: https://www.theguardian.com/books/2001/mar/17/society.martinamis (accessed 17 June 2019).
Amis, Martin, *London Fields* (London: Vintage, [1989] 2003).
Amis, Martin, *Yellow Dog* (London: Vintage, [2003] 2004).
Amis, Martin, *The House of Meetings* (London: Jonathan Cape, 2006).
Amis, Martin, *The Pregnant Widow* (London: Jonathan Cape, 2010).
Amis, Martin, *Lionel Asbo: State of England* (London: Jonathan Cape, 2012).
Amis, Martin, *The Zone of Interest* (London: Jonathan Cape, 2014).
Amis, Martin, *The Rub of Time: Bellow, Nabokov, Hitchens and Other Pieces, 1994–2016* (London: Jonathan Cape, 2017).
Anderson, Amanda, *Bleak Liberalism* (Chicago: University of Chicago Press, 2016).
Annie Hall, [Film] dir. Woody Allen (USA: United Artists, 1977).

Apte, Mahadev L., *Humor and Laughter: An Anthropological Approach* (Ithaca, NY: Cornell University Press, 1985).

Aristotle, *Poetics*, in *Classical Literary Criticism*, 2nd edn, ed. and trans. Penelope Murray and T. S. Dorsch (London: Penguin, 2000), pp. 57–95.

Arts Council England, *Literature in the 21st Century: Understanding Models of Support for Literary Fiction*, 15 December 2017. Available online: https://www.artscouncil.org.uk/publication/literature-21st-century-understanding-models-support-literary-fiction (accessed 29 April 2019).

Attardo, Salvatore, *Linguistic Theories of Humor* (Berlin: Mouton de Gruyter, 1994).

Attardo, Salvatore, *Humorous Texts: A Semantic and Pragmatic Analysis* (Berlin: Mouton de Gruyter, 2001).

Attardo, Salvatore (ed.), *The Routledge Handbook of Language and Humor* (New York, NY: Routledge, 2017).

Auer, Peter and Eastman, Carol M., 'Code-Switching', in *Society and Language Use*, eds Jürgen Jaspers, Jef Verschueren and Jan-Ola Östman (Amsterdam: John Benjamins, 2010), pp. 84–112.

Bakhtin, Mikhail, *Problems of Dostoevsky's Poetics*, trans. Caryl Emerson (Minneapolis, MN: University of Minnesota Press, [1963] 1984).

Bakhtin, Mikhail, *Rabelais and His World*, trans. Hélène Iswolsky (Bloomington, IN: Indiana University Press [1965] 1984).

Barker, Ronnie and Corbett, Ronnie, 'Answering the Question Before Last' [video], YouTube (recorded 1980, uploaded 18 December 2007), https://www.youtube.com/watch?v=y0C59pI_ypQ (accessed 17 June 2019).

Barker, Nicola, *Love Your Enemies* (London: Faber and Faber, [1993] 1994).

Barker, Nicola, *Reversed Forecast* (London: Faber and Faber, [1994] 1995).

Barker, Nicola, *Small Holdings* (London: Faber and Faber, 1995).

Barker, Nicola, *Heading Inland* (London: Faber and Faber, 1996).

Barker, Nicola, *Wide Open* (London: Faber and Faber, 1998).

Barker, Nicola, *Five Miles from Outer Hope* (London: Faber and Faber, 2000).

Barker, Nicola, *Behindlings* (London: Flamingo, 2002).

Barker, Nicola, *Clear* (London: Fourth Estate, 2004).

Barker, Nicola, *Darkmans* (London: Fourth Estate, 2006).

Barker, Nicola, *Burley Cross Postbox Theft* (London: Fourth Estate, 2010).

Barker, Nicola, *The Yips* (London: Fourth Estate, 2012).

Barker, Nicola, *In the Approaches* (London: Fourth Estate, 2014).

Barker, Nicola, *The Cauliflower®* (London: William Heinemann, 2016).

Barker, Nicola, *H(A)PPY* (London: William Heinemann, 2017).

Barker, Nicola, 'The Goldsmiths Writers' Centre Presents Nicola Barker', interview at Goldsmiths, University of London, 24 January 2018.

Barker, Nicola, *I Am Sovereign* (London: William Heinemann, 2019).

Barnes, Julian, 'Diary', *London Review of Books*, 12 November 1987. Available online: https://www.lrb.co.uk/v09/n20/julian-barnes/diary (accessed 8 May 2019).

Barnes, Julian, *England, England* (London: Picador, [1998] 1999).
Barstow, David, Craig Susanne and Buettner, Russ, 'Trump Engaged in Suspect Tax Schemes as He Reaped Riches from His Father', *New York Times*, 2 October 2018. Available online: https://www.nytimes.com/interactive/2018/10/02/us/politics/donald-trump-tax-schemes-fred-trump.html?module=inline (accessed 26 April 2019).
Bataille, Georges, 'Attraction and Repulsion I: Tropisms, Sexuality, Laughter and Tears' [1938], in *The College of Sociology, 1937–39*, ed. Denis Hollier, trans. Betsy Wing (Minneapolis: University of Minnesota Press, [1979] 1988), pp. 103–12.
Bataille, Georges, 'Attraction and Repulsion II: Social Structure' [1938], in *The College of Sociology, 1937–39*, ed. Denis Hollier, trans. Betsy Wing (Minneapolis: University of Minnesota Press, [1979] 1988), pp. 113–24.
Bataille, Georges, 'Laughter' [1944], trans. Bruce Boone, in *The Bataille Reader*, eds Fred Botting and Scott Wilson (Oxford: Blackwell, 1997), pp. 59–63.
Bataille, Georges, 'Un-knowing: Laughter and Tears' [1953], trans. Anne Michelson, October, 36 (1985), 89–102.
Bataille, Georges, *Inner Experience*, trans. Leslie Anne Boldt (Albany, NY: State University of New York Press, [1954] 1988).
Baum, Devorah, *The Jewish Joke: An Essay with Examples (Less Essay, More Examples)* (London: Profile, 2017).
BBC News, 'Howard Jacobson Wins Booker Prize', 12 October 2010. Available online: https://www.bbc.co.uk/news/entertainment-arts-11526278 (accessed 29 April 2019).
BBC News, 'Pound Coin Gag Scoops Best Edinburgh Fringe Joke Award', 22 August 2017. Available online: https://www.bbc.co.uk/news/uk-scotland-40999000 (accessed 16 July 2019).
Beckett, Samuel, *Watt* (New York: Grove Press, [1953] 1994).
Benchley, Robert, 'Why We Laugh—Or Do We? (Let's Get This Thing Settled, Mr. Eastman)', *New Yorker*, [2 January 1937] 16 February 2010. Available online: https://www.newyorker.com/magazine/1937/01/02/why-we-laugh-or-do-we (accessed 3 June 2019).
Benedictus, Leo, 'Early Swerves', review of Magnus Mills, *The Scheme for Full Employment, London Review of Books*, 6 November 2003. Available online: https://www.lrb.co.uk/v25/n21/leo-benedictus/early-swerves (accessed 9 July 2019).
Benjamin, Walter, 'Fate and Character' [1921], trans. Edmund Jephcott, in *Selected Writings, vol. 1: 1913–1926* (Cambridge, MA: Harvard University Press, 2004), pp. 201–6.
Bennett, Alice, *Contemporary Fictions of Attention: Reading and Distraction in the Twenty-First Century* (London: Bloomsbury, 2018).
Bennett, Catherine, 'The Blaine Bashers Make Me Proud to Be British', *Guardian*, 11 September 2003. Available online: https://www.theguardian.com/uk/2003/sep/11/britishidentity.comment (accessed 7 February 2019).
Bentley, Nick, *Radical Fictions: The English Novel in the 1950s* (Oxford: Peter Lang, 2007).

Bentley, Nick, 'Re-writing Englishness: Imagining the Nation in Julian Barnes's *England, England* and Zadie Smith's *White Teeth*', *Textual Practice*, 21:3 (2007), 483–504.

Bentley, Nick, 'Mind and Brain: The Representation of Trauma in Martin Amis' *Yellow Dog* and Ian McEwan's *Saturday*', in *Diseases and Disorders in Contemporary Fiction: The Syndrome Syndrome*, eds T.J. Lustig and James Peacock (New York: Routledge, 2013), pp. 115–29.

Bentley, Nick, *Martin Amis* (Tavistock: Northcote House, 2015).

Berger, Peter L., *Redeeming Laughter: The Comic Element of Human Experience*, 2nd edn (Berlin: Walter de Gruyter, 2014).

Bergonzi, Bernard, *The Situation of the Novel*, 2nd edn (Basingstoke: Macmillan, 1979).

Bergson, Henri, 'Laughter: An Essay on the Meaning of the Comic' [1900], trans. Cloudesley Brereton and Fred Rothwell, in *Comedy*, ed. Wylie Sypher (New York: Doubleday, 1956), pp. 61–190.

Berlant, Lauren, *Cruel Optimism* (Durham, NC: Duke University Press, 2011).

Berlant, Lauren and Ngai, Sianne (eds), 'Comedy: An Issue', special issue *Critical Inquiry*, 43:2 (2017), 223–589.

Bevis, Matthew, *Comedy: A Very Short Introduction* (Oxford: Oxford University Press, 2013).

Beynon, Huw, *Working for Ford* (London: Allen Lane, 1973).

Bhabha, Homi K., 'Foreword: Joking Aside: The Idea of a Self-Critical Community', in *Modernity, Culture and 'the Jew'*, eds Bryan Cheyette and Laura Marcus (Cambridge: Polity, 1998), pp. xv–xx.

Billig, Michael, *Laughter and Ridicule: Towards a Social Critique of Humour* (London: Sage, 2005).

Blackburn, Tony, *Poptastic!: My Life in Radio* (London: Cassell, 2007).

Boltanksi, Luc and Chiapello, Eve, *The New Spirit of Capitalism*, trans. Gregory Elliott (London: Verso, [1999] 2007).

Boord, Andrew, 'The First and Best Part of Scoggins Jests. Full of Witty Mirth and Pleasant Shifts, Done By Him in France and Other Places: Being a Preservative against Melancholy' [1626], gathered by Andrew Boord, Doctor of Physicke, London, Printed for Francis Williams, in *Old English Jest-Books*, 3 vols, ed. W. Carew Hazlitt (London: Willis and Sotheran, 1864), pp. 37–161.

Boym, Svetlana, *The Future of Nostalgia* (New York: Basic Books, 2001).

Brauner, David, *Post-War Jewish Fiction: Ambivalence, Self-Explanation and Transatlantic Connections* (Basingstoke: Palgrave Macmillan, 2001).

Brauner, David, 'Fetishizing the Holocaust: Comedy and Transatlantic Connections in Howard Jacobson's *Kalooki Nights*', *European Judaism*, 47:2 (2014), 21–9.

Bown, Alfie, *In the Event of Laughter: Psychoanalysis, Literature and Comedy* (London: Bloomsbury, 2019).

Boyd, Brian, *On the Origin of Stories: Evolution, Cognition, and Fiction* (Cambridge, MA: Harvard University Press, 2009).

Bracke, Astrid, *Climate Crisis and the 21st-Century British Novel* (London: Bloomsbury, 2019).
Bradford, Richard, *The Novel Now: Contemporary British Fiction* (Oxford: Blackwell, 2007).
The Britannia Inn: Universal and International Exhibition, Brussels (London: Whitbread, 1958).
Brooker, Joseph, *Flann O'Brien* (Tavistock: Northcote House, 2004).
Brooker, Joseph, 'Satire Bust: The Wagers of *Money*', *Law and Literature*, 17:3 (2005), 321–44.
Brooker, Joseph, 'The Middle Years of Martin Amis', in *British Fiction Today*, eds Phillip Tew and Rod Mengham (London: Continuum, 2006), pp. 3–14.
Brooker, Joseph, 'Jonathan Coe's Stories of Sadness', in *Jonathan Coe: Contemporary British Satire*, ed. Philip Tew (London: Bloomsbury, 2018), pp. 35–50.
Brown, Mark, 'Howard Jacobson Wins Booker Prize 2010 for *The Finkler Question*', *Guardian*, 12 October 2010. Available online: https://www.theguardian.com/books/2010/oct/12/howard-jacobson-the-finkler-question-booker (accessed 29 April 2019).
Bruns, John, *Loopholes: Reading Comically* (New Brunswick, NJ: Transactions, 2014).
Bullock, Barbara E. and Toribio, Almeida Jacqueline, 'Themes in the Study of Code-switching', in *The Cambridge Handbook of Linguistic Code-switching*, eds Barbara E. Bullock and Almeida Jacqueline Toribio (Cambridge: Cambridge University Press, 2009), pp. 1–18.
Butler, Judith, *Precarious Life: The Power of Mourning and Violence* (London: Verso, 2004).
Byrt, Anthony, 'The World Cracked Open' *New Zealand Listener*, 19 January 2008. Available online: https://www.noted.co.nz/archive/listener-nz-2008/the-world-cracked-open/ (accessed 25 February 2019).
Calvino, Italo, *The Literature Machine*, trans. Patrick Creagh (London: Secker and Warburg, [1980] 1987).
Carroll, Noël, *Humour: A Very Short Introduction* (Oxford: Oxford University Press, 2014).
Carter, Angela, *Burning Your Boats: Collected Short Stories* (London: Vintage, 1996).
Cavaliero, Glen, *The Alchemy of Laughter: Comedy in English Fiction* (Basingstoke: Macmillan, 2000).
Chadderton, Helena, 'Translating Class in Jonathan Coe', *The Translator*, 23:3 (2017), 269–78.
Chapman, James, '50,000 Drain Covers Stolen "To Be Sold as Scrap in China and India"', *Daily Mail*, 14 August 2008. Available online: https://www.dailymail.co.uk/news/article-1044676/50-000-drain-covers-stolen-sold-scrap-China-India.html (accessed 22 August 2019).
Charlton, Matt, 'How Satire Gave Boris Johnson His Persona', *Vice*, 20 August 2018. Available online: https://www.vice.com/en_uk/article/8xb7vv/how-satire-gave-boris-johnson-his-persona (accessed 13 June 2019).

Charney, Maurice, *Comedy High and Low: An Introduction to the Experience of Comedy* (New York: Oxford University Press, 1978).

Cheyette, Bryan, 'Wedded to the Umlaut', review of Howard Jacobson, Kalooki Nights, *Guardian*, 8 July 2006. Available online: https://www.theguardian.com/books/2006/jul/08/featuresreviews.guardianreview24 (accessed 11 March 2019).

Cheyette, Brian, 'British-Jewish Literature', in *The Routledge Encyclopedia of Jewish Writers of the Twentieth Century*, ed. Sorrel Kerbel (New York: Routledge, 2010), pp. 7–10.

Cheyette, Bryan, *Diasporas of the Mind: Jewish and Postcolonial Writing and the Nightmare of History* (New Haven, CT: Yale University Press, 2013).

Childs, Peter, *Julian Barnes* (Manchester: Manchester University Press, 2011).

Childs, Peter and Green, James, *Aesthetics and Ethics in Twenty-First Century British Novels* (London: Bloomsbury, 2013).

Coe, Jonathan, 'Satire and Sympathy: Some Consequences of Intrusive Narration in *Tom Jones* and Other Comic Novels', PhD thesis, Warwick University, 1986.

Coe, Jonathan, *What a Carve Up!* (London: Penguin, [1994] 1995).

Coe, Jonathan, *The House of Sleep* (London: Penguin, [1997] 1998).

Coe, Jonathan, *The Accidental Woman* (London: Penguin, [1987] 2000).

Coe, Jonathan, *A Touch of Love* (London: Penguin, [1989] 2000).

Coe, Jonathan, *The Dwarves of Death* (London: Penguin, [1990] 2001).

Coe, Jonathan, *The Rotters' Club* (London: Penguin, [2001] 2002).

Coe, Jonathan, *Like a Fiery Elephant: The Story of B.S. Johnson* (London: Picador, 2004).

Coe, Jonathan, *The Rain Before It Falls* (London: Viking, 2007).

Coe, Jonathan, *The Closed Circle* (London: Penguin, [2004] 2008).

Coe, Jonathan, *The Terrible Privacy of Maxwell Sim* (London: Penguin, 2010).

Coe, Jonathan, *Expo 58* (London: Viking, 2013).

Coe, Jonathan, 'Expo 58', Jonathan Coe Personal Website, 2013, http://www.jonathancoewriter.com/books/expo58.html (accessed 16 August 2016).

Coe, Jonathan, *Marginal Notes, Doubtful Statements: Non-Fiction, 1990–2013* [Kindle edn] (London: Penguin, 2013).

Coe, Jonathan, 'Winshaw Playing Cards', Jonathan Coe Personal Website, 2013, http://www.jonathancoewriter.com/books/winshawCards.html (accessed 17 June 2019).

Coe, Jonathan, 'David Nobbs 1935–2015', Jonathan Coe Personal Website, 2015, http://www.jonathancoewriter.com/blog.php/?p=475 (accessed 17 June 2019).

Coe, Jonathan, 'Is Martin Amis right? Or will Jeremy Corbyn Have the Last Laugh?' *Guardian*, 30 October 2015. Available online: https://www.theguardian.com/books/2015/oct/30/martin-amis-jeremy-corbyn-humour-jonathan-coe (accessed 17 June 2019).

Coe, Jonathan, *Number 11, or Tales that Witness Madness* (London: Viking, 2015).

Coe, Jonathan, 'Will Satire Save Us in the Age of Trump?' *Guardian*, 6 January 2017. Available online: https://www.theguardian.com/books/2017/jan/06/jonathan-coe-will-satire-save-us-in-the-age-of-donald-trump?CMP=share_btn_link (accessed 16 July 2019).

Coe, Jonathan, *Middle England* (London: Viking, 2018).

Coe, Jonathan, 'How Brexit Broke Britain', *Time*, 6 June 2019. Available online: https://time.com/5601982/how-brexit-broke-britain/ (accessed 7 June 2019).

Coe, Jonathan, 'How Bad Can It Get? Reflections on the State We're In', *London Review of Books*, 15 August 2019. Available online: https://www.lrb.co.uk/v41/n16/the-state-were-in/how-bad-can-it-get#coe (accessed 12 August 2019).

Cohen, Ted, *Jokes: Philosophical Thoughts on Joking Matters* (Chicago: University of Chicago Press, 1999).

Colebrook, Claire, *Gilles Deleuze* (London: Routledge, 2002).

Colebrook, Claire, *Irony* (London: Routledge, 2004).

Condren, Conal, 'Satire and Definition', *Humor*, 25:4 (2012), 375–99.

Connor, Steven, *Samuel Beckett: Repetition, Theory and Text*, rev edn (Aurora, CO: Davies Group, 2007).

Cook, William, 'Have Donald Trump and Brexit Killed off the Dark Art of Political Satire?' *Independent*, 18 January 2018. Available online: https://www.independent.co.uk/news/long_reads/donald-trump-satire-politics-late-shows-us-president-paradox-john-oliver-stephen-colbert-a8165401.html (accessed 26 April 2019).

Cooper, Anthony Ashley, Third Earl of Shaftesbury, *Characteristics of Men, Manners, Opinions, Times* (Cambridge: Cambridge University Press, [1711] 1999).

Cornwell, Neil, *The Absurd in Literature* (Manchester: Manchester University Press, 2006).

Corrigan, Robert W. (ed.), *Comedy: Meaning and Form*, 2nd edn (New York: Harper and Row, 1981).

Cowper, William, *The Task: A Poem in Six Books* (Ann Arbor, MI: University of Michigan Library, [1785] 2007) [online edn], ii, pp. 57–62. Available online: http://quod.lib.umich.edu/cgi/t/text/text-idx?c=ecco;idno=004792652.0001.000, (accessed 17 June 2019).

Crews, Brian, 'Martin Amis and the Postmodern Grotesque', *Modern Language Review*, 105:3 (2010), 641–59.

Critchley, Simon, *On Humour* (London: Routledge, 2002).

Critchley, Simon, 'Repetition, Repetition, Repetition: Richard Prince and the Three r's', in *Lacan, Psychoanalysis and Comedy*, eds Patricia Gherovici and Manya Steinkoler (New York: Cambridge University Press, 2016), pp. 237–42.

Crosthwaite, Paul (ed.), *Criticism, Crisis, and Contemporary Narrative: Textual Horizons in an Age of Global Risk* (New York: Routledge, 2011).

Crown Prosecution Service, 'Anti-Social Behaviour Orders on Conviction (ASBOs)', 2014. Available online: http://www.cps.gov.uk/legal/a_to_c/anti_social_behaviour_guidance/ (accessed 4 May 2017).

Cuder-Domínguez, Pilar, 'Ethnic Cartographies of London in Bernardine Evaristo and Zadie Smith', *European Journal of English Studies*, 8:2 (2004), 173–88.

Curran, Kieran, *Cynicism in British Post-War Culture: Ignorance, Dust and Disease* (Basingstoke: Palgrave Macmillan 2015).

Currie, Mark, 'Introduction', in *Metafiction*, ed. Mark Currie (Harlow: Longman, 1995), pp. 1–18.

Curthoys, Ned, 'Howard Jacobson's *The Finkler Question* as Holocaust Pedagogy', *Holocaust Studies*, 19:3 (2013), 1–24.

Dango, Michael, 'Camp's Distribution: "Our" Aesthetic Category', *Social Text 131*, 35:2 (2017), 39–67.

Dauber, Jeremy, *Jewish Comedy (A Serious History)* (New York: Norton, [2017] 2018).

Davies, Ben, *Sex, Time and Space in Contemporary Fiction: Exceptional Intercourse* (Basingstoke: Palgrave Macmillan, 2016).

Davies, David, *Aesthetics and Literature* (London: Continuum, 2007).

Davies, Helen and Ilott, Sarah, 'Mocking the Weak? Contexts, Theories, Politics', in *Comedy and the Politics of Representation: Mocking the Weak?* (Basingstoke: Palgrave Macmillan, 2018).

David, Murray S., *What's So Funny? The Comic Conception of Culture and Society* (Chicago: University of Chicago Press, 1993).

Dawson, Paul, *The Return of the Omniscient Narrator* (Columbus, OH: Ohio State University Press, 2013).

De Cristofaro, Diletta, *The Contemporary Post-Apocalyptic Novel: Critical Temporalities and the End Times* (London: Bloomsbury, 2019).

Deleuze, Gilles, *Masochism: Coldness and Cruelty*, trans. Jean McNeil (New York: Zone Books, [1967] 1989).

Deleuze, Gilles, *Difference and Repetition*, trans. Paul Patton (London: Continuum, [1968] 2004).

Deleuze, Gilles, *The Logic of Sense*, trans. Mark Lester (London: Continuum, [1969] 2004).

Dern, John A., *Martians, Monsters and Madonna: Fiction and Form in the World of Martin Amis* (New York: Peter Lang, 2000).

Des Pres, Terrence, 'Holocaust Laughter', in *Writing into the World: Essays 1973–1987* (Harmondsworth: Penguin, 1981), pp. 277–86.

Di Bernardo, Francesco, 'A Terrible Precariousness: Financialization of Society and the Precariat in Jonathan Coe's *The Terrible Privacy of Maxwell Sim*', in *Jonathan Coe: Contemporary British Satire*, ed. Philip Tew (London: Bloomsbury, 2018), pp. 141–54.

Díaz Bild, Aída, '*Kalooki Nights* or the Sacred Duty to Remember the Holocaust', *Holocaust Studies*, 23:3 (2018), 265–86.

Dickens, Charles, *Great Expectations* (Oxford: Oxford University Press, [1861] 2008).

Dickie, Simon, *Cruelty and Laughter: Forgotten Comic Literature and the Unsentimental Eighteenth Century* (Chicago: University of Chicago Press, 2011).

Diedrick, James, *Understanding Martin Amis*, 2nd edn (Columbia, SC: University of South Carolina Press, 2004).

Dolar, Mladen, 'The Comic Mimesis', in 'Comedy: An Issue', eds Lauren Berlant and Sianne Ngai, special issue *Critical Inquiry*, 43:2 (2017), 570–89.

Doten, Mark, *Trump Sky Alpha* (Minneapolis, MN: Graywolf Press, 2019).
Double, Oliver, *Getting the Joke: The Inner Workings of Stand-Up Comedy*, 2nd edn (London: Bloomsbury, 2014).
Douglas, Mary, 'Do Dogs Laugh? A Cross-Cultural Approach to Body Symbolism', in *Implicit Meanings: Essays on Anthropology* (London: Routledge, [1975] 1993), pp. 83–9.
Dowland, Douglas and Ioanes, Anna (eds), 'Violent Feelings: Affective Intensities in Literature, Film, and Culture', special issue *Lit: Literature Interpretation, Theory*, 30:1–2 (2019), 1–169.
Driscoll, Lawrence, *Evading Class in Contemporary British Literature* (New York: Palgrave Macmillan, 2009).
Duggan, Robert, *The Grotesque in Contemporary British Fiction* (Manchester: Manchester University Press, 2013).
Eagleton, Terry, 'Theydunnit', review of *What a Carve Up!*, *London Review of Books*, 28 April 1994, p. 12.
Eagleton, Terry, *Humour* (Newhaven, CT: Yale University Press, 2019).
Eastman, Max, *Enjoyment of Laughter* (London: Hamish Hamilton, 1937).
Eve, Martin, 'Sincerity', in *The Routledge Companion to Twenty-First Century Literary Fiction*, eds Daniel O'Gorman and Robert Eaglestone (Abingdon: Routledge, 2019), pp. 36–47.
Eco, Umberto, 'The Comic and the Rule', in *Travels in Hyperreality: Essays*, trans. William Weaver (San Diego, CA: Harcourt Brace, 1983), pp. 269–79.
Eco, Umberto, 'The Frames of Comic "Freedom"', in *Carnival!* ed. Thomas A. Sebeok (Berlin: Mouton, 1984), pp. 1–9.
English, James F., *Comic Transactions: Literature, Humor, and the Politics of Community in Twentieth-Century Britain* (Ithaca, NY: Cornell University Press, 1994).
English, James F., *The Economy of Prestige: Prizes, Awards, and the Circulation of Cultural Value* (Cambridge, MA: Harvard University Press, 2005).
Ermida, Isabel, *The Language of Comic Narratives: Humor Construction in Short Stories* (Berlin: Mouton de Gruyter, 2008).
Fahrenthold, David A., 'Trump Recorded Having Extremely Lewd Conversation about Women in 2005', *Washington Post*, 8 October 2016. Available online: https://www.washingtonpost.com/politics/trump-recorded-having-extremely-lewd-conversation-about-women-in-2005/2016/10/07/3b9ce776-8cb4-11e6-bf8a-3d26847eeed4_story.html?noredirect=on&utm_term=.7bfa10a4e7c1.
Fahrenthold, David A. and O'Connell, Jonathan, 'How Donald Trump Inflated His Net Worth to Lenders and Investors', *Washington Post*, 28 March 2019. Available online: https://www.washingtonpost.com/graphics/2019/politics/trump-statements-of-financial-condition/?utm_term=.3be0102388d6 (accessed 26 April 2019).
Fears, Christine, 'An Interview with Will Self', *The Literateur*, 6 February 2010. Available online: http://literateur.com/an-interview-with-will-self (accessed 9 July 2019).
Felski, Rita, *Uses of Literature* (Oxford: Blackwell, 2008).

Fielding, Steven, 'Comedy and Politics: The Great Debate', 29 September 2011. Available online: http://nottspolitics.org/2011/09/29/comedy-and-politics-the-great-debate/ (accessed 17 June 2019).

Fischer, Susan Alice, '"A Glance from God": Zadie Smith's *On Beauty* and Zora Neale Hurston', *Changing English: Studies in Culture and Education*, 14:3 (2007), 285–97.

Fletcher, Angus, *Comic Democracies: From Ancient Athens to the American Republic* (Baltimore, MD: Johns Hopkins University Press, 2016).

Fludernik, Monika, *Towards a 'Natural' Narratology* (Abingdon: Routledge, 1996).

Ford, Russell (ed.), 'Why So Serious (Philosophy and Comedy)', special issue *Angelaki*, 21:3 (2016), 1–152.

Forster, E. M., *Aspects of the Novel* (Harmondsworth: Penguin, [1927] 1962).

Freud, Sigmund, 'Humour' [1928], trans. Joan Rivier, in *The Standard Edition of the Complete Psychological Works of Sigmund Freud, Vol. 21: The Future of an Illusion, Civilization and Its Discontents, and Other Works*, ed. James Strachey (London: Vintage, [1964] 2001), pp. 159–66.

Freud, Sigmund, *The Joke and Its Relation to the Unconscious*, trans. Joyce Crick (London: Penguin, [1905] 2002).

Freud, Sigmund and Breuer, Josef, 'On the Psychical Mechanism of Hysterical Phenomena: Preliminary Communication (1893)', in *The Standard Edition of the Complete Psychological Works of Sigmund Freud, Vol. 2: Studies On Hysteria*, ed. and trans. James Strachey (London: Vintage, [1955] 2001), pp. 1–18.

Friedman, Sam, *Comedy and Distinction: The Cultural Capital of a 'Good' Sense of Humour* (Abingdon: Routledge, 2014).

Frye, Northrop, *Anatomy of Criticism: Four Essays* (Princeton, NJ: Princeton University Press, [1957] 2000).

Galligan, Edward L., *The Comic Vision in Literature* (Athens, GA: University of Georgia Press, 1984).

Ganteau, Jean-Michel, 'Innocent Abroad: Jonathan Coe's Expo 58 and the Comedy of Forgiveness', in 'Focus on Comic Representations in Post-Millennial British and Irish Fiction', ed. Barbara Puschmann-Nalenz, special issue *Anglistik: International Journal of English Studies*, 27:1 (2016), 19–29.

Gąsiorek, Andrzej, *Post-War British Fiction: Realism and After* (London: Edward Arnold, 1995).

Gąsiorek, Andrzej, '"A renewed sense of difficulty": E. M. Forster, Iris Murdoch and Zadie Smith on Ethics and Form', in *The Legacies of Modernism: Historicising Postwar and Contemporary Fiction*, ed. David James (Cambridge: Cambridge University Press, 2011), pp. 170–86.

Gąsiorek, Andrzej, 'Michael Chabon, Howard Jacobson, and Post-Holocaust Fiction', *Contemporary Literature*, 53:4 (2012), 875–903.

Genette, Gerard, *Narrative Discourse: An Essay in Method*, trans. Jane E. Lewin (Ithaca, NY: Cornell University Press, [1972] 1980), pp. 113–17.

Germanà, Monica and Mousoutzanis, Aris (eds), *Apocalyptic Discourse in Contemporary Culture: Post-Millennial Perspectives of the End of the World* (New York: Routledge, 2014).

Ghosh, Amitav, *The Great Derangement: Climate Change and the Unthinkable* (Chicago: University of Chicago Press, 2017).

Gibbons, Rob, Gibbons, Neil, Iannucci, Armando and Coogan, Steve I, *Partridge: We Need to Talk about Alan* (London: HarperCollins, 2011).

Gilbert, Ruth, *Writing Jewish: Contemporary British-Jewish Literature* (Basingstoke: Palgrave Macmillan, 2013).

Gilroy, Paul, *After Empire: Melancholia or Convivial Culture?* (Abingdon: Routledge, 2004).

Gilroy, Paul, 'The Closed Circle of Britain's Postcolonial Melancholia', in *The Literature of Melancholia: Early Modern to Postmodern*, eds Martin Middeke and Christina Wald (Basingstoke: Palgrave Macmillan, 2011), pp. 187–204.

Gimbel, Steven, *Isn't that Clever: A Philosophical Account of Humor and Comedy* (New York: Routledge, 2018).

Gladwell, Malcolm, *Desert Island Discs*, 10 August 2015, BBC Radio 4. Available online: http://www.bbc.co.uk/programmes/b04d0xfx (accessed 17 June 2019).

Gladwell, Malcolm, 'The Satire Paradox' [podcast], *Revisionist History*. Available online: http://revisionisthistory.com/episodes/10-the-satire-paradox (accessed 23 August 2016).

Glass, Charles, 'It's Best to Roll with the Big Cats Forget the Jealous Snipers – If Amis Can Get £500,000 for His Novel He Deserves It', *Guardian*, 10 January 1995.

Goldsmith, Stuart *The Comedian's Comedian* [podcast]. Available online: http://www.comedianscomedian.com/ (accessed 23 August 2016).

Greenberg, Jonathan, *The Cambridge Introduction to Satire* (Cambridge: Cambridge University Press, 2019).

Greenman, Ben, 'Is Satire Possible in the Age of Trump?' *New York Times*, 8 March 2019. Available online: https://www.nytimes.com/2019/03/08/books/review/mark-doten-trump-sky-alpha.html?smid=tw-nytbooks&smtyp=cur (accessed 26 April 2019).

Gregson, Ian, *Character and Satire in Postwar Fiction* (London: Continuum, 2006).

Greif, Mark, 'You'll Love the Way It Makes You Feel', *London Review of Books*, 23 October 2008. Available online: https://www.lrb.co.uk/v30/n20/mark-greif/youll-love-the-way-it-makes-you-feel (accessed 23 July 2019).

Griffin, Dustin, *Satire: A Critical Reintroduction* (Lexington, KY: University Press of Kentucky, 1994).

Griffiths, Trevor, *Comedians* (London: Faber and Faber, 1976).

Groes, Sebastian, *British Fictions of the Sixties: The Making of the Swinging Decade* (London: Bloomsbury, 2009).

Groes, Sebastian, '"Please don't hate me, sensitive girl readers": Gender, Surveillance and Spectacle after 9/11 in Nicola Barker's Clear', in *Women's Fiction and Post-*

9/11 Contexts, eds Peter Childs, Claire Colebrook and Sebastian Groes (London: Lexington, 2015), pp. 159–77.

Guignery, Vanessa, *Novelists in the New Millennium: Conversations with Writers* (Basingstoke: Palgrave Macmillan, 2013).

Guignery, Vanessa, *Jonathan Coe* (Basingstoke: Palgrave Macmillan, 2016).

Guignery, Vanessa, 'An Interview with Jonathan Coe—Looking Backwards and Forwards', *Études britanniques contemporaines*, 54 (2018). Available Online: https://journals.openedition.org/ebc/4396 (accessed 16 July 2019).

Gurewitch, Morton, *Comedy: The Irrational Vision* (Ithaca, NY: Cornell University Press, 1975).

Gutwirth, Marcel, *Laughing Matter: An Essay on the Comic* (Ithaca, NY: Cornell University Press, 1993).

Hackett, Paul, 'Howard Jacobson Wins Man Booker for Comic Novel', *Globe and Mail*, 12 October 2010. Available online: https://www.theglobeandmail.com/arts/books-and-media/howard-jacobson-wins-man-booker-for-comic-novel/article4328936/ (accessed 29 April 2019).

Haffenden, John, *Novelists in Interview* (London: Methuen, 1985).

Hale, Dorothy J., 'On Beauty as Beautiful? The Problem of Novelistic Aesthetics by Way of Zadie Smith', *Contemporary Literature*, 53:4 (2012), 814–44.

Halliday, M. A. K. and Hassan, Ruqaiya, *Language, Context and Text: Aspects of Language in a Social-Semiotic Perspective*, 2nd edn (Oxford: Oxford University Press, 1989).

Harper, Graeme (ed.), *Comedy, Fantasy and Colonialism* (London: Continuum, 2002).

Head, Dominic, *The Cambridge Introduction to Modern British Fiction, 1950–2000* (Cambridge: Cambridge University Press, 2002).

Head, Dominic, 'The Demise of Class Fiction', in *A Concise Companion to Contemporary British Fiction*, ed. James F. English (Oxford: Blackwell, 2006), pp. 229–47.

Heilman, Robert Bechtold, *The Ways of the World: Comedy and Society* (Seattle: University of Washington Press, 1978).

Heise, Ursula K., *Imagining Extinction: The Cultural Meanings of Endangered Species* (Chicago: University of Chicago Press, 2016).

Heller, Agnes, *Immortal Comedy: The Comic Phenomenon in Art, Literature, and Life* (Oxford: Lexington, 2005).

Hensher, Philip, '*NW* by Zadie Smith: Review', *Telegraph*, 3 September 2012. Available online: http://www.telegraph.co.uk/culture/books/9508844/NW-by-Zadie-Smith-review.html (accessed 9 July 2019).

Herman, David, *Story Logic: Problems and Possibilities of Narrative* (Lincoln, NE: University of Nebraska Press, [2002] 2004).

Hicks, Heather J., *The Post-Apocalyptic Novel in the Twenty-First Century: Modernity beyond Salvage* (Basingstoke: Palgrave Macmillan, 2016).

Higgins, Kathleen Marie, *Comic Relief: Nietzsche's Gay Science* (Oxford: Oxford University Press, 2000).

Hill, Robert H., *Tales of the Jesters* (Edinburgh: W.M. Blackwood and Sons, 1934).

Hitchens, Christopher, 'Between Waugh and Wodehouse: Comedy and Conservatism', in *On Modern British Fiction*, ed. Zachary Leader (Oxford: Oxford University Press, 2002).

Holmes, Christopher, 'The Novel's Third Way: Zadie Smith's "Hysterical Realism"', in *Reading Zadie Smith: The First Decade and Beyond*, ed. Philip Tew (London: Bloomsbury, 2013), pp. 141–53.

Holt, Jim, *Stop Me If You've Heard This: A History and Philosophy of Jokes* (London: Profile, 2008).

Hot Chip, 'Over and Over', in *The Warning* [Music Album] (UK: EMI, 2006).

Houser, Heather, *Ecosickness in Contemporary U.S. Fiction: Environment and Affect* (New York: Columbia University Press, 2016).

Houser, Tammy Amiel, 'Zadie Smith's *NW*: Unsettling the Promise of Empathy', *Contemporary Literature*, 58:1 (2017), 116–48.

Houswitschka, Christopher, '"Show me a novel that's not comic…:" Howard Jacobson's *The Finkler Question*', in 'Focus on Comic Representations in Post-Millennial British and Irish Fiction', ed. Barbara Puschmann-Nalenz, special issue *Anglistik: International Journal of English Studies*, 27:1 (2016), 45–59.

Hubble, Nick, 'What Became of the People We Used to Be? *The House of Sleep* (1997) and the 1970s Sitcom, *Whatever Happened to the Likely Lads?* (1973–5)', in *Jonathan Coe: Contemporary British Satire*, ed. Philip Tew (London: Bloomsbury, 2018), pp. 95–108.

Hühn, Peter et al. (eds), *The Living Handbook of Narratology*, Hamburg: Hamburg University. Available online: http://www.lhn.uni-hamburg.de/ (accessed 17 June 2019).

Hungerford, Amy, 'On the Period Formerly Known as Contemporary', *American Literary History*, 20:1–2 (2008), 410–19.

Hutcheon, Linda, *Narcissistic Narrative: The Metafictional Paradox* (Waterloo, ON: Wilfrid Laurier University Press, 1980).

Hutcheon, Linda, *A Poetics of Postmodernism* (London: Routledge, 1988).

Hutcheon, Linda, *Irony's Edge: The Theory and Politics of Irony* (London: Routledge, 1994).

Hutcheon, Linda, *The Politics of Postmodernism*, 2nd edn (London: Routledge, 2002).

Hutchinson, Colin, *Reaganism, Thatcherism and the Social Novel* (Basingstoke: Palgrave Macmillan, 2008).

Huyssen, Andrea, 'Foreword: The Return of Diogenes as Postmodern Intellectual', in *Critique of Cynical Reason*, ed. Peter Sloterdijk, trans. Michael Eldred (Minneapolis, MN: University of Minnesota Press, [1983] 1987), pp. ix–xxv.

Ilott, Sarah, *New Postcolonial British Genres: Shifting the Boundaries* (Basingstoke: Palgrave Macmillan, 2015).

Jabukiak, Katarzyna, 'Simulated Optimism: The International Marketing of *White Teeth*', in *Zadie Smith: Critical Essays*, ed. Tracey L. Walters (New York: Peter Lang, 2008), pp. 201–18.
Jacobson, Howard, *Coming from Behind* (London: Abacus, [1983] 1986).
Jacobson, Howard, *Peeping Tom* (London: Penguin, [1984] 1993).
Jacobson, Howard, *Roots Schmoots: Journeys among Jews* (Woodstock, NY: Overlook Press, 1994).
Jacobson, Howard, *Seriously Funny: From the Ridiculous to the Sublime* (London: Viking, 1997).
Jacobson, Howard, *The Mighty Walzer* (London: Vintage, [1999] 2000).
Jacobson, Howard, *The Making of Henry* (London: Vintage, [2004] 2005).
Jacobson, Howard, *Kalooki Nights* (London: Vintage, [2006] 2007).
Jacobson, Howard, 'Let's See the "criticism" of Israel for What It Really Is', *Independent*, 18 February 2009. Available online: https://www.independent.co.uk/voices/commentators/howard-jacobson/howard-jacobson-letrsquos-see-the-criticism-of-israel-for-what-it-really-is-1624827.html (accessed 10 April 2019).
Jacobson, Howard, *The Finkler Question* (London: Bloomsbury, [2010] 2011).
Jacobson, Howard, 'Guardian Book Club Week Three: Howard Jacobson on Writing Kalooki Nights', *Guardian*, 2 October 2010. Available online: https://www.theguardian.com/books/2010/oct/02/book-club-howard-jacobson-kalooki (accessed 15 April 2019).
Jacobson, Howard, 'Howard Jacobson on Taking Comic Novels Seriously', *Guardian*, 9 October 2010. Available online: https://www.theguardian.com/books/2010/oct/09/howard-jacobson-comic-novels (accessed 21 March 2019).
Jacobson, Howard, 'On Being Taught by FR Leavis', *Telegraph*, 23 April 2011. Available online: https://www.telegraph.co.uk/culture/books/8466388/Howard-Jacobson-on-being-taught-by-FRLeavis.html (accessed 29 April 2019).
Jacobson, Howard, *Zoo Time* (London: Bloomsbury, [2012] 2013).
Jacobson, Howard, *Pussy* (London: Jonathan Cape, 2017).
Jacobson, Howard, 'Howard Jacobson on Why He Wrote *Pussy*, a Furious Dedication to Trump', *Penguin Books*, 12 April 2017. Available online: https://www.penguin.co.uk/articles/2017/howard-jacobson-on-pussy/ (accessed 26 April 2019).
Jacobson, Howard, 'Why the Novel Matters', *Times Literary Supplement*, 4 July 2018. Available online: https://www.the-tls.co.uk/articles/public/importance-fiction-modern-times-jacobson/ (accessed 29 April 2019).
James, David, '"Style is Morality"? Aesthetics and Politics in the Amis Era', *Textual Practice*, 26:1 (2012), 11–25.
James, David (ed.), *The Cambridge Companion to British Fiction since 1945* (Cambridge: Cambridge University Press, 2015).
James, David, 'Worlded Localisms: Cosmopolitics Writ Small', in *Postmodernism, Literature and Race*, eds Len Platt and Sara Upstone (Cambridge: Cambridge University Press, 2015), pp. 47–61.

James, David, *Discrepant Solace: Contemporary Literature and the Work of Consolation* (Oxford: Oxford University Press, 2019).

Johnson, B. S., *Christie Malry's Own Double Entry* (London: Picador [1973] 2001).

Johnson, B. S., *Well Done God! Selected Prose and Drama of B.S. Johnson*, eds Jonathan Coe, Philip Tew and Julia Jordan (London: Picador, 2013).

Jones, Owen, *Chavs: Demonization of the Working Class* (London: Verso, 2011).

Jordison, Sam, 'Booker Prize Disdains Comedy? What a Joke', *Guardian*, 14 October 2010. Available online: https://www.theguardian.com/books/booksblog/2010/oct/14/booker-prize-disdains-comedy-joke (accessed 29 April 2019).

Kafka, Franz, *The Complete Short Stories*, ed. Nahum N. Glatzer (London: Vintage, 2005).

Karl, Alissa G., 'The Zero Hour of the Neoliberal Novel', *Textual Practice*, 29:2 (2015), 335–55.

Karpf, Anne, 'Satire Won't Rid Us of Trump, But It Will Make Us Feel Better', *Guardian*, 26 December 2016. Available online: https://www.theguardian.com/commentisfree/2016/dec/26/satire-donald-trump-bigotry-prejudice-humour-escapism (accessed 26 April 2019).

Keller Simon, Richard, *The Labyrinth of the Comic Theory and Practice from Fielding to Freud* (Tallahassee, FL: Florida State University Press, 1985).

Kelly, Adam, 'David Foster Wallace and the New Sincerity', in *Consider David Foster Wallace*, ed. David Hering (Los Angeles: SSMG Press, 2010), pp. 131–46.

Kermode, Frank, 'Here She Is', *London Review of Books*, 6 October 2005. Available online: https://www.lrb.co.uk/v27/n19/frank-kermode/here-she-is (accessed 9 July 2019).

Kim, Jong-Seok, '"Getting History Wrong": The Heritage/Enterprise Couplet in Julian Barnes's *England, England*', *Critique*, 58:5 (2017), 587–99.

Knopp, Eva, '"There Are No Jokes in Paradise": Humour as a Politics of Representation in Recent Texts and Films from the British Migratory Contact-Zone', in *Translation of Cultures*, eds Petra Rüdiger and Konrad Gross (Amsterdam: Rodopi, 2009), pp. 59–74.

Koestler, Arthur, *The Act of Creation* (London: Arkana, [1964] 1989).

Konstantinou, Lee, *Cool Characters: Irony and American Fiction* (Cambridge, MA: Harvard University Press, 2016).

Konstantinou, Lee, 'Four Faces of Postirony', *Metamodernism: Historicity, Affect and Depth after Postmodernism*, eds Robin van den Akker, Alison Gibbons and Timotheus Vermuelen (London: Rowman and Littlefield, 2017), pp. 87–102.

Kottman, Paul A., 'Slipping on Banana Peels, Tumbling into Wells: Philosophy and Comedy', *Diacritics*, 38:4 (2008), 3–14.

Kozintsev, Alexander, *The Mirror of Laughter*, trans. Richard P. Martin (New Brunswick, NJ: Transaction, [2007] 2012).

Kundera, Milan, *Testaments Betrayed: An Essay in Nine Parts*, trans. Linda Asher (New York: HarperCollins, [1993] 1995).

Laity, Paul, 'A Life in Writing: Jonathan Coe', *Guardian*, 29 May 2010. Available online: https://www.theguardian.com/books/2010/may/29/life-writing-jonathan-coe (accessed 16 August 2016).

LaMarre, Heather L., Landreville, Kristen D. and Beam, Michael A., 'Political Ideology and the Motivation to See What You Want to See in *The Colbert Report*', *International Journal of Press/Politics*, 14:2 (2009), 212–31.

Lanone, Catherine, 'Mediating Multi-Cultural Muddle: E. M. Forster Meets Zadie Smith', *Études anglaises*, 60:2 (2007), 185–97.

Larose, Nicole, 'Reading *The Information* on Martin Amis's London', *Critique*, 46:2 (2005), 160–76.

Lassner, Phyllis, *Colonial Strangers: Women Writing the End of the British Empire* (New Brunswick, NJ: Rutgers University Press, 2004).

Lawson, Mark, 'Molars, Money and Martyrdom', *Independent*, 14 March 1995.

Lee, Katy, 'So Many Manhole Covers Are Stolen in China That One City Is Tracking Them with GPS', *Vox*, 22 March 2015. Available online: https://www.vox.com/2015/3/22/8267829/move-over-smart-watch-in-china-the-smart-manhole-cover-has-arrived (accessed 22 August 2019).

Lee, Stewart, *How I Escaped My Certain Fate: The Life and Deaths of a Stand-Up Comedian* (London: Faber and Faber, 2010).

Leech, Geoffrey and Short, Mick, *Style in Fiction*, 2nd edn (Harlow: Pearson, [1981] 2007).

Lever, James, 'Unshutuppable', review of Nicola Barker, *Burley Cross Postbox Theft*, *London Review of Books*, 9 September 2010. Available online: https://www.lrb.co.uk/v32/n17/james-lever/unshutuppable (accessed 1 February 2019).

Lewis, Wyndham, 'The English Sense of Humour', *Spectator*, 15 June 1934, pp. 915–16.

Lewis, Wyndham, *Men Without Art*, ed. Seamus Cooney (Black Sparrow Press: Santa Rosa, CA [1934] 1987).

Lezard, Nicholas, 'Counting the Cost of Martin's Money', *Independent*, 11 January 1996.

Little, Judy, *Comedy and the Woman Writer: Woolf, Spark, and Feminism* (Lincoln, NE: University of Nebraska Press, 1983).

Littlewood, Jane and Pickering, Michael, 'Heard the One about the White Middle-class Heterosexual Father-in-law? Gender, Ethnicity and Political Correctness in Comedy', in *Because I Tell a Joke or Two: Comedy, Politics and Social Difference*, ed. Stephen Wagg (London: Routledge, 1998), pp. 291–312.

Lockyer, Sharon, '"Dad's Army Side to Terrorism": Chris Morris, *Four Lions* and Jihad Comedy', in *No Known Cure: The Comedy of Chris Morris*, eds James Leggott and Jamie Sexton (London: BFI, 2013), pp. 197–211.

Lockyer, Sharon and Pickering, Michael (eds), *Beyond a Joke: The Limits of Humour*, 2nd edn (Basingstoke: Palgrave Macmillan, 2009).

Lodge, David, *The Art of Fiction* (London: Penguin, 1992).

Loveness, Jeff, 'This Is the Political Satire that Finally Stops Trump', *McSweeney's*, 23 January 2017. Available online: https://www.mcsweeneys.net/articles/this-is-the-political-satire-that-finally-stops-trump (accessed 12 July 2019).

Lusin, Caroline, 'The Condition of England Novel in the Twenty-First Century: Zadie Smith's *NW* (2012) and Jonathan Coe's *Number 11, or Tales that Witness Madness* (2015)', in *The British Novel in the Twenty-First Century: Cultural Concerns – Literary Developments – Model Interpretations*, eds Vera Nünning and Ansgar Nünning (Trier: Wissenschaftlicher Verlag Trier, 2018), pp. 247–63.

Lyall, Sarah, 'Martin Amis's Big Deal Leaves Literati Fuming', *New York Times*, 31 January 1995. Available online: http://www.nytimes.com/books/98/02/01/home/amis-bigdeal.html (accessed 17 June 2019).

Malcolm, Norman, *Ludwig Wittgenstein: A Memoir*, 2nd edn (Oxford: Oxford University Press, [1958] 2001).

Marcus, David, 'Post-Hysterics: Zadie Smith and the Fiction of Austerity', *Dissent* (2013). Available online: https://www.dissentmagazine.org/article/post-hysterics-zadie-smith-and-the-fiction-of-austerity (accessed 6 March 2018).

Marsh, Huw, 'Nicola Barker's *Darkmans* and the "vengeful tsunami of history"', *Literary London*, 7:2 (2010). Available online: http://www.literarylondon.org/london-journal/september2009/marsh.html (accessed 29 January 2019).

Marsh, Huw, *Beryl Bainbridge* (Tavistock: Northcote House, 2014).

Masters, Ben, *Novel Style: Ethics and Excess in Fiction since the 1960s* (Oxford: Oxford University Press, 2017).

Martin, Theodore, *Contemporary Drift: Genre, Historicism and the Problem of the Present* (New York: Columbia University Press, 2017).

Matthews, Graham, *Ethics and Desire in the Wake of Postmodernism: Contemporary Satire* (London: Bloomsbury, 2012).

Marx, Nick and Sienkiewicz, Matt (eds), *The Comedy Studies Reader* (Austin, TX: University of Texas Press, 2018).

McClennen, Sophia A., 'Hitting Trump Where It Hurts: The Satire Troops Take Up Comedy Arms against Donald Trump', *Salon*, 11 February 2017. Available online: https://www.salon.com/2017/02/11/hitting-trump-where-it-hurts-the-satire-troops-take-up-comedy-arms-against-donald-trump/ (accessed 26 April 2019).

McGraw, Peter and Warren, Caleb, 'Benign Violations: Making Immoral Behavior Funny', *Psychological Science*, 21:8 (2010), 1141–9.

McGraw, Peter and Warner, Joel, *The Humor Code: A Global Search for What Makes Things Funny* (New York: Simon and Schuster, 2014).

McHale, Brian, *Postmodernist Fiction* (London: Routledge, 1987).

McHale, Brian and Platt, Len (eds), *The Cambridge History of Postmodern Literature* (Cambridge: Cambridge University Press, 2016).

McKenzie, John, *Perform or Else: From Discipline to Performance* (London: Routledge, 2001).

McKinnie, Michael, 'Olympian Performance: The Cultural Economics of the Opening Ceremony of London 2012', *Public*, 53 (2016), 49–57.

Medhurst, Andy, *A National Joke: Popular Comedy and English Cultural Identities* (Abingdon: Routledge, 2007).

Meinig, Sigrun, '"What's more important than a gesture?": Jewishness and Cultural Performativity', in *Anglophone Jewish Literature*, ed. Axel Stähler (Abingdon: Routledge, 2007), pp. 65–75.

Meredith, George, 'An Essay on Comedy' [1877], in *Comedy*, ed. Wylie Sypher (New York: Doubleday, 1956), pp. 1–57.

Michaud, Jon, 'Eighty-Five from the Archive: Robert Benchley', *New Yorker*, 16 February, 2010. Available online: https://www.newyorker.com/books/double-take/eighty-five-from-the-archive-robert-benchley (accessed 3 June 2019).

Miles, Margaret, 'Carnal Abominations: The Female Body as Grotesque', in *The Grotesque in Art and Literature: Theological Reflections*, eds James Luther Adams and Wilson Yates (Grand Rapids, MI: William B. Eerdmans, 1997), pp. 83–112.

Miller, Andy and Mitchinson, John, 'Episode 3 – David Nobbs' [podcast], *Backlisted Podcast*, 23 December 2015. Available online: https://soundcloud.com/backlistedpod/episode-3-david-nobbs (accessed 17 June 2019).

Miller, J. Hillis, *Fiction and Repetition: Seven English Novels* (Oxford: Basil Blackwell, 1982).

Mills, Eleanor, 'Don't Mention the Buses', *The Sunday Times*, 4 October 1998, section Features, p. 7.

Mills, Magnus, *The Restraint of Beasts* (London: Flamingo, 1998).

Mills, Magnus, *The Scheme for Full Employment* (London: Harper Perennial, [2003] 2004).

Mills, Magnus, *Explorers of the New Century* (London: Bloomsbury, [2005] 2006).

Mills, Magnus, 'This Much I Know', *Observer*, 26 July 2009. Available online: https://www.theguardian.com/lifeandstyle/2009/jul/26/magnus-mills-this-much-i-know (accessed 9 July 2019).

Mills, Magnus, *The Maintenance of Headway* (London: Bloomsbury, [2009] 2010).

Mills, Magnus, *Screwtop Thompson and Other Tales* (London: Bloomsbury, 2010).

Mills, Magnus, *All Quiet on the Orient Express* (London: Bloomsbury, [1999] 2011).

Mills, Magnus, 'Small Talk', *Financial Times*, 30 September 2011. Available online: https://www.ft.com/content/047168ca-ea8a-11e0-b0f5-00144feab49a (accessed 9 July 2019).

Mills, Magnus, *A Cruel Bird Came to the Nest and Looked In* (London: Bloomsbury, [2011] 2012).

Mills, Magnus, *The Field of the Cloth of Gold* (London: Bloomsbury, 2015).

Mills, Magnus, *The Forensic Records Society* (London: Bloomsbury, 2017).

Mills, Magnus, 'My Favourite Books', *Guardian*, undated. Available Online: https://www.theguardian.com/books/top10s/top10/0,6109,99334,00.html (accessed 9 July 2019).

Mitchell, Kaye, *Intention and Text: Towards an Intentionality of Literary Form* (London: Continuum, 2008).

Moncrieff, Seán, 'Welcome to the Death of Satire', *Irish Times*, 19 January 2019. Available online: https://www.irishtimes.com/life-and-style/people/se%C3%A1n-moncrieff-welcome-to-the-death-of-satire-1.3751287 (accessed 26 April 2019).

Mookerjee, Robin, *Transgressive Fiction: The New Satiric Tradition* (Basingstoke: Palgrave Macmillan, 2013).
Moran, Joe, 'Artists and Verbal Mechanics: Martin Amis's *The Information*', *Critique*, 41:4 (2000), 307–17.
Morreall, John, *Taking Laughter Seriously* (Albany, NY: State University of New York Press, 1983).
Morreall, John (ed.), *The Philosophy of Laughter and Humor* (Albany, NY: State University of New York University Press, 1987).
Morreall, John, *Humor Works* (Amherst, MA: HRD Press, 1997).
Morreall, John, *Comic Relief: A Comprehensive Philosophy of Humor* (Chichester: Wiley-Blackwell, 2009).
Moretti, Franco, 'Serious Century', in *The Novel*, ed. Franco Moretti, 2 vols (Princeton, NJ: Princeton University Press, 2006), i, pp. 364–400.
Moseley, Merritt, *Understanding Jonathan Coe* (Columbia, SC: University of South Carolina Press, 2016).
Muir, Hugh, 'Manhole Covers Vanish in the Night', *Guardian*, 25 October 2004. Available online: https://www.theguardian.com/uk/2004/oct/25/ukcrime.prisonsandprobation (accessed 22 August 2019).
Mulkay, Michael, *On Humour: Its Nature and Its Place in Society* (Cambridge: Polity, 1988).
Munnery, Simon, *And Nothing But* [Stand-up Comedy DVD] (UK: Go Faster Stripe, 2015).
Nash, Walter, *The Language of Humour* (Abingdon: Routledge, [1985] 2013).
Nelson, T. G. A., *Comedy: An Introduction to Comedy in Literature, Drama, and Cinema* (Oxford: Oxford University Press, 1990).
Ngai, Sianne, *Ugly Feelings* (Cambridge, MA: Harvard University Press, 2005).
Ngai, Sianne, *Our Aesthetic Categories: Zany, Cute, Interesting* (Cambridge, MA: Harvard University Press, 2012).
Nietzsche, Friedrich, *The Gay Science, with a Prelude in Rhymes and an Appendix in Songs*, trans. Walter Kaufmann (New York: Vintage, [1882] 1974).
Nikulin, Dmitri, *Comedy, Seriously: A Philosophical Investigation* (New York: Palgrave Macmillan, 2014).
Nobbs, David, *The Fall and Rise of Reginald Perrin* (London: Mandarin, [1975] 1990).
North, Michael, *Machine-Age Comedy* (Oxford: Oxford University Press, 2009).
North, Michael, *What Is the Present?* (Princeton, NJ: Princeton University Press, 2018).
O'Brien, Flann, *The Third Policeman* (London: Harper Perennial, [1967] 2007).
O'Brien, Flann (Myles na Gopaleen), *The Best of Myles: A Selection from the 'Cruiskeen Lawn'*, ed. Kevin O'Nolan (London: Picador, [1968] 1977).
Olson, Kirby, *Comedy after Postmodernism: Rereading Comedy from Edward Lear to Charles Willeford* (Lubbock, TX: Texas Tech University Press).
O'Neill, Patrick, *The Comedy of Entropy: Humour, Narrative, Reading* (Toronto: University of Toronto Press, 1990).

Osborne, John. *Radical Larking: Seven Types of Technical Mastery* (Basingstoke: Palgrave Macmillan, 2014).
O'Toole, Laurence, 'A Right Carrion', review of *What a Carve Up!*, *New Statesman*, 29 April 1994, p. 7.
Palmer, D. J. (ed.), *Comedy: Developments in Criticism* (Basingstoke: Macmillan, 1984).
Palmer, Jerry, *The Logic of the Absurd: On Film and Television Comedy* (London: BFI, 1987).
Palmer, Jerry, *Taking Humour Seriously* (London: Routledge, 1994).
Palmeri, Frank, *Satire in Narrative: Petronius, Swift, Gibbon, Melville, and Pynchon* (Austin, TX: University of Texas Press, 1990).
Parkin, John and Phillips, John (eds), *Laughter and Power* (Oxford: Peter Lang, 2006).
Partington, Alan, *The Linguistics of Laughter: A Corpus-Assisted Study of Laughter-Talk* (Abingdon: Routledge, 2006).
Partington, Alan, 'From Wodehouse to the White House: A Corpus-Assisted Study of Play, Fantasy and Dramatic Incongruity in Comic Writing and Laughter-Talk', *Lodz Papers in Pragmatics*, 4:2 (2008), 189–213.
Parvulescu, Anca, *Laughter: Notes on a Passion* (Cambridge, MA: MIT Press, 2010).
Peters, Susanne, 'A Proletarian Comedy of Menace: Martin Amis's *Lionel Asbo*', in 'Focus on Comic Representations in Post-Millennial British and Irish Fiction', ed. Barbara Puschmann-Nalenz, special issue *Anglistik: International Journal of English Studies*, 27:1 (2016), 85–97.
Pettersson, Bo, *How Literary Worlds Are Shaped: A Comparative Poetics of Literary Imagination* (Berlin: Walter de Gruyter, 2016).
Pfister, Manfred (ed.), *A History of English Laughter: Laughter from Beowulf to Beckett and Beyond* (Amsterdam: Rodopi, 2002).
Phiddian, Robert, 'Satire and the Limits of Literary Theories', *Critical Quarterly*, 55:3 (2013), 44–58.
Pirandello, Luigi, *On Humor*, trans. Antonio Illiano and Daniel P. Testa (Chapel Hill, NC: University of North Carolina Press, [1908/1920] 1960).
Pirker, Eva Ulrike, 'Approaching Space: Zadie Smith's North London Fiction', *Journal of Postcolonial Writing*, 52:1 (2016), 64–76.
Platt, Len, *Writing London and the Thames Estuary: 1576–2016* (Leiden: Brill, 2017).
Plessner, Helmuth, *Laughing and Crying: A Study of the Limits of Human Behavior*, 3rd edn, trans. James Spencer Churchill and Marjorie Grene (Evanston, IL: Northwestern University Press, [1961] 1970).
Postal Museum website, 'Post Office Statistics: #11. Letters Delivered by the Royal Mail, 1920–2010', 2011. Available online: https://www.postalmuseum.org/discover/collections/statistics/ (accessed 22 February 2019).
Pritchett, V. S., *George Meredith and English Comedy* (London: Chatto and Windus, 1970).
Provine, Robert R., *Laughter: A Scientific Investigation* (New York: Penguin, [2000] 2001).

Prusak, Bernard G., 'The Science of Laughter: Helmuth Plessner's *Laughing and Crying* Revisited', *Continental Philosophy Review*, 38 (2006), 41–69.

Purdie, Susan, *Comedy: The Mastery of Discourse* (Hemel Hempstead: Harvester Wheatsheaf, 1993).

Puschmann-Nalenz, Barbara (ed.), 'Focus on Comic Representations in Post-Millennial British and Irish Fiction', special issue *Anglistik: International Journal of English Studies*, 27:1 (2016), 1–162.

Rabaté, Jean-Michel, *Kafka L.O.L.* [Kindle edn] (Macerata: Quodlibet, 2018).

Ramsey-Kurz, Helga, 'Humouring the Terrorists or the Terrorised? Militant Muslims in Salman Rushdie, Zadie Smith, and Hanif Kureishi', in *Cheeky Fictions: Laughter and the Postcolonial*, eds Susanne Reichl and Mark Stein (Amsterdam: Rodopi, 2005), pp. 73–86.

Rankin, Jennifer and Waterson, Jim, 'How Boris Johnson's Brussels-bashing Stories Shaped British Politics', *Guardian*, 14 July 2019. Available online: https://www.the guardian.com/politics/2019/jul/14/boris-johnson-brussels-bashing-stories-shaped-politics (accessed 30 July 2019).

Raskin, Victor, *Semantic Mechanisms of Humor* (Dordrecht: D. Riedel, 1985).

Raskin, Victor (ed.), *The Primer of Humor Research* (Berlin: Mouton de Gruyter, 2008).

Redfern, Michael, *French Laughter: Literary Humour from Diderot to Tournier* (Oxford: Oxford University Press, 2008).

Redfern, Walter, *Puns: More Senses than One*, 2nd edn (London: Penguin, [1984] 2000).

Robins, John, *A Robins amongst the Pigeons*, 2015. Available online: https://arobins amongstthepigeons.tumblr.com/ (accessed 15 May 2019).

Romanska, Magda and Ackerman, Alan, *Reader in Comedy: An Anthology of Theory and Criticism* (London: Bloomsbury, 2017).

Roof, Judith, *The Comic Event: Comedic Performance from the 1950s to the Present* (New York: Bloomsbury, 2018).

Rose, Jacqueline, 'Why Howard Jacobson Is Wrong', *Guardian*, 24 February 2009. Available online: https://www.theguardian.com/commentisfree/2009/feb/23/howard-jacobson-antisemitism-caryl-churchill (accessed 10 April 2019).

Ross, Michael, *Race Riots: Comedy and Ethnicity in Modern British Fiction* (Montreal and Kingston: McGill-Queen's University Press, 2006).

Roston, Murray, *The Comic Mode in English Literature: From the Middle Ages to Today* (London: Continuum, 2011).

Roth, Philip, *Sabbath's Theater* (London: Vintage, [1995] 1996).

Rozik, Eli, *Comedy: A Critical Introduction* (Eastbourne: Sussex Academic Press, 2011).

Rudrum, David and Stavris, Nicholas (eds), *Supplanting the Postmodern* (New York: Bloomsbury, 2015).

Russo, Mary, *The Female Grotesque: Risk, Excess and Modernity* (New York: Routledge, 1994).

Rustin, Susanna, 'A Life in Writing: Nicola Barker', *Guardian*, 1 May 2010. Available online: https://www.theguardian.com/books/2010/may/01/nicola-barker-life-in-wr iting (accessed 13 June 2019).

Sacks, Mike, *Poking a Dead Frog: Conversations with Today's Top Comedy Writers* (New York: Penguin, 2014).

Sage, Victor, 'The Ambivalence of Laughter: The Development of Nicola Barker's Grotesque Realism', *Review of Contemporary Fiction*, 32:3 (2012), 87–97.

Sale, Charles, *The Specialist* (London: Putnam and Co., 1930).

Salisbury, Laura, *Samuel Beckett: Laughing Matters, Comic Timing* (Edinburgh: Edinburgh University Press, 2012).

Sanderson, David, 'Rise of Trump Makes Satire Unnecessary, Says Armando Iannucci', *The Times*, 1 October 2018. Available online: https://www.thetimes.co.uk/article/rise-of-trump-makes-satire-unnecessary-says-armando-iannucci-vpdncxr9f (accessed 26 April 2019).

Sansom, Ian, 'Review of Magnus Mills, *A Cruel Bird Came to the Nest and Looked In*', *Guardian*, 23 September 2011. Available online: https://www.theguardian.com/books/2011/sep/23/cruel-bird-nest-magnus-mills-review (accessed 9 July 2019).

Schoene, Berthold, 'Twenty-First-Century Fiction', in *The Oxford History of the Novel in English, vol. 7: British and Irish Fiction since 1940*, eds Peter Boxall and Bryan Cheyette (Oxford: Oxford University Press, 2016), pp. 549–63.

Schopenhauer, Arthur, *The World as Will and Representation [1818–19]*, trans. E. F. J. Payne, 2 vols (New York: Dover, 2000).

Scott, Jeremy, *The Demotic Voice in Contemporary British Fiction* (Basingstoke: Palgrave Macmillan, 2009).

Segal, Erich, *The Death of Comedy* (Cambridge, MA: Harvard University Press, 2001).

Self, Will, *Walking to Hollywood: Memories of Before the Fall* (London: Bloomsbury, 2010).

Self, Will, 'A Point of View: That Joke Isn't Funny Any More', *BBC News*, 22 August 2014. Available online: http://www.bbc.co.uk/news/magazine-28881335 (accessed 9 July 2019).

Sell, Jonathan P. A., 'Experimental Ethics: Autonomy and Contingency in the Novels of Zadie Smith', in *The Ethical Component in Experimental British Fiction since the 1960's*, eds Susana Onega and Jean-Michel Ganteau (Newcastle: Cambridge Scholars Press, 2007), pp. 150–70.

Shaw, Katy, *Crunch Lit* (London: Bloomsbury, 2015).

Shaw, Katy, 'Will Self: Why His Report on the Death of the Novel Is (still) Premature', *Independent*, 20 April 2018. Available online: https://www.independent.co.uk/arts-entertainment/books/will-self-report-death-novel-is-still-premature-literature-a8289716.html (accessed 29 April 2019).

Shaw, Kristian, *Cosmopolitanism in Twenty-First Century Fiction* (Basingstoke: Palgrave Macmillan, 2017).

Sicher, Efraim and Weinhouse, Linda, *Under Postcolonial Eyes: Figuring the 'Jew' in Contemporary British Writing* (Lincoln, NE: University of Nebraska Press, 2010).

Silcoff, Mireille, 'Booker Prize winner Howard Jacobson on Zionism, English Literature and Why Serious Stuff Is Better than Froth', *National Post*, 29 October 2010.

Available online: https://nationalpost.com/afterword/mireille-silcoff-booker-prize-winner-howard-jacobson-on-zionism-english-literature-and-why-serious-stuff-is-better-than-froth (accessed 21 March 2019).

Silverblatt, Michael, *Bookworm*, 'Jonathan Coe: *The House of Sleep*' [podcast], KCRW, 19 March 1998. Available online: http://www.kcrw.com/news-culture/shows/bookworm/jonathan-coe-the-house-of-sleep (accessed 17 June 2019).

Simpson, Paul, *Stylistics* (London: Routledge, 2004).

Singh, Anita, 'Man Booker Prize: Howard Jacobson Is Surprise Winner', *Telegraph*, 12 October 2010. Available online: https://www.telegraph.co.uk/culture/books/booker-prize/8060132/Man-Booker-Prize-Howard-Jacobson-is-surprise-winner.html (accessed 29 April 2019).

Skinner, Quentin, 'Hobbes and the Classical Theory of Laughter', in *Leviathan after 350 Years*, eds Tom Sorrell and Luc Foisneau (Oxford: Clarendon Press, 2004), pp. 139–66.

Sloterdijk, Peter, *Critique of Cynical Reason*, trans. Michael Eldred (Minneapolis, MN: University of Minnesota Press, [1983] 1987).

Smith, Barry and Skelton, Paul, 'Britannia, 41 Townhall Street', *Dover Kent Archives*. Available online: http://www.dover-kent.com/Britannia-Townwall-Street.html (accessed 16 August 2016).

Smith, Zadie, *White Teeth* (London: Penguin, [2000] 2001).

Smith, Zadie, 'This Is How It Feels to Me', *Guardian*, 13 October 2001. Available online: https://www.theguardian.com/books/2001/oct/13/fiction.afghanistan (accessed 9 July 2019).

Smith, Zadie, *The Autograph Man* (London: Penguin, [2002] 2003).

Smith, Zadie, 'Love, Actually', *Guardian*, 1 November 2003. Available online: https://www.theguardian.com/books/2003/nov/01/classics.zadiesmith (accessed 9 July 2019).

Smith, Zadie, *On Beauty* (London: Penguin, [2005] 2006).

Smith, Zadie, *Changing My Mind: Occasional Essays* (London: Penguin, 2009).

Smith, Zadie, *Swing Time* (London: Hamish Hamilton, 2016).

Smith, Zadie, *Feel Free: Essays* (London: Hamish Hamilton, 2018).

Spark, Muriel, 'The Desegregation of Art', in *The Golden Fleece: Essays*, ed. Penelope Jardine (Manchester: Carcanet, 2014), pp. 26–30.

Stallybrass, Peter and White, Allon, *The Politics and Poetics of Transgression* (London: Methuen, 1986).

Stonebridge, Lyndsey and MacKay, Marina (eds), *British Fiction after Modernism: The Novel at Mid-Century* (Basingstoke: Palgrave Macmillan, 2007).

Stott, Andrew, *Comedy*, 2nd edn (Abingdon: Routledge, 2014).

Su, John, 'Beauty and the Beastly Prime Minister', *ELH*, 81:3 (2014), 1083–110.

Swift, Jonathan, 'Thoughts on Various Subjects', in *The Battle of the Books and Other Short Pieces* (London: Cassell, 1886). Available online: http://www.gutenberg.org/files/623/623-h/623-h.htm (accessed 26 April 2019).

Tait, Theo, 'First One, Then Another, Then Another, Then Another after That', review of Magnus Mills, *The Restraint of Beasts*, in *London Review of Books*, 26 November 1998. Available online: https://www.lrb.co.uk/v20/n23/theo-tait/first-one-then-another-then-another-then-another-after-that (accessed 9 July 2019).

Tancke, Ulrike, '*White Teeth* Reconsidered: Narrative Deception and Uncomfortable Truths', in *Reading Zadie Smith: The First Decade and Beyond*, ed. Philip Tew (London: Bloomsbury, 2013), pp. 27–38.

Tate, Andrew, *Apocalyptic Fiction* (London: Bloomsbury, 2019).

Taylor, D. J., *A Vain Conceit: British Fiction in the 1980s* (London: Bloomsbury, 1989).

Tew, Philip, *The Contemporary British Novel*, 2nd edn (London: Continuum, 2007).

Tew, Philip, *Zadie Smith* (Basingstoke: Palgrave Macmillan, 2010).

Tew, Philip, Celebrity, Suburban Identity and Transatlantic Epiphanies: Reconsidering Zadie Smith's *The Autograph Man*', in *Reading Zadie Smith: The First Decade and Beyond*, ed. Philip Tew (London: Bloomsbury, 2013), pp. 53–68.

Tew, Philip, 'Comedy, Class and Nation', in *The Oxford History of the Novel in English, vol. 7: British and Irish Fiction since 1940*, eds Peter Boxall and Bryan Cheyette (Oxford: Oxford University Press, 2016), pp. 161–73.

Tew, Philip (ed.), *Jonathan Coe: Contemporary British Satire* (London: Bloomsbury, 2018).

Thatcher, Margaret, 'Speech to Conservative Party Conference', 12 October 1979. Available online: http://www.margaretthatcher.org/document/104147 (accessed 9 July 2019).

Thatcher, Margaret, 'Speech to Parliamentary Press Gallery', 5 December 1979. Available online: http://www.margaretthatcher.org/document/104185 (accessed 9 July 2019).

Thomas, Susie, 'Zadie Smith's False Teeth: The Marketing of Multiculturalism', *Literary London*, 4:1 (2006). Available online: http://www.literarylondon.org/london-journal/march2006/thomas.html (accessed 9 July 2019).

Thurschwell, Pamela, 'Genre, Repetition and History in Jonathan Coe', in *British Fiction Today*, eds Philip Tew and Rod Mengham (London: Continuum, 2006), pp. 28–39.

Todd, Richard, 'The Intrusive Author in British Postmodernist Fiction: The Cases of Alasdair Gray and Martin Amis', in *Exploring Postmodernism*, eds Matei Calinescu and Douwe Wessel Fokkema (Amsterdam: John Benjamins, 1990), pp. 123–38.

Tolan, Fiona, '"Painting While Rome Burns": Ethics and Aesthetics in Pat Barker's *Life Class* and Zadie Smith's *On Beauty*', *Tulsa Studies in Women's Literature*, 29:2 (2010), 375–93.

Torrance, Robert M., *The Comic Hero* (Cambridge, MA: Harvard University Press, 1978).

Tovey, Josephine, 'Satire Is a Pointed Weapon in the Age of Trump', *Sydney Morning Herald*, 8 February 2017. Available online: https://www.smh.com.au/opinion/satire-is-a-pointed-weapon-in-the-age-of-trump-20170208-gu808r.html (accessed 26 April 2019).

Trahair, Lisa, *The Comedy of Philosophy: Sense and Nonsense in Early Cinema Slapstick* (Albany, NY: State University of New York Press, 2007).

Trexler, Adam, *Anthropocene Fictions: The Novel in a Time of Climate Change* (Charlottesville, VA: University of Virginia Press, 2015).

Triezenberg, Katarina E., 'Humor in Literature', in *The Primer of Humor Research*, ed. Victor Raskin (Berlin: Mouton de Gruyter, 2008), pp. 523–42.

Trimm, Ryan, 'After the Century of Strangers: Hospitality and Crashing in Zadie Smith's *White Teeth*', *Contemporary Literature*, 56:1 (2015), 145–72.

Upstone, Sarah, 'Do Novels Tell Us How to Vote?' in *Brexit and Literature: Critical and Cultural Responses*, ed. Robert Eaglestone (Abingdon: Routledge, 2018), pp. 44–58.

Valman, Nadia, 'Jewish Fictions', in *The Oxford History of the Novel in English, vol. 7: British and Irish Fiction since 1940*, eds Peter Boxall and Bryan Cheyette (Oxford: Oxford University Press, 2016), pp. 347–67.

Vandaele Jeroen, 'Narrative Humor (I): Enter Perspective', *Poetics Today*, 31:4 (2010), 721–85.

Vandaele, Jeroen, 'Narrative Humor (II): Exit Perspective', *Poetics Today*, 33:1 (2012), 59–126.

van den Akker, Robin, Gibbons, Alison and Vermuelen, Timotheus (eds), *Metamodernism: Historicity, Affect and Depth after Postmodernism* (London: Rowman and Littlefield, 2017).

Vermeulen, Timotheus and van den Akker, Robin, 'Notes on Metamodernism', *Journal of Aesthetics and Culture*, 2 (2010), 1–14.

Virno, Paulo, *Multitude: Between Innovation and Negation*, trans. Isabella Bertoletti, James Cascaito and Andreas Casson (Los Angeles: Semiotext(e), 2008).

Wagg, Stephen, 'You've Never Had It so Silly: The Politics of British Satirical Comedy from *Beyond the Fringe* to *Spitting Image*', in *Come On Down? Popular Media Culture in Post-war Britain*, eds Dominic Strinati and Stephen Wagg (London: Routledge, 1992), pp. 254–84.

Wallace, David Foster, 'E Unibus Plurum: Television and U.S. Fiction' [1993], in *A Supposedly Fun Thing I'll Never Do Again* (London: Abacus, 1998), pp. 21–82.

Waters, Tracey L., 'Still Mammies and Hos: Stereotypical Images of Black Women in Zadie Smith's Novels', in *Zadie Smith: Critical Essays*, ed. Tracey L. Walters (New York: Peter Lang, 2008), pp. 123–39.

Waterstones, 'Jonathan Coe Discusses Expo 58' [video], YouTube (uploaded 29 August 2013), https://www.youtube.com/watch?v=E9e4eVLNC1I (accessed 16 August 2016).

Watt, Ian, *The Rise of the Novel: Studies in Defoe, Richardson and Fielding* (London: Penguin, [1957] 1972).

Watt-Smith, Tiffany, *Schadenfreude: The Joy of Another's Misfortune* (London: Profile, 2018).

Waugh, Patricia, 'The Naturalistic Turn, the Syndrome, and the Rise of the Neo-Phenomenological Novel', in *Diseases and Disorders in Contemporary Fiction: The*

Syndrome Syndrome, eds T. J. Lustig and James Peacock (New York: Routledge, 2013), pp. 17–34.

Waugh, Paul, 'The Donald Trump and Boris Johnson Show: UK And US Braced for the New "Special Relationship"', *Huffington Post*, 1 June 2019. Available online: https://www.huffingtonpost.co.uk/entry/donald-trump-and-boris-johnson-will-blond-ambition-be-enough-to-forge-a-new-special-relationship_uk_5cf292dbe4b0e346ce7ef269 (accessed 14 June 2019).

Weems, Scott, *Ha! The Science of When We Laugh and Why* (New York: Basic Books, 2014).

Weitz, Eric, *The Cambridge Introduction to Comedy* (Cambridge: Cambridge University Press, 2009).

Wells, Lynn, 'The Right to a Secret: Zadie Smith's *NW*', in *Reading Zadie Smith: The First Decade and Beyond*, ed. Philip Tew (London: Bloomsbury, 2013), pp. 97–110.

Welsh, Alexander, *The Humanist Comedy* (New Haven, CT: Yale University Press, 2014).

Westwood, Robert and Rhodes, Carl (eds), *Humour, Work and Organization* (Abingdon: Routledge, 2007).

White, Allon, '"The Dismal Sacred Word": Academic Language and the Social Reproduction of Seriousness', in *Carnival, Hysteria and Writing: Collected Essays and Autobiography* (Oxford: Clarendon Press, 1993), pp. 122–34.

Wilkinson, Katharine, 'The Persistence of Letters in Contemporary Fiction' (PhD, Queen Mary University of London, 2019).

Wille, Anna, '"Born and bred, almost": Mimicry as a Humorous Strategy in Zadie Smith's *White Teeth* and Hanif Kureishi's *The Buddha of Suburbia*', *Anglia*, 129:3–4 (2011), 448–68.

Williams, Heathcote, *Boris Johnson: The Beast of Brexit*, 2nd edn (London: London Review of Books, 2019).

Wisse, Ruth R., *No Joke: Making Jewish Humour* (Princeton, NJ: Princeton University Press, 2013).

Wittgenstein, Ludwig, *Philosophical Investigations*, 3rd edn (Oxford: Blackwell, [1953] 1968).

Woloch, Alex, *The One vs. the Many: Minor Characters and the Space of the Protagonist in the Novel* (Princeton, NJ: Princeton University Press, 2003).

Wood, Heloise, 'Bollinger Everyman Wodehouse Prize withheld for First Time', *Bookseller*, 16 May 2018. Available online: https://www.thebookseller.com/news/bollinger-everyman-wodehouse-prize-comic-fiction-withheld-first-time-786381 (accessed 8 May 2019).

Wood, James, 'A Terrible Privacy', interview with Toni Morrison, *Guardian*, 18 April 1992, section Weekend, p. 5.

Wood, James, *The Broken Estate: Essays on Literature and Belief* (London: Jonathan Cape, 1999).

Wood, James, *The Irresponsible Self: On Laughter and the Novel* (London: Jonathan Cape, 2004).

Wood, James, 'Member of the Tribe: Howard Jacobson's *The Finkler Question*', *New Yorker*, 1 November 2010. Available online: https://www.newyorker.com/magazine/2010/11/08/member-of-the-tribe (accessed 4 June 2019).

Wood, James, 'Books of the Year', *New Yorker*, 17 December 2012. Available online: https://www.newyorker.com/books/page-turner/books-of-the-year (accessed 9 July 2019).

Zahar, Isabelle, 'The Artist as Critic, Style as Ethics: Amis's American Stylists and Self's Stylisation', *Textual Practice*, 26:1 (2012), 27–42.

Žižek, Slavoj, *In Defence of Lost Causes* (London: Verso, 2008).

Žižek, Slavoj, *The Sublime Object of Ideology* (London: Verso, [1989] 2008).

Žižek, Slavoj, *Violence* (London: Profile, 2008).

Zupančič, Alenka, *The Odd One In: On Comedy* (Cambridge, MA: MIT Press, 2008).

Index

Adams, Ann Marie   91 n.56
affect, *see also* laughter
  comic varieties of   2, 132
  deadpan   104, 105, 106–12, 114
  as kynical letting go (Sloterdijk)   42
  labour and performance   205–10
  laughter as   15, 25 n.22, 86–94
  negative   6, 7
  passions *vs.* emotions   86–7, 91
  and tone   21 n.2
Ahmed, Sara   6 n.22
Alexander, Victoria N.   53 n.2
allegory   39, 104, 111, 115 n.54, 120–1, 200
Allen, Woody   182 n.54
Amis, Kingsley   11, 22, 80, 167
  dismissive attitude towards style   54
  Jake's Thing   8
  Lucky Jim   32 n.51
Amis, Martin   12, 14–15, 40, 53–76, 80, 95, 101, 116, 131, 132
  Dead Babies   131 n.2
  Experience   54
  The House of Meetings   64
  The Information   56, 62–4, 72–3
  Lionel Asbo   64–6, 70–2, 73–6
  London Fields   58, 59–61, 63, 74
  Money   54–5, 56, 57–8, 63, 69, 158
  The Moronic Inferno   72 n.64
  The Pregnant Widow   64
  The Rachel Papers   58
  'State of England'   73 n.67
  Success   58
  Yellow Dog   64–5, 66–9, 73 n.68, 75 n.71
  The Zone of Interest   64
Anderson, Amanda   6 n.21
anti-Semitism   178–80, 186, 191–5
Aristophanes   3
Aristotle   31, 135
aspect seeing (Wittgenstein)   164–5

Attardo, Salvatore   30 n.46, 60, 101, 102 n.7
Auer, Peter   70 n.55
Austen, Jane   168–9, 180
Auster, Paul   128 n.105

Bainbridge, Beryl   11, 35–6
Bakhtin, Mikhail   23, 27, 84, 144–7, 149, *see also* carnivalesque; grotesque
Barker, Nicola   5, 12, 131–65
  In the Approaches   155–64
  Behindlings   134 n.12, 164–5
  Burley Cross Postbox Theft   132–7, 140–4, 147–9, 154–5
  The Cauliflower®   132, 137–40, 155, 163
  Clear   149–53
  Darkmans   131 n.3, 134, 150–1
  Five Miles from Outer Hope   145–6, 155
  H(A)PPY   131, 155, 163
  Heading Inland   145, 164
  I Am Sovereign   139–40, 160–1, 165
  Love Your Enemies   145
  Reversed Forecast   131 n.2, 147
  Small Holdings   145
  Wide Open   146, 157
  The Yips   146 n.59, 157
Barker, Pat   12
Barnes, Julian   1 n.1, 12
  England, England   18–19, 105, 204–10
Bataille, Georges   16, 79, 90 n.52, 95, 98–100
bathos   107, 115, 139, 163, *see also* upgrading as comic technique
  Martin Amis and   61, 66, 68, 71–2, 76
Baudrillard, Jean   204
Baum, Devorah   187–8
Beckett, Samuel   16, 21, 103, 106, 117, 121
  Waiting for Godot   3
  Watt   104, 118, 125–6

Bellow, Saul   53–4, 55
Benchley, Robert   19–20
Benjamin, Walter   103
Bennett, Alice   95 n.67
Bentley, Nick   53 n.2, 56, 57 n.12, 66, 68 n.46, 204
Berger, Peter L.   29 n.39, 42 n.85, 179–80
Bergonzi, Bernard   53 n.1
Bergson, Henri
  and distancing effect of laughter   88, 107
  and fleetingness of laughter   99 n.81
  and machine-age comedy   16, 103, 106, 108–9, 117, 123, 207
  and pedantry   135, 137
  and repetition   128–9
Berlant, Lauren   3 n.13, 5, 6 n.21, 7
Bevis, Mathew   31
Beynon, Huw   112–13, 127 n.103
Bhabha, Homi K.   188 n.73
Billig, Michael   2 n.6, 83, 150
Blackburn, Tony   4
Blaine, David   144, 149
Booker Prize   1 n.1, 104, 167–8, 170
Bown, Alfie   2 n.6, 8, 79 n.9, 174, 177
Boxall, Peter   13
Boyd, Brian   102 n.4
Boym, Svetlana   209
Bracke, Astrid   6 n.21
Bradbury, Malcolm   11, 22, 36
Bradford, Richard   68–9, 131 n.4, 164 n.125
Brauner, David   191
Brexit   14, 18, 35, 201–4, 210
British Association for Contemporary Literary Studies (BACLS)   13
British Fiction after Modernism (Stonebridge and MacKay)   53 n.1
British-Jewish fiction   180–1
British Literature in Transition, 1980–2000 (Schoene and Pollard)   12–13
Brooker, Joseph   21 n.3, 75, 128
Brooke-Rose, Christine   11
Brophy, Brigid   11
Brown, Roy 'Chubby'   169, 173
Bruce, Lenny   87–8
Bullock, Barbara E.   70 n.55
Bunyan, John   115 n.54
Burney, Fanny   10

Butler, Judith   6 n.21

Calvino, Italo   139
The Cambridge History of Postmodern Literature (McHale and Platt)   157 n.103
The Cambridge History of the English Novel (Caserio and Hawes)   12
caricature   28, 75–6, 84, 195, 197
carnivalesque   146–53
Carter, Angela   131, 146, 148, 152
Cavaliero, Glen   11 n.38, 134 n.10
Cervantes, Miguel de   10, 168
Chadderton, Helena   39 n.75
Chaplin, Charlie   103, 104
Chappelle, Dave   175
Charney, Maurice   102, 138
Cheng, Ken   30
Cheyette, Bryan   82 n.24, 180
Childs, Peter   204 n.13
class
  in Barker, *Burley Cross*   144
  carnivalesque upheaval of   146
  as indexed by comic style   62–76
  in Smith, *NW*   95–6
cliché (as comic device)   59–60, 66
code-switching, *see* style, shifting
Coe, Jonathan   13–14, 18, 21–51, 132, 170, 201–4
  The Accidental Woman   21
  A Touch of Love   21
  The Closed Circle   44 n.91, 50, 202
  The Dwarves of Death   21
  Expo 58   22, 29, 34–40, 41, 42, 209–10
  The House of Sleep   44 n.91, 51
  Middle England   202–3
  Number 11   29, 41, 42–50
  The Rotters' Club   50–1, 202, 203
  The Terrible Privacy of Maxwell Sim   22, 29, 31–4
  What a Carve Up!   21, 22–9, 40, 41, 44 n.91, 45, 51
The Colbert Report   24–5 n.22
Cold War   35, 36
Colebrook, Claire   158
The Comedian's Comedian (podcast)   48 n.109
The Comedians (television programme)   173
comedy, *see also* humour; laughter

and binaries   139–40
boundaries of   17–18, 167–200
and class   62–76
correction *vs.* forgiveness (Wood)   71 n.59, 79–81
definition of   1–3 (*see also* comedy, *vs.* humour (Eco))
distinction from jokes   102
distinction from satire   28
English   10–11
ethics of   18, 160–1
and forgiveness   155–64
metacomedy   45–50
narrative structure of   102
New   3
Old   169
and paradox   131–65
and pedantry   134–7, 141, 142, 143, 163
and performance (*see* performance)
political efficacy of   21–51, 84–6, 132, 201
romantic   161
and seriousness   6–7, 9–10, 168, 210
stand-up   46, 48, 61, 140, 169, 170–5, 178–80
and temporality   102
vs. humour (Eco)   153–4
and work (*see* work)
zany (*see* Ngai, Sianne, zany aesthetic)
comic licence, *see* comedy, boundaries of
comic novel
   Booker Prize and   167
   definition of   8–10, 21, 131
   history of   10–13
   perceived decline of   172–3
   purported Englishness of   8–9
   as tautology   168
comic turn   4–6, 11, 19, 204, 208, 210
Condren, Conal   26 n.26, 40
Connor, Steven   125
contemporary (challenge of defining)   13
Cornwell, Neil   105 n.20, 129 n.110
Cowper, William   45
cricket   164
Critchley, Simon   8, 27, 109, 154
Crosthwaite, Paul   6 n.23
Crowhurst, Donald   31–2
cultural capital   62, 64
Currie, Mark   49

Curthoys, Ned   184 n.61
cynicism   41–2, 49, *see also* satire
   as enlightened false consciousness   41
   vs. kynicism (Sloterdijk)   42

Dango, Michael   80 n.17
Dauber, Jeremy   180–1 n.48, 183, 190 n.85
Davidson, Jim   173, 175
Davies, Helen   175
Dawson, Paul   131 n.4
deadpan humour, *see under* affect
De Cristofaro, Diletta   6 n.23
Deleuze, Gilles   16, 103, 117, 119, 124, 187
Dern, John A.   64 n.32
Desani, G.V.   11
Descartes, René   86
Des Pres, Terrence   181
DeWitt, Helen   104
Diary of a Nobody (Grossmith and Grossmith)   133–4
Díaz Bild, Aída   187, 189
Di Bernardo, Francesco   34 n.56
Dickens, Charles   80, 131, 133, 149, 168, 169, 171, 176
Dickie, Simon   10 n.32, 150–1
Diedrick, James   58 n.19, 73 n.67
Diogenes   42
Dolar, Mladen   102
Dostoevsky, Fyodor   146, 168
Doten, Mark   198–9
Double, Oliver   48, 173 n.20
Douglas, Mary   91
Dowland, Douglas   6 n.22
Drabble, Margaret   11
Driscoll, Lawrence   73, 76
Dryden, John   40
Duggan, Robert   67 n.43, 71 n.57, 144
Dyer, Jeff   2 n.10

Eagleton, Terry   22 n.9, 28 n.34, 179
Eastman, Carol M.   70 n.55
Eastman, Max   19
Eco, Umberto
   comedy *vs.* humour   17, 153–5, 159
   critique of carnival laughter   24 n.18, 148–9, 152
Eliot, George   11, 168
embedded language, *see* matrix language

éndoxa 31, *see also under* Jokes
English, James 7, 11 n.36, 47 n.104, 95, 167 n.3
Englishness 18
   and comic tradition 55, 80
   instability as concept 208
   and performance (*see* performance)
   and sense of humour 36, 39
   and style 55–6
epistolary novel 133
Ermida, Isabel 101 n.2
Esslin, Martin 105 n.20
European Union 35, 38, 201, *see also* Brexit
Eve, Martin 158

Farrell, J.G. 167
Felski, Rita 87
Ferris, Joshua 104
Fielding, Henry 10, 21, 55 n.7, 58, 64, 169
Fielding, Steven 28 n.37
Flaubert, Gustave 133
Fludernick, Monika 58 n.18
fools (wise or holy) 137–8
football (language of) 59–60, 61–2
Forster, E.M. 22 n.7, 77, 91
Four Lions 86
Franzen, Jonathan 15, 78, 158
Frayn, Michael 35, 36
Free to Choose (Friedman and Friedman) 44–5
Freud, Sigmund
   'Humour' 80, 188
   The Joke and Its Relation to the Unconscious 29–30, 93, 188
   and laughter 79
   'On the Psychical Mechanism of Hysterical Phenomena' 93
   puns 32
   relief theory of humour 26 n.25, 93, 174 n.24
   tendentious jokes 181
   third person in jokes 31
Friedman, Sam 171 n.14
Frye, Northrop 27, 40, 142, 155 n.93
funny turn 4–5, *see also* comic turn

Ganteau, Jean-Michel 39–40

Gąsiorek, Andrzej 53 n.1, 91 n.56, 190, 195
Genette, Gerard 103 n.10
genre 10, 16, 20, 103–4, 131, 168, *see also* comedy; satire
   comedy as 1–4
   crunch lit (Shaw) 34
   Now We Know Better (Greif) 38
Germanà, Monica 6 n.23
Ghosh, Amitav 6 n.21
Gilbert, Ruth 182 n.55, 190
Gilroy, Paul 6 n.21, 23
Gimbel, Steven 179 n.43
Gladwell, Malcolm 25 n.22
Gray, Alisdair 32
Greenberg, Jonathan 142
Greenman, Ben 198–9
Gregson, Ian 28, 40
Greif, Mark 38
Griffiths, Trevor 178–80
Groes, Sebastian 53 n.1, 144, 149
grotesque
   aesthetic 67 n.43
   ambivalent function of 140, 144–8
   characterization of 66, 159
Guignery, Vanessa 38 n.72, 47 n.103, 209–10
   allusion in Coe, *Expo 58* 35 n.62
   Coe and Beckett 21 n.5
   Coe's critical reception 22 n.11
   satire in Coe 41

Haffenden, John 15 n.44, 76 n.74
Halliday, M.A.K. 58 n.20
Hancock, Tony 96
Hassan, Ruqaiya 58 n.20
Have I Got News for You 25–6
Head, Dominic 53 n.1, 76, 148 n.64
Heise, Ursula K. 6 n.21
hell (as comic plot) 126–8
Heller, Agnes 2, 84, 88 n.45, 134
Hensher, Philip 94–5
Herman, David 15 n.45, 69–70, 71, 74, 75
Hicks, Heather J. 6 n.23
Higgins, Kathleen 89–90
Hill, Robert H. 151 n.79
Hitchcock, Alfred 39
Hitchens, Christopher 29 n.39, 67
Hobbes, Thomas 47, 86

Holmes, Christopher 79 n.8, 81
Holocaust 111, 170, 181, 184
   and comedy 186–95
   denial 185–6, 194
   humour and 190 n.85
Hot Chip (band) 101
Houser, Heather 6 n.22
Houser, Tammy Amiel 96
Houswitschka, Christopher 169 n.8
Hubble, Nick 51 n.115
Humour, Work and Organization
      (Westwood and Rhodes) 105
      n.19
Humour, *see also* comedy; laughter
   absurd 107, 112, 117–18, 119, 129
   classic theories of 8
   deadpan 105, 107, 109 (*see also under*
      affect)
   definition of 4 (*see also* Humour, *vs.*
      comedy (Eco))
   and empathy 80
   incongruity theory 17, 29–30, 60, 61,
      101–2, 109, 132, 136–40, 163
   internet 199
   and mockery 27, 38, 50, 80, 85, 118,
      150–2, 162, 195
   register-based 58–62, 64, 66, 68, 83–4
   relief theory 26, 93, 151, 174
   and repetition 101–29
   script opposition theory 60
   semantic script theory 30 n.46
   and spite 149–50, 162
   and style (*see* style)
   superiority theory 79 n.10, 103, 108,
      117, 135–7
   and surprise 101–2, 110–11
   vs. comedy (Eco) 153–4
Hutcheon, Linda 49–50, 157 n.102
Hutchinson, Colin 50, 207–8, 209
Huyssen, Andreas 41
hyperreality 204, 209

Ilott, Sarah 175
intentionality 4, 175, 179–80, 186
interdisciplinarity 8, 56, 210
Ioanes, Anna 6 n.22
Ionesco, Eugène 3
irony 17, 132, 142, 148, 193
   ironic reversal 71 n.57
   militant (Frye) 27
   retrospective 38
   vs. sincerity 132, 157–63
Ishiguro, Kazuo 12

Jabukiak, Katarzyna 77 n.1
Jacobson, Howard 6 n.20, 12, 9–10,
      17–18, 151 n.83, 167–200
   Coming from Behind 168, 175–8
   The Finkler Question 167, 169 n.8,
      170, 172, 181–6, 187–8, 200
   Kalooki Nights 171 n.11, 186–95,
      197, 200
   The Making of Henry 171 n.11
   The Mighty Walzer 188
   Peeping Tom 188–9, 190
   Pussy 170, 196–200
   Roots Schmoots 185 n.63
   Seriously Funny 10, 169, 173–4,
      178–80, 181, 195 n.97
   Zoo Time 170–2
James, David 6 n.22, 53 n.1, 54–5, 94
Jewish comedy and humour 170, 180–6
   and essentialism 183–5
   internalised anti–Semitism 194
   and self-mockery 187–8, 195
Johnson, Boris 13–14, 18
   constructed persona of 25–6, 201–3
Johnson, B.S. 11, 21, 28, 46 n.100
Jokes, *see also* puns
   as coping mechanism 88
   as dominant focus of humour
      studies 102
   and *éndoxa* 31, 33–4
   and incongruity 30
   as innovative action 29–40
   insider *vs.* outsider 182–6, 194
   Jewish jokes (*see* Jewish comedy and
      humour)
   and joke-telling communities 183
   and misogyny 169, 179
   as philosophy 165
   right to tell 194
   and surprise 101–2
Jones, Owen 65 n.37

Kafka, Franz 111, 113, 168
Kant, Immanuel 47, 101, 136
Keller Simon, Richard 10

Kelly, Adam 158 n.107
Kelman, James 76 n.75
Kermode, Frank 77, 87
Kierkegaard, Søren 47, 103, 129 n.111
Kim, Jong-Seok 204 n.13
Knopp, Eva 81
Koch, Ilse 189–90
Konstantinou, Lee 83, 159, 163
Kozintsev, Alexander 2 n.6
Kundera, Milan 47
Kureishi, Hanif 84

Lacan, Jacques 103, 118
The Lady Vanishes 39, 46 n.99
Lanone, Catherine 91 n.56
Lassner, Phyllis 84
late capitalism 34, 205, 208
laughter 77–100, *see also* comedy; humour
   carnivalesque 146, 149
   as catharsis 28, 44
   as communication 91–94
   and community 95–99
   corrective function of 103
   and crying 90, 92–4
   cynical *vs.* kynical 42
   in the dark 82, 84
   as emotion 86–94
   as enemy of emotion 88
   fleeting nature of 98–100, 203
   as judgement 84
   political force of 23–4
   political limitations of 24–29, 50, 85–6 (*see also* satire)
   as reinforcement of ideology 24–5 n.22, 174
   relation to comedy 1–2
   rhetorical force of 83
   as substitute for thought 26, 28
   unifying effects of 50–1
   as yielding of control 90–1
   and Zadie Smith 77–100
The League of Gentlemen 123, 128
Leavis, F.R. 168–9, 180
Lee, Stewart 173
Lehmann, Rosamond 22 n.7
Lever, James 144, 146
Levi, Primo 110
Lewis, Wyndham 11, 103, 117 n.59, 204 n.11

Little, Judy 11 n.35
Littlewood, Jane 173
Lively, Penelope 167
Lockyer, Sharon 86 n.37, 178
Lodge, David 8–9, 11, 22
Loveness, Jeff 199 n.107
Lusin, Caroline 98 n.79

McEwan, Ian 12, 67
McGraw, Peter 2 n.6, 8, 112
McKenzie, Jon 205–6
McKinnie, Michael 202–3
Manning, Bernard 169, 173–5, 177
Martin, Theodore 3
masochism 117–18, 188–90, 191, 192, *see also* Deleuze, Gilles
Masters, Ben 69, 71
matrix language 70–1, 72
Matthews, Graham 129
Medhurst, Andy 12 n.39, 173
Meinig, Sigrun 89 n.49
metacomedy, *see under* comedy
metafiction 49–50, 142, 156–64
metalepsis 157
Metamodernism (van den Akker, Gibbons and Vermeulen) 158 n.107
Michaud, Jon 19 n.53
Miles, Margaret 145
Miller, J. Hillis 124
Mills, Magnus 5, 16, 101–29, 135, 187
   A Cruel Bird Came to the Nest and Looked In 104, 112, 113
   All Quiet on the Orient Express 104, 106, 107–8, 123–7
   Explorers of the New Century 104 n.16, 113
   The Field of the Clot of Gold 104, 121
   The Forensic Records Society 112
   The Maintenance of Headway 104, 105, 106, 112, 112–21, 122–3
   The Restraint of Beasts 104, 105, 106–12, 113, 120 n.74, 123, 126–9
   The Scheme for Full Employment 104, 106, 112–21
   This Much I Know 105
   Three to See the King 104, 113
Mitchell, Kaye 4 n.14
mockery, *see under* humour
Molière 135

Mookerjee, Robin   64
The Morecambe and Wise Show   50–1, 203
Moretti, Franco   10
Morreall, John   8, 26 n.25, 101, 105, 136 n.18, 190 n.85
Morrison, Toni   32
Moseley, Merritt   39 n.75, 49 n.110
Mousoutzanis, Aris   6 n.23
Munnery, Simon   136

Nabokov, Vladimir   53, 54, 55, 137
Naipaul, V.S.   11, 80
narration
   authorial *vs.* character   57–8, 71–3, 74, 81
   and ethics   160–1
   eye-dialect   71
   idiolect   58
   inverted free indirect discourse   66
   matrix language and embedded language   70–1, 72
   skaz   58
Nelson, T.G.A.   137–8
neoliberalism   43–5
The New Spirit of Capitalism (Boltanski and Chiapello)   205–6
Ngai, Sianne   6 n.22, 7, 18
   commedification of culture   5
   hybridity of comedy   3 n.13
   tone   21 n.2
   zany aesthetic (*Our Aesthetic Categories*)   18, 205–7, 210
Nietzsche, Friedrich   103, 124–5, 129 n.111
Nikulin, Dmitri   2 n.7
9/11   82, 85
Nobbs, David   21–22, 32–3, 46 n.99, 49 n.110
North, Michael   13, 103–4, 117 n.59
nostalgia   36, 39, 44, 203, 208–9
'Notes on Metamodernism' (van den Akker and Vermeulen)   163

O'Brien, Flann   16, 59, 106, 121, 125
   At Swim-Two-Birds   157
   The Third Policeman   126–9
The Office   104, 105 n.19
Orton, Joe   107
The Oxford History of the Novel in English (Boxall and Cheyette)   12

Palmer, Jerry   17, 107, 137, 138 n.24, 179
Parker, Emma   28
Partington, Alan   61, 71
Partridge, Alan   4, 133
Parvulescu, Anca   2 n.6, 86–7, 91, 98
pedantry, *see under* comedy
performance   5, 7, 18–19, *see also* comedy, stand-up
   'Above the Below' (Blaine)   149, 151–3
   and Englishness   201–3, 204–10
   and foolery   138 n.24
   and work   105, 204–10
Peters, Suzanne   55 n.7
Pettersson, Bo   111, 120 n.74
Pfister, Manfred   11 n.38, 79
Pickering, Michael   173, 178
Pirandello, Luigi   153–4
Pirker, Ulrike   78 n.7
Plato   102, 124, 135, 164
Platt, Len   144 n.47
Plessner, Helmuth   15, 90, 93
'Political Ideology' (LaMarre, Landreville and Beam)   24–5 n.22
Pope, Alexander   40, 197
pornography   64–5, 67–8, 172
postmodernism   35, 40–1, 132, 157, 159, 163
post-postmodernism   159–63
post-war consensus   43
The Prisoner   123
Pritchett, V.S.   10
Provine, Robert R.   2 n.5
Pryor, Richard   175
puns   93, 112, 182, 194, *see also* jokes
   multiplicity of   164
   prevalence in one-liners   30 n.33
purgatory, *see* hell (as comic plot)

Rabaté, Jean-Michel   113
Rabelais, François   149, 168, 169, 172
race and racism   63, 173–80
Ramsey-Kurz, Helga   84–5
Raskin, Victor   30 n.46, 60, 101
Reader in Comedy (Ackerman and Romanska)   8
Redfern, Walter   164 n.125, 174–5
register humour, *see under* humour
repetition, *see under* humour
Richardson, Dorothy   22 n.7

Richardson, Samuel   10
Richter, Jean Paul   153 n.89
Robins, John   4 n.15
Robinson, Richard   55
Roof, Judith   1–2, 6, 8, 109 n.34, 199–200
Rose, Jacqueline   183–4 n.59
Ross, Michael   8, 175, 177
Roston, Murray   11 n.38
Roth, Philip   40, 168, 169, 180–1
The Routledge Companion to Twenty-First Century Literary Fiction (O'Gorman and Eaglestone)   13
Rushdie, Salman   12, 67, 78, 81, 84, 95, 167
Russo, Mary   145

Sacks, Mike   19 n.54
Sage, Victor   131 n.3, 144, 155
St Aubyn, Edward   55
Sale, Charles   119
Salisbury, Laura   117, 178
Sansom, Ian   112
satire   21, 40–5, 49, 185, 189–90, 201, *see also* comedy; genre; humour
　as catharsis   28
　contemporary impediments on   196–200
　and cynicism   41
　definition of   40–1
　distinction from comedy   28
　grotesque and carnivalesque   140–53
　limitations of   24–29, 195, 196–200, 209
　Menippean   142–4, 146, 159
　post-war boom   25
　potential of   27
　as thesis art (Kundera)   47
Saturday Night Live   199
Saunders, George   158
Schoene, Berthold   12 n.40
Schopenhauer, Arthur   17, 101
　and incongruity   136–7
　and pedantry   141
Scogin, John   150–1
Scott, Jeremy   57–8, 68
Scourge of the Swastika (Russell)   188–9
Segal, Erich   2 n.7, 3–4
self-deprecation   201–2
Self, Will   40, 73, 101

Selvon, Sam   11
7/7 bombings   85
Shaftesbury, Earl of (Anthony Ashley Cooper)   23, 26 n.25
Shakespeare, William   78
Shaw, Katy   34, 171 n.15
Shaw, Kristian   97 n.75
Shiels, Barry   55
Shteyngart, Gary   2 n.10
Simpson, Paul   70 n.55, 76 n.75
sincerity, *see under* irony
Sinclair, May   22 n.7
skaz, see under narration
Sloterdijk, Peter   14, 41–2
Smith, Zadie   12, 15–16, 77–100, 132, 158
　The Autograph Man   77, 87–91, 92
　The Embassy of Cambodia   78 n.7
　NW   77, 78, 94–99
　On Beauty   77, 91–4
　Swing Time   77, 99–100
　White Teeth   77, 78, 79–86, 87
Smollett, Tobias   10, 169
Spark, Muriel   27, 40, 80, 156, 157
Spencer, Herbert   26 n.25
Spinoza, Baruch   86
Sri Ramakrishna   137–40
stand-up comedy, *see under* comedy
stereotypes
　anti-Semitic   194–5
　comic potential and pitfalls   28, 76 n.75, 146 n.59, 175–80
　national   38
　racist and sexist   170, 173
Sterne, Laurence   10, 81
Stetz, Margaret   7
Stott, Andrew   1, 2, 8
style   53–76
　and class   70–6
　and comedy   57
　and ethics   53–6, 58, 69, 75–6
　hierarchies of   57–62, 72–73
　and immorality   55
　and judgement   54, 59–64, 68, 70–6
　and nationality   55–6
　shifting   69–75
　vs. content   54, 57, 69
Style in Fiction (Leech and Short)   71
Su, John   22 n.8, 209

Supplanting the Postmodern (Rudrum and Stavris)   158 n.107
Swift, Jonathan   39, 196, 197, 200

Tait, Theo   111, 128 n.105
Tancke, Ulrike   85
Tate, Andrew   6 n.23
Taylor, D.J.   53 n.1
Tew, Philip   11 n.37, 14 n.43, 73, 77 n.1, 82, 88
Thatcher, Margaret   28 n.37, 45, 120, 121
Thatcherism   22, 27–8, 45, 120, 209
Thomas, Susie   84
Thurber, James   190–1
Thurschwell, Pamela   22–3
Todd, Richard   57 n.12
Tolan, Fiona   91 n.56
tone
    in Coe   32–40
    comic *vs.* serious   5, 9
    definition of   21 n.2
    tragicomic   32
Toribio, Almeida Jacqueline   70 n.55
tragedy
    and comedy   3, 103, 137, 139, 191
    history as   23
    and humour (Pirandello)   154
    Jacobean   22
    as sublimation (Zupančič)   109
tragicomedy   32, 78, 81, 84
Trahair, Lisa   91
Trexler, Adam   6 n.21
Triezenberg, Katarina   102
Trump, Donald   18, 170, 196–200
2018 financial crisis   33–4
2012 Olympic Games   202–3
The Two Ronnies   51 n.116

Under Postcolonial Eyes (Sicher and Weinhouse)   192
Updike, John   8–9
upgrading as comic technique   71–2, 76, *see also* bathos
Upstone, Sarah   146 n.59

Valman, Nadia   180–1, 187 n.69
Vandaele, Jeroen   4 n.14, 8 n.25, 102
violence   64–5, 67–8
    objective *vs.* subjective (Žižek)   110–11
    and work   109–12
Virno, Paolo   14, 29–31, 34, 40
voice, *see* narration

Wagg, Stephen   25–6 n.24
Wallace, David Foster   15, 78, 83, 103, 158, 159
Walters, Tracey L.   89
Warner, Joel   2 n.6
Warren, Caleb   8
Waterhouse, Keith   11, 133
Watt, Ian   10
Watt-Smith, Tiffany   142
Waugh Evelyn   11, 35, 80
Waugh, Patricia   32 n.52
Weitz, Eric   5, 105 n.20
Weldon, Fay   11
Wells, Lynn   95–6
Welsh, Irvine   76 n.75
Wharton, Edith   69–70, 71
White, Allon   7 n.24
White, E.B.   19
Wilkinson, Katharine   133 n.6
Wille, Anna   84
Williams, Heathcote   25 n.23, 202
Williams, Nigel   133
Wisse, Ruth R.   184–5, 190 n.85
Wittgenstein, Ludwig   2, 27, 30, 164–5
Wodehouse, P.G.   11, 28, 29, 39, 202
Wodehouse Prize   1–3, 36, 61
Woloch, Alex   156 n.99, 160 n.113
Wood, James   9, 32, 55–6
    comedies of correction and forgiveness   71 n.59, 154, 160
    hysterical realism   15, 78–86
Woolf, Virginia   11
work   104–29, *see also under* violence
    and affect (*see under* affect)
    comedies of work (definition)   105
    as doctrine   116
    Fordism   113
    as hell   128
    and performance   105, 204–10
    post-Fordist   205–7, 209
    seriality of   124–6
    and tyranny   112
    and violence   109–12
    working to rule   117, 119–20
workplace humour   105

Zahar, Isabelle 57
Žižek, Slavoj 110–11
Zupančič, Alenka 8, 117
    automatism 129
    comedy and/as repetition 16, 103, 106
    comedy and master signifiers 118–19
    comedy and tragedy 109
    comic sequence *vs.* joke 102

www.ingramcontent.com/pod-product-compliance
Lightning Source LLC
Chambersburg PA
CBHW072141290426
44111CB00012B/1939